BOURBON STREET

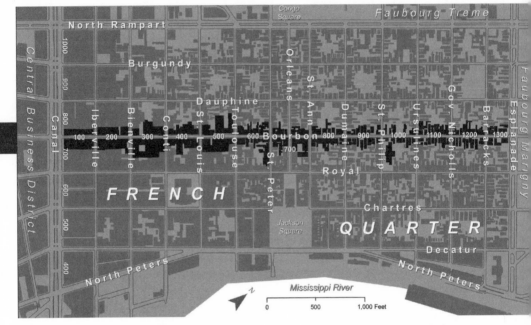

French Quarter street names, numbers, and structural footprints, with buildings on Bourbon Street–facing parcels shown in black.

BOURBON STREET

A HISTORY

RICHARD CAMPANELLA

LOUISIANA STATE UNIVERSITY PRESS)|(BATON ROUGE

Publication of this book is made possible in part by support from the Zemurray Foundation.

Published by Louisiana State University Press

Copyright © 2014 by Louisiana State University Press

Manufactured in the United States of America

FIRST PRINTING

DESIGNER: *Mandy McDonald Scallan*
TYPEFACE: *Whitman*
PRINTER AND BINDER: *Maple Press, Inc.*

All maps and graphs were created by the author.

Library of Congress Cataloging-in-Publication Data

Campanella, Richard.
  Bourbon Street : a history / Richard Campanella.
    pages cm
  Includes bibliographical references and index.
  ISBN 978-0-8071-5505-9 (cloth : alkaline paper) — ISBN 978-0-8071-5506-6 (pdf) — ISBN 978-0-8071-5507-3 (epub) — ISBN 978-0-8071-5508-0 (mobi) 1. Bourbon Street (New Orleans, La.) —History. 2. New Orleans (La.) —History. 3. New Orleans (La.) —Social life and customs. 4. New Orleans (La.) —Social conditions. I. Title.
  F379.N575B682 2014
  976.3'35—dc23

2013030627

The paper in this book meets the guidelines for permanence and durability of the Committee on Production Guidelines for Book Longevity of the Council on Library Resources. ∞

For Marina and Jason

Here we are in the Rue Bourbon! Heavens, what associations!

— LOUIS FITZGERALD TASISTRO, touring New Orleans in 1842

CONTENTS

ILLUSTRATIONS

GRAPHS

PREFACE

Hundreds of millions. That's how many people, over the past two generations, have crammed themselves into a minor and rather middling artery in a secondary city on America's Third Coast. They made it into one of the most famous streets in the nation, a brand that has diffused worldwide both nominally and phenomenologically, a metaphor in the English language, and the greatest sustained homegrown economic success of its host city. People by the thousands beeline for this narrow space, and parade up and down it nightly, because a rather curt and crusty cohort of shrewd locals figured out what pleasured them and delivered it with panache, while battling constantly police, patricians, preservationists, and pontificators. The street is named Bourbon, the city is New Orleans, and the story is fundamentally American.

Bourbon Street emerged from an inward shift in the urban geography of "sin" in the late nineteenth century. It gained momentum with the rise of leisure tourism in the early twentieth century, and catapulted into national fame during World War II. It has hummed ever since, round the clock, 365 days a year—all without the benefit of a corporate structure, a team of experts, a board of directors, or a marketing branch. Formed inadvertently by working-class characters toiling individually but prospering collectively through the clever use of space and the adaptive commodification of culture, Bourbon Street today is at once "the biggest disorganized street in the whole country," as Earl Bernhardt has stated, and a well-honed economic engine that employs thousands, pumps millions of outside dollars into the city's economy, and single-handedly generates imagery and reputation about an entire metropolis.

For some, that Bourbon Street image is a delectable mélange of historicity and hedonism; for others it's iniquitous, crass, phony, and offensive. No one is lukewarm about Bourbon Street; people either love it or loathe it. Bourbon Street is also a treasure trove of American history, a living museum of Enlightenment-era urban planning and Creole architecture, and a fascinating and complex social phenomenon. It is as old as the city itself, and has been famous for longer than the French and Spanish colonial eras combined—indeed for nearly one-third of New Orleans's entire existence.

And yet Bourbon Street has been almost completely ignored by scholars. Not a single book has been written about its history, much less an in-depth scholarly investigation. Only a handful of academic articles, a few planning documents, a smattering of popular pieces, and one local television documentary have been devoted to the subject. New Orleans, meanwhile, has become a hot topic worldwide; books, anthologies, dissertations, theses, articles, and films about the city have been released by the hundreds just since Hurricane Katrina. Yet the city's most famous, most infamous, and most visited spot remains unexamined.

The oversight is not an accident; it's an acerbic snub and a contemptuous dismissal. The most that "serious" researchers usually allot to Bourbon Street is a patronizing reminder to their audience that it does not represent "authentic" New Orleans, and that such amateurish delusions must be set aside before the forthcoming cultural enlightenment may commence. Even professional tourism marketers unctuously suggest that visitors venture beyond Bourbon Street to experience the "real" New Orleans. Most locals, particularly the cultural clerisy, wholeheartedly agree with this sentiment and hate Bourbon Street as an odious affront to their city. Educated newcomers and sophisticated visitors figure out quickly that declaring disdain for Bourbon Street is the first step toward showcasing their taste and gaining insider status, and they do so with the zeal of a convert. That millions of plebian rubes absolutely love Bourbon cinches the argument that anyone with even a hint of respectability and intellect must eschew The Street.

I myself marched obediently to this beat as I began studying the historical geography of New Orleans nearly twenty years ago. The deeper I delved into the subject, the more I succumbed to the social pressure to think of Bourbon Street as an ersatz and degrading freak show best viewed as cultural negative space. I avoided it in my perambulations, glibly denounced its inauthenticity (as if I were the arbiter of reality), and discouraged newcomers from going there. A voice inside winced at my arrogance, particularly since I had long been curious about Bourbon Street's origins and inner workings.

What changed my interpretation was Hurricane Katrina. I bore witness to the storm and ensuing deluge, and after fleeing on the fifth day of the multiact apocalypse, joined millions of others in watching newscasts of a metropolis I loved drowning in its own filth. It was gut-wrenching.

But amid all the televised tragedy, one sign of life came across the airwaves. It came from Bourbon Street. A bar had remained open and became a community locus. A few buskers gathered nearby and played music. Sweaty neighbors joined them, mustered up some pluck, and managed wistful and defiant smiles for the world to see. Soon, nearby bars and clubs reopened, offering respite to exhausted responders trying to resuscitate a city. In ensuing weeks, Bourbon Street became the liveliest and happiest place in a city of death and misery. It provided an invaluable counterpoint to viewers tuning in worldwide expecting to see a municipal funeral. It was the first place in the city to return to work, turn up the music, put on a party face, pump cash into employees' pockets, and send revenue to city coffers. In my mind, Bourbon Street had redeemed itself by keeping the human heart beating in this fragile, ancient experiment called New Orleans. Yet Bourbon did not seek redemption, awaited no accolades, and hardly recognized that it had done something important. It just wanted to get back to being successful—and I couldn't think of a better model for the city to emulate.

So inspired, my curiosity grew: How did this straight line form in this sinuous environment? Who lived there centuries past, and what were their Bourbon Street lives like? How and where did the nocturnal entertainment scene form, who created it, and why did it prosper? How does it work? Why do so many people love it, while others despise it ardently, almost histrionically? Love, hate, fame, infamy, music, food, liquor, sex, money, mobsters: there had to be an interesting story here. I mulled these questions privately as I researched and wrote other books about the city. Finally, with the encouragement of a friend, I decided to sate my scandalous curiosity and figure out how Bourbon Street happened.

Part cultural history and geography, part investigative analysis, *Bourbon Street: A History* explores this mile-long urban space from its inception in colonial times, through the tumultuous nineteenth century, to the Great War, Prohibition, the Depression, World War II, the civil rights movement, to the famous and infamous entertainment strip it has become today. Local, national, and world events interleave with the Bourbon Street story; characters ranging from presidents to prostitutes, showgirls to "shot girls," mavens to mobsters have played roles on its stage. The book contemplates Bourbon Street dispassionately, as a curious artifact informing on New Orleans and American society, past and present. It argues that the modern phenomenon that is Bourbon Street emerged rather spontaneously, locally and from the bottom up, without planning or centralized control—something that led me to originally entitle the book "How Bourbon Street Happened" (and thus the chapter names in Part II). The book also views Bourbon Street as an element of the built environment with a municipal history, population, architecture, and economy, and as a battleground over notions of space and culture. The book explains how Bourbon Street operates on a typical night, how it affects and reflects (or offends) the city of New Orleans, how it has diffused worldwide as a sort of public-domain brand, and how it generates passionately polarized reactions. The book is neither a defense nor a condemnation of Bourbon Street, but rather a nonjudgmental analysis of a complex phenomenon from many angles. Hundreds of millions of people, after all, can't be ignored.

My appreciation goes to the following people for their support over the three years of this project: Tulane University Provost Michael A. Bernstein and Dean Kenneth A. Schwartz of the Tulane School of Architecture; Executive Editor Rand Dotson and the staff of the Louisiana State University Press; editors Catherine L. Kadair and Susan A. Murray; historian Lawrence N. Powell; Bourbon Street "mayors" Earl Bernhardt and Chris Owens; geographer Julie Hernandez and students Evan Nicholl and Elyse Monat; jazz historian Bruce Raeburn; Americanist Joel Dinerstein and the Tulane University New Orleans Center for the Gulf South, where I am a Monroe Fellow; journalist Jack Davis; archivists Keli Rylance and Irene Wainwright; Michael Sartisky of the Louisiana Endowment for the Humanities; scholar S. Frederick Starr; sociolinguist Christina Schoux Casey; historian Judith Kelleher Schafer; geographer Verena Rienke of Germany, who translated some German texts; photographer Del Hall, who captured scenes of circa-1960 Bourbon Street and kindly provided them to me; and World War II veteran John Tambasco, my uncle. Appreciation also goes to the many Bourbon Street and French Quarter informants who shared their experiences with me. I also acknowledge the following institutions and their helpful staffs for access to archival documents, research materials, datasets, and analytical tools used in this volume: Tulane University School of Architecture; Louisiana Division of the New Orleans Public Library; The Historic New Orleans Collection–Williams Research Center; U.S. Library of Congress; Howard-Tilton Library at Tulane University; Tulane University Special Collections; Tulane University Southeastern Architectural Archive; Louisiana State Museum; U.S. Census Bureau; New Orleans Notarial Archives; Greater New Orleans Community Data Center; and the Louisiana Collection and Special Collections of the Earl K. Long Library at the University of New Orleans. Special thanks to Marcel Wisznia of Wisznia Architects for access to the Maritime Building roof to photograph Bourbon Street from certain vantage points.

Deepest appreciation goes to my parents, Mario and Rose Campanella, both of whom passed away during the course of this project; to my wife, Marina Campanella, for her love and support; and to Jason Campanella, our son, born August 3, 2012—the first native-born New Orleanian in our family.

I
ORIGINS

A Straight Line in a Sinuous Space
Creating Rue Bourbon, 1682–1722

There are no straight lines in nature. Nor are there any right angles. Rather, intricate arcs and fractures merge and bifurcate recurrently, like capillaries in a plant leaf or veins in an arm. Nowhere is this sinuous geometry more evident than in deltas, like that of the Mississippi River. Starting eighteen thousand years ago, warming global temperatures melted immense ice sheets across North America. The runoff aggregated to form the lower Mississippi River and flowed southward bearing vast quantities of sediment. The bluffs and terraces that confined the channel to a broad alluvial valley petered out roughly between present-day Lafayette and Baton Rouge in Louisiana, south of which lay the Gulf of Mexico.

Into that sea disembogued the Mississippi, its innumerable tons of alluvium smothering the soft marshes of the Gulf Coast and accumulating upon the hard clays of the sea floor. So voluminous was the Mississippi's muddy water column that it overpowered the (relatively weak tides and currents of) the Gulf of Mexico, thus prograding the deposition farther into the sea. Occasional crevasses in the river's banks diverted waters to the left or right, creating multiple river mouths and thus multiple depositions. High springtime flow also overtopped the river's banks and released a thin sheet of sediment-laden water sideways, further raising the delta's elevation.

In this manner, southeastern Louisiana rose from the sea. The process took about 7,200 years, making the Mississippi Delta, as Mark Twain put it, "the youthfulest batch of country that lies around there anywhere."[1] Young, dynamic, fluid, warm, humid: flora and fauna flourish in such conditions, as evidenced by the verdant vegetation and high productivity of the delta's ecosystem. Humans, on the other hand, view these same conditions as inhospitable, dangerous, even evil, and endeavor to impose rigidity and rectitude upon them, so as to exploit better the delta's resources.

When French colonials came to establish a city on this fluidity, they imposed river-restraining levees, runoff-draining canals, rational urban grids, delineated parcels, and defendable ramparts toward exerting control over this threatening and distant land. The premier spatial signature of these interventions was the one geometric shape utterly absent in nature: the straight line. From the European standpoint, Euclidean geometry—clean lines, orthogonal angles, neat triangles, perfect circles—introduced order to disorder, civilization to wilderness, godliness to the heathen, and the power of the Crown to the cowering native.

Straight lines arrived into the toolbox of colonialism via ancient architectural sources, starting with Hippodamus, who is credited with the first planned gridded street system in Piraeus in the fifth century BC, and with Marcus Vitruvius Pollio, whose *De architectura* did for buildings what Hippodamus had done earlier for cities. Vitruvius's tome disappeared after Rome's fall—a loss that can be viewed as symbolic, because progressive thought on urban design in the West subsequently waned.[2] The Renaissance reinvigorated European thinking about cities, and in the late 1400s, Vitruvius's *De architectura* fortuitously reappeared. The opus taught a new generation that buildings should be *firmitas, utilitas,* and *venustas*—strong, useful, and beautiful. So too should cities: a civil engineer and planner by today's definitions, Vitruvius articulated the values of *ordinatio* (measured and incremented order), *symmetria,* and *eurythmia* (graceful adaptiveness) in urban design, manifested by central plazas and orthogonal street grids and paying homage, ultimately, to the human body.[3]

Vitruvian ideas particularly resonated with officials in Spain. Throughout their aggressive New World colonization, Spanish colonials produced hundreds of urban grids with central plazas fronted by institutions of church and state. Similar designs appeared in European cities during the 1600s and 1700s, taking "hold among the French at the very moment that the Bourbon monarchy was expanding its imperial domain on the Continent."[4] That domain spread across the Atlantic and took root in France's two enduring but dissociated New World colonial regions. One was in Canada; the other was in the Caribbean.

French Canadian René-Robert Cavelier, sieur de La Salle sought to expand his king's empire while figuring out how Canada and the Caribbean were geographically associated. In 1682, La Salle sailed across the Great Lakes and floated down the Illinois and Mississippi Rivers. That spring he and his crew became the first Europeans to describe what would become, decades later, the site for New Orleans. They proceeded to the mouth of the Mississippi, where, in the words of a crew member, "on the ninth of April, with all possible solemnity, we performed the ceremony of planting the cross and raising the arms of France, [taking] possession of that river, of all rivers that enter it and of all the country watered by them."[5] The Mississippi Basin, in La Salle's mind, now belonged to France. He named it Louisiane to honor his king, Louis XIV, grandson of the first monarch in the Bourbon dynasty. Recognizing the strategic advantage afforded by the Mississippi River, La Salle sailed home to recommend to the Sun King the establishment of a fortification near the river's mouth. "[A] port or two" there, he declared, "would make us masters of the whole of this continent."[6]

Louisiana arrived into Bourbon France's imperial docket at roughly the same time that Sébastien Le Prestre, Seigneur de Vauban emerged as the Crown's premier military engineer. Vauban integrated new principles of military defense with Vitruvian and Hippodamian notions of symmetrical urban order. He designed plats with narrow streets (to funnel invading troops) which ran in straight lines (to allow local regimes to be readily summoned) and set them within fortifications angled to expose any attacker to maximum firepower. Vauban's influential field manual instructed generations of engineers on how:

> To make the Streets in a Fortress . . .
> Of the principal Angles of a Fortress . . .
> Of the Streets, Places of Arms, Corps de Garde, and Magazines . . .
> Of the Advantages and Disadvantages of a Place situated on the side of great Rivers.[7]

The concept of neatly fortified cities appealed to the Crown's absolutist aspirations. Eager to inscribe his power into the landscape, King Louis XIV deployed engineers trained by Vauban and his successor, the Marquis d'Asfeld, across the French countryside to build roads and bridges connecting villages with Paris. Villages that were once largely autonomous and vulnerable now became part of a national effort and dependent on the Crown for defense.

Likewise, French claims in the New World came to be viewed as tabulae rasae for similar Vauban-designed imperial envelopment. Urban planning worked hand in hand with national expansion; in the words of one historical anthropologist, it represented "a conscious conviction that spatial control yielded political control."[8] It was during this era, and under this paradigm, that Louisiana became a French possession.

Establishing a colony in Louisiana came at a slow pace and great cost. La Salle himself perished in a mutiny after getting lost on his 1684 return trip. Henri de Tonti sought to continue La Salle's mission, cautioning French officials of English and Spanish interests, but the War of the League of Augsburg distracted their attention.

Not until 1697 did the Crown return to Louisiana matters. It directed French Canadian warrior Pierre Le Moyne, sieur d'Iberville to seek "the mouth [of the Mississippi River,] select a good site that can be defended with a few men, and block entry to the river by other nations."[9] Charged to establish Louisiana, Iberville set sail from France in late 1698 with two ships and two hundred men, among them his nineteen-year-old brother, Jean Baptiste Le Moyne, sieur de Bienville.

The 1699 voyage of Iberville and Bienville achieved only the first directive. A "good site" proved hard to find along the lower Mississippi, and the place where Iberville eventually established a fort (Maurepas, near present-day Biloxi) would not block other nations from the river. The French needed to be *on* the river and near its mouth—but where? And how? "All this land is a country of reeds and brambles," bemoaned Iberville; "I climbed to the top of a nut tree . . . but saw nothing other than canes and bushes, [much of it] inundated."[10] With that water-logged terrain, however, came plentiful resources. "We regarded this beautiful river with admiration," recalled crew members; "The water is . . . very good to drink. . . . The country [is] everywhere covered with splendid trees [and] wild game, such as ducks, geese, snipe, teal, bustards, and other birds." Blooming vines entangled mature live oaks and blackberry patches, forming a junglelike scene. The crew spotted three alligators and killed a buffalo.

Iberville first viewed the future site of downtown New Orleans probably on March 7, 1699. There, he and his crew met a group of Annocchy Indians, with whom they traded tools and trinkets for buffalo meat, bear meat, and geographical intelligence. American bison grazed on the natural levees of future New Orleans; that morning, the crew "saw three buffaloes lying down on the bank," which promptly disappeared into the "thick forest and cane-brakes."[11] These are among the first surviving descriptions of what the landscape around future Bourbon Street looked like three hundred years ago.

Iberville's explorations spawned a colonial French society scattered thinly along the Gulf coast. Following the establishment of Fort Maurepas in 1699, Bienville built a small blockhouse on a flood-prone site along the lower Mississippi River in 1700. Two years later, he and Iberville established Fort Louis de Louisiana on the Mobile River, where draftsman Charles Levasseur designed a Vauban-style bastion and a small town plat. "La Mobile," France's first attempt at a street grid in Louisiana, grew over the next five years to host a solid fort, nearly a hundred structures, and eighty-one resident families, until scarce resources and flooding forced its relocation downriver in 1711. There, officer Jacques Barbizon de Pailloux laid out another Vauban fortification and urban grid. Streets were named to reify the Crown's involvement: Rue Conti, Rue Dauphin, Rue Royale. All three toponyms remain in downtown Mobile, Alabama, today.[12]

Scarcity, hunger, pestilence, natural disaster, official inattention, and a desperate lack of settlers made life in early Louisiana a dreaded hardship. Frustrated and pessimistic, the Crown in 1712 ceded a monopoly to a prominent financier named Antoine Crozat for the commercial development of Louisiana. Privatizing Louisiana relieved the Crown of the hassle of management, while chancing that commercialization might actually prove lucrative. That hope was soon dashed: lack of mineral riches, scarcity of agriculturalists, and limited commercial interaction with Spain, coupled with mismanagement, feuding, and Indian tensions, doomed the speculative venture. "The colony of Louisiana is a monster that has no form of government," grumbled authorities in 1716. Governor Cadillac was more blunt: "Bad country, bad people," he called Louisiana.[13]

When Crozat retroceded his monopoly in 1717, Louisiana's prospects seemed dim. Yet a number of important events occurred during the Crozat years. The colony gained four new forts on key positions on the Red, Mississippi, Coosa-Tallapoosa, and Tombigbee Rivers. It was also during the Crozat era that King Louis XIV died (1715) and left the throne to his five-year-old great-grandson Louis XV, for whom Philippe, Duc d'Orléans would act as regent of France. Among the Duc d'Orléans's many business associates was a brilliant and flamboyant Scotsman peddling a bold proposition. His name was John Law.

Born in Edinburgh in 1671, Law grew rich through econometric wizardry parlayed into high-risk financial affiliations with European aristocracy. His dazzling intellect seeking a laboratory for his economic theories, Law settled with his millions in Paris and allied himself with the newly empowered Duc d'Orléans. The regent, impressed with Law's fiscal acumen and something of a kindred spirit, authorized Law to establish the Banque Générale in 1716. It succeeded, reflecting favorably on Law's thinking on fiat currency and emboldening him to seek a bigger experiment. He caught wind of Crozat's surrender of an exotic and intriguing place that some people called Louisiana and others Mississippi. Law pounced, proposing to the regent a land-development plan than would enrich all investors while enlarging the empire. He envisioned the colony producing tobacco and raw materials in a mercantilist relationship with the mother country, while weaning France off the prized leaves grown by English colonists in the Chesapeake region. Equity in the company would pay off the national debt, and riches would follow. In this bold new experiment called Louisiana, France would also have an opportunity to learn from its mistakes in other New World ventures and finally get colonialism right. Part scheming gambler in search of a good hand, part brilliant economist striving to put theory into practice, Law found the right patron for a high-risk, high-reward adventure of breathtaking proportions. "The beguiling inclusiveness of Law's plan," wrote historian Lawrence N. Powell, "—its promise to retire the national debt, revive the French domestic and overseas economy, and establish an autarkic source of tobacco—is what drew the Regent to Law's theories."[14]

Less than a month after Crozat formally relinquished Louisiana, John Law's new Company of the West received a twenty-five-year monopoly charter to develop commercially the Louisiana colony. Committed to populate it with six thousand settlers and three thousand slaves in the next ten years, the Company then launched an unprecedented marketing campaign across the continent to drum up investment in Louisiana stock and land, and to inveigle the lower classes to immigrate. Although based on scandalously exaggerated estimations of commercial viability, Law's so-called Mississippi Company thrust Louisiana into the forefront of European attention. It also decided resolutely to found a city to be called La Nouvelle-Orléans.

"Resolved to establish, thirty leagues up the river, a burg which *should be called* New Orleans, where landing would be possible from either the river or Lake Pont-chartrain."[15] Those words, scribed in the Company register for September 9, 1717, set in motion the foundation of the riverside settlement first envisioned by La Salle thirty-five years earlier.[16] The name explicitly honored the royal sponsor, unlike the exotic monikers of earlier outposts such as Biloxi, Mobile, Natchitoches, and Natchez. It also made it clear to stockholders that this enterprise enjoyed the backing of the Crown and intended to extend the absolutist power of the king.

The stipulated site came from intelligence gathered from Indians over the previous eighteen years regarding a strategic shortcut to the Mississippi River. Rather than sailing forty treacherous leagues up the lower Mississippi (the river route) amid fog and sand bars, against the current and sometimes against the wind, voyagers instead traversed the open waters of the Mississippi Sound into the protected waters of Lake Pontchartrain and up a little inlet called Bayou St. John. They would then disembark and trek a short Indian trail—today's Bayou Road— along a slight upland now called the Esplanade Ridge, to reach the banks of the Mississippi. To Bienville, this lake route circumvented the dangers of the river route and mitigated concerns about the feasibility of a riverside settlement. Based on this geographical reckoning and amid a paltry array of viable alternatives, Bienville selected this site for New Orleans. In late March or early April 1718, six vessels bearing forty-three men anchored along the riverfront terminus of the portage to Bayou St. John. "M. de Bienville cut the first cane," recalled colonist Jonathan Darby. Thirty workers, all convicts, proceeded to clear the "dense canebrake" around the present-day intersection of Conti and Decatur Streets.[17] Behind those bankside reeds lay the hardwood forests of the natural levee, which the axmen cleared next. Six carpenters got to work building provisional shelters— "log cabins," in Darby's words. "We are working at present on the establishment of New Orleans thirty leagues above the entrance to the Mississippi,"[18] is about all Bienville wrote about his city's earliest moments.

Unlike in Mobile, initial urbanization in New Orleans occurred without the surveying of a street grid. But neither was early development completely indiscriminate. Bienville, possibly with the collaboration of Jacques Barbizon de Pailloux (who had helped designed Mobile in 1711), laid out a straight baseline about 700 feet from the river. Today it would be situated between and parallel to Charters and Royal Streets. It was angled by 37 degrees, southwest to northeast, so that it fronted the sharp meander of the river like a board balanced atop a bent knee. In doing so, Bienville correctly saw the river as being more pertinent to the geography of his city than cardinal directions. The angled baseline thus faced approaching river traffic, as if Bienville expected a fully articulated urban grid and fortification to be forthcoming. That rotation angle would later drive the orientation of the entire city, including Bourbon Street.[19]

Bienville's baseline did not prevent early development from occurring irregularly. The disorder may have arisen from a sense that Bienville's site could not withstand flood threats from the Mississippi (it inundated in 1719), and might be supplanted by more viable options at Mobile, Manchac, or Natchez. It did not help that John Law's land-development scheme—"built on speculation, deception, and inflation"[20] and explicitly invested in a city to be called New Orleans—imploded in 1720, instigating riots in Europe and wreaking havoc on Louisiana's already dubious reputation. Although the Company survived the crash (sans Law, who fled France), prospects for its New Orleans project were not auspicious. One observer described the isolated settlement as comprising "about a hundred forty barracks, disposed with no great regularity, a great wooden warehouse, and . . . a few inconsiderable houses, scattered up and down, without any order or regularity . . . [they] would be esteemed common and ordinary buildings in a European village. *New Orleans*, in 1720, made a very contemptible figure."[21] What further affronted New Orleanians was the recent decision by the Company to designate New Biloxi, a coastal position located across the bay from Iberville's ca. 1699 Fort Maurepas ("Old Biloxi"), as headquarters and capital of the Louisiana colony. Chief Engineer Louis-Pierre Le Blond de la Tour proceeded to design plans for the new capital, and, having served under Marquis d'Asfeld, Vauban's successor, rendered a star-shaped fort design with a symmetrically positioned street grid, *place d'armes*, and church.[22]

La Tour soon fell ill and, with orders from Paris, dispatched his assistant, Adrien de Pauger, also a protégé of d'Asfeld and Vauban, to New Orleans to bring similar order to that "contemptible" outpost. Described by one researcher as a "proud, proper, and religiously devout man [who] was one part idealist engineer and one part hot-tempered rogue," Pauger did not see eye to eye with his boss, and like any superior threatened by an ambitious underling, La Tour harbored feelings of jealousy and competition.[23]

Pauger arrived at New Orleans on March 21, 1721, carrying La Tour's Biloxi plans in his baggage. Although three years had passed since Bienville's men had first swung their axes, vegetation had been cleared only within a swath stretching 1,500 feet along the river and extending inland by half that distance, an area that did not include present-day Bourbon Street.[24] The engineer explored the terrain, surveyed its topography and soils, observed its relationship to the curvaceous river, and got to work. While doing so, Pauger seems to have gotten along with Bienville, who also locked horns with La Tour. Sharing a common enemy and working together on a common problem, the two men would play key roles in creating the city of New Orleans and laying out Bourbon Street.[25]

Pauger's progress may be reconstructed from his communiqués with superiors. He sent a letter to Paris on April 14, twenty-four busy days after arriving, in which he enclosed "the plan of the city projected at New Orleans." He sent another copy to La Tour on the same day, in which he explained. "the changes I [made] because of the situation of the terrain, which being higher on the river bank, I have brought the town site . . . closer to it, so as to profit from the proximity of the landing place [and] the breezes that come from it."[26] Had Pauger not shifted his grid 700 feet toward the river from Bienville's baseline, Bourbon Street today would be located along what is now Burgundy, the cathedral would be four blocks from the river, and roughly half the French Quarter would occupy what is now the Faubourg Tremé. It was a wise move because it gave the city two extra feet of topographic elevation, enough to evade high water in the backswamp.

The April 1721 sketches have been lost, but another one, dated August 9, 1721, probably resembled them given that its title read *Plan de la Ville de la Nouvelle Orleans projettée en Mars 1721*. This crude drawing, which covers only the riverfront blocks, represents the earliest surviving depiction of the urban grid that was eventually realized. It also shows the first street names: Rue de Chartres and Rue de Conty (both comprising present-day Chartres Street), Rue de Bienville, and Rue de St. Louis. Bourbon Street appears neither in name nor shape.[27]

What this map did not show was the smattering of huts, sheds, gardens, and paths paying no heed to Pauger's orderly vision. Worse yet, villagers continued building willy-nilly as they had since 1718, and reacted with indignation when this lordly newcomer told them to do otherwise. A city census had enumerated 327 free townspeople (as well as 171 black slaves and 21 Indian slaves), so there were plenty of potential relocation conflicts to resolve.[28]

The arrival of Pauger's plans in Paris, probably in November, may have triggered a key decision on the destiny of New Orleans. The Company and the Crown at that time found themselves in economic chaos following the bursting of John Law's Mississippi Company "bubble." Officials had been concurrently contemplating which site would serve optimally as the capital and headquarters for Louisiana, but, distracted as they were with the fiscal crisis, that colonial matter ranked a distant second priority, vulnerable to capricious decision making. Into this messy moment arrived Pauger's beautiful, orderly plans for New Orleans. According to historian Marc de Villiers du Terrage, the appearance of Pauger's map in Paris probably "had weight in the Company's final decision, since the regent, god-father to the new capital, was necessarily flattered to see the project put into effect,"[29] particularly after enduring three years of bad news about the floods and primitive huts in his namesake settlement. Momentum started to build for

Bienville's site. It had amassed a population of 446 within the confines of today's French Quarter, and nearly triple that figure within the modern metro area. "The year 1721 had been generally favourable to New Orleans," wrote Villiers du Terrage. "From a military post, a sales-counter, and a camping-ground for travellers, it had become, in November, a small town, and the number of its irreconcilable enemies began to decrease."[30] On December 23, 1721, a month after the arrival of Pauger's plans, the Company officially decided to transfer the general management of Louisiana from Biloxi to New Orleans.

Word of the status upgrade would not reach New Orleans for months. Meanwhile, Pauger's plan remained on paper into the new year. This is evidenced by a January 1722 eyewitness account of a Jesuit traveler, Father Pierre François Xavier de Charlevoix. "Imagine to yourself," Charlevoix wrote later that month, "two hundred persons . . . sent out to a build a city . . . waiting till a plan is laid out for them, and till they have built houses according to it. . . . Pauger . . . has just shown me a plan of his own invention; but it will not be so easy to put into execution, as it has been to draw [on] paper."[31] The plan that Charlevoix saw was not the crude 1721 sketch but rather the predecessor of a more articulated version that Pauger's superior La Tour had signed off on April 23, 1722. La Tour most likely got back into the picture upon hearing rumors of New Orleans's promotion. Having designed Biloxi and advocated for it to remain the capital, La Tour was pained to see his rivals prevail without him. To New Orleans he bolted to reposition himself in New Orleans's design team. Whatever tension his reappearance might have caused, it did not affect the quality of the work. The April 23 *Plan de la Ville de la Nouvelle Orleans* beautifully depicted a nine-by-six grid, which, angled to match Bienville's 37-degree baseline, neatly exploited the natural levee while positioning corner bastions to confront enemy ships. Each full block measured precisely 50 *toises* (320 English feet) on each side, a toise being six *pieds,* the French foot. Within the blocks were twelve parcels: two sets of five oriented perpendicularly to the river separated by two slightly larger properties parallel to the river.[32] Pauger designed the parcels so that each lot "may have the houses on the street front and may still have some land in the rear to have a garden, which here is half of life."[33]

In the principal cell of the urban grid, Pauger created a *place d'armes,* to be fronted by edifices of church and state in Vitruvian symmetry, overlooking the Mississippi. Pauger also split the blocks evenly behind the church with an additional street (Orleans)—a feature derived from La Tour's plan for Biloxi and suggesting a mentor-protégé influence, despite the animus. Surrounding the urban grid was the angled Vauban fortification. The map labeled the longitudinal streets as, starting downriver, Rue de l'Arsenal (positioned at the urban fringe, per Vauban's instructions), Rue St. Philippe, Rue Dumaine, Rue St. Anne, Rue d'Orleans, Rue St. Pierre, Rue de Toulouse, Rue St. Louis, and Rue Bienville. On the latitudinal streets, starting from the river, were Rue du Quay, Rue Chartres (which farther downriver became Rue de Conty), Rue Royalle (Royale), and finally Rue de Bourbon—the first cartographic depiction of that now-famous toponym. Other names (Dauphine and Burgundy) were added shortly thereafter; still others were relocated, changed, or appended over the centuries. With the exception of Rue Quay (now Decatur), all other street names paid homage to the monarchy in general, or to key Crown figures or their relatives, lineages, titles, or patron saints. Most remain in place today, changed only by anglicization.[34]

Who selected and positioned the street names? It was not John Law, who by this time had fled France in disgrace. Other Parisian authorities would have been more likely to *approve* site-level decisions from the colonies, rather than generate them. Bienville and La Tour, on the other hand, worked on-site, ranked highest in local authority, and knew which egos had to be stroked, including their own. These two men plus Pauger deserve credit for choosing and placing New Orleans's first street names. Evidence come from the self-flattering Rue de Bienville and the probability that Rue St. Pierre and Rue St. Anne discreetly inscribed La Tour (whose first name was Pierre) and his wife, Marie-Anne Le Sueur, into the map. Adrien de Pauger attempted to do the same with Rue St. Adrien, but he seems to have been trumped—perhaps by an indignant La Tour—because that name was soon changed to Rue de l'Arsenal (now Ursulines). Pauger originally wanted Royalle-Bourbon to be used for what is now Royal Street, and Conti to be used for today's Bourbon Street, but someone, perhaps Bienville, intervened, removing the hyphenated name for Royal and transferring "Bourbon" to Bourbon.[35]

Rue de Bourbon honored any one of a number of Louisiana-involved members of the reigning house of France, a family lineage traceable to the thirteenth century and dominant in the region since 1589. Which? One candidate was "Louis Henri, *prince de Condé,* who was duc de Bourbon, a member of the Regency Council, and prime minister from 1723 to 1726," but as historian Charles Edwards O'Neill noted, the founders had already honored him with Rue de Condé. "Was the name Bourbon given in honor of the young prince de Bourbon-Conti, born in 1717, when New Orleans was about to be founded?," O'Neill asked.[36] Probably not, because there was already a Rue de Conti. Count of Toulouse Louis-Alexandre de Bourbon? Rue de Toulouse. Louis-Auguste de Bourbon? Louis-Charles de Bourbon? Other Bourbons? The namers surely realized that such clever ambiguity worked to their advantage, allowing any number of potentially useful narcissists in the House of Bourbon to feel like they now had ownership in this enterprise called New Orleans.

Placement of certain names was strategic: Rue de Orleans, for example, went to the grid's prominent Y-axis to flatter the Company's most critical sponsor, while throughout the other longitudinal streets, the "saint" toponyms interleave those of the royals, for reasons of symmetry and duality of deference to church and state. There is no particular reason why the fourth latitudinal street from the quay got assigned "Bourbon," thus the personality or dynasty it honors bears no insight into the nature of the street, or vice versa.

Pauger's plan represented to the European eye everything that the wild, watery delta was not. It embodied the Vitruvian value of *ordinatio* in its measured and incremented blocks. It bespoke *symmetria* in its perfect proportionality. It exhibited *eurythmia* in its graceful adaptiveness to natural topography, hydrology, climate—and expansion. An updated plan appeared later in 1722, in which the nine-by-six grid grew by two additional streets, yielding a total of sixty-six blocks plus parcel delineation and enumeration, an expanded fortification, and proposed locations for sixteen city features. This map represented the first full surviving cartographic articulation of Bourbon Street and the present-day French Quarter.[37]

On May 26, 1722, word of the Company's decision to designate New Orleans as capital reached Biloxi. "It appears to me that a better decision could not have been made," beamed Bienville to the Council; "we have accordingly transported here all the goods that were at Biloxi."[38] A splendid new urban plan, capital-city status, new people and resources arriving: circumstances appeared to favor New Orleans in the summer of 1722, but for the existing hodgepodge still impeding Pauger's execution of the plan. Surely he eventually would have mustered official forces to clear away those first four years of indiscriminate development, but nature beat him to it. Pauger wrote that at 9:00 a.m. on September 11, 1722, "a great wind" swept the settlement, "followed an hour later by the most terrible tempest and hurricane that could ever be seen."[39] Not until 4:00 a.m. on September 13 did the gusts abate, at which time "they set to work to repair the damage done." This included thirty-four houses, the city's entire flotilla of five ships, flatboats and pirogues, plus cargo and cannons.[40] Yet New Orleans's first major hurricane proved to be a blessing in disguise. Wrote La Tour: "All these buildings were temporary and old, not a single one was in the alignment of the new town, and they were to have been pulled down. Little harm would have been done."[41]

Dumont described the events that followed. La Tour "cleared a pretty long and wide strip [present-day Decatur Street] along the river, to put in execution the plan he [and Pauger] had projected." They traced "the streets and quarters [of] the new town [and] to each settler who [petitioned] they gave a plot ten fathoms front by twenty deep [60 by 120 English feet]. . . . Those who obtained these plots [must] inclose them with palisades, and leave all around a strip at least three feet wide, at the foot of which a ditch was to be dug."[42] By the end of 1722, nine parcels facing Bourbon Street had new houses on them, mostly between Toulouse and Orleans. By the mid-1720s, all of the street's blocks had been surveyed, named, cleared, and cursorily drained with moat-like ditches around each "isle" (block), though structural development would not come for a while.[43] A built environment subsequently arose within the cells of Pauger's grid. The "palisade cabins" typical of Biloxi, built entirely of pine, transformed in the new New Orleans to ones built of "brick, or half-brick and half-wood," using cypress. "New Orleans," wrote Dumont of this era, "began to assume the appearance of a city."[44]

In this manner, French colonials brought Hippodamian rectitude and Vitruvian symmetry to the desultory delta, and Bourbon Street ranked among the very first constitutional elements. At the broadest level, the French Crown—via its Enlightenment-era attempt to perfect the art of colonialism in the test bed called Louisiana—deserves credit for the creation of Bourbon Street and its vicinage. Specifically, it was La Salle who identified the ideal geographical situation that New Orleans would later be created to seize, while John Law, the Duc d'Orléans, and the Company of the West initiated the city's foundation. Bienville and his native informants deserve credit for selecting this particular site to host New Orleans, while he and possibly Pailloux oriented the future street grid to its 37-degree azimuth. Pauger deserves the lion's share of the credit for Bourbon Street, giving it its exact location, length, width, block, and parcel delineations. La Tour influenced and imposed himself into Pauger's work, while both engineers plus Bienville share credit for naming the street.

Nighttime revelers on Bourbon Street startle to the sight of the dramatically backlit statue of Christ in St. Anthony's Garden, which casts an ethereal shadow upon the rear wall of St. Louis Cathedral. Some observers ponder the visage's spiritual message; others might regret their evening's indulgences. Whatever the interpretation, all owe their presence at that spot largely to a man interred beneath that shadow. Adrien de Pauger lies below the marble floors of the cathedral, having died of "the fever and dysentery" in June 1726, within three years of

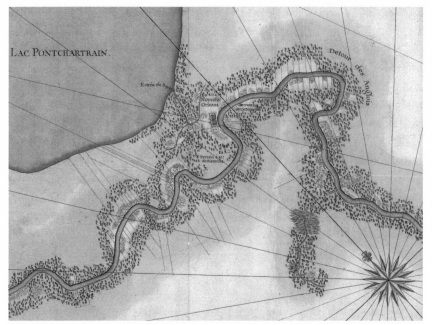

Straight lines in a sinuous space: rectilinear New Orleans perched upon the wending Mississippi, ca. 1732. Detail of *Carte du cours du fleuve St. Louis depuis dix lieues audessus de la Nouvelle Orleans. Library of Congress.*

the deaths of Le Blond de la Tour, the Duc d'Orléans, and John Law.[45] Law, for his part, has been redeemed by economics if not history; while his Louisiana failure is remembered today as history's first stock market crash and a real estate scam for the ages, Law's theories form the bases of modern monetary policy, and New Orleans today is the "unintended consequence" of Law's attempt to put his ideas into practice.[46] The rectitude of the original city plat, meanwhile, bears the imprint of enlightened thinking dating back to ancient times. Of the men most responsible for creating the straight line of Bourbon Street in this sinuous space, only Bienville would see it come to fruition as a place for people.

A Streetscape Emerges

Rue Bourbon and Calle Borbon, 1722–1803

We stand at the intersection of Rue Bourbon and Rue Bienville in January 1732. Gazing southwestwardly, Rue Bourbon ends abruptly one block away, barricaded by an unimposing stockade lined with a loathsome moat "largely unfinished[,] only *un pouce* deep."[1] In the distant left is a smattering of "houses . . . built with wooded-front and mortar, whitewashed, wainscoted and latticed," their roofs "covered with shingles[,] thin boards [with] the appearance and beauty of slate."[2] Greased paper or cloth *plastille* covers those windows that are not shuttered, as glass is a scarce luxury. Wisps of gray smoke rise from mud-clad central chimneys. Around the rustic hovels are sheds, chicken coops, dovecotes, rabbit hutches, fallow gardens, and scrubby fields with the occasional leafless fruit tree or mulberry bush, the latter planted in the hope of developing a local silkworm industry. Far away, a rickety windmill churns with the winter breezes sweeping off the river. A network of narrow drainage ditches, some lined with crude picket or seven-board fences, demarcate parcels regardless of the improvements therein—their proprietors apparently aware of the relationship between possession and the law. Farm animals wander more or less freely; some pigs wallow in fetid puddles. Rue Bourbon manages to be at once dusty and muddy, desolate yet persevering.[3]

In the distance to our right is a rather foreboding line of dense forest strewn with slash and debris. Villagers refer to this direction as the "woods" side of town—"back" toward the swamps, as opposed to the "river" side, or "front." Along this wild edge toil enslaved black men, furnished by their masters "to cut down the trees at the two ends of the town as far as Bayou St. John . . . to clear this ground and to give air to the city and to the [wind]mill."[4] The landscape before us, little resembling Pauger's original majestic vision, evokes any number of French colonial experiments throughout the circum-Caribbean world, and it appears equally unpromising. No wonder. Most denizens come from the geographic and economic fringes of the Francophone world: the lower strata of societies in France or French Canada, Saint-Domingue, and the West Indies, via the nascent coastal outposts of Pensacola, Mobile, and Biloxi. For every *concessionaire,* company employee, or soldier, there are more than a few *engagés* and *forçats*—indentured servants and forced immigrants deported from France for criminality, penury, indebtedness, or other undesirable traits. Nearly half the city's population, including the field laborers we see around Rue Bourbon, arrived in chains in the past decade from the Senegambia region of West Africa or from other French slave colonies. As in the Caribbean, a small caste of free people of color (initially called *affranchis* and later *gens de couleur libres*) materialized between the free white and enslaved black castes. A few miles upriver, German and Swiss farmers settled about a decade ago, and now produce a disproportionate share of the city's sustenance—something of which the local Francophones seem incapable. What we see from this corner of Rue Bourbon falls short of the great expectations of the founder generation and its royal patrons.

Looking downriver, we see hints of city life. On the first corner of Rue Bourbon lives the widow Laforge on a property she rents from a man named Dauphin. Her neighbor, La Sonde, also a widow, lives with her child, her slave, and her slave's child in a compound of three structures. The next two lots, granted "to one named Desloriers" and "to one named Jean Foutre," are developed with little houses but currently unoccupied. What surprises our eye, to our right, is the ornamental garden with a symmetrical serpentine design, recalling the more enlightened aspirations once held for this forlorn outpost.[5] It is the exception, however; mostly we see humble abodes. "The greatest part of the houses," writes one resident, "is of brick; the rest are of timber and brick[;] many habitations [live] close together[,] each making a causey to secure his ground from inundations, which fail not to come every year with the spring."[6] Most houses on Rue Bourbon are of the standard one-story cross-timber type, in which locally made bricks cemented with a mortar of sand and lime—or, alternately, a mass of mud entangled with hay or other resilient grasses or stems—fill the X-frame of hand-hewn timbers. Their roofs, covered with cypress shingles or bark, are universally hipped in their configurations, many with Norman-style double-pitches that extend anywhere from a *pied* (a French foot) to a *toise* (six *pieds*) beyond the walls, providing shelter from rain or sun. The internal layout is of the *salle et chambre* variety: two abutting rooms, the *salle* for dining and the *chambre* for sleeping,

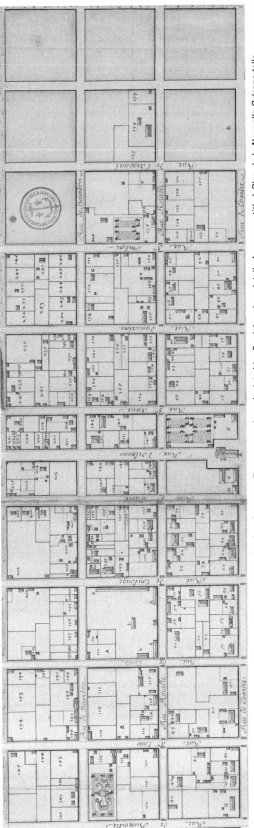

Bourbon, Royal, and Chartres Streets a decade after they were first surveyed, as depicted by Gonichon in a detail of a map entitled *Plan de la Nouvelle Orleans telle qu'elle estoit au mois de dexembre 1731. Library of Congress.*

sharing a common two-hearth central chimney. A gallery usually lines at least one side of the structure, sometimes all four, creating an airy sheltered buffer between private and public space. The rear gallery is more like a loggia, with built-in cabinets, functional storage bins, and chests. Wall-mounted chimneys are rare; hallways (corridors) are all but unknown; stairways are usually set within the exterior gallery space; and kitchens stand separately from residences for fire safety. We also see some hovels, reminiscent of those from the city's first years, comprising a palisade of wooden stakes driven into the ground, encased with muddy hay, and topped with a bark or wood-tiled roof.[7]

Crossing Rue Conti (which in 1732 was called St. Louis) brings us to the homes of this first Bourbon community. They are occupied by the likes of La Roche Castel the blacksmith; Becquet the locksmith; Barbaud, who has the largest household on Rue Bourbon; and Marseau. Most have families; some have slaves. They also have rules for living here. Officials mandate that proprietors dig drainage ditches five *pieds* from their lots so that the soil dries and become a sidewalk, but few comply, giving rise to deeply puddled, filthy water. It's a source of great inconvenience, and necessitates that raised wooden walkways, *banquettes*, be built in lieu of earthen sidewalks. Ditches, wooden bridges, dust, fallow gardens, picket fences, simple cottages belonging to French-speaking families with heads of household like Brosset the surgeon, Rafflot the roofer, La Pierre the hairdresser, Commercy the knife maker, and Angebaud the carpenter characterize the rest of our stroll down Rue Bourbon. There are exceptions: around St. Ann lives Marie, a free black woman, one of only two black property owners on Rue Bourbon, and one of her neighbors is the city's first English-speaking Protestant family.[8]

Arriving at the Dumaine block of Rue Bourbon puts us in the lower fringes of the developed city. To our left begins the road to Bayou St. John, on which arrives everything from bricks made in Chantilly, to timber cut from the backswamp, to fish and game drawn from Lake Pontchartrain, to colonists in transit from Mobile and Biloxi. After the properties of Vincent and Cape at the St. Philip corner, Rue Bourbon becomes mostly empty, save for the irregular posts, palisades, and ditches. And in the distance to our left is that daunting line of dark, dense timber.

Present-day lovers and loathers of Bourbon agree on only one thing: that the street is atypical of the French Quarter neighborhood and of the city of New Orleans. The opposite, however, was the case in the colonial era: Rue Bourbon typified the city's original nineteen streets. It was a representative microcosm of local society;

its people and built environment reflected the heart of the city's statistical bell-shaped curve in terms of population, density, age and family structure, class, architecture, and municipal conditions. Few eyewitnesses who recorded accounts of eighteenth-century New Orleans found anything particularly salient on Rue Bourbon. It was pedestrian, unpretentious, and utterly unexceptional.

Census data bear this out. While the street in 1726 did have more residents (152, or 20 percent of the city's population) than any other except Royal (168), this was mostly a product of its longer length. When normalized, Rue Bourbon falls into an intermediary rank, with 2.5 people per household, double the peripheral streets' household density of 1.3 and half that of the riverfront blocks' 5.2. Little had changed by the census of 1727, when Rue Bourbon's population of 171 people fell behind Royal's 226, its household density of 3.1 ranked below the city average of 3.6, and its proportion of servants and slaves (3 percent, all servants) paled in comparison to the city's 17 percent and the inner-city's 30–40 percent.

The year 1731 brought ministerial change to Louisiana when, after years of disappointment, the flailing Company finally relinquished the colony to the Crown. Whatever lofty designs the French had for New Orleans as a lucrative quasi-commercial imperial experiment, it now looked like just another mediocre financial and administrative responsibility. A census in January 1732 indicated that the malaise had a corollary on city streets. That headcount enumerated only 111 people on Rue Bourbon, 60 fewer than five years earlier.[9]

Low prioritization from Paris did not completely incapacitate New Orleanians. They had work to do. Levees were erected to prevent, or rather minimize, river flooding. Charity Hospital (1736) and the Ursulines Convent (built in 1751 for the nuns who arrived in 1727) brought health care and education to residents. A sawmill powered by a river diversion helped speed up house construction. Population steadily increased, though by no means dramatically, as the founding cohort died off and the first Creole (locally bred) generation took its place. New Orleans's meager progress hardly won the attention of the Crown in the 1750s and 1760s because its attention focused on the worldwide hostilities that came to be known as the Seven Years' War.

England's crushing defeat of France in the North American theater of that conflict—what English-speakers would call the French and Indian War—radically realigned the geography of European empire. France retained only a few Canadian and Caribbean islands, while England gained French Canada, French Louisiana east of the Mississippi, and Spanish West Florida. It would have won Louisiana west of the Mississippi as well had King Louis XV not secretly ceded those vast lands to his Spanish cousin King Carlos III a year earlier through the Treaty of Fontainebleau. Included in the clandestine offer was New Orleans, whose terrain was deemed an "isle" on account of the Bayou Manchac distributary, and was thus cartographically detached from the east-of-the-Mississippi mainland. The clever deal compensated a friend (Spain) for the loss of its territory (Florida) to the British, while keeping a key city (New Orleans) out of the hands of a triumphant enemy (England). We can only imagine what New Orleans might look like today had it become British. Instead, Spain accepted Louisiana in late 1762; after the secret transfer became public in 1764, the dominion of New Orleans passed from France to Spain politically in 1766 and militarily in 1769.

The populace, however, generally retained its creolized Francophone Caribbean culture, and many administrators sent from Spain (*peninsulares*) married into the Creole elite. French predominated linguistically; only official documents and discourse regularly occurred in Spanish. As is often the case in regime changes, toponyms were altered to remind residents of their new governors; thus, *rue* became *calle*, and *Bourbon* became *Borbon* or *Burbon*. The street itself changed only incrementally. Calle Borbon from the 1760s to the 1790s hosted a villagelike streetscape of cottages and fenced gardens as it did in French colonial times, only with more people and edifices.

Visualizing daily life on late-eighteenth-century Calle Borbon entails an understanding of Spanish colonial municipal management and dispute resolution. "Reactionary" would be an apt description. Only when enterprises emitted nuisances that incommoded neighbors, or were thought to threaten public health, did authorities of the Cabildo (City Hall) intervene; there were no land-use ordinances or zoning to speak of, and certainly no planning commission. The retailing of seafood provides a case in point. Fishermen, who traditionally sold their catch "in the plaza [or] in the heat of the sun" on street corners, raised residents' ire when they dumped "blood, gills and other waste" at their doorsteps. The Cabildo responded by ordering fish vendors "to a designated place" in the recently constructed market, predecessor of today's French Market. In another case, authorities intervened regarding "the public gambling place owned by Boniquet" and "the freedom enjoyed by slaves of both sexes in going to dances [at] Coquet's house," because of the "detriment caused to the public moral[,] tranquility, good order[,] and cleanliness of this city."[10] While no records detail the enterprises on Calle Borbon in this era, we do know that "taverns, inns . . . rooming houses, billiard halls, restaurants and soft drink establishments" and "a very large number

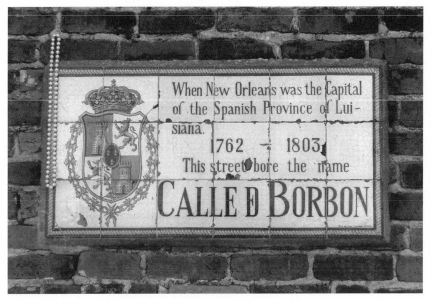

Designation for Bourbon Street during the Spanish period. *Photograph by author.*

of Cabarets" abounded citywide. Many were run by Catalonians from Barcelona, others by Creoles. "There is almost not a single street," growled a Spanish official, "where there is not one or more cabarets in sight of the citizens [—] places of idleness and vices so disgraceful and . . . degrading to humanity." Bourbon surely had its share, but given its distance from the river, it generally hosted less commercial activity than Royal, which in turn had less than Chartres and Levee (Quay) along the busy riverfront. For this and other reasons, the Cabildo, when it divided New Orleans into administrative wards in 1779, used Calle Borbon as a border, because it conveniently separated blocks with denser populations and activities from quieter areas in the rear of the city.[11]

Like today, streets in colonial New Orleans required constant maintenance. Authorities required that property owners construct *puentes*—wooden planks arranged like bridges across drainage ditches—in front of their properties, but widespread noncompliance forced the Cabildo to let the work to city publicans. The puddles, hoofs, feet, wheels, and wind eroded Calle Borbon unevenly, requiring additional publicans to regrade the streets using fill and a water-level device to ensure proper inclination.[12] Circulating all around were horses and carriages, pedestrians, frolicking children, stray dogs, occasional livestock, the Cabildo-paid town crier, and peddlers offering, in singsong French Creole, everything from "fresh beef, fresh pork, salted meat and sausages[,] mutton, venison[,] rice, fresh and dry vegetables" to "wild fowl of all kinds and fresh fish"[13]

The Spaniards also created a street sanitation service using mule-drawn carts. The beasts fertilized the streets with their droppings, as did those pulling carriages, not to mention the occasional head of livestock. With the mud, stagnant water, potholes, ditches, and planks, a walk down Calle Borbon in the late 1700s could be a hazardous and disgusting adventure—worse so at night. When "loiterers or people of bad character" successfully evaded authorities one too many times, the Cabildo acted on the need for nighttime illumination by mandating owners of corner properties to erect gas lanterns with reflective tin backing. The "reflectors" cast about as much light as an alacritous firefly. Two years later, the Cabildo ordered eighty-six oil lamps from Philadelphia and hired Brion the blacksmith to determine their best placement at intersections citywide. Brion advised installing wooden posts at each corner, with an iron arm extending the glass-encased lamp into the intersection and a counterweight at the opposite end. Costs for the "oil, cotton, sulphur, wicks, flints, and steel . . . to make sparks," plus nightly lighting and maintenance, was borne by property owners based on their frontage, although this was later changed to a chimney tax and a flour tax. Fuel for lamps included fish oil, bear oil, and pelican grease; costly whale oil, which burned clean and bright, was reserved for indoor lighting. To save money, street lamps were lit only twenty-two nights monthly, "based on the decrease or increase of the light of the moon."[14]

Colonial New Orleans changed forever on Good Friday 1788. Around 1:30 p.m., a woman in the state treasurer's home at Chartres and Toulouse, two blocks from Calle Borbon, "crown[ed] her devotion by making a small altar [and] left several candles burning. [A] candle fell on some ornaments which took fire, and the house in an instant was in flames."[15] Winds swept the fire two blocks in either direction on Chartres, and, abetted by "the powders which the merchants had in their stores," the blaze exploded across six blocks of Royal Street and seven along Calle Borbon. Dauphine and Conti Streets finally broke the conflagration, and by late afternoon, "4/5 of the populated section of this City was reduced to ashes, [including] the Parish Church and House, Cabildo and Jail." Worse yet, the destroyed district comprised "the part of the City most important and best situated."[16] At least twenty squares were charred utterly, including twelve fronting Calle Borbon from Conti to beyond Dumaine, making it the most-devastated street in the city. In all, 856 "fine and commodious houses valued on an average at three thousand dollars each, were destroyed,[17] including most of the aging French-era buildings, with their cross-timbered walls and double-pitched hip roofs. Because the fire burned out just before reaching the St. Philip intersection with Calle Borbon, it spared a corner cottage with precisely those early-colonial architectural traits, despite that it postdated the French colonial era. That edifice also miraculously survived the nineteenth and twentieth centuries, and operates today as the now famous but once utterly mundane tavern known as Lafitte's Blacksmith Shop. This Bourbon Street landmark rates among the best surviving examples of the building types that once predominated throughout colonial New Orleans.

The Good Friday fire was the most physically destructive disaster ever to befall Bourbon Street, obliterating half its edifices. Roughly 80 percent of the city lay in ruins. Yet New Orleans proved resilient in the aftermath, thanks to the leadership of Governor Esteban Miró, the Cabildo's provisioning of food and shelter, the generosity of Spanish benefactor Don Andres Almonaster y Rojas, the easing of trade regulations, and a construction boom in the city's first *suburbia*. The speed and quality of the recovery, however, fell short of citizens' expectations. For example, a May 1789 real estate transaction described present-day 636–640 Bourbon as "an ordinary lot of ground with all of the debris and ruins found thereon," indicating that the charred "house of wood and brick" had not been cleared fourteen months after the blaze.[18]

New houses eventually arose in the fire zone, and they generally exhibited the same designs of earlier decades. Although hundreds of French colonial structures disappeared in the blaze, the French colonial architectural tradition, infused with West Indian influences, survived. The Spanish made no attempt to change it in the name of fire prevention. Instead, they adopted a policy of fire suppression, requesting from their superiors "four pumps . . . 60 leather buckets . . . two hooks with a chain . . . rope . . . and six hooks with long wooden handles."[19]

Governor Miró was replaced by the equally capable Governor Hector de Carondelet in 1792. Among the many municipal achievements of Carondelet's era were the city's first theater, newspaper, police force, and navigation canal. Of particular significance to Bourbon Street was the decision by surveyor Carlos Trudeau, who laid out Suburbia Santa Maria (now the Central Business District) upriver from the original city, to give the new streets new names rather than continue the old ones. What would otherwise have been Bourbon Street's extension instead gained the name Calle de San Francisco, later Calle de Carondelet. To this day, none of the French Quarter street names save Rampart extend nominally upriver from Canal Street.

Governor Carondelet's administration saw nearly as many disasters as achievements; three hurricanes and two fires struck during 1792–94 alone. The last of these traumas heralded a turning point in the city's architectural history. On December 8, 1794, boys playing in a Royal Street courtyard ignited flames that swept southward with autumn winds. Within three hours, 212 structures were charred. Flames licked Calle Borbon but destroyed only two of its structures.[20]

Unlike in 1788, the Cabildo this time moved to *prevent* future fires by clearing away hazards and by looking to their own building traditions to codify a more fire-resistant cityscape. It stipulated that new houses "must be built of bricks and a flat roof or tile roof," their walls "covered with cement of at least one inch thick."[21] Other Spanish features unrelated to fire safety, such as arched openings on the ground floor, pilasters, balconies, courtyards, a sense of symmetry, and façades flush with the banquette rather than set back, accompanied the architectural transformation. Soon the fenced gardens and wooden galleries of a French village gave way to the stuccoed brick walls and wrought-iron balconies of a Spanish city. The American administration subsequently mandated brick construction and slate roofs for the inner city, permitting wooden structures only in the back-of-town.[22] Time and the elements have claimed many of these early post-1794 edifices, but the styles and sensibilities instilled by the Spanish codes still abound in the modern-day Bourbon streetscape. Perhaps the best surviving example is the Old Absinthe House at 240 Bourbon, erected three years after the departure of the dons but nevertheless representative of their architectural legacy.

Fire transformed the streets of New Orleans in the same era that revolution rocked the Atlantic world—in the British colonies (1776), in France proper (1789, which toppled the House of Bourbon), and in France's Saint-Domingue sugar colony (1791), where a complex caste war exploded into a major slave insurrection. Concurrently, technological breakthroughs began to alter southern agriculture, boding well for the future of New Orleans. Eli Whitney's 1793 patent for the "cotton engine" made lint production lucrative and drove the spread of cotton into the lower Mississippi Valley. Two years later, Jean Etienne de Boré of New Orleans succeeded in granulating Louisiana sugarcane at a commercially viable scale, making it exportable and profitable at the same time that war-torn Saint-Domingue's productivity plunged. Sugarcane cultivation swiftly replaced crops such as indigo, rice, and tobacco throughout southern Louisiana. The breakthroughs raised the value of arable land, rekindled the plantation system, breathed new life into chattel slavery, and made Louisiana suddenly relevant in the Atlantic economy. Shipments of cotton and sugar had only one economical way to reach that economy: by floating down the Mississippi for deposit at New Orleans and transshipping to world markets, where new steam-engine technology revolutionized the processing of cotton textiles. The Port of New Orleans was starting to look more attractive.

Dramatic political news punctuated the local excitement. Spain, waning in power and apprehensive about the United States' mounting interest in New Orleans, secretly retroceded in 1800 its Louisiana colony to Napoleon's militarily powerful France and, two years later, prohibited Americans from depositing goods there. Upon learning of these provocations, an alarmed President Thomas Jefferson aspired to gain control of the once-marginalized, now-valued port city, as France boldly returned to the North American stage. But where Jefferson saw strategic advantage, Napoleon saw economic subservience: the future emperor viewed his regained Louisiana colony as little more than a breadbasket to feed the astonishingly profitable sugar colony of Saint-Domingue—once, of course, its insurgent slaves were crushed.

Instead, Napoleon's twenty thousand troops, sent to Saint-Domingue in 1802 to restore order, were vanquished through lethal yellow fever outbreaks and bloody battles. Loss of the keystone colony undermined whatever passive interest Napoleon had in Louisiana. Wary of overextending his empire, in need of money, and in light of impending war, Napoleon decided to sell the entire colony to the United States, which had bargained previously only for New Orleans. "A vast and unlimited territory [became American] without the loss of a drop of blood," marveled one westerner of the Louisiana Purchase.[23] The eighty-five-year-old port once envisioned to command that territory for France instead became the new American city of New Orleans.

Officials ceremoniously lowered the French tricolor for the last time on December 20, 1803. In only a few years, New Orleans's fortunes had dramatically reversed. For decades, the colony played the role of rogue or orphan to two distracted Old World monarchies which viewed New Orleans, at best, as a portal into unknown hinterland; now the city found itself treasured by an ascendant and unabashedly capitalistic New World democracy which saw it as kingpin in westward expansion. Prominent observers routinely predicted that this new American

city would "doubtless one day become the greatest [city on the] continent, perhaps even in the world."[24] Another went further, foreseeing New Orleans as "one
of the greatest commercial cities in the universe."[25]

To incoming Anglo-Americans, royalistic names like "Bourbon" reeked of
musty Old World "bombastic pride and ostentation."[26] Nevertheless, American
authorities retained most colonial-era street names, not wanting to offend local
sensibilities any more than necessary. They did bring their English language to
this Francophone city, however, and Anglophonic pronunciations increasingly
permeated discourses and led to relabeled toponyms. Nueva and Nou-velle Or-le-
ans became New Orl-eans; Luisiana and Louisiane became Lou-isi-ana; and Calle
Bor-bon and Rue Bour-bon became Bourbon Street. These would be the least of
the changes to come.

A Transect of Antebellum Society

Ethnicity, Race, Class, and Caste on Bourbon Street, 1803–1860

Shortly after the Louisiana Purchase, New Orleans was officially incorporated as an American city with a government and legal status. Among the first orders of business: "a general survey of the inhabitants of this City and suburb."[1] Conducted by Matthew Flannery during May–August 1805, the enumeration determined that New Orleans and immediately adjacent areas had 8,475 inhabitants, 177 percent more than in 1778.[2] The population had changed spatially, as it expanded into the upper suburb of Santa Maria (which the Francophones called "Faubourg Ste. Marie" and the Anglophones "St. Mary" or "the American quarters") and shifted within the inner city. Whereas Bourbon Street consistently claimed an intermediary population rank throughout the colonial era, now it topped the list: Flannery's census enumerated more people residing on Bourbon (697) than on any other street, including prominent Royal with its 645 denizens. Bourbon also had the highest number of white residents (316) and the highest percentage of people below the age of sixteen, an indicator of familial domesticity and rootedness in a port known for single male transients.

What ca.1805 Bourbon was *not* was the richest street; ten other arteries had more slaveholders, and higher ratios of enslaved to free people. Those tonier residences tended to be located in the front and center of town. Nor was Bourbon the most racially diverse; twelve other streets had higher nonwhite percentages, and they generally lay in the rear or lateral fringes of town.[3] Bourbon Street in the early 1800s, as in colonial times, was neither particularly powerful nor disenfranchised, neither bustling nor sleepy, and not at all notorious. It was, rather, a reasonably priced place for light commerce and homemaking among the working and middle classes, with smaller numbers of poorer and wealthier families as well. Bourbon had, however, declined since colonial times in its share of the city's total population: whereas one out of five New Orleanians lived there in 1727 and one in eight 1732, now, in 1805, one in twelve called that street home.[4]

Bourbon's growth matched the temper of the times. Consider, from the American perspective, the excitement over the Louisiana Purchase. An exotic and strategic port city suddenly lands in friendly hands, just as thousands of Americans migrate westward down the Ohio River Valley, convert forests into farmlands, and find themselves in need of a downriver emporium to cash out their harvests. Opportunity motivated waves of Anglo-Americans to cast their lot with the curious city. Some newcomers derived from English stock and hailed from New England and the mid-Atlantic states; others were of Celtic, Upland Scottish, or Irish heritage and arrived from the Upper South. Nearly all were Anglophone Protestants of American nationality and culture. Many were self-selected for traits of ambition, savvy, and risk-taking. When newcomers' numbers began to mount in the 1810s, so did locals' consternation. "The Americans [are] swarming in from the northern states[,] invading Louisiana as the holy tribes invaded the land of Canaan," wrote the last French official to oversee Louisiana. "Each one turn[s] over in his mind a little plan of speculation."[5] They jolted the city's economy, turned a deaf ear to its lingua franca, and complicated the social terrain in just about every way imaginable.

Native-born New Orleanians felt rather unsettled by all the excitement—and woefully unprepared for the changes ahead. Compared to their new compatriots, they spoke a different language, practiced a different religion, and followed distinct legal philosophies. They perceived race and managed slavery differently. They surveyed land and built houses their own way. They ate different foods, celebrated different festivals, and honored different heroes. They even entombed their dead differently. Their leaders for the previous century had been appointed to them, not elected among them. New Orleanians were told, not polled; decisions and policies flowed from the top down, with little feedback tolerated from the bottom up. Provincial, culturally conservative, resistant to change, often unlettered, naïve to the ways of republican government, and ill-equipped for the fiercely competitive world of free-market capitalism, New Orleanians fretted, then resented, then resisted the onslaught of les Américains.

In the face of this impending threat, New Orleans's mostly Catholic Francophone population came to view its shared colonial-era heritage and deep-rooted

Louisiana nativity as a unifying bond—a panracial, place-based sort of ethnicity that distinguished them from English-speaking Protestant Anglo-Americans from elsewhere. In certain contexts, the natives described themselves as the *ancienne population;* in others, including vernacular speech, they were known far and wide as the Creoles—a modification of the old Spanish *criollo* and Portuguese *crioulo* ("bred"), which originally meant the first generation born locally, in the New World colony, to parents of the charter or founder generation, who were born elsewhere. Other appellations loosely dropped on this group by contemporary Anglos included "the French," "the Gallics," "the Gauls," or "the Latins." Racial identification within Creolism usually derived from context. Advertisements offering "Creole Slaves," for example, implied that these were black Creoles, while an article on Creole voting trends would indicate that these were whites Creoles, because blacks were denied suffrage. The *gens de couleur libres* (free people of color—mixed in racial ancestry, Catholic in faith, and Franco-American in culture) occupied a special caste between white and black, and were often described as Creoles of color or black Creoles.

Anglo-Americans were not the only *arrivistes:* more than nine thousand refugees—roughly equally divided among whites, free people of color, and the enslaved—arrived in 1809 via Cuba from former Saint-Domingue, now Haiti. These Francophones breathed new life into New Orleans's Franco-Afro-Caribbean language and culture, but they further complicated the position of the Creoles, who now had to share power, resources, and living space with a third faction. Such also was the Creoles' relationship with immigrants arriving directly from France, who like the Americans tended to be worldly—but like the Creoles spoke French, practiced Catholicism, and exhibited Latin cultural ways. Immigrants from the Spanish-speaking world additionally diversified New Orleans's ethnic landscape, arriving since the 1770s from Mexico, Cuba, Central and South America, the Canary Islands, and the Spain mainland. At least a few representatives of nearly every society of the greater Atlantic Basin, and many beyond, circulated in New Orleans and on Bourbon Street in the early 1800s. "What is the state of society in New Orleans?" pondered a visitor in 1819; "[One] might as well ask, What is the shape of a cloud?"[6]

The Americans also rearranged the city's ethnic geography. A first clue as to how appears in the aforementioned 1805 census, which lists for Bourbon Street a who's who of classic French and Spanish Creole surnames, e.g., Beauregard, Dreaux, Duplessis, Castillion, Peyroux, Lefevre, and Lamouroux. They overwhelmingly lived in the lower part of the neighborhood. Rare were the Anglo names, despite the recently installed American authority. A notable exception was census-taker Matthew Flannery, who recorded himself living at "71 Rue de Bourbon S.," in the uppermost part of Bourbon between present-day Iberville and Bienville. Most of the remaining handful of Anglo-sounding names on Bourbon Street (Hinson, Moore, Durnford) belonged to Flannery's immediate neighbors.

More clues come from an 1808 land-ownership map. At first glance, the chart's symmetrical arrangement of proprietors' names exudes a sense of civic regularity. A closer inspection, however, uncovers a burgeoning social-geographical dichotomy that would soon expand citywide. Scanning Bourbon's interior and lower blocks, we see among the landowners the same Creole predomination as in the 1805 census. But among the uppermost blocks of Bourbon—where Flannery lived—we see more Anglo surnames: Jackson, Kennedy, Duncan, McCormick, John[s]ton, among others. The pattern holds true at coarser scales: in the eleven lower blocks of Bourbon (from Bienville to Barracks), fully 96 percent of proprietors had French or Spanish Creole surnames, and only 4 percent were Anglo. But above Bienville Street, those percentages shift to 59 percent Creole and 41 percent Anglo.[7]

What Bourbon Street exhibited in 1805–8 foretold nineteenth-century New Orleans's premier cultural-geographical chasm: a predominately Creole, Francophone, Catholic, Old World–oriented downtown, versus a more culturally American, Anglophone, and Protestant uptown. Bourbon and other French Quarter streets straddled that lower-Creole/upper-Anglo ethnic divide for much of the nineteenth century, forming a fine transect of local society. The Anglicized nature of upper Bourbon partially explains why the first Protestant church in New Orleans arose on its corner with Canal Street. Built in 1815, the small octagonal Christ Church was designed by an Anglo-American (Henry S. Latrobe) in a style popular among Anglo-Americans (Gothic) for Anglo-American congregants of the Episcopal faith.[8]

Creole New Orleans's slow and often painful absorption into the United States would define the city's and Bourbon Street's experience for decades to come. The ethnic tension ran deep and endured many years. "To my grandmother, an American was nothing, absolutely," asserted a member of the old French Creole clan of Masson. "They were just trespassers who had no business there," she continued, "and it was a disgrace to think that my mother had married an American. . . . The Americans thought the French were beneath them too. . . . There really were two worlds on either side of Canal Street."[9] Mildred Masson Costa, born in 1903 into a strictly French-speaking household in the French Quarter, spoke those memories into a tape recorder in 1985.

Culture colored the competition, but what was really at stake was money. Along the riverfront and in the banks and exchanges, the serious business of business hummed. Now that the colonial obstructionists had been shunted aside, New Orleans's long-recognized geographical advantage enabled commerce to come calling from all directions. Statehood brought political and legal order to the Louisiana Territory in 1812, the same year that steamboat technology arrived to the city's docks, solving the problem of contra-current shipping. Insatiable demand for labor made the city the nation's premier slave mart, handling domestic importations of humanity sold out of the old Upper South into the fertile cotton and sugarcane plantations of the new Southwest. New Orleans came to a different sort of national prominence in 1815 for its merciless rout of invading professional British troops in what proved to be the culminating battle of the War of 1812. The victory helped introduce this isolated and exotic outpost to the rest of the American people and envelop it into the national fold; Anglo-American migration subsequently increased, as did foreign immigration. By 1820, the city's population had more than tripled since Americanization, with 27,176 people in the city proper and 41,351 throughout the lower-river region. New suburbs sprouted above (Faubourgs Duplantier, Solet, La Course, and L'Annunciation, 1806–10) and behind (Faubourg Tremé, 1810) the original city.

Despite the upriver expansion, century-old Bourbon Street still retained its rank as the most populated street in the city. Its 1,307 people in 1820 outnumbered Canal Street's 1,198 and Dauphine's 1,147. More whites and enslaved blacks called Bourbon home than any other street (647 and 376, respectively), and more African Americans both enslaved and free (660) lived here than on all other streets except neighboring Dauphine, which had 694. Bourbon also had the highest number of women, who, at 763, represented nearly three-fifths of the street's population. Nearly one out of every twenty New Orleanians had a Bourbon Street address, the highest street-level proportion citywide. But Bourbon's share of the city's total population continued to shrink, as one would expect, given its fixed length in a growing city. Whereas 20 percent of New Orleanians lived on Bourbon in 1727, only 12 percent lived there in 1732, 8 percent in 1805, and by 1820, 4.8 percent.

Because the six river-parallel streets of the French Quarter—Levee (now Decatur), Chartres, Royal, Bourbon, Dauphine, and Burgundy—share the same length, width, orientation, and developmental era, they present a fine comparative human geography of antebellum New Orleans. They also help us understand Bourbon Street's place in local society.

A key explainer of spatial patterns in this era was proximity to the river or swamp, a geography that rendered two perceptual urban spaces: the "front" and "back" of town. Areas fronting the Mississippi hosted most of the city's economic activity. There lay also the highest and best-drained lands. Commercial activity and prosperity generally gravitated toward the front of town—but not *too* close, because the river's actual edge was replete with bustling traffic and malodorous port activity. This explains why the Levee Street corridor, now Decatur and North Peters, proliferates to this day with storehouses and warehouses rather than residences.

Areas back from the river, along and behind Burgundy Street, saw none of those riverfront annoyances. Instead, however, they suffered from low topographic elevation and proximity to the flood-prone mosquito-breeding swamps. Far away from the commercial heartbeat of the city, the low-rent back-of-town attracted *les petit gens*—the working class, the poor, and the disenfranchised. This relegation explains why Burgundy Street and neighborhoods behind it abound to this day with simple cottages and shotgun houses, with relatively few storehouses, townhouses, or mansions.

Areas between the riverfront and the back-of-town afforded the benefits of the bustling inner-city economy and high elevation, while also maximizing the distance from both riverfront nuisances and backswamp hazards. That spatial positioning translated to a more illustrious social position, higher real estate values, better housing, and thus a wealthier demographic—*les grands*—that was more likely to comprise members of the master class. This explains why Chartres and Royal Streets had the highest percentage of slaves in 1820, with 37.3 and 34.8 percent respectively. It explains why John Adems Paxton observed in the 1820s that on "the streets nearest the river, the houses are principally of brick . . . but in the back part of the town, they are generally of wood."[10] It also explains why, to this day, opulent townhouses and mansions are common along Chartres and Royal but scarce on Burgundy. Bourbon and Dauphine represent increments between the two social spaces, thus Bourbon's appeal to the white working and middle classes. Bourbon and Dauphine were 30 percent enslaved, markedly less than Chartres and Royal but more than the back-of-town.

We see these human geographies manifested with striking linearity in the 1820 census. Each street's percentage of white residents decreased steadily with increasing distance from the river. Levee Street, closest to the river, was 60.4 percent white; next, Chartres Street, was 56.9 percent; Royal 56.6 percent; Bourbon 49.5 percent; Dauphine 39.5 percent; and back-of-town Burgundy at only 33.4 percent. Why? Whites, occupying the most privileged position in New Orleans's three-caste social structure, had more fiscal and legal wherewithal to position themselves closer to amenities, conveniences, and commerce, and farther from urban nuisance and environmental risk. Bourbon's middling spatial position put it almost precisely in an intermediary racial-composition position, nearly matching the city's 46 percent white overall population.

Similarly linear patterns emerge when we map free people of color. While some members of this mixed-race caste gained upper-class status, most were working-class denizens of the back-of-town. This is corroborated in our 1820 data: Burgundy Street had the highest percentage of free people of color among our six streets, at 37.6 percent. That proportion steadily decreased as we move closer to the river, higher in elevation, and upward in real estate value: Dauphine had 29.3 percent; Bourbon 21.7 percent; Royal 8.6 percent; and Chartres and Levee only 5.8 and 5.6 percent. Free people of color, who were Creole in ethnicity, also predominated in the downriver sections of the city: lower Bourbon had more than upper Bourbon, for reasons relating to the Anglo/Creole geographies described earlier. However, we cannot measure this numerically because the 1820 census recorded only street names, not house numbers.

The racial alloy of Bourbon Street's residents might seem surprising vis-à-vis the harsh realities of codified racial subjugation. But in fact, slavery fostered racially mixed settlement. The legal infrastructure that enslaved the black population and suppressed free people of color was so effective in segregating the castes socially, economically, and politically that the spatial proximity of the races in residential settlement patterns presented zero threat to the free white caste. A wealthy white family living on Bourbon Street in the 1820s would not have felt socially threatened by working-class free people of color living next door, or slaves living behind, because no one would ever presume that those three neighboring families occupied the same social caste. Only when that legal infrastructure began to be dismantled did the races spatially disassociate. That moment was still 40 to 140 years in the future.

In sum, we may characterize ca. 1820 Bourbon Street as well populated but not crowded, as ethnically diverse as the city but no more, mostly middle class, generally residential, and mostly Francophone, Catholic, and Creole in all but its uppermost Anglicized blocks.

Enslaved New Orleanians lived with or near their masters throughout New Orleans, and Bourbon Street was no exception. Those who labored as domestics or clerks usually resided in slant-roofed quarters appended behind townhouses and cottages. Two Bourbon Street real estate ads depict this architecturally accommodated racial integration:

> FOR SALE. A fine house situated at the corner of Toulouse and Bourbon streets[,] built on a full lot . . . divided into seven rooms with plenty of space, a fine store, kitchen, rooms for negroes, etc.

> FOR SALE—A new two story brick house, covered with flat tiles, containing 12 double rooms, kitchen, negro cabins for each apartment, a well and privies . . . at the corner of Bourbon and St. Peter street.[11]

Other slaves, ranging from skilled craftsmen and artisans to hired-out laborers, lived in detached group quarters on back alleys close to the abodes of their masters. Proximity abetted the master's financial interest and personal comfort by allowing for the monitoring of slave movement and promptness of service, so masters naturally built their compounds accordingly. Nevertheless, the city put the force of law behind the practice. An ordinance in 1817 prohibited slaves from living "in any house, out-house, building, or enclosure" not owned by their master or representative, else the slave face jail time and twenty lashes, and the master a five-dollar fine. An 1857 city ordinance reads similarly to its predecessor from forty years earlier: "That it shall not be lawful for any slave to lodge or sleep in any house or premises other than that of his owner or master," with fines and lashes awaiting white and black lawbreakers respectively.[12] This so-called back-alley settlement pattern imparted an ironic spatial integration into New Orleans's antebellum racial geography, despite the extreme social oppression of chattel slavery.

Ethnic tensions among Creoles, Anglo-Americans, and immigrants underscored city life. At stake, from the Creoles' perspective, was their control of the city's culture and political power in the face of a mounting Anglo presence. The hard way to ease such tensions is to negotiate compromises. The easy way is to get a divorce—and that is, in effect, what New Orleans did. In 1836, the Americans won legislative consent to divide the city into three semi-autonomous municipalities, each with its own council, recorder, and officers, unified under a single mayor and General Council.[13] Most Creoles and foreign French would be concentrated in the First Municipality (the French Quarter, between Canal and Esplanade) and Third Municipality (below Esplanade, which also had a high immigrant population), while most Americans would govern themselves in the Second Municipality (above Canal Street, also home to many Irish and German immigrants). Bourbon fell squarely in the First Municipality, and both the street and the Quarter were further sliced into that municipality's First, Third, Fourth, and Sixth Wards. For the next sixteen years, residents elected councilmen, paid taxes, recorded deeds, managed the port, and participated in civic affairs differently than New Orleanians who lived across Canal or Esplanade. Each municipality even had its own seal.

Profoundly stupid, the municipality system triplicated costly municipal functions while pitting neighborhoods against each other. "Had the Legislature sought, by the most careful efforts," wrote the Third Municipality's *Daily Orleanian* in 1849, "to create a war of races, to make distinction between Creole and American, they could not have chosen a better means . . . than the present division."[14] Bourbon Street found itself on the wrong side of the Anglo-Creole rift, and while the antebellum economic boom would continue to make Bourbon a fairly decent address, the future did not bode well.

Archival documents fall short of providing a comprehensive quantitative tabulation of late-antebellum Bourbon Street society. Population schedules of the U.S. Census neglected to record street names and house numbers, while city directories included only a select portion of local society. For all its shortfalls, we look to *Cohen's New Orleans & Lafayette Directory* for 1851 to understand the social makeup of late antebellum Bourbon Street. New Orleans, according to this source, had a population of 119,460 in 1850. If we assume that 3 to 4 percent lived in Bourbon Street, based on earlier data, then roughly 4,000 people called Bourbon home that year. When Cohen's field workers did their survey in 1850, they compiled 284 heads of household with Bourbon Street addresses. If we assume that each household comprised on average six members, then roughly 40 percent of Bourbon Street families gained a mention in Cohen's directory. Who were these people? Recognizing the shortfall of statistical representativeness, Bourbon Street society (or rather, its upper half) in 1850 comprised

- 21 percent people with skilled trades, including shoemakers (12), dressmakers (9), carpenters (7), tailors (6), jewelers (3), midwifes (3), bakers, cigar makers, dyers, repairers, and tinsmiths (two each), and an artist, a blacksmith, a bricklayer, a cabinetmaker, a hat maker, a locksmith, a mattress maker, a maker of musical instrument, a painter, a pointer, and a turner;

- 18 percent shopkeepers, coffeehouse (saloon) owners, restaurateurs, and innkeepers. Shopkeepers numbered 37, making theirs the single most common occupation of Bourbon Street residents; there were eleven coffeehouse/saloon owners, two restaurateurs, and two innkeepers;

- 17 percent professionally employed people, including merchants (9), eight professionals of unspecified fields, lawyers (7), dentists, doctors, engineers, and professors (3 each), bankers, brokers, and inspectors (2 each), and an accountant, trader, auctioneer, and druggist;

- 6 percent clerks, who, numbering 17, generally worked as employees for those engaged in any of the above occupations and/or their affiliated firms;

- 2 percent unskilled, such as launderers, horse holders, a fisherman, and a student (this figure would be much higher if the city directory consistently included lower-class households);

- 35 percent with unspecified occupations. Many of these were women, and some were listed as widows.[15]

Upper Bourbon deserves particular attention in this era. The first two blocks hosted the Fisk Free Library, predecessor to the New Orleans Public Library; the Jefferson Academy, an exclusive private school offering a classical education; and a Jewish synagogue and Hebrew school.[16] These institutions may seem surprising for a street like Bourbon. What explains them is the fact that upper Bourbon both reflected and served the better-educated, more cosmopolitan Anglo-American populace across Canal Street more so than the mostly working-class Creole lower Bourbon. Both the academy and library had Anglo cultural origins: Professor G. J. Lord ran the academy, while Massachusetts-born merchants Abijah and Alvarez Fisk created the city's first library by donating a house at the riverside/upriver corner of Bourbon and Customhouse and stocking it with books.[17]

Ethnic patterns on ca. 1850 Bourbon Street may be gleaned from surnames listed in the 1851 *City Directory*. Of the names of the 285 Bourbon residents listed,

- 66 percent sounded French (for example, Boudousquie, Le Gardeur, Rousseau);

- 17 percent English (Barkley, Robertson, Wilkinson);
- 5 percent Germanic or Dutch (Gerstenneger, Mascendorff, Van Rooten);
- 5 percent Spanish (Alvarez, Hernandez, Gomez);
- 3 percent Italian (Baratino, Siroti, Valletti);
- 2 percent Jewish (Adler, Klein, Rosenberg);
- 1 percent Portuguese or Greek (Da Silva, Thalamass).[18]

It should be noted that city directories usually underreported lower-class households. Those with African ancestry were completely excluded if enslaved, and grossly underrepresented if free. Only two entries were denoted as "f.m.c." (free men of color), an innkeeper and a turner, despite that hundreds of free people of color lived on antebellum Bourbon Street. Inclusion of this caste, as well as poor and working-class whites, would substantially increase the percentage of French surnames.

When we map the English-sounding names, we see further validation for the uptown-Anglo/downtown-Creole pattern. Fully 25 percent of those with Bourbon's Anglo surnames lived on the first block right off Canal Street, while another 14 percent lived on the second block. Stated another way, nearly 40 percent of Bourbon's Anglos lived on the uppermost 15 percent of Bourbon's space. The first block had nearly a two-to-one ratio of English to French surnames (eleven to six), despite that French outnumbered English surnames nearly four to one on the street as a whole.

Iterating this ethnic geography was a corresponding religious element. Anglo-American citizens erected at the corner of Canal and Bourbon this Catholic city's first Protestant house of worship, Christ Church, built in 1815 in a Gothic style and an octagonal shape from designs by Henry S. Latrobe. When local Episcopalians outgrew the small church, they had it replaced in 1835–37 with an imposing Ionic-style church designed by Gallier and Dakin. For the next twenty years, this columned temple formed a city landmark and a prominent gateway to Bourbon Street. But therein lay the problem: Canal and Bourbon had grown into quite a bustling intersection by the 1840s, particularly on Sundays. Because of New Orleans's jolly indifference to national standards regarding the Sabbath, a stream of "regimental drills, parades, and gayety" came down Bourbon Street on the Christian day of worship, disturbing the congregation and scandalizing visitors. Elders considered seeking approval from the city to place a chain across Bourbon, the first attempt to create a pedestrian mall on the street. Instead they used the problem to justify their request for permission to sell the site.[19] They suc-

One of the earliest photographic images of New Orleans, a daguerreotype by Jules Lion (*top*), a French-born free man of color, captured Canal Street between Bourbon and Royal in the mid- to late 1840s. Note the former Christ Church at the Bourbon/Canal corner, which by this time was a *shul* for the Dispersed of Judah congregation. The same block in 2013 appears at bottom. *Jules Lion image from Marshall Dunham Photograph Album, Mss. 3241, Louisiana and Lower Mississippi Valley Collections, LSU Libraries, Baton Rouge, LA; modern photograph by author.*

ceeded—and sold it to Rhode Island–born Judah Touro in 1847, who converted the former church into a *shul* for his Dispersed of Judah congregation. Jews in this era, mostly English speakers and American in nationality, tended to reside with the Anglo population and generally avoided the Creole side of town. So it comes as no surprise that two-thirds of the handful of likely Jewish surnames on Bourbon Street had addresses on Bourbon's Anglo-dominant first block. Touro Synagogue, plus an adjoining Hebrew school as well as Judah Touro's residence, established a brief but intensive Jewish presence on upper Bourbon.[20] The spatial correlation of Anglos and Jews continued in the late nineteenth century, when both congregations and institutions shifted uptown. Christ Church and Touro Synagogue, both Bourbon-borne, today operate within a dozen blocks of each other on St. Charles Avenue.

The remainder of Bourbon may best be described as a representative transect of New Orleans society. The street formed a backdrop of normalcy against which everything in New Orleans that was perceived by outsiders as deviant, novel, famous, and odd stood in contrast. For this reason, very few first-person descriptions of Bourbon Street appear in antebellum literature. One example of this ignored normalcy at first appears to be an exception to the rule, but in fact only proves it. In *Random Shots and Southern Breezes* (1842), Louis Tasistro takes his readers through the "French part of New-Orleans," down "Rue de Chartres" and into "the famous St. Louis Exchange," to "the ancient Cathedral," and past "the famous *Calaboose.*" Finally, he writes, "Here we are in the Rue Bourbon! Heavens, what associations!" Unfortunately, any hope of an inquisitive description is quickly dashed, because the only associations Tasistro had with Rue Bourbon involved the French royals for whom it was named. Nothing else on the street called Tasistro's attention.[21]

In fact, Bourbon Street did have a distinction. In this town smitten with performance, theaters of one sort or another dotted the cityscape, and the central French Quarter had its fair share. In the late 1850s, Bourbon Street scored a coup. A new Parisian owner had taken possession of the nearby Théater d'Orleans, long renowned for featuring touring European companies. The Frenchman planned to keep that success going, but because he failed to negotiate a lease with the theater's manager, New Orleanian Charles Boudousquié, the local impresario decided to outdo the Parisian with a superior venue for French opera. Boudousquié formed the New Orleans Opera House Association in March 1859, raised more than one hundred thousand dollars from aficionados, purchased a 193.5' x 191.5'

The Old French Opera House on Bourbon Street at the Toulouse intersection (*top*), photographed around 1900, and a detail of Bourbon Street (*bottom*) extracted from the lower left of the original photo. Note the streetcar rails and approaching car (later part of the famous Desire line), the granite paving blocks, and the wooden planks on the sidewalk (banquette). *Library of Congress.*

lot, and contracted to build a splendid opera house "at the corner of Bourbon and Toulouse Streets, in accordance with the plans and elevations made by [architectural firm] Gallier and Esterbrook."[22] Work commenced in May and, with an eye on the fall social calendar, proceeded round the clock aided by nighttime lighting coming from large bonfires erected in the adjacent streets. It must have been a magnificent sight, as yellow-orange illumination danced off the rising walls of what a local newspaper predicted would be "a handsome structure of the Italian order [that will] rise like a Colossus over everything in that vicinity."[23] The grand opening occurred on the evening of December 1, 1859, with a performance of Rossini's *Guillaume Tell.* It was a triumph that would be remembered for years. "Superb . . . magnificent . . . spacious and commodious . . . a spectacle . . . richly worth viewing [at] a scale of great elegance," raved the reviews of the gleaming white New French Opera House.[24]

Theaters were a big deal in these times: featuring not only plays and musicals but reenacted historical and current events, magicians and "natural philosophers," balls, dances, and socials, they were foci of social activity. The French Opera House and nearby competing venues such as the St. Peter Street and Orleans theaters stoked the twilight bustle and gave entrepreneurs an opportunity to serve that same conveniently gathered pool of potential clients with food, drink, lodging, and diversions. Antoine's Restaurant, for example, noted on its calling card that it catered to patrons of the nearby theaters. In this manner, a nocturnal food, drink, and entertainment district began to form in the central French Quarter, and because the grandest of all the venues was the French Opera House, Bourbon Street found itself as the axis. Thus was planted one of the seeds from which, decades later, the modern-day Bourbon Street night scene would germinate—but more on this later. For now, we contemplate the question of why Charles Boudousquié chose this particular spot on Bourbon at Toulouse for his project. No evidence exists that he eyed this corner to the exclusion of others; it more likely came to his attention opportunistically. Surely he desired to be in the heart of the city, and, as a French Creole impresario whose patrons were usually fellow Francophones, Boudousquié probably wanted his French Opera House to be on the Creole side of town. Where exactly? The lower streets below St. Philip were too residential and gritty, as were the rear streets behind Burgundy. The uppermost streets like Canal and Customhouse, as well as all riverfront streets, were too commercial. This left the heart of the French Quarter; now it was a matter of finding enough adjacent property owners forming a sufficiently large space who would all be willing to sell quickly at an acceptable price. Perhaps it

mattered that the five parcels at the corner of Bourbon and Toulouse were unusually large—four of them measured 60' x 120'—which reduced the total number of
sales required. In any case, Boudousquié and his company had the right amount
of money to convince these five landowners to part with their properties; all sales
were made on March 23–24, 1859, after which demolitions immediately ensued.
Thus, a broad site-selection strategy and a fair dose of happenstance landed the
French Opera House at the corner of Bourbon and Toulouse. Had it not, we
might perceive Bourbon Street quite differently today.

For the next sixty years, despite Civil War, federal occupation, declining fortunes, multiple managers, and a few missed seasons, what became known and
beloved as the Old French Opera House played host to a litany of famous names
and performances, not to mention countless Carnival balls and society events.
Culturally, it served as a home away from home for a steady stream of French
and other European performers at a time when New Orleans's connection to the
Old World grew increasingly tenuous, and when Gallic syllables became less frequently heard in local streets. And magnificent it remained, particularly at night:
wrote one observer, "The building, with its fresh coat of whitewash, glimmers
like a monster ghost in the moonlight."[25]

A Smell So Unsavory

Managing Bourbon Street in the Mid-1800s

New Orleans's population, which doubled roughly every fifteen years throughout the early 1800s, exerted constant pressure on living space. Demand for new housing prompted a question in the minds of planters who owned agrarian land abutting the city: Can my plantation yield more profit by another season in agriculture or by subdivision for new homes? The closer the plantation lay to the inner city, the more likely that the planter would eventually choose to develop, and hire a surveyor to start the process. This individualized decision making, which would drive urban expansion for the next seventy years sans the oversight of a city planning commission, put surveyors in the position of contemplating whether to extend existing street names and trajectories into their new subdivisions or to start afresh. Bourbon Street was among those subjected to this decision, with lasting implications for the future urban geography of the city.

Carlos Trudeau, who first considered street extensions when he laid out Suburbia Santa Maria in 1788, opted for new names and angles. His decision prevented Bourbon Street from extending upriver. The next land subjected to subdivision was Bernard Xavier Philippe de Marigny de Mandeville's plantation immediately below the city. Marigny hired Nicholas de Finiels in 1805 to design a plat, a tricky task because of a sharp bend in the river. Finiels situated the faubourg's central artery along an old sawmill canal and named it after Paris's Champs-Élysées, today's Elysian Fields. He then aligned to that axis his own grid of forty-two blocks and adjoined it to the Old City—which lay ajar by 45 degrees—with polygonal blocks. Finiels's design meant that some Old City streets elbowed downriver, while others forked both downriver and lakeside. Bourbon was the only one that elbowed solely in a lakeside direction.

Marigny, who would later earn a reputation as a colorful maverick, relished the opportunity to stamp his creation with his own street names. Chartres/Conde thus became Moreau; Royal forked into Casa Calvo and L'Union; Bourbon became Bagatelle; Dauphine became Grand Homme; and Burgundy became Craps. That decision prevented Bourbon Street from expanding downriver nominally. Bourbon did, however, grow by one block in each direction over the next few years. Shortly after the creation of Faubourg Marigny, the city's lower fortification was subdivided to become today's Esplanade Avenue corridor. Around the same time (1810), the upper-fortification commons was subdivided into today's Canal Street. Urbanizing these interstices seamlessly conflated Pauger's 1722 bourg with Trudeau's 1788 and Finiels's 1805 faubourgs. Today, these are the "100 blocks" between Canal and Iberville, and the "1300 blocks" between Barracks and Esplanade.

Westerners in the early 1800s pressed their political representatives for what Americans at the time called internal improvements—that is, transportation infrastructure. New Orleanians did the same locally, and at the top of their list of priorities were better city streets. Much upgrading needed to be done: American-era streets deviated little from colonial times, a failure that Anglos unreservedly blamed on the Creole political establishment. Not until 1817 did the city finally gain its first stone-paved street, Gravier between Tchoupitoulas and Magazine, and it would be an additional five years before it launched a citywide paving campaign. That 1822 effort, which started with Royal Street, hardly solved the problem.[1] Residents continued to hop among puddles, ditches, and feces much like their ancestors did a century prior. Even worse were the sidewalks, which were called footpaths, footways, and causeways in English, and *trottoirs* and *banquettes* in French. Old wooden sidewalks were replaced with brick ones starting in 1820, but that project proceeded only when funds became available. An 1827 city ordinance taxed property owners whose parcels abutted already improved streets to pay for new sidewalks, and specified that work begin from the front to the back of town: Royal first, then Levee, then Bourbon, Dauphine, Burgundy, and finally Rampart.[2] Two years later, however, Bourbon's *trottoirs* continued to generate complaints: "The sidewalks on Bourbon st. from one extremity to the other are in the most wretched state. The bricks are torn up, the gutters sunk and the edgings of the walks rotten, and in many places the walking at night is dangerous."[3] In the street proper, hackmen and their passengers had their teeth rattled as carriages bounced along washboard surfaces. Wheels and hoof-beats deepened potholes, which collected water, which in turn stagnated and produced mosquitoes, algae, slime, and stench. "We were the whole of yesterday assailed by so unsavory a smell," bemoaned one informant in 1826; "the whole street from Bourbon to Royal suffered alike. . . . [S]uch nuisances . . . will give us yellow fever in abundance."[4] Bourbon Street, despite its center-of-town position, seemed to suffer back-of-town street conditions and became something of a rallying cry for street improvements. An ordinance in 1835 resolved to contract one Mr. Claudot-Dumont "to pave, according to his method, Bourbon street from Canal to Esplanade street," using granite curb and gutter stones (measuring 4 inches thick and at least 36–42 inches long) for the street edges, and "hard square paving stones" (12' x 8' x 8') for the surface.[5] Whether Claudot-Dumont did his job is unclear; what is clear is that Bourbon Street's rough condition continued to generate a disproportionate number of citizen complaints. The city in 1838 sent around men in carts loaded with sediment to smooth over perturbations, but this too proved problematic. "Bourbon street . . . is in filthy condition," growled a local newspaper; "the dirt carts not having been along for several days. This is wrong, and the person to whose charge this business is entrusted, should attend to his duty."[6]

Contrast Bourbon's rustic state to that of moneyed Royal and Chartres Streets, where banks, hotels and commercial exchanges, auction houses, publishers, and other professional offices attracted more investment and better infrastructure. To equalize improvements among the competing streets of the First Municipality, the City Council in the late 1830s used Bourbon as an experiment for a new type of paving. It involved brick and bitumen, a viscous tar-like petroleum that, when mixed with mineral aggregates, formed asphalt. "The paving of Bourbon street . . . from Canal to Toulouse . . . so far, promises success," reported the *Picayune* in 1839; "we would not be surprised to see the plan adopted throughout the city."[7] Costs were borne, or at least shared, by property owners; an 1839 real estate contract declared that the new owner, cotton broker Auguste O'Duhigg, "binds himself to pay for the bitumen paving laid in front of [his] 60' front on [present-day 626–632] Bourbon."[8]

The new technique worked well at first, to the point that "many a drayman, hackman, or cabman [went] squares out of his way" to use Bourbon's smooth surface. Problem was, the bitumen crumbled, in part because it attracted heavy traffic but mostly for reasons of application, material, and subsurface.[9] It had to be done again. "They are *re-bitumenising* Bourbon street," huffed a reporter, as workers tried to fix the problem.[10] In 1841, the municipality abandoned the great Bourbon Street "asphaltum experiment," resolving instead to pave it with simpler but bumpier round stones imported as ship ballast or on barges from the upcountry.[11] Other paving materials used on antebellum streets included

Canal Street at the Bourbon intersection around 1864 (*top*) and in 2013 (*bottom*). Note the granite paving blocks, which would have been similar to those on Bourbon Street, and the D. H. Holmes department store, which operated on this block until 1989. *Historic photograph by W. D. McPherson, Marshall Dunham Photograph Album, Mss. 3241, Louisiana and Lower Mississippi Valley Collections, LSU Libraries, Baton Rouge, LA; modern photograph by author.*

cobblestones, square block and flat granite stones, rangia shells dredged from the bottom of Lake Pontchartrain, bricks, and wooden planks and gunwales stripped from flatboats.[12] Relics of these materials may be seen today whenever utility cuts are excavated on Bourbon Street.

Even more critical to daily lives was domestic water. New Orleans needed it to drink, cook, bathe, and clean both inside and outside: an 1817 public-health law mandated that residents water down the dusty streets and banquettes fronting their houses daily.[13] Bourbon denizens obtained water from street vendors, or tasked their domestics or children to scoop it directly from the Mississippi. Others would collect rain running off roofs, or dig wells in courtyards, and store the water in cisterns. Each method required much labor and yielded little potable water, creating a niche for entrepreneurs: enter the private water system. One attempt worthy of biblical times came in 1810 on the levee at Ursulines Street. Slaves pumped river water into a raised tank, which thence flowed by gravity through hollow cypress logs to subscribers. Famed architect Benjamin H. B. Latrobe designed a better system a few years later, in which a steam engine mounted in a three-story pump house would draw water from the Mississippi, store it in raised cast-iron reservoirs, and distribute it through a network of cypress pipes to subscribing residences or to cast-iron boxes at street corners. Latrobe's waterworks served the city from 1823 to 1836.[14] Subsequently, the Water Works Company assumed responsibility for water distribution, and in the spring of 1853 installed "large new main pipes in Bourbon street . . . in place of the old small ones" from Latrobe's system. "We have been struck," wrote a reporter, "with the depth to which the workmen dig without reaching water."[15]

Garbage was collected on antebellum Bourbon Street six days a week by a city contractor with a mule-drawn cart, into which residents deposited "dirt, filth and kitchen offals" brought out in "tubs, hampers, [or] baskets." Strictly forbidden were "dung, chips, shavings and feculent matter," which individuals had to discard themselves.[16] Feces could only be moved through the streets at night and "emptied into the current of the river"—the water source for folks downstream.[17] For garbage collection, citizens had to bring their debris outside just as the cart approached; the contractor did not pick up anything from the curb except for dead animals and street litter. The policy forced residents to wait endlessly listening for the cart to approach. An 1819 ordinance corrected this flaw by allowing the storage of garbage in containers "placed near the gutter of the foot way, opposite to their respective building."[18] This was the precursor of a standard element of the modern-day Bourbon streetscape: the daily collection of stinking refuse via a standing army of massive black plastic receptacles.

As in colonial times, illumination on Bourbon Street in the early 1800s came from oil lamps "suspended to iron chains, which are stretched from the corners of houses or high posts, diagonally across the junctions." They were maintained by city-paid lamplighters who doubled as "city guards," or policemen.[19] Smaller oil-fueled lamps and candles provided lighting inside Bourbon and all other New Orleans homes, until, in 1834, the New Orleans Gas Light and Banking Company commenced operating its plant in the rear of the American sector. Lines laid throughout St. Mary and the French Quarter, including on Bourbon Street, allotted gas to paying residential, industrial, and commercial subscribers, particularly theaters and exchange hotels. By the 1850s, gas also fueled city streetlights, although many lanterns still used oil. The city contracted with the gas company to service both gas and oil street lamps, scheduling their daily lighting and extinguishing to take full advantage of diurnal and lunar cycles and penalizing the company for malfunctioning lamps. Until electrification arrived at the end of the century, the lamplighter's task formed an integral part of the daily ritual that was life on Bourbon Street.[20]

As the city expanded, finding a particular person or business in the metropolis became increasingly difficult. The seemingly mundane solution—house numbering—nevertheless had frustrated New Orleanians since the city's inception. Not until the early American years did a system finally materialize. Who better to create it than Matthew Flannery, the contractor who took the 1805 census? Flannery's method rested on three suppositions. First, that the Mississippi River and Orleans Street formed the city's principal X and Y axes—fair enough, given Pauger's design. Second, Flannery construed Orleans Street to be oriented east-west, thus making downriver "north" and upriver "south" of Orleans. This was not so wise, given that Orleans angled by 37 degrees. Third, he enumerated houses in the order they occurred—a flat-out bad idea, because it ignored vacant lots and future changes in density. So he doubled all numbers, to give the system elbowroom. His 1805 directory shows fifty-eight houses on "Rue de Bourbon S.," which would have been distributed from present-day Iberville to Orleans, plus another fifty-four houses on "Rue de Bourbon N." from Orleans to Barracks. Flannery himself lived at 71 South Bourbon, which meant the thirty-fifth or thirty-sixth house from Orleans counted in a southern, or upriver, direction. Between which blocks? We can't tell, and therein lies another flaw in Flannery's system.[21] Nevertheless, the City Council approved Flannery's system and mandated that every street corner be marked with two pairs of wooden signs mounted at right angles, one in French and one in English. Occupants had to pay Flannery two and a half bits for a tin plaque with their house number to affix to their abode.[22]

Inevitably, Flannery's system failed to gain traction. The city intervened in 1831, requiring every twenty feet of street space citywide to be enumerated with even numbers for the downriver side of those streets perpendicular to the Mississippi, as well as the river side of those (like Bourbon) parallel to the river. Odd numbers would be assigned to those upriver or lakeside. No other systemwide rule was stipulated, although the law did specify how houses should post their signage. Searching for an address on Bourbon Street in the 1830s and 1840s would have entailed seeking an oval-shaped tin or iron plate above each building's door, or to its right at least ten feet above the soil, with the house number painted at least three inches high in black oil and varnished to protect it from rain. (How many residents abided by these requirements is unknown.) Streets signs, a municipal responsibility under the direction of the city surveyor, were conveniently color-coded: black lettering on a yellow field if the street ran perpendicular to the river, and white letters on a black field for those like Bourbon that paralleled the river.[23]

The year 1852 brought major changes to the administration of New Orleans. The inefficient municipality system, which since 1836 had divided the city into three semi-autonomous municipalities, was finally abandoned—but only after the Americans had allied with uptown German and Irish immigrants to guarantee numerical superiority over the Creoles. City Hall moved out of the Creole quarter and into the American sector; the fulcrum of commerce and publishing did the same; speakers of English increased their numbers; and Creole cultural influence gradually began to wane. The 1852 reforms also brought changes in political geography. First, the former municipalities were renamed "municipal districts" and were confusingly renumbered such that Bourbon Street found itself out of the old First Municipality and *in* the new Second Municipal District (where it remains today). Next, the city of Lafayette in neighboring Jefferson Parish (present-day Garden District and Irish Channel) was annexed into New Orleans. This expansion did not affect Bourbon Street, but it did further the uptown spread of the Americanizing city, which always made downtown denizens anxious. Third, the city's wards, which served electoral and statistical purposes and had been reconfigured four times previously, had to be redrawn again to accommodate the 1852 changes. Because Felicity Street had long marked New Orleans's upper limit, the new ward enumeration began at Felicity (First Ward) and continued consecu-

The full length of Bourbon Street viewed from the cupola of the former Hibernia Bank Building (*top*), and from the opposite perspective (*bottom*). *Photographs by author, 2011–13.*

tively downriver. To equalize populations within wards, the high-density French Quarter was sliced into the narrowest wards (Fourth, Fifth, and Sixth), while the less-populated lower faubourgs allowed for broader wards (Seventh, Eighth, and Ninth). Bourbon Street's ward lines remain today precisely where they were delineated in 1852, Canal to St. Louis being the Fourth Ward, St. Louis to St. Philip the Fifth, and St. Philip to Esplanade the Sixth Ward. City fathers also in 1852 tweaked the ever-problematic house-address system; it persisted until the adoption of the superior 100-block "decimal system" in 1894, which remains in service today.[24]

One final change in 1852 affected Bourbon Street morphologically. The city decided to dispense with the name Bagatelle for the street that angled off lower Bourbon into the Faubourg Marigny. After 130 years of measuring 4,600 perfectly straight feet, Bourbon Street now elbowed into another neighborhood and continued indeterminately, progressing lakeward as New Orleanians drained and built farther and farther into the backswamp.

A Place to "See the Elephant"
Antecedents of Modern-Day Bourbon Street

Collective memory benefits from an associated structural framework—that is, a place or object that evokes a mental image or recollection. As we individually cherish souvenirs and mementos to commemorate times past and loved ones lost, societies collectively save old buildings, erect monuments, name and rename streets, and protect historical cityscapes so that citizens may synchronize their narratives of who they are as a people, where they came from, and where they should be going.

As a city with a colorful past and a modern-day economy based on marketing it, New Orleans proliferates in structurally based social memory. It uses the French Quarter, for example, to preserve the social memory of antebellum Creole society. It points to the Garden District to recall wealthy nineteenth-century Anglo society, and upholds Tremé to remind us of the free people of color.

Preservation is intrinsic to this arrangement; without it, we would forget, or fail to convince newcomers, of these narratives. Cases in point: the destruction of the South Rampart Street commercial corridor, Louis Armstrong's neighborhood, and Storyville so impaired the social memory of jazz that tourists regularly come away disappointed when they learn that the "birthplace of jazz" is more of a municipal slogan than a visitable place. Out of sight, out of mind—and conversely, in sight, in mind. Hence the power of preservation.

The power goes beyond specific sites or buildings. The collective perception of New Orleans as unique and exceptional, which is an article of faith among residents and a cornerstone of civic pride, may be largely traced to architectural preservation. Had the decaying old neighborhood known colloquially as "the French quarters" been demolished and modernized, as was routinely suggested as recently as the late 1930s, the tourism industry never would have germinated; the sense of exoticism instilled by legions of local-color writers would have dissipated; culinary and musical traditions would have been deprived of a space for paying customers; and iconic photographs of iron-lace galleries never would have been taken. It's not the only factor—Mardi Gras plays a major role—but without the French Quarter, the cherished mantra of civic uniqueness would have gone unsung, and New Orleans might have ended up with a collective memory and a nationwide reputation little different than that of Mobile or Galveston.

Instead, the French Quarter was saved, and wisely so, because, in addition to bearing the aforesaid fruits, it diffused preservationist activism into other historical neighborhoods. Today, locals and visitors alike utilize that structural substratum—thousands of nineteenth-century buildings bearing a magnificent Euro-Caribbean-American urban aesthetic—to substantiate and justify a collective memory that strums many appealing chords: Frenchness. Creoleness. Joie de vivre. An air of mystery and a sense that something different happened here; a certain subtropical brand of eccentricity; a whiff of Caribbean escapism; a tolerance for indulging in the pleasures of the moment. It's appealing stuff, and it's only convincing when it rests on a tactile, visible structural foundation. Try selling this in Peoria and see what happens.

Additionally, downtown New Orleans benefits from a high level of urban granularity—that is, a cityscape that is intricate, multifaceted, heterogeneous, minimally set back from the street, and most importantly, walkable. Its constituent parts include narrow streets crowded with galleries, steep-pitched roofs punctuated with chimneys, and dark alleys and *portes-cochères* disappearing into hidden courtyards. "The general effect is very pleasing," wrote Lafcadio Hearn in 1881; "no one with an artistic eye can avoid loving the zigzag outline of peaked roofs with the pretty dormers; the iron arabesques of graceful balconies, the solid doors and . . . shutters, so brightly green."[1] This pointillistic urban texture, replete with nooks and crannies, fosters a sense of intrigue, and piques a curiosity to seek what's behind those doors, what lurks down that dark alley. Walkability is key because it facilitates the tantalizing possibility of social interaction with strangers while maintaining anonymity and, if one chooses to indulge, ambulatory ebriety. Walt Whitman recognized, in the words of a modern writer, the "continually tantalizing, pullulating field of sexual potential" walking among crowds of strangers; in "City of Orgies," the poet rhapsodized "as I pass O Manhattan, your frequent and swift flash of eyes offering me love."[2] Recalling his visit to New Orleans, he versed:

High urban granularity: Bourbon Street at the peak of Mardi Gras, 2012. *Photograph by author.*

Once I pass'd though a populous city imprinting my brain for
    future use with its shows, architecture, customs, traditions,
Yet now of all that city I remember only a woman I casually met
    there who detain'd me for love of me.[3]

What Whitman sensed in crowded nineteenth-century urbanity emanates still from the twenty-first-century French Quarter. Perambulating aimlessly and namelessly in a cozy, complex old cityscape lends itself to capricious experimentation—drinking in public, slipping into an exotic show, hooking up with a stranger, crossing a racial or gender Rubicon—in ways that motoring identifiably across a suburban environment does not. It's worth noting that the New Orleans lover mentioned by Whitman in "Once I Pass'd Through a Populous City" was long thought to be a woman of color, while handwritten drafts suggest it was in fact a man. Both relationships would have been verboten at the time, yet possible in the social milieu of the crowded city. And whoever it was, there's a good chance the tryst took place in the intimacy of the French Quarter.[4]

Bourbon Street represents an extreme case of structurally based social memory. It is the modern-day space in which New Orleans's centuries-old reputation for hedonism is exaggerated, concentrated, showcased, commoditized, and sold—noisily, round the clock, year-round, for a tidy profit. It is participatory street theater in perpetual motion, pounded by music, tantalized by sexuality, and dazed by alcohol. It is a carefully crafted sociological "backspace" within which newcomers, tutored by T-shirt slogans and window props, are persuaded to view deviance as acceptable, and restraint as deviant.[5] And what seals the deal is the same structural corroboration that supports New Orleans's broader social memory and validates its claim to exceptionalism: the ancient buildings, the iron-lace balconies, the old-time gas lamps, the *tout ensemble* of steamy, sultry, subtropical urbanism at the apogee of the Caribbean basin—all nestled tightly, yours to explore, on foot, anonymously.

Which all begs the question, where *did* this piquant reputation come from?

That question has a number of answers. First, great ports in general, like frontier cities, regularly develop economic sectors that cater to pleasure and escapism because steady streams of mostly male transients traveling alone make such enterprises biologically rational, and potentially lucrative. Ports were gendered spaces, and historic New Orleans, often the first or last stop on a long riverine or oceanic voyage, was no exception. Males outnumbered females substantially, and in some riverfront districts overwhelmingly, particularly during October through May, when transients ("strangers") settled into exchange hotels or rented rooms to work the commercial season. Some were northern businessmen; others were foreign sailors, upcountry boatmen, soldiers, traders, travelers, opportunity-seekers on the make, immigrants in transit, or vagrants. Their numbers were substantial: in 1831, when New Orleans had roughly 55,000 permanent residents, one journalist estimated that "there are frequently from 25 to 50,000 strangers in the place" during the winter. Another in the late 1840s estimated that while the city's official population exceeded one hundred thousand, "a transient population of thirty or forty thousand [departs] in swarms . . . as soon as the warm season commences, [and returns like] wild geese . . . on the first appearance of a flake of snow."[6]

Flush with cash and released from the responsibilities and restraints of home, men arrived to this port city with pent-up demand for immediate gratification. Some came looking for trouble. "Probably no city of equal size in christendom receives . . . a greater proportion of vicious people than New Orleans," surmised a public health official in 1851; "The crimes against persons and property are committed chiefly by this floating population."[7] Other transients gleefully found

themselves separated from the mothers, wives, sisters, and aunts of their domestic lives, a notion that one flatboatman in 1834 pondered with mischievous
naiveté: "Men thrown together from all parts of the United States and in deed
from the whole world with ther [sic] various manners and habits unrestrained by
the presence of female influance exhibits a scene of extraordinary novelty and
is probably one of the best places for a man to acquire a knowledge of *human
nature*."[8] In the words of an enigmatic nineteenth-century expression, such men
sought to "see the elephant" in New Orleans—that is, to witness the utmost, to
see everything you expected, to complete a journey and live the experience to
the fullest. This phrase, popular from the 1840s to the end of the century, may
trace its origins to traveling carnivals, which often held out their most popular
exhibit, a live elephant, as a climax. "To see the elephant" meant to raise one's
expectations for a journey or destination, and to live it to its fullest. An 1848
article reporting an intoxicated robbery victim as "having but lately arrived from
the upper country [with] a strong desire to see the 'elephant'" could have been
referring to any one of thousands of men hoping to sow their wild oats in the
Queen City of the South.[9]

Exploiting the crossroads of anonymity, desire, and opportunity, New Orleans
catered to the itinerant male seeking "the elephant" by creating innumerable outlets for liquor, sex, games of chance, entertainment, and victuals. Because profit
could be made in the business of pleasure, stakeholders lobbied authorities to
keep such activities as legal as possible, in as many places and times as possible,
often in the face of citizen resistance and temperance activism. Bars and brothels
were geographically widespread in historic New Orleans, and because transients
arrived at all hours, the pleasure industry made itself available round the clock,
the Sabbath be damned.

A second answer to the reputation question involves the geography of tolerance. Tiny towns and interior cities can maintain monocultural communities
because few differentiating outsiders come knocking on their door. But port cities
must meet halfway, however grudgingly, the varied hordes disembarking at their
docks, and the larger their hinterlands and forelands, the greater the diversity of
the strangers. Thus, international ports were, and remain, typically more cosmopolitan than interior cities and more tolerant of behavior that would not fly
elsewhere. By no means was New Orleans unusual in this regard; the "lax" morals reported in hundreds of historical sources on New Orleans may also be found
in literature about the Liverpools and New Yorks and San Franciscos of the world,
although not necessarily in the same form or proportions.

Third, ports of the southern Atlantic and Caribbean basins were additionally informed by the Latin Catholic cultures of Mediterranean France, Spain, and Italy, which lacked the judgmental verve of Anglo-American societies and viewed alcohol as part of the daily bread rather than an escapist's vice. So we should not be surprised that New Orleans gained roughly the same laissez-faire reputation of Havana, San Juan, Vera Cruz, Cartagena, Salvador, Rio de Janeiro, and other nodes of the so-called Creole Atlantic. It is no coincidence that many of those sister cities celebrate some form of Carnival, recite romanticized narratives of their histories, take pride in their sexualized and roguish reputations, nurture tourist industries based on historical architecture, and designate spaces for Bourbon Street–like activity. New Orleans's brand of pleasure-seeking did not form independently or internally, but rather orbited as a social trait and an economic niche throughout the ports and portals of the Atlantic-Caribbean system. What distinguished it was the fact that it happened to be situated at the northernmost apogee in that system, at the terminus of the Mississippi River system, and, after 1803, within the expanding borders of the Unites States.

Finally, regardless of activities elsewhere, New Orleans gained a hedonistic reputation because it earned one, deserved one, and wasted no time in developing one. It was not merely a passive importer of external influences, but an active producer, molder, and exporter of culture. Eyewitnesses by the score attest to this, and while they are not without their nationalistic biases and epistemological shortcomings, their testimonies provide ample evidence that New Orleans was a raucous, sexualized, and often hellacious place fueled by copious quantities of alcohol—all provenances of the core ingredients of today's Bourbon Street.

The reports start at the dawn of the colonial era. As early as 1720, as John Law's "Mississippi Bubble" burst and ruined multitudes of investors, depictions of Louisiana as a debauched society circulated in European presses. It did not help that much of the colony's white population comprised *forçats*, immigrants forced out of the mother country for, among other reasons, depravity and vice. Nor did it help that the colony's economy, particularly after 1730, increasingly broke loose of the sanctioned mercantilist trading relationship with the mother country, and settled instead into a rogue smuggling role serving the Mississippi and Caribbean trading regions. Contraband was fenced in taverns, grog shops, and saloons in the rear quarters of the city and along isolated ingresses and egresses, away from official eyes. Where there were rogues making money, there was indulgence. Alcohol of various origins—the local rum *tafia*, beer made from corn, wine, brandy—flowed copiously.[10] An anonymous critic noted in 1744 that even men of little means "are seldom without wine in their cellars; the tradesmen is seldom a week without drinking it beyond moderation; but that is nothing in comparison with the soldier."[11] The geographies of contraband, transshipment, and human transience in New Orleans coincided with the geographies of hedonism, bacchanalianism, sybaritism—the perfect arrangement for a rambunctious reputation to form, intensify, and spread.

New Orleans's infamy grew as shipping activity bustled, multitudes circulated, and word spread. "This place is one of the worst I ever witnessed," wrote a homesick newcomer in 1817; "the chief amusements are gambling and drinking [and] quarrels and even murders are very frequent here."[12] John H. B. Latrobe, who visited in 1834, carped that "cafés and barrooms were open" on the Sabbath, and that "rum and gin, Monongahela [rye whiskey], and Tom and Jerry [sweetened hot rum] here live in palaces [with] whole army of bottles . . . of all colours lin[ing] the shelves in close array.[13] Another man, describing in 1847 the city's varied and low-priced eateries, reported that "the profit is on the liquor," as evidenced by "the immense patronage these establishments enjoy. . . . [T]hey monopolize the corners of every square; whole rows of them may be found in some localities, and new ones are springing up every day."[14] "The city's more than twenty-five hundred taverns are always filled with drinkers . . . especially during election time," wrote Elisée Réclus during his 1853 visit; "[They] fuel the most violent passions with brandy and rum."[15] A hyperbolic exposé written anonymously in 1850 excoriated the local embrace of spirits. "Of [all] the sources of evil and cause of contamination," it raged, "there is none . . . so glaring as the immense number of drinking houses in every part of the city." In descriptions that bring to mind modern-day Bourbon Street, it reported that "grog shops . . . are found in whole blocks—on three of every four corners . . . from street to street, every door leading into a drinking house. . . . [T]hree-fourths of the men . . . are confirmed drunkards, [taking] up to twenty-five to thirty [drinks] a day, and yet these are all high-minded, *sober,* and respectable *gentlemen,* full of *Southern chivalry*[!]"[16] Grog shops alone, by one estimate, brought in one hundred thousand dollars' revenue to city coffers annually in the late 1830s. This amounts to well over six hundred outlets—and those were just the law-abiding ones.[17]

New Orleans's notoriety grew so universal that it earned the metropolis a slew of sobriquets, among them the "Great Southern Babylon," "Necropolis of the South," and most commonly, "Sodom and Gomorrah." An 1812 *New-York Gazette* piece saw New Orleans's recent bouts with hurricanes and fires as retribution for its status as "a second Sodom . . . exhibiting, particularly on the Sabbath, scenes of the most licentious wickedness."[18] A missionary minister visiting in 1823 reminded his readers that "New Orleans is of course exposed to greater varieties of human misery, vice, disease, and want, than any other American town. . . . Much has been said about [its] profligacy of manners . . . morals . . . debauchery, and low vice. . . . [T]his place has more than once been called the modern Sodom."[19] The aforementioned 1850 exposé catalogued the city's other moral transgressions in subchapters entitled "Concubinage," "Kept Mistresses," "Extent of Licentiousness," "Regular Prostitutes" and "Prostitution of Wives," "Amalgamation," "A Man Selling His Own Children," "Slave Girls Hired As Bed Companions," "Disregard of the Sabbath," "Bull Fighting," "Drinking Houses," "Vagrants," "Women Whipping on the Plantations," and "Depravity of Slaveholders," among others. The anonymous author held back when he (or she) characterized New Orleans as "this Babel of all Babels, this Sodom of all Sodoms . . . this modern Golgotha."[20]

Another factor forming New Orleans's reputation may seem to undercut the eyewitness accounts cited above, but it actually bolsters them. Most of those testimonies were produced by visitors, not locals, and disproportionately they hailed from Anglo-American New England and the mid-Atlantic states, which tended to view askance all things Franco-Hispanic, not to mention Afro-Caribbean. Like tourists today, the newcomers' attention gravitated to that which deviated from their perceived norms. They scribbled in their journals about what surprised, offended, shocked, thrilled, or intrigued them, and ignored what seemed familiar and quotidian. No surprise, then, that spectacles such as tippling bons vivants, brawling boatmen, quadroon balls, Carnival revelry, and reprehensible "continental Sabbaths" got plenty of coverage, while caring parents, diligent laborers, and responsible authorities went unrecorded. Thus the danger of overrelying on travel writers to understand past peoples and places: their skewed lenses created an inverted reality in which the exception seemed the norm, and the normal became exceptional. This is not to say their representations are false, but rather that they are prone to selectivity, disproportion, and incompletion—not to mention misunderstanding, prejudice, sensationalism, or hidden agendas. Historians counter this methodological problem by consulting sources untainted by intermediary interpreters, such as personal diaries and letters, municipal and sacramental records, licenses and legal documents, censuses, and archeological evidence. For our purposes, however, visitor representations are fair game because we are investigating the origin of a *reputation*—a perception. Testimonies about New Orleans did not have to be accurate or valid to justify the formation of an urban image; like gossip, they just had to be believed. And people believed them. Whatever "reality" existed in the streets and parlors of historic New Orleans, visiting writers represented them in ways that constructed a metropolitan notoriety and infamy, which resonated with readers and produced a subsequent generation of notepad-toting visitors—who further ensconced the reputation as their preconceived expectations were inevitably confirmed. What resulted was a metabelief of New Orleans's social deviancy, diffused through a many-to-many network of thousands of readers absorbing hundreds of travelogues, and reinforced through either ground-truth or through the process of confirmation bias. Add to this the widely read local-color writers of the late 1800s; the rise of the tourism industry and professional travel marketing in the early 1900s; cinema, television, and modern telecommunications; and finally the nightly Bourbon Street bacchanalians, and the reputation of New Orleans becomes gospel believed worldwide. It is even embraced locally, not as a slanderous stigma but as a romanticized social memory: New Orleanians love to be viewed as carpe-diem epicureans with a devilish flair, regardless of their actual lifestyles. So formed the perceptual backstory that underlies (and reinforces) Bourbon Street's success, and while the average nightly reveler might not articulate it as such, most feel that their indulgent behavior is socially sanctioned because they've heard repeatedly that this is what people have always done here.

Bourbon Street has more than a historical reputation, a social memory, and a convincing structural framework to back it up. It also has geographical antecedents. In surveying New Orleans's historical geography of sin to find these proto-Bourbons, two geographical histories emerge: an era of "soft" concentrations from the 1700s to 1857, during which vice occurred hither and yon; and an era of "hard" districts, from 1857 to 1917, when city authorities limited vice to specified areas.

Vice, abundant as it was, generally scattered throughout colonial and antebellum New Orleans. Grog shops and tippling houses, caravanserai (flophouses), music and dance halls, gambling dens, and brothels popped up wherever demand and supply shook hands, and that meant most neighborhoods, if not most blocks. Adding to the spatial ubiquity was the fact that, unlike in other cities, prostitutes in New Orleans generally rented the roofs over their heads. Landlords could charge more for a houseful of whores using their beds to earn money, than for family members using their beds to sleep. Property owners eagerly followed suit, and lobbied the city to leave their productive tenants alone.[21]

Yet concentrations did occur, for the same reason that "concerns akin assemble together" in industries as varied as "the grocery and provision lines, the import coffee trade, the iron works, the printing and publishing houses, [or] the horse and mule markets": to take advantage of mutual clients, supply chains, employee pools, and economies of scale.[22] Police reports, court records, and news articles about illegal sex activity for the period 1846 to 1862, gathered by historian Judith Kelleher Schafer and mapped by this researcher, show that most prostitution—which was usually accompanied by drinking and gambling and sometimes by violence—occurred in three principal zones. One was located in middle-rear edge of town; another in the upper edge; and the third along the lower riverfront.

In the First District—that is, the French Quarter and Faubourg Tremé—the vice zone lay around the intersection of Customhouse (renamed Iberville in 1901) and Burgundy Streets. Schafer unearthed at least seventy-five illegal-sex reports from court records and other sources, many of them involving scores of arrests, with addresses on Customhouse, Burgundy, Dauphine, Conti, Bienville, Basin, Franklin, and adjacent streets. Why here? This was the rear of the Old City—none too elegant, none too pricey, yet conveniently proximate to clients galore in the city core. Better yet, the nearby Old Basin (Carondelet) Canal turning basin and its attendant industries, plus the popular Globe Ballroom, drew a steady stream of potential johns.[23]

In the Second District (today's Warehouse District, Central Business District, Superdome area, and Lower Garden District), a crescent-shaped sin space spanned from the rears of Gravier and Perdido Streets, up Phillippa (now University Place, O'Keefe, and Dryades), and down Girod and Julia to the Mississippi River. Therein could be found the raffish back-of-town near Charity Hospital, the turning basin of the New Basin Canal and its leatherneck workforce, the heavy-labor industries along the semi-rural periphery, and above all, the uptown wharf along the Mississippi River. From the 1790s to the 1860s, thousands of young western males guided flatboats down from the upcountry to this dock, whereupon they unloaded hinterland cargo, vended it, dismantled the vessel, and sold the scrap wood. Flush with cash, the boatmen usually treated themselves to a few days or weeks "footloose" in the big city, free to see the elephant. Venues served them along the flatboat wharf (present-day South Peters Street), in part because the lads utilized their docked vessels as rent-free base camps. One visitor reported seeing flatboats "used as huckster shops, dwellings, pigpens, museum[s], coopers shops, etc."[24] Others disdained the mile-long "line of gambling-shops" formed by the flatboats on Sundays, not to mention the boatmen themselves, who, by one springtime 1830 account, numbered "5000 or 6000," or 10 percent of the entire city's population.[25]

Once boatmen were finally crowbarred out of their floating lairs, they spilled into adjacent streets to seek affordable room and board. The high-rent arteries of the Second District, such as St. Charles, Camp, and Magazine Streets, generally eschewed the scruffy vagabonds. Back streets, however, were a different story: these semi-urbanized margins were a bit more forgiving, with their enticingly discreet and dimly lit shelters and refuges. To this area (mostly) young single male transients gravitated, with time on their hands, cash in their pockets, and the freedom of anonymity. Phillippa Street bore witness to a remarkable concentration of brothels, particularly around Gravier, Perdido, and Girod, and with them were all the affiliated antics, scams, and crimes.

An incident in 1855 illustrates how these activities intersected. One night, at 213 Phillippa near Girod, a man named Abraham Rosenthal made an "appointment" with one Mrs. Sinkovitz. As he began to kiss her, out popped from under the bed Mr. Sinkovitz, who "arose in his wrath, and threatened to exterminate the unfortunate Rosenthal with a hatchet." Rosenthal begged and prayed for mercy, and finally offered to buy it, at which point the Sinkovitzes relieved him of everything he had, "laughing in their sleeves." Rosenthal later reported the entrapment and the Sinkovitzes ended up in prison—a fortunate outcome, because this common scam often resulted in bloodshed.[26]

The most adventurous males debauched in a sketchy purlieu known as "The Swamp." Located a dozen blocks inland from the flatboat wharf, where Julia and Girod petered out into the backswamp, this area took in all that civilized New Orleanians threw out: the eerie Girod Street Cemetery (1822); the smelly New Basin Canal (1832); Charity Hospital and its pestilential patients (1835), not to mention gas works, garbage dumps, shantytowns, and city stables. So it comes as no surprise that the boatmen's den of iniquity ended up here as well. Like Bourbon Street today, The Swamp, located a stone's throw from the Girod Street Cemetery, repelled some visitors but enticed others. "The captains or owners of the flatboats were of the more provident sort" and generally avoided the district, "but the hired men seldom cared to save their money" and "usually stayed here until they had spent or gambled the results of their trip away, then left for home by land."[27]

Girod Street, connecting the riverfront wharves with the New Basin Canal, hosted a disproportionate share of vice venues and crime. Out-of-state newspa-

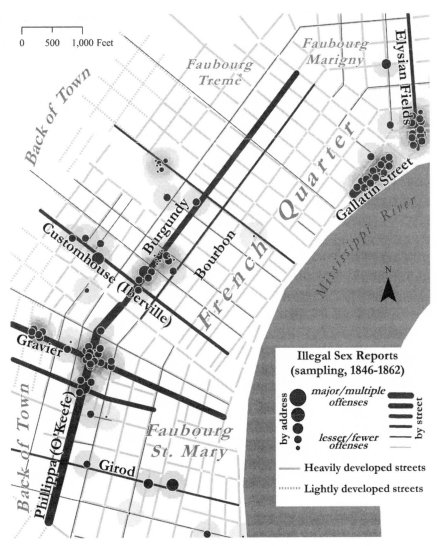

Illegal sex concentrations in antebellum New Orleans, based on police reports, court records, and news articles (1846–1862) gathered by Judith K. Schafer, published in her book *Brothels, Depravity, and Abandoned Women,* and mapped by the author.

pers noted that Girod Street "is said to be the den of cut-throats, gamblers, and other infamous persons, and it is proposed to root them out by tearing down the houses and widening the street," an early example of conflating a social problem with its structural environment.[28] Locals called Girod "a sink of pollution" with "scarcely a decent house in the whole street." Detailed descriptions of the Girod vice scene (possibly the street's rear terminus at the swamp) come from an 1852 *Picayune* article. "Rows of low tenements . . . leaning against one another, [their] fronts shattered and broken, [with] a few crazy, creaky steps lead[ing] to each door," lined the infamous corridor. A closer look revealed the activity inside: "There is a red curtain in every window, and drunkenness and vice seem to peep through patched panes." The woman of the house—such enterprises were usually run by females, likely madams—"enlarges her business by accommodating board-ers and lodgers." Upstairs, strangers paid a dime or a *picayune* for a rude bunk, depending on how cramped was the room, and endured "men in a beastly state of intoxication, with bloody clothes . . . a broken jaw, a stab in the body; while slovenly bloated women hang around them." The "desperate rascal who would rob or murder, [with] police . . . in pursuit," found refuge in the hovels of Girod Street. "This is not a fancy picture," the article concluded.[29]

Last but not least of the "soft" concentrations of antebellum vice was the Gallatin Street area. Only two blocks long, Gallatin probably comes closest to an antebellum proto-Bourbon, except that it was incomparably more violent and unconstrained than the bourgeois fête of today. Newspapers described the strip as "filled with low groggeries[,] the resort of the worst and most abandoned of both sexes."[30] The raucous space ranked among the few streets in the city to achieve metaphor status in the local lexicon, such that if one spoke of a woman having a "career on Gallatin Street," or of "the frail daughters of Gallatin Street," everyone knew what that meant. Few New Orleanians would have challenged the journalist who, in inventorying the city's geography of sin in 1855, wrote that "worst among the worse is Gallatin street . . . sons of fraud, treachery and blood meet there the daughters of the night, and with them hold high wassail and unhallowed revelry. There is no redeeming feature to this street of streets."[31] Nevertheless, more wickedness lay a short distance downriver, around the dogleg-shaped inter-section of Elysian Fields Street: here operated the Sign of the Lion (Lion's Den), the Stadt Amsterdam, the Mobile, the Pontchartrain House, the Whitehall, and Tivoli Gardens, known together as "Sanctity Row."

Gallatin Street plus Sanctity Row formed the highest concentration of illegal sex, drinking (licensed or otherwise), violence, robberies, pickpockets, and scams in late antebellum New Orleans. Why here? It lay at the periphery of the French or Creole Market, the city's largest municipal emporium, which buzzed with stalls, conveyances, errand-runners, day-hires, cheap food, running water, distractions, amusements, shelter, and a steady stream of customers round the clock. Such activity attracted loiters, transients, curiosity-seekers, and adventurers, to whom bars, brothels, and gambling dens catered. The adjacent streets also ranked fairly low socioeconomically; one visitor called this area "the St. Giles of New Orleans . . . where poverty and vice run races with want and passion." It attracted troublemakers with its cheap rents, and lacked the civic clout to keep them out.[32] The nearby U.S. Mint, a smoky industrial operation, further suppressed the cost of living and added to the foot traffic, as did the international shipping wharves at the foot of Esplanade. And on Elysian Fields was the Pontchartrain Railroad Station, which landed visitors from Mobile via Lake Pontchartrain (hence the Mobile and the Pontchartrain House saloons). For many disoriented coastwise travelers, this spot formed the back-end gateway to New Orleans. Railroads, ships, markets, low rents, cheap eats, a quick buck, strangers coming and going at all hours: perfect ingredients for a vice district.

Select incidents help paint a picture of the seediness of Gallatin Street. One night in 1849, for example, a hapless chap named Chambers fell for the same dangerous trap that Rosenthal would on uptown's Phillippa Street (see earlier). Chambers got a room in a Gallatin Street boardinghouse, and, predictably, soon found himself "having a chat" with a lady named Miss Bridget. As she cunningly excused herself to get water, a man by the name of Warden suddenly appeared, "asserting [to Chambers] in very strong terms that he was the husband of the lady who had just gone out. As is usual in such cases, a fight ensued." By dawn, Chambers found himself robbed of fifteen dollars; he and Warden found themselves cut and bruised; and Miss Bridget and her accomplice found themselves in the slammer. "This is an old game," admonished the *Picayune*, "and the young gentleman had not paid as dearly as many before him have for seeing the 'elephant.'"[33]

Such Gallatin Street antics would have elicited the same head-shaking discountenance from decent folk in mid-1800s as Bourbon Street scams and rows do in the early 2000s. Yet Bourbon in the mid-1800s was nothing like this. In the 284 spatially referenced reports of vice incidents culled by Schafer in her research, not a single one had occurred on Bourbon Street, nor hardly any on Royal or Chartres. Bourbon instead continued its moderate, middle-class mixed residential-commercial status in this era, neither rich nor poor, nor particularly bustling, quiet, proper, nor scandalous. Surely some vice did occur in these heart-of-town streets, but very little compared to the three "soft" vice concentrations of Custom-house Street, the Phillippa/Girod area, and around Gallatin and Elysian Fields.

Laws had been on the books for years targeting "lewd and abandoned women," but they mainly prohibited "occasion[ing] scandal or disturb[ing] the tranquility" rather than paid sex per se.[34] The ubiquity and profitability of prostitution, how-ever, impelled city authorities to augment their intervention. In March 1857, the City Council passed "An Ordinance concerning Lewd and Abandoned Women," a sixteen-act, thrice-amended piece of legislation said to be the first of its kind in the United States. Dubbed the Lorette Law after the French slang for whores, the ordinance restricted the sex trade by taxing, in certain areas, prostitutes $100 and brothel keepers $250 annually.[35] The law's spatial restrictions aimed to make the sex trade invisible, not illegal: harlots could not occupy any one-story building, or the lower floor of any structure, nor could they "stand upon the sidewalk . . . or at the alley way, door or gate . . . nor sit upon the steps [with] an indecent posture [nor] stroll about the streets of the city indecently attired."[36] The Lorette Law also mandated that white and free colored prostitutes not occupy the same house, and banned public women from soliciting johns in cabarets or coffeehouses. Most significantly, it directed these restrictions to certain spaces defined with hard legal limits, ending the era of widespread prostitution and softly concentrated vice areas. This new era of legally delineated geographies of sin would last for the next sixty years, and helped pave the way for the rise of Bourbon Street.

Generally speaking, the Lorette Law taxed and curtailed prostitution in the front-of-town, and thus pushed it to the rear and lower outskirts of the city.[37] Although it remained legal to sell sex from an upper floor within this zone so long as it was quiet, unnoticeable, and licensed, the Lorette Law marked the beginning of the end of the old "soft" Phillippa/Girod and Gallatin/Elysian Fields vice concentrations, not to mention the scores of dispersed brothels. However, one old concentration evaded the new delimitations. Because the Lorette Law did not restrict prostitution on the swamp (lake) side of Basin Street between Canal Street and Toulouse, the old Customhouse Street concentration around the Franklin intersection managed to persist—with great consequence forty years later.[38] As for Bourbon Street, it fell well within the restricted zone, and saw little change because the street harbored few if any brothels at the time.

The Lorette Law came under legal attack immediately. One madam, Eliza Costello, refused to pay the $250 fee and ran her case to the Louisiana Supreme Court, which in January 1859 ruled the ordinance unconstitutional on licensing technicalities. Sex workers celebrated with a vulgar victory parade through the streets of the inner city. Authorities fought back. "For the next forty years," wrote historian Judith Kelleher Schaffer, "city leaders passed eight new versions of the Lorette Law, all of which attempted unsuccessfully to control, regulate, or just make money on prostitution."[39] Licensing fees and penalties were tweaked variously, but the spatial limits of the law generally remained the same as in 1857. This meant that, by default, the one place in the city where sex workers could ply their trade with no costs, minimal police interference, and maximum proximity to populations, was directly lakeside of the upper French Quarter: Customhouse, Bienville, St. Louis, and Conti Streets, extending for a few blocks lakeside of Basin Street toward the backswamp. That space would, in time, form an opportunity for the city to attempt its greatest corralling of vice, one that would cinch New Orleans's notorious national reputation and lay the groundwork for today's Bourbon Street.

Of the myriad personalities who resided on nineteenth-century Bourbon Street, two in particular serve as exemplars of its society, and as architects of the violent civil trauma it would endure. By a remarkable coincidence, they may well have occupied the same building, an elegant Greek Revival townhouse with distinctive crossed-arrows cast-iron railings. It was built in 1835 by the prominent Creole August St. Martin, whose daughter Natalie wed a newcomer by the name of Judah P. Benjamin. The young couple lived here briefly in the late 1830s. Years later, Benjamin, who was born in England of Jewish ancestry, would become a Louisiana lawyer and senator as well as attorney general, secretary of war, and secretary of state for the Confederate States of America. That the house at 327 Bourbon gained the residency of a man of St. Martin's socioeconomic status, and of Benjamin's ambition, attests to the appeal of antebellum Bourbon Street to the upper class, despite the surprising proximity of families of lesser means. Just two doors down, for example, on the corner of Conti, stood a humble ca. 1820s Creole cottage, typical of the working class. It still stands today, home to the Famous Door Bar.

Benjamin secretly fled the defeated Confederacy and, incredibly, reinvented himself as a distinguished British counsel in the 1870s. Meanwhile, in New Orleans, a certain newcomer to the city scribed in 1876 a letter to his wife, in which he stated that he had

taken a parlor and chamber on the first floor of a house on Bourbon Street, two squares below Canal Street . . . once the resident of our friend Mr.

Gaskett, and is now kept as a lodging house by an old mulatto woman. She does not furnish meals, and says since the war she cannot get along with servants. From her remarks she must have owned them formerly.[40]

The city directory listed a "W. A. Gasquet" residing at 65 Bourbon Street, which, "two squares below Canal Street," is today's 327 Bourbon—the Judah Benjamin House. The writer of that letter was none other than Jefferson Davis, president of the vanquished Confederacy and Benjamin's former boss. If the "Gaskett" in Davis's letter is indeed the "Gasquet" of 65 Bourbon, then both men resided in the same Bourbon Street space, twenty-five years before and eleven years after the war they oversaw. It is especially intriguing to imagine the erstwhile Confederate president paying his Bourbon Street rent to a mulatress who herself owned slaves.[41]

Today the Judah Benjamin House is a strip club.

II
FAME AND INFAMY

How Bourbon Street Germinated
1860s–1910s

American cities changed after the Civil War, and New Orleans, its singularity not-withstanding, was no exception. The metropolis's inner core, traditionally home to a wide range of classes and all three of the antebellum city's social castes (free white, free people of color, and enslaved black), grew congested, industrialized, anonymous, raffish, and less appealing as a place to live. Prosperous families, many of whom had lost their fortunes to the war, departed the aged streets and crumbling mansions of the French Quarter (the Second District) for new neighborhoods developing uptown or toward Bayou St. John. Middle-class families wanted out too, and with them went many merchants. "The French Quarter can no longer compete with the upper city, which outstripped [it] in a short time," lamented the *New-Orleans Tägliche Deutsche Zeitung* in 1869. "The traders [above] Canal Street realize that the [French Quarter] has already seen the 'good days' pass."[1] The city's expanding network of streetcar and omnibus lines facilitated the exodus from the old city to the new banlieus cum faubourgs.

Emancipation also motivated the moving. The main reason why such a re-markably economically and racially mixed population comingled in the antebellum French Quarter was because chattel slavery and codified discrimination so effectively segregated the classes and castes in economic, political, and social ambits that additional segregation in residential settlement patterns was simply unnecessary. A wealthy white family living on Bourbon Street in the 1820s, for example, would not have felt socially threatened by neighbors who were working-class free people of color, or by the slaves living in the back alley, because everyone knew that their spatial proximity bore zero relationship to their social propinquity. Emancipation changed all this; poor black neighbors would now present a threat to the social prestige of the wealthier white family next door.

Whites increasingly viewed nonwhite neighbors with displeasure, and, in time, would seek legal means to resegregate the races as much as possible. For now, however, they mostly fled uptown.

Fine boutiques, fancy hotels, professional offices, and houses of worship departed as well. "Every week closes another shop on Chartres and Royal street and the owners of these shops move to the 1st District [Faubourg St. Mary, today's CBD]," reported the *Tägliche Deutsche Zeitung*.[2] Publishers left Chartres Street for Camp Street's growing Newspaper Row. Bankers abandoned Royal Street for the emerging financial district around Carondelet and Gravier. City Hall, which had decamped the old Spanish Cabildo on the Place d'Armes a few years earlier, brought its legions of clerks to the new uptown Lafayette Square edifice. They displaced, among others, the Irish and German immigrant families who dwelled in common-wall cottages during antebellum times, and the upcountry flatboatmen, whose notorious wharf fell victim to modernization, and whose infamous old haunts became folk memories. Farther upriver, the old sugarcane plantations that once stretched to Carrollton and beyond had been, by the 1860s and 1870s, largely subdivided into faubourgs. Uptown was en vogue in postbellum New Orleans; downtown was passé and déclassé.

Those who remained in the French Quarter found their real estate devalued by the changing demographics. Streets that once saw wealthy Creoles neighboring working-class immigrants now had working-class Creoles neighboring poor Sicilians or destitute African Americans. Dropping real estate values enticed malodorous industries such as breweries, food processing, and sugar refining to move into spaces once dedicated to residential and retail uses, which further undermined land values. New Orleans's historical inner city, including Bourbon Street, began to transform from the high-density mélange of classes, activities, and land uses to a modernizing American downtown that was increasingly commercialized and industrialized in its nonresidential areas, and increasingly poor and squalid in its residential districts. The spatial momentum of the postbellum city mobilized phenomena in three directions: it sent affluence and amenities upriver; it moved poverty, urban nuisances, and environmental hazards backward toward the swamp; and it positioned Dickensian congestion into the narrow streets and alleys of the inner core. Downtown New Orleans became dirty, depressed, and dodgy. Matters got so bad that a proposal floated in 1869 to widen Bourbon Street from Canal Street to the French Opera House at Toulouse, to "raise hope in the French Quarter of new vital business life." A newspaper correctly predicted that the widening project, which would have radically altered Bourbon Street as we

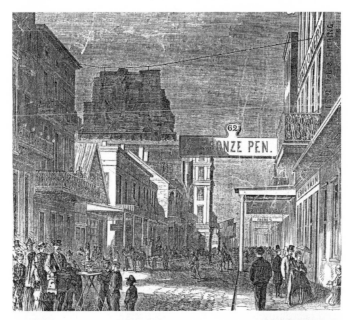

Ca. 1870s sketch of present-day 300 block of Bourbon Street, looking downriver toward the French Opera House (*top*), paired with a modern perspective (*bottom*). *Courtesy City of New Orleans, Vieux Carré Commission; 2013 photograph by author.*

know it today, "will probably not get enough support to be realized [because] such a project needs—apart from the financial aspect—public spirit, community initiative, and energy, and these are exactly [what is lacking] in the French Quarter."[3] They were right.

The geography of indulgence and vice shifted correspondingly. Formerly prevalent in the urban fringe, the saloon and gambling scene now flourished in the central city. Of the 468 saloons licensed by the city's Comptroller's Office during the first six months of 1868, fully 181, or three out of every eight, were located in the urban core—within a half mile of the Royal/Canal intersection—an area that was home to only one out of every eight residents. Saloons constituted over 6 percent of all businesses, including tiny ones like peddlers and draymen, a testimony to the importance of drinking to the local economy.[4] That figure rises when we include unlicensed ad-hoc operations like these described contemptuously by one local journalist: "[At] the foot of Canal street . . . are a number of dirty looking doggeries and low gambling houses . . . crowded day and night by lazy, filthy, ragged negroes, who lounge around in a state of idleness, gambling, drinking and carousing, making the whole neighborhood a perfect plague spot."[5] The commentary featured an illustration of an elegantly dressed white lady suffering a "swarm of greasy, drunken negroes" as she exited the nearby Louisville and Nashville train depot, leaving the writer to worry about "the impression made on the mind of visitors." That concern was shared by others in the commercial class, who increasingly recognized the potential economic value of leisure travelers and fretted how they might react to inner-city debauchery. Only later would they recognize that a certain brand of iniquity actually attracted visitors.

Brothel districts, stanched as they were by the Lorette Law, otherwise reflected the same centripetal spatial shift of the saloon and gambling dens. Of the antebellum sex-industry concentrations, only the one around Customhouse and Franklin, which was excluded from the law's limits, gained momentum. That area, particularly the three riverside blocks of Franklin Street from Canal to Bienville, would form a locus for black roustabouts unwinding after a day of hard labor on the riverfront. Places with names like the Honky Tonk, the Pig Ankle, and the Hot Cat sold whisky for five cents and a mixture of claret, water, and cocaine for a dime. In the back were kitchens frying cheap victuals; next door were long halls for dancing and gambling; and upstairs were cribs for sleeping and copulating. A fair number of "slumming white tourists" could be found among the mostly black clientele.[6] To its detractors, Franklin Street came to be viewed as the worst of the postbellum districts—"slums and dives [with] the most loathsome, filthy, hotbeds of vice and debauchery ever permitted to befoul . . . any city," hosting "orgies . . . throughout the livelong night." An exposé that touched upon nearly every social flashpoint of this time and place—sex, race, miscegenation, class, hygiene, intemperance, crime, gambling, corruption—described Franklin Street's

> ball room crowded with negroes of all stages of . . . depravity[,] raggedness and filth. Here male and female, black and yellow, and even white, meet on terms of equality and abandon themselves to . . . obscenity and lasciviousness. . . .

> In the corners of the room are the gaming tables around which pull, tug and jostle a motley crew of men, women and boys[; nearby] sit several greasy, filthy wretches, almost in rags, while several tattered, half drunken rousters treat them to the poisonous stuff there dispensed at five cents a glass.

> Not only are these vile haunts, which have been the scene of dozens of murders, permitted to remain open and flaunt their debaucheries . . . they are actually licensed by the Mayor, and [protected by] policemen.[7]

Franklin Street found itself increasingly competing with an emerging nighttime district in the upper French Quarter. Royal and Bourbon Streets in particular saw new saloons, gambling dens, entertainment venues, hotels, and restaurants opening for adventurous male clients. They also catered to a new breed of leisure travelers spawned by the rising disposable income of the bourgeois class, which enjoyed increasing mobility on account of nationally expanding passenger railroad lines. Visitors generally dallied near their downtown hotels, further motivating the establishment of a coterminous entertainment cluster as an alternative to dangerous dives yonder. Theaters, dance halls, ballrooms, circuses, and vaudeville venues provided some of that inner-city entertainment. On Orleans Street, for example, the Clio opened in 1867, offering plays, performances, and "an elegant bar [offering] the best of wines and Liquors." Next door at the corner with Bourbon Street, the Crescent City Circus brought more amusement-seeking foot traffic to the area.[8] A few years later, on Bourbon and St. Ann, entrepreneur

Frederick "Faranta" Stempel set up a tent theater and did well enough to upgrade to a corrugated-iron-covered pavilion which was as much an eyesore—"Faranta's New Iron Theater," it was called—as it was a hit with hoi polloi.[9]

But a gentleman on the town could only take so much zany theatrical diversion before craving something a bit more interactive, a bit more intimate. For those who sought wine, women, and song, a controversial new offering appeared on the emergent downtown night scene: the concert saloon.

Concert saloons, an American variation of the English music hall and a forerunner of vaudeville and burlesque, brought together a number of ploys to compete in the nighttime entertainment market. Premier among them was sexualized performance, most famously the iconic cancan, in which a chorus line of high-kicking girls in close-reefed corsets suggestively swirled their petticoats to reveal shapely black-stockinged legs. Daft and danceable music filled the air, emanating from rollicking piano, orchestras, or the latest self-playing instruments—an early example of Bourbon Street's forte as a local testing grounds for imported fads (think karaoke today). Darting among the crowd in concert saloons were "pretty waiter girls"—or "beer jerkers," as they were indelicately called—who personalized the sexual atmosphere by interacting individually with patrons, another tactic that persists on modern Bourbon Street (think "shot girls" today). Finally, and most importantly from a moneymaking perspective, concert saloons sold large quantities and varieties of beer, wine, and spirits, and did so with the sort of panache that convinces patrons that they are partaking of upscale exclusivity.[10]

Concert saloons first appeared in New York during the Civil War, and flourished to the point that the city passed a law against them. They soon diffused to other ports, including, in the late 1860s, New Orleans. A hit with "young men, not only of this city, but of all the country tributary to New Orleans," the boisterous venues raised the eyebrows of the local establishment, earning accusations of intemperance, promiscuity, and criminality. Religious reformers, predecessors of the proselytizers on Bourbon Street today, targeted concert saloons as "places where . . . the most good could be accomplished [to] win souls to Christ." In one 1869 incident, "a young and pretty lady" bravely ventured into a number of concert saloons and commandeered the piano for the purpose of performing "music unknown to the saloon"—church hymns. The response ranged from awkward silence to catcalls.[11] Owners responded with indignation, insisting "that they are doing the public a benefit by keeping young fellows, who come to see the elephant, from seeing it in a gambling house," and "deem themselves the best friend in the world of homeless and poverty stricken women," some of whom earned a tidy twenty to thirty dollars weekly. By the end of the 1860s, two concert saloons operated uptown, the St. Nicholas at 109 St. Charles and Louis Bauer's Pavillion at Baronne and Poydras (site of today's Le Pavillon Hotel), and another four found a home in the upper French Quarter. On Royal Street were The Napoleon, a favorite rendezvous for Francophiles, and The Bismarck, where Germans downed five barrels of imported Cincinnati lager nightly ("The Bismarck sells no city beer," it boasted) to piano musical accompaniment. On Chartres just off Canal, the Conclave "illuminates and enlivens [the] neighborhood" with the help of four beer jerkers "kept pretty busy . . . until midnight." And on Bourbon Street stood a concert saloon and beer garden that, in retrospect, ranks as the first venue offering the type of entertainment for which Bourbon Street would become famous decades later. City licensing records show that on February 2, 1868, H[enry] Wenger paid a $250 annual license fee (the same fee that a commission merchant or big grocery distributor would pay) for his place at 11 (now 119–125) Bourbon, on the lake side of the block between Canal and Customhouse (now Iberville).[12] "Wenger," as everyone called both the chap and his joint, "runs four girls as 'jerkers,'" wrote one observer in 1869, and "makes Bourbon street musical with the remarkable machine [called] a self-acting organ. Through some manipulation that the looker on cannot discover, music fills the establishment, and good music at that." Pretty girls, liquor, music, and atmospheric manipulation: to call Wenger's the seed from which modern Bourbon Street would sprout is justified on a number of levels.[13]

Licensing records show how concert saloons changed New Orleans nightlife after the Civil War. The Comptroller Office's Register of Licenses for 1868, for example, granted 468 licenses for "coffeehouses"—a loan translation of the French *maison de café*, or simply *café*, which to this day in Paris refers to an establishment that serves coffee in the morning and alcohol later. Coffeehouses in nineteenth-century New Orleans were traditional saloons in which men of the establishment class conducted business and drank in a rather sedate and often sophisticated setting; the spaces were generally not rowdy or boisterous and rarely sexualized. The proprietors of coffeehouses felt little need to advertise: although the owners of 468 such enterprises paid for licenses in 1868, only one appeared in the *City Directory* that year.[14] In the parlance of the day, "coffeehouse" was *not* synonymous with bar, barroom, or grog shop.

Over the next eleven years later, things changed. Coffeehouses still abounded by 1879; a partial listing of license records that year enumerates 225, some affiliated with groceries, oyster saloons, or restaurants. But the records also list 38 "barrooms," including two "Bar Room[s] with Instrumental & Vocal Music" at 32 and 42 Royal Street; three "Coffee House[s] with Theatrical Performances" at 36 Royal, at the corner of Chartres and Conti, and a few blocks away at 8 Poydras; and, last but not least, Wenger's at 11–13 Bourbon, which had to pay a steep extra fee because of the ruckus it raised. The comptroller described the Bourbon Street concert saloon as a "Bar Room with Instrumental or Vocal Music as Per Sec 64 of ordinance no. 4789 a.S. This License with $75.00 already Paid[;] Makes $700 for said business."[15] Wenger's and its competitors—such as Joseph Zeigler's Beer Saloon on Royal, which imported its own beer on ice—together offered the nightly spectacle of music, dance, sexuality, and spirits within a few blocks of each other. Traditional coffeehouses, which constituted nearly 100 percent of the licensed saloon scene in 1868, fell to 85 percent in 1879. That other 15 percent was getting more and more of the clientele—and all of the attention.[16]

Wenger's reputation grew notorious in the 1870s. Some described the three-story brick Bourbon Street joint as a concert saloon, a music hall, or a beer garden; others called it pure trouble. Evidence came one Saturday night in May 1875, when a "war at Wenger's" erupted between rival uptown and downtown gangs, spilled onto Bourbon Street, and turned bloody on ever-rough Customhouse Street. Next evening saw a near repeat, when a "male beer-swiller got at loggerheads with a female beer-slinger," and turned his rage toward owner Henry Wenger when he intervened. As the two men came to blows, in came Mrs. Wenger to the melee, "fearing for her husband's safety" and wielding a half-gallon tin pot, which she proceeded to "flatten . . . across [the beer-swiller's] cranium." Off he darted into Bourbon Street, only to be pursued and captured by other Wenger's patrons, who seem to have savored a rare opportunity to feel morally outraged. Local newspapers suggested that Wenger's should "employ a peeler"—a bouncer, another modern-day Bourbon Street fixture.[17]

Such incidents apparently persuaded Henry Wenger to rethink his gambit, because shortly thereafter he remodeled his space into an elegant performance hall, comparable to New York's Gilmore Garden.[18] Rebranded as Wenger's Garden, billed as "the only place of this kind in the United States," and inaugurated in January 1876, the new venue featured 250 colored gas jets for illumination, "the finest and choicest wines," "a first-class restaurant," and special family rooms with separate entrances. It also dispensed with "the waiter girl system" and "those diabolical symphonies, known as concert hall music."[19] The new Wenger's, now managed by the founder's son, earned itself a recommendation in an early visitors' guide as "handsomely lighted[;] an agreeable spot to spend an evening."[20] But reformers weren't buying the reincarnation. The local weekly *Mascot*, which specialized in investigating sleaze, likened Wenger's to "a nigger dive on Franklin street" for its brawling, its cozy relationships with officials, and its use of "women as decoys to attract custom[ers]."[21] An illustration accompanying the incensed exposé depicted a riotous scene of dozens of men tangled in fracases amid screaming dames and billy-clubbing cops, as "Old Wenger" tried to maintain order at the top of the heap and "Son Henry" hid under a table. Captioned "Pitfalls for the Unwary," it represents the first published illustration decrying Bourbon Street mayhem—the first of many.

The racial vitriol evident in the *Mascot's* vocabulary bespoke the temper of the times. Resentment over the Confederacy's defeat, followed by the humiliation of federally propped progressive biracial Reconstruction government, fanned the flames of white supremacy during the 1860s and 1870s. After the Compromise of 1877 repositioned white southerners in control of local and state government, one of the first orders of business was to reverse Reconstruction attempts to undo antebellum state laws and city ordinances that kept free blacks off voting rolls and segregated (or banned) them on public transportation and in restaurants, saloons, theaters, opera houses, hotels—even in jails, hospitals, and cemeteries. The ensuing Constitution of 1879 plus a slew of state and local laws resegregated nearly every aspect of life. "The federal Civil Rights Act of 1875 prohibiting segregation in public accommodations might as well have never been passed," wrote historian Liva Baker. "Color barriers reappeared. Hospitals, churches, sporting events, restaurants, theaters . . . even New Orleans' brothels began to observe the color line."[22] Bourbon Street, like any other place in the state, would for the next eighty years comprise two legally recognized racial spaces. The streetcar running down it, the opera house on it, the saloons and eateries catering to it, the hotels lodging its visitors: all had to divide space by white skin or black, or, more popularly, exclude the latter outright.

Calculating year-by-year trends in Bourbon businesses is a difficult task because of the paucity of optimal and consistent sources. City licensing records, the premier primary documentation, have been partially or totally lost for most years, and those that survive employed frustratingly irregular protocols of inclusion and categorization, making temporal comparisons suspect. City directories, while available annually, were also selective and fickle in their listings, and Sanborn fire insurance maps recorded only a fraction of commercial tenants. While these problematic sources yield rather erratic year-to-year trend lines of business and industries, they nevertheless paint a general picture of postbellum Bourbon Street. Focusing on the years 1868, 1879, 1885, 1897, and 1908, we see that, with the significant exceptions of Wenger's, the French Opera House, and some saloons, Bourbon Street still mostly hosted a humble society of working-class folks. Much as in the 1730s and the 1820s, the Bourbon Street of the late 1800s was a place for tradesmen and traders working for their neighbors, with limited direct interaction with the rest of the nation and world. It was ordinary in a decent, stoic, salt-of-the-earth way.

This prevailing working-class normalcy brings into relief those few enterprises that deviated, and their presence, while limited at first, would gradually increase. The number of hotels on Bourbon, for example, went from zero to three during from 1868 to 1908, the landmark Cosmopolitan plus two others near the French Opera House. Add to these nearly a dozen boardinghouses, described as "furnished rooms" in the Underwriters Inspection Bureau of New Orleans's 1897 street survey, and we now have hundreds of guests spending the night on Bourbon Street. Lodgers need to eat, and in that same time period, the number of restaurants on Bourbon increased from one to five (eight according to the 1897 Underwriters survey). They drink too, and we see the number of saloons increasing from eight to sixteen (twenty-one according to the Underwriters). All these figures represent license-paying legal enterprises; if we included informal boardinghouses, eateries, and taverns, the numbers would rise markedly. Bourbon Street by the early 1900s gradually moved away from the tradesmen-and-traders economy of the 1800s and edged toward the new economy appearing throughout downtown, one based on pleasure.[23]

Districts gain traction when they reach a critical mass and the whole becomes greater than the sum of its parts. Downtown's growing night scene comprised concert saloons in the upper French Quarter, dozens of restaurants, billiards halls, coffeehouses, barrooms, groceries that sold liquor, and social clubs and clubhouses with in-house bars. Particularly noteworthy were the gambling dens strewn along upper Royal Street and lower St. Charles Avenue, where men crowded day and night playing keno and other games of chance. The dens were widely known to pay hush money to a city-controlled gamblers' fund supposedly for charity, but actually destined for politicians' pockets.[24] Blamed by reformers as emblematic of local corruption and "the main cause of [economic] hard times," the cluster of "notorious keno halls [on] Royal Street, hell holes of depravity and vice," nightly transferred thousands of dollars from the pockets of hundreds of "poor laboring men" to the coffers of the downtown vice industry, "while their families starve at home."[25] A night at Royal's keno halls was often preceded, or followed, by drinks, dancing, and skirt-chasing, which nearby enterprises legally or otherwise accommodated. So grows a district.

The forces transforming old Creole New Orleans into a modern American downtown tracked similar changes nationwide. In the French Quarter, for example, industrial food and beverage processing increasingly crowded out local tradesmen, merchants, and residents. The sugar-processing industry dominated the river side of North Peters, while Jax built a brewery barely a block from St. Louis Cathedral. On Conti off Bourbon was a smelly vinegar plant that the American Brewing Company acquired in 1890 and soon expanded across the entire 300 block of Bourbon Street. Smokestacks punctuated the skyline, and grime filled the air. The agrarian days from before the war had faded. Old neighborhoods grew bleak; cities were industrializing; the nation was changing, and Americans began to feel nostalgic.

People looking for a reprieve found it in a new literary style gaining popularity for its representation of quaint regional folkways and its ability to generate nostalgia for simpler times. "Local color" dominated fiction in the late 1800s, and Louisiana regionalist writers, rich with untapped material, featured prominently in the genre. The style affected nonfiction as well, instilling in selected works of writers such as Lafcadio Hearn, George Washington Cable, and Grace King sentimental and heroic themes in narratives about New Orleans's past. The era also saw the publication of canonical histories of New Orleans by the likes of Charles Gayarré and Alcée Fortier, whose works were subsequently cited in newspaper articles and school lessons, forming the public understanding of the city's past which survives to this day. Though lacking in any premeditated intention, local-color literature effectively construed for nationwide readers a sense of exoticism and exceptionalism about New Orleans, and rendered its Creoles seemingly romantic and mysterious. The built environment fared well too, as pen-and-ink illustrations of gorgeous courtyards with cascading wisteria, of iron-filigree galleries crowding quaint narrow streets, brought imagery to words and made readers curious about the city—and eager to visit it. Local-colorists discovered, revised, and in some cases invented a new geography, history, and vocabulary for New Orleans. The crumbling old neighborhood known loosely for generations as "the French section" or "the Creole quarters," for example, was retrospectively rebranded the "Vieux Carré." Street names like Goodchildren, Tchoupitoulas, Love, and Craps offered a literary opportunity for Lafcadio Hearn to wax eloquent on "a history full of incident and romance."[26] A brutal crime at a Royal Street mansion in 1834 was revived by Cable in 1889 as the "Haunted House in Royal Street," a favorite of local lore (and ghost tours) to this day. Aging landmarks once taken for granted—the Old Ursuline Convent, St. Louis Cemetery, St. Roch Chapel, the Dueling Oaks—were presented by Grace King in 1895 as poignant peculiarities lovingly sketched in splendorous decay. Bourbon Street in particular benefited from local color: the French Opera House featured majestically in postwar retrospection, despite that its prewar career had lasted all of sixteen months. A nameless saloon on the corner of Bienville that had been brooding in business for decades became "the Old Absinthe House," suddenly famous despite itself. And a picturesque hovel at the corner of St. Philip, which had been serving liquor for as long as anyone could remember, gained a swashbuckling new identity as "Lafitte's Blacksmith Shop."[27] Local-colorists succeeded in instilling romance and charm to an urban personality that had previously been stigmatized by violence and depravity. Scholar S. Frederick Starr went so far as to credit Lafcadio Hearn, who lived steps off Bourbon Street, with "inventing New Orleans"—an invention that would underpin the modern leisure travel industry.[28]

Few Americans traveled purely for pleasure before the Civil War. Crossing long distances was simply too grueling, slow, dangerous, and costly to do for fun. Few leisure travelers meant few amenities to ameliorate the journey, which further discouraged touring. So disassociated were cities across the United States that each synchronized its clocks to the sun rather than each other.

Circumstances changed in the decades following the war, forged by advances in travel infrastructure, in the supply and demand of travel services, and in the transforming spatial and cultural psyche of middle-class Americans. The main infrastructural advancement was railroads. By 1869, four decades after their inception, rails linked the nation coast to coast; by 1885, six railroad lines connected New Orleans to every regional city of consequence, and all others beyond.[29] Train travel became faster, cheaper, safer, and comfortable to the point of luxurious. Train schedules forced regions to standardize their clocks, while telegraph and later telephony allowed travelers to communicate while on the road. The nation shrunk even as it expanded.

Similar technologies reworked spatial relationships locally. Streetcar lines had been expanding citywide since the war, and in response to petitions from residents, rails were finally installed on Bourbon and Royal in 1873–74.[30] Bourbon's service was designed as a downriver extension of the uptown Clio/Carondelet line, which looped around the foot of Canal Street and turned down Bourbon to Elysian Fields (later to Desire Street) and returned on Royal.[31] Because tracks had to be unidirectional, lines on narrow arteries required that one-way directionality be officially mandated for all vehicles on that street. Thus traffic on Bourbon had to flow downriver, while Royal's moved upriver. Residents and visitors alike could now circulate to and through Bourbon Street faster and farther for everything from housing to work to school and recreation.

The streetcar lines became electrified in 1893, during an era that saw electrification adopted by merchants (late 1880s) and by residents into the early 1900s. Power for downtown customers came from the coal-fired Claiborne Power Plant at the foot of Elysian Fields Avenue (1896), which needed a network of substations to convert and distribute the electricity. Scanning the cityscape for sites, the Railway Realty Company in 1908 purchased a lot at 311 Bourbon because it was centrally located amid downtown power needs. The lot was cleared, and in 1922, a substantial new brick building, filling the rearmost fifty-two feet of the lot, was erected to house the equipment. For decades, the Bourbon Street Electric Substation "housed direct current equipment [for] the downtown business area and to serve the transit system; [later] it provided alternating current to the downtown network area."[32] Early-twentieth-century Bourbon Street was illuminated by shepherd's crook lampposts at the intersections, and for blocks in between, by a necklace-like arrangement of incandescent bulbs hung every two or three feet along wires secured to the same L-shaped poles that held electrical cables for the streetcar. Years later, the substation was donated to the city as a pocket park named Edison Place; today it is Music Legends Park.

Electricity, telephony, elevators, and load-bearing steel frames set on pilings enabled the construction of high-rise edifices in this era, many of them designed with the emerging leisure-travel industry in mind. By 1884, five major hotels in downtown New Orleans offered a hundred or more rooms each, and the top dozen had more than a thousand rooms lodging more than three thousand guests.[33] Food services changed as well; dining out became less of a necessity and more of an experience. The first generation of New Orleans cookbooks repackaged local cooking traditions as "Creole cuisine" and depicted is as inimitable and titillating as the people and the place. Mardi Gras, too, had transmuted from the disorganized street mayhem of antebellum days to a spectacular midwinter processional ritual increasingly aimed at drawing visitors and generating positive

Looking down Bourbon Street into the smoky, semi-industrialized French Quarter in the early 1900s (*top image*); rephotographed from the same spot in 2012 (*bottom*). *Historic photograph Library of Congress; modern photograph by author.*

press for the city. Last but not least, theaters, concert saloons, coffeeshops, keno halls, and brothels satisfied the tastes and desires of the supply side of the leisure-travel industry.

The demand side rose commensurately. Increasing amounts of disposable income in this pre–income tax era gave more Americans the means to travel, while the advent of photography and a boom in literary magazines (which relished travelogues) imbued them with curiosity for new sights and experiences. Intrepid easterners set out to see their country in every direction. Why tour Europe? asked the travel industry; "See America First" became its marketing slogan. New Orleans drew its share of sightseers, but suffered a competitive disadvantage for the tourist dollar because of the lingering stigma of postbellum strife. What better way to show the world that the Queen of the South was open for business than to throw a municipal festival worthy of an international audience—a world's fair.

The idea for a major exposition in New Orleans originated with the National Cotton Planters' Association in 1882. Approved by Congress in early 1883, the event was given the cumbersome name World's Industrial and Cotton Centennial Exposition, ostensibly to commemorate the first American cotton export in 1784. Upper City Park, a fallow uptown plantation that was never subdivided, was selected to host the event because it afforded sufficient space as well as direct streetcar access to downtown. After that wise decision, however, things went downhill. Behind-schedule construction, sparse funds, erratic exhibitor participation, and an opening day in late 1884 that even boosters described as "sadly unfinished" got the event off to a rocky start.[34] It never really gained its footing during the main stint in 1885. For years afterward, the standard narrative held that the exposition did more harm than good to New Orleans's interests, but retrospection has since softened this assessment. It succeeded in showcasing Louisiana arts and culture in a way that resonates to this day. It accelerated inspired residential real estate development in the sparsely developed blocks around the exposition grounds, and created a leafy urban environment that would eventually attract two beautiful university campuses and spawn the creation of magnificent Audubon Park. The exposition also gave impetus, form, and vocabulary to the various players—hoteliers, restaurateurs, entertainment impresarios, and railroad agents—of what we now think of as the tourism trade. As if to document the birth of the industry, the exposition inspired the first generation of tour guides—predecessors of today's *Fodors* and *Frommers*, which, with their pithy characterizations and chipper recommendations, play so significant a role in forming visitor perceptions. James S. Zacharie's archetypal *New Orleans Guide* presents an inventory of tourism tropes, ca. 1885, that strike notes familiar today. Within his table of contents, for example, are sections entitled "Routes to New Orleans"; "Baggage and Cab Tariff"; "Hotels and Restaurants," "Social Manners and Customs"; "Amusements and Holidays"; "Car Excursions"; "Sights of the City"; "Walk[s] in the Old City"; "Excursions Out of the City"; and a handy "Outlines of the History of Louisiana," a section that concluded with "Louisiana Reconstructed."

Victorian Age visitors traveled to New Orleans in part to see the "famous" sights they had read about. But men in particular came for pleasure—an interest handled discreetly by tour guides. Wenger's specialized in those pleasures, and lower Bourbon had developed quite a little cluster of hot spots offering the same. Next door to Wenger's in the late 1880s were Gus August Brill's Saloon, Curry and Verneuille's poker room, the Elk's Club and its barroom, a cigar shop, a confectionary, and a pawnbroker, all of which benefited from the pedestrian traffic generated by Cluverius Tyler's pharmacy, Runkel's dry goods, Schwartz's general merchandise corner store, and a number of musical instrument retailers. Games of chance could be found in abundance nearby ("the moon was full . . . last night," rued one observer; "So were the gambling houses").[35] Organ-grinders, street entertainers, and peddlers of snacks and knickknacks materialized whenever crowds formed, and that was often: businesses stayed open late and street traffic remained as heavy at 11:00 p.m. as at 11:00 a.m. "The corner of Canal and Bourbon [ranked as] probably the most frequented in the city."[36]

But then fiery disaster struck—twice. The first ignited on Mardi Gras night 1890 and severely damaged half the first block of Bourbon. Affected businesses had mostly rebuilt and reopened by the second anniversary of the blaze, when, on February 16–17, amid "a ceaseless procession [of] merry, happy" people patronizing "saloons, restaurants, and other places," a second fire started at Schwartz's and spread rapidly. The flames "crossed [Bourbon] street in a bound," and eventually destroyed three Touro Row units, adjacent storehouses, and at least thirteen major enterprises, at a cost of $2 million.[37] Among the charred ruins was Wenger's Garden and its three stories of gaudy interiors. Henry Wenger might have rebuilt except that D. H. Holmes, who owned the famed department store around the corner on Canal Street, had been eyeing his space for expansion. When the price was right, Wenger sold the space to Holmes. Having been fully insured for his building and business, Wenger relocated his enterprise to the corner of Burgundy and Customhouse, where the nearby Varieties Theater and a number of other ribald venues had for years helped give this vicinity a nighttime entertainment economy. Holmes expanded its presence on the first block of Bourbon Street, and held it into modern times.[38]

The 1892 blaze, the last great downtown conflagration in the city's history, had the potential to thwart or redirect Bourbon's transformation. In fact, it sustained it, because the destruction opened up key space through which the new Cosmopolitan Hotel on Royal Street, with its hundreds of nightly touring guests, could establish a valuable second entrance on Bourbon Street. Now the tallest structure on Bourbon Street, the Cosmopolitan Hotel Annex would draw a steady flow of overnight visitors to the area.[39] Their presence created demand for nighttime services, dining, entertainment, potations, games of chance—even a Turkish Bath (Osbourne's, at 111–115 Bourbon), which opened in 1895 near the old Wenger's and, like concert saloons, represented a fad (for saunas) that diffused from Europe through New York in the 1860s and eventually found a home on Bourbon Street. New enterprises specializing in food and drink opened nearby and advertised for employees; a "Fashion Saloon [at] Customhouse and Bourbon," for example, sought in 1893 "a Young Man who is a good oyster opener and understands something about barkeeping," two skills that can land a job on Bourbon Street to this day.[40] Victor Bero's and Eugene Camor's restaurant at 31 Bourbon—Victor's, the choice eatery in town, operating in a space to which today's Galatoire's would move in 1905—offered an eight-course dinner complete with *café noir* and a half-bottle of claret for one dollar, and served it under "new patent electric lights and fans" in a gentlemen's dining room with a "Cafe for Ladies attached."[41] Such dazzling new amenities lured more visitors to the upper French Quarter and incentivized the construction of additional lodging; the Grunewald Hotel, for instance, opened just one year after the structurally similar Cosmopolitan and only 800 feet away, serving the same growing leisure and business travel market.

The mounting bustle inevitably attracted sex workers into the urban core. Prostitutes sought johns at the new male spaces downtown, and experimented with sundry ways to extract money from their pockets. Sometimes they went sour. One night, a country visitor named John Elliston escorted a woman named Mamie Lucius to her cottage at present-day 618 Bourbon Street. As Elliston made himself comfortable, a second man burst into the bedroom: it was, inevitably, Mamie's purported spouse. The "husband" feigned outrage and unsheathed a weapon; the john pleaded to "prevent exposure and scandal"; and the scammers eventually made off with fifty dollars and the police in hot pursuit. It was the same "husband game" documented on Gallatin Street at the lower end of town in 1849, on Phillippa Street at the upper rear sections in 1855 (see chapter 5), and in countless other incidents—only now it was occurring on Bourbon Street.[42] Such incidents made the news only when the police were involved; what went unrecorded were the routine bodily transactions between lustful men with cash and public women with few alternatives. The whores lived in group quarters on upper Dauphine and Burgundy Streets and up Customhouse toward Franklin, and worked places like Wenger's, the Royal Street keno halls, the inns near the theaters, and the Cosmopolitan Hotel so regularly that, to keep up appearances, the establishments created separate men's and women's entrances.

One night a curious fifteen-year-old girl ventured into the women's entrance of the Cosmopolitan. She later recollected the scene inside: "I could see all these girls decked out in diamonds and beautiful clothes[,] eating sumptuous meals [and] drinks, having a ball." Intrigued, she sought entrée into their demimonde, only to be dissuaded by them—purportedly on account of her young age, but more likely because "they weren't about to let me hustle on their territory." Instead the ladies of the evening pointed her to a "landlady" who had set up house on Dauphine Street. "Why don't you go [there], learn how to do it?" She did, and later became the longest-working and last old-style French Quarter madam. Norma Badon Wallace's career in the downtown sex industry lasted over half a century, and it began at the ladies' entrance to the Cosmopolitan Hotel.[43]

The increasing visibility of the sex trade motivated reformers to, once again, experiment with legislation to rein in vice. Segregation seemed particularly plausible in this era, a time when progressive urban planning encouraged the separation of land uses, when *Plessy v. Ferguson* sanctioned the segregation of races, when fancy new residential parks kept the classes apart in housing, and when new "local option" laws led to regulating where and when alcohol could be sold.[44]

The first sex segregation attempt came in 1890, when the City Council, aiming to curb prostitution downtown, tightened the limits of the old Lorette Law from Poydras to Claiborne to St. Louis to the Mississippi River. The revision proved ineffective, and the problem only deepened. A late-1890s street survey by the Underwriters Inspection Bureau of New Orleans, for example, identified sixteen "female boarding houses," one of which was affiliated with the notorious madam Josie Arlington, packed into the first four blocks of Burgundy Street, forming the densest concentration in the city despite the law.[45] The 300 block of Burgundy was particularly wild—Smoky Row, folks called it—and would remain

Looking down Bourbon Street from the Canal intersection in the early 1900s (*top*), and in 2012 (*bottom*). The six-story Cosmopolitan Hotel appears on the right of the 1900s image. *Historic photograph Library of Congress; modern photograph by author.*

so for decades.[46] That's precisely where Henry Wenger reestablished his former Bourbon Street concert saloon after the 1892 fire.

A more radical solution was needed, and in early 1897, a newly elected councilman named Sidney Story, scion of a prominent New Orleans family, came forth to present it. In the words of Alecia Long, Alderman Story and his allies in City Hall, "acknowledging their belief that sins of the flesh were inevitable, looked Satan in the eye, cut a deal, and gave him his own address."[47] Story proposed spatially isolating prostitution to a compact area bounded by Basin, Customhouse, Robertson, and St. Louis Streets—the very heart of the pre-1857 soft-vice zone around Customhouse and Franklin, and the same area excluded from the vice-curtailing limits of the Lorette Law after 1857. Although spanning barely sixteen blocks, a fraction of the Lorette footprint, Story's ordinance deviated radically from its antecedent in that it banned prostitution outright throughout the rest of the city. By default, then, prostitution became freely and legally practicable therein, and, better, stipulated no licenses or taxes for sex services. The Lorette laws, by contrast, curbed (but did not ban) prostitution within a large delimited area, and left it unmolested beyond. Story's prostitution solution was indeed radical, and subsequent amendments helped made it unique in the nation for its rigor and clarity. One modification stipulated that public women not only had to ply their avocation exclusively in the designated area, but they also had to establish their permanent residency there. This led to concerns, only partially in jest, that those sixteen blocks, which were already home to two thousand people, could not accommodate a vast throng of migrating harlots. A later proviso made it "unlawful for any prostitute of the colored or black race to occupy any house outside the limits of Perdido, Gravier, Franklin, and Locust streets," creating a so-called "uptown district" that also matched an old antebellum vice concentration.[48] Another called for opaque windows on all houses of ill-repute. Significantly from the perspective of Bourbon Street, yet another addendum to Story's ordinance made his district—or, as the whores sardonically called it, "Storyville"—a depot for "any concert-saloon or place where can-can, clodoche or similar female dancing or sensational performance are shown." Starting on January 1, 1898, Storyville alone became "the only physical space in the city where concert saloons and other sexually oriented entertainment establishments could be legally established."[49] The amendment shifted the full suite of risqué nighttime entertainment businesses out of streets like Bourbon, and across Basin Street into the sixteen blocks of Storyville. The upper French Quarter reeled from the loss of business. To add injury to insult, yet another major fire—the third in eight years—blackened the first block of Bourbon Street in 1898, this one destroying the Turkish Bath House.[50]

In the opening years of the 1900s, Storyville formed what all of New Orleans's earlier vice concentrations had not: a crisply delineated legal cluster of sex, drinking, dancing, music, and wagering venues. Business boomed, and in the process, the vice industry invented its own neighborhood. It created a signature streetscape in the form of Basin Street (dubbed "The Line," the same nickname given to Broadway in Manhattan's Tenderloin District), where magnificent mansions became gaudy "sporting houses" and prostitutes called down from balconies to men walking "down The Line." It produced an iconic gateway to "The District," in the form of Tom Anderson's famous Basin Street saloon. It had accessibility, being located minutes from the French Quarter, Central Business District, and Canal Street, and steps from a new train station which deposited out-of-towners directly onto "The Line." It boasted, only three years into its existence, 230 brothels, 60 houses of assignation, and scores of cribs, concert saloons, bars, cafés, and restaurants—this despite a steep five-thousand-dollar licensing fee for concert saloons mandated by a 1903 ordinance.[51] Storyville also generated employment for pianists and other musicians, nurturing the development of what would later be called "jass," or jazz. Most of all, it garnered national fame and infamy, and, to the chagrin of reformers, breathed new twentieth-century life into New Orleans's eighteenth- and nineteenth-century reputation for sin. For its first decade and a half, Storyville succeeded in corralling the sex trade and put the freeze on the drink-and-dance scene on inner-city streets such as Bourbon. But the seeds had already been planted, and when Storyville faltered in the 1910s, the fulcrum of the indulgence industry would drift back in Bourbon Street's direction.

How Bourbon Street Blossomed

1910s–1920s

When the Cosmopolitan Hotel opened on Royal and expanded onto Bourbon in 1892, it ushered in a new era of handsome high-rise hotels appealing to leisure travelers. The Grunewald opened the next year on Baronne near Canal, followed by the "million dollar[,] distinctly individual" Hotel De Soto ("Famous for its Creole Cuisine") on Perdido in 1904 at the site of the old Pavillion concert saloon. Eight years later arose the Monteleone ("Finest Hotel in New Orleans"), towering twelve stories above upper Royal. On a smaller scale were the Country, the Commerce, the Henrietta, and the Planters, all on or within one block of upper Bourbon. At least sixteen other downtown hotels were operating by 1920. Competition led to expansion and innovation; the Grunewald, for example, added scores of luxury rooms in 1908 and four years later converted a utilitarian basement into a dazzling venue designed like a cavern. Complete with stalactites and stalagmites, "The Cave" gained fame for nocturnal dining, drinking, and music, and came to be viewed as the prototype for a new concept: the nightclub.

Older hotels adapted to the new leisure market. The venerable St. Charles, operating in its third edifice since 1837 three blocks from Bourbon, proved adroit in making the transition. It abandoned the "exchange" model of lodging, which, in an era when travel was slow and need-driven, provided a mostly male extended-stay business clientele with everything from accommodations and comestibles to banking, auctions, and conference rooms. Now, with railroads moving people swiftly and comfortably, more and more couples and families traveled for fun, zipped around town effortlessly in streetcars and autos, and sought novelty and amenity in dining and lodging.

The rise of tourism in the early 1900s inspired powerful local forces to pool their resources for mutual benefit. Chief among the new promotional agencies was the Association of Commerce and its Convention and Tourism Bureau, whose very name reified an industry that, a few decades earlier, barely had a name, let alone a lobby. Professional pitchmen scanned the horizon for visitation opportunities and converted them into tourism dollars. In one case, the association capitalized on the closure of European cities during the Great War by pitching New Orleans as an alternative Old World destination for domestic conventions and tours.[1] In another case, the association endeavored to reposition New Orleans *against* the hoteliers' "City That Care Forgot" brand, which, to its chagrin, made "life in New Orleans seem little more than 'a series of parades and Bacchanalian debaucheries.'"[2] The association instead coined the more investment-friendly "America's Most Interesting City," at one point printing a hundred thousand stickers bearing that motto for packages mailed worldwide, and posting the slogan on signs at train stations.[3] Modern tourism had arrived.

While many French Creoles departed the French Quarter after the Civil War, enough remained to maintain a Francophone society in this and adjacent neighborhoods for at least two decades into the twentieth century. Dotting downtown were about twenty tiny private institutes or academies, "French schools," often taught by aging French Creole society gentlemen (like Alcée Fortier) with no formal pedagogical training but troves of traditional knowledge. One such one-room school was the Guillot Institute on the 1300 block of Dauphine, which steered its pupils toward all things French—language, history, culture—and only secondarily to anything American. It conducted most of its curriculum in French; Anglophone teachers were usually relegated to teach math. Homes in which the primary language was French were not at all uncommon on early-twentieth-century Bourbon Street; and bilingual children playing in the neighborhood were the rule rather than the exception, with American English, New Orleans French, and Sicilian Italian being the top three languages.[4]

Bourbon Street was central to many of the childhood memories of this generation. Recalled Mildred Masson, who was born into a strictly Francophone home in 1903: "I can remember sitting [at] the corner of Bourbon and Canal . . . waiting for the parade. . . . We saw all the [Mardi Gras] parades from that particular vantage point."[5] Her neighbor Madeline Archinard, born in 1900, recalled eighty-two years later how she used to watch parades from the Bourbon Street stoop of one Mrs. Parmaris while her parents attended balls at the Old French Opera House. "The little house . . . on Bourbon Street is still there. It's a little shop now, but it reminds me of the past every time I go there."[6]

Above all, Creoles of the French Quarter adored the Old French Opera House on the corner of Bourbon and Toulouse. Quarter children would attend Sunday matinees for twenty-five cents and were seated in a special section downstairs. "I was brought up in that way[,] to enjoy music," recalled Archinard; "even as young children[,] we learned to love music in that way."[7] Mildred Masson described the grand edifice as "my second home. . . . I practically lived there[,] three nights a week, and then we had the matinee on Sunday." Because she arrived early with her grandfather, little Mildred would run around in the dressing rooms and get free ballet lessons from the dancers. Then came the performance. She recalled with a laugh: "The very first thing I saw was Faust, and when the devil came out, with the smoke and the drumbeat, yours truly got panicky and I flew backstage to my grandfather! . . . I was two years old; it was more than I expected. I met the devil afterwards, and he was very charming."[8] Even better for the precocious little French-speaking New Orleanian was what came *after* the performance. "The foyer was right in the front, upstairs, on the second floor," she recalled three-quarters of a century later; "and there they used to always serve punch for the ladies[;] there was never a man in the place." The men went "down in the bar in the basement," on Bourbon Street—and that's where Mildred wanted to be. She "used to slip underneath . . . the double swinging doors" of the saloon to visit her grandfather in the bar, where they would "sit me on the bar, and I was given a glass of Maraschino cherries . . . in a Sazerac glass . . . at nine or ten o'clock at night!" By the time the performance ended, it was nearly midnight, but perish the thought that this meant bedtime. Rather, Mildred would accompany her grandfather to Johnny's, a little eatery across Bourbon Street: "All my grandfather's cronies would gather at Johnny's . . . and at one o'clock in the morning, I was eating fried oysters and I was eating rum omelets. I *loved* rum omelets! I loved to see these little purple flames go up and down and I can still see it there. Then we walked home."[9] Everyone in the Quarter went to the Opera House on Bourbon, although blacks were relegated to inferior seating. Another reason, however, explained Mildred's devotion: her grandfather belonged to the volunteer organization, Les Pompiers de L'Opéra (Opera Firemen), whose members pledged to attend operas nightly and, in exchange for enjoying the production gratis, would check for fire hazards before, during, and after the event. They took their jobs very seriously. "When there was a fire to be built upon the stage," explained Mildred in 1985, "they were the ones who built it, and they were the ones who put it out." "Before they went home—well, me too because I was there—they used to go over *every single seat* to see that not a cigarette was left under those seats." Because managers saw the hazard of fire primarily deriving from audiences, the Pompiers worked only on performance nights, not rehearsals. That proved to be a fatal distinction.

Just before midnight on December 3, 1919, the concert master of the French Opera House and his colleague from the New Orleans Grand Opera Company went out for drinks following a rehearsal of *Carmen*. As the two men headed down Bourbon Street at 2:30 a.m., they noticed a plume of smoke wafting from the theater's second-story window. To a nearby saloon they darted to alert the central fire station. Flames of unknown origin had proceeded to ignite highly combustible props, costumes, and scenery, and soon engulfed the upper floors. Neighbors awoke to witness the terrible sight, as fire crews struggled to prevent the blaze from spreading. By dawn, wrote one local journalist, "the high-piled debris, the shattered remnants of the wall still standing, the wreathing smoke, all made the historic site resemble a bombarded cathedral town."[10]

The allusion to the recent fighting in Europe was apropos. The Great War weakened the already tenuous cultural exchange that French institutions struggled to maintain with the former colonies of their fading empire. Old-guard New Orleanians at the receiving end of that exchange took special pride in their French Opera on Bourbon Street—"the one institution of the city," wrote a local editorialist, "above all which gave to New Orleans a note of distinction and lifted it out of the ranks of merely provincial cities . . . [an] anchor of the old-world character of our municipality [preventing] our drifting into Middle-Western commonplacity."[11] Mildred Masson, by this time a teenager, was among those devastated by the loss, particularly since her own grandfather toiled pro bono as a Pompier to ensure this would never happen. "You see, the fire burned the night after a rehearsal, not after a performance." Her voice betraying agitation and indignation even sixty-six years later, she declared the Pompiers "were not responsible for being there during rehearsals because you weren't supposed to use the rest of the theater, you were supposed to be on the stage, and they thought the actors or the singers would have the sense enough not to smoke. You can't very well smoke and sing anyway."[12]

Now, with the destruction of the city's last best French cultural toehold, even the Grand Opera Company admitted that it had suffered "a severe blow to the artistic and social life of New Orleans."[13] So intrinsic was the theater to the Bourbon Street neighborhood that some pondered whether the fire would "sound the death knell of that entire quarter of the city, with its odd customs that charm the stranger."[14] Just three years earlier, another major antebellum landmark, the former St. Louis Exchange Hotel on St. Louis Street, a block off Bourbon, was razed for the damage inflicted by the Great Storm of 1915. A few years before that, officials leveled an entire block of Creole townhouses across from the hotel, and replaced it with a gigantic Beaux Arts courthouse intended the save the French Quarter from itself. Newspaper editors received hundreds of letters pleading with Grand Opera Company authorities to rebuild at the same site, but all too aware of its decaying vicinage, they demurred. When officials finally erected a comparable multiuse auditorium ten years later, they located it well off Bourbon Street and in a different neighborhood.[15] Most New Orleanians by then viewed the French Quarter as a dirty and dangerous slum—Little Palermo, they called it, and not flatteringly—and some advocated for wholesale demolition. Two Creoles born in the Quarter in 1900 and 1903, the previously quoted Madeline Archinard Babin and Marie Pilkington Campbell, testified clearly in their elder years that it was after the Great War, which coincided with these cultural and structural losses, that the last wave of old French Creole families finally departed the French Quarter.[16]

The Great War affected New Orleans in other ways. Economically, it was a godsend. Local leaders lobbied successfully for a major naval training facility, for "quartermaster depot" status as a storage and distribution point, and for the modernization of dock facilities, all of which created thousands of jobs and valuable new infrastructure. Mississippi River traffic boomed after decades of decline, as vast quantities of matériel heading for the front had overwhelmed the nation's rail system and forced the federal government to reinvigorate the inland waterways system with a vast fleet of modern tow-barges. Men by the thousands circulated downtown, embroiled in the war effort through local employment or destined for Europe. The hotels and restaurants originally intended for leisure travelers now catered to men in uniform.

Sending their sons into a foreign war was bad enough, but many southerners fretted additionally that their boys would succumb to retail booze and bosoms while transshipping through the City That Care Forgot. Reformers worried that sin merchants would turn likely lads into lascivious Lotharios and further legitimize their lecherous line of work. They saw Storyville as the heathens' lair and targeted it for cleansing. Legal as the district was, however, they redirected their outrage at a secondary cluster of illegal "cabarets [around] Iberville, Bienville, Conti, and North Rampart streets." Forming a connecting corridor between upper Bourbon/Royal and Storyville, this sub rosa cabaret belt represented a twentieth-century continuation of the antebellum soft-vice concentration of Iberville Street, which in 1901 had been renamed "to sponge away some of the febrile memories of the naughty Customhouse Street."[17] Seasoned with the Latin exoticism in vogue at the time, the Iberville/Rampart area became known as the Tango Belt, and its businesses and denizens competed with those of Storyville a few blocks lakeward. Sometimes antagonisms between the two red-light districts got out of hand. In March 1913, a violent feud among rival Franklin Street dance halls erupted into a deadly shoot-out and brought public attention to the ongoing "Tenderloin War." Storyville was becoming dangerous; its colorful reputation darkened. Musicians departed for safer and more lucrative northern cities like Chicago and later New York, and brought jazz with them.[18] By the mid-1910s, Storyville had lost a share of its prostitute population and entertainment action to the Tango Belt at the edge of the French Quarter, where, according to one enraged reformer in 1916, "there is more vice in one hour than in the so-called tenderloin district [Storyville proper] in twenty-four hours." A journalist referred to the Tango Belt as the "abode of Merrymaking and Brazen Vice; twin sister of [the] Restricted District."[19]

Such protests met with stony silence at City Hall because authorities like Mayor Martin Behrman knew all too well that the damned dives practically minted money. Behrman and the "ring Democrats" were also suspected by reformers to be in the pocket of tenderloin bigwigs like Basin Street saloonkeeper Tom Anderson. City Hall's fiscal calculus changed, however, when the U.S. Navy, concerned about its sailors, threatened to withdraw wartime investments from key American cities if local governments did not clean up their prostitution problems. New Orleans topped the Navy's list because of its large and uniquely legal sex district. In a remarkable commentary on the importance of the sex trade to the city's economy, Mayor Behrman, to the outrage of reformers (who dubbed him "Champion of the Red Light District"), travelled personally to Washington to persuade the Navy to spare Storyville. Arguing that policing, monitoring, and the recent racial segregation of the district—viewed at the time as a long-overdue progressive reform—should allay the Navy's concerns, Behrman initially met with success. But sentiments changed as the matter went up the Navy's ladder. Closure orders were issued, and on November 12, 1917, Sidney Story's twenty-year-old experiment to segregate seediness officially ceased.[20]

Storyville's closure sent New Orleans's geographies of pleasure en masse back across Basin Street. Laid-off musicians sought new gigs in the French Quarter, at spots such as the Lyric Theater at Burgundy and Iberville, which would become a premier black vaudeville playhouse—or else hit the road. First-generation jazzmen like Tony Jackson, Bill Johnson, Jelly Roll Morton, Freddie Keppard, Sidney Bechet, Kid Ory, and Louis Armstrong all headed north.[21] Prostitutes ousted from their sporting houses and cribs resettled in the soft-vice concentrations of old, particularly around Iberville Street. That the Tango Belt had formed there during the 1910s, despite its illegality and the presence of its larger and more famous legal counterpart only two blocks lakeside, testified to the increasing pull of the upper French Quarter in the riverward shift of vice. Soon, along St. Louis and Dauphine Streets, post-Storyville prostitutes positioned themselves in windows, Amsterdam-style, trolling for johns. Recalled a French Quarter madam whose career commenced in the late 1910s: "From the river to Rampart I can't tell you how many whores there were. Between Iberville and St. Louis Streets and from Bourbon to Rampart, every door had a girl hustling in it."[22] Another eyewitness identified the French Quarter and the neighborhoods behind it as "the most open and well-known district" for the sex trade, and broke down the racial patterns therein. All "is divided at Rampart," he noted. Behind Rampart and Basin Streets, "Negro prostitution predominates. . . . As one goes back from Basin west the white women are older and less attractive and more solicitous, and at the very last lap of the division is a Mexican woman of the type that solicits either whites or blacks. This is at Conti and Crozat. From here back to Claiborne is all Negroes."[23] The upper French Quarter, conversely, drew prostitutes who were more likely to be white or otherwise "fancier," and demanded higher prices from a larger and more moneyed white client pool.

Upper Bourbon, Royal, and Chartres similarly benefited from Storyville's closure by reclaiming the nighttime entertainment trade. Gambling dens—the Bee Club, the Acme, the Grand, and the Olympic—continued to infest upper Royal, while the Smokehouse polluted Iberville Street. Set amid this action, Bourbon Street during 1917–19 found itself well positioned to control the new business of bacchanal, vis-à-vis high demand from doughboys en route to or from the front, burgeoning leisure travel, an emerging sense of social liberation among women, an inventory of picturesque "sites of historic interest," and the sudden disappearance of its twenty-year-old competition across Basin Street. When authorities busted the Tango Belt repeatedly during 1916–21 for everything from prostitution to drugs to violating Sunday blue laws, Bourbon Street benefited again.

With this mix of factors at play, we might ask why Bourbon Street did not become world-famous in the 1920s. The loss of the French Opera House certainly set it back, but mostly what thwarted Bourbon's rise was the chief priority of antivice social reformers: temperance.[24]

As old as the Republic, the American temperance movement gained momentum in the early twentieth century when its sensibilities accorded with Progressive political and social causes. Rural Protestants in particular took offense at the sexually and racially loose crapulence of cosmopolitan cities, whose populations swelled with, according to one prohibitionist, "illiterate aliens from wine-growing countries."[25] They funneled their energies into the Anti-Saloon League, which took their complaints to state capitals and to Washington. In Louisiana, the movement met with increasing success in the north; the "local option" on alcohol control was granted to voters in 1902, and, seven years later, new laws prohibited gambling in saloons, segregated drinking establishments by race, and banned alcohol sales within 300 feet of schools and churches. War against Germany furthered the dry cause, as alcohol production came to be viewed as an unpatriotic waste of scarce grains, and resistance to prohibition from German Americans (read: breweries) fell silent. Wartime dry laws gave New Orleans its first taste of life without liquor starting in November 1918, despite the armistice. By decade's end, more than half of Louisianans lived in dry parishes, most of them in the Anglo-Saxon Protestant north. The Franco-Creole Catholic south, in contrast, rolled its collective eyes at the movement, and New Orleanians scorned it with particular vehemence. But statewide and nationally, the "wets" failed to mobilize their opposition, and when the "drys" maintained their momentum even after the war ended, enough states, including Louisiana, ratified the Eighteenth Amendment to make it the law of the land effective January 1920.[26]

Confusion reigned in New Orleans. Frantic wholesalers exported all their stock whiskey before it became contraband. Retailers repackaged themselves or folded. The Sazerac Bar, whose "reputation overspread a continent," converted to a cafeteria. Ramos' Bar, know for a gin fizz "which not only made the imbiber see the angels but actually talk to 'em," shut its doors, as did the Gem on Royal Street, whose mint julep "would have turned . . . Jeremiah into a bubbling optimist." Bourbon Street—now "surely misnamed," quipped a New York journalist—saw its famous Old Absinthe House "wabbl[ing] as a soft drink emporium, feebly bidding for trade on the strength of its wicked past."[27] The Cosmopolitan Hotel closed down the "famous hallway" between its Bourbon lobby and the cabaret on the Royal side of the building, through which "have trod the political feet of

Louisiana . . . to the pulsating heart of political activities [in the] thirst parlors of Rue Royal."[28] The raids made business at the Old Absinthe House so untenable that the owner surreptitiously moved its famous bar-top dripping fountain to an empty building two blocks down, which came to be called the Absinthe Bar.

City licensing records show how dealers abided, at least ostensibly, by the new law. While liquor outlets still received licenses to conduct business—including Galatoire's on Bourbon—their occupations were no longer described as "saloons," "barrooms," or by the old euphemism "coffee house," but rather as distributors of "Malt liquor" or "Retail Malt, 2%." The reason: the law allowed for the sale of malt, which is extract made from water-soaked germinated grain that is then dried and crushed, so long as it fermented no further. Dealers sold it winkingly as an ingredient for baked goods, but everyone knew it went straight into home-brewed beer. By summer 1920, the rush for liquor outlets to convert to malt was in full swing. On July 1, a parade of twenty-eight law-abiding capitalists lined up at City Hall to pay their twenty-five dollars for a license to "retail malt liquor, less than 2%." Another forty-nine followed just in the next two weeks. Malt retailers and a suspiciously high number of confectionaries blossomed citywide, particularly in places like West End, Spanish Fort, Iberville Street and Bourbon Street, all known watering holes. July 1920 also saw the licensing of nearly eighty newly minted malt retailers and thirty-four enthusiastic entrepreneurs starting confectionary businesses.[29]

Bourbon Street not only sold alcohol ingredients, it also produced them. The massive ca. 1890s American (Regal) plant on the 300 block, like other local breweries, adapted by selling alternatives such as "near beer" (less than 0.5 percent alcohol), root beer, and soft drinks. Because near beer could only be made from full beer, breweries endured the temptation to sell the hotly demanded illegal product for top dollar rather than the unwanted tepid piss for pennies. Nearly all succumbed, and American itself was raided and fined thousands of dollars.[30]

The shift from spirits to sweets accounts for the rise of confectionaries. Soft-drink retailers and soda fountains exploded nationally during Prohibition because they filled the social niche left open by bars; the number of businesses listed under "Soft Drinks" in the city directory increased from zero to more than three hundred in the first year of Prohibition.[31] Whether they served as fronts is difficult to ascertain, but not unlikely; nationwide, businesses that were legally licensed as confectionaries and soda fountains were nearly as likely as restaurants and clubs to serve illegal beverages. An old colloquialism for unlicensed liquor outlets, the "speak-easy," reentered the national parlance. It referred to the hushed tones in which the provider and imbiber conducted their business—and they had plenty to conduct.

Tones were hushed because Prohibition made criminals out of ordinary people. By eliminating the legal supply of a substance in high demand, the law inadvertently but inexorably inflated its price. Delighted bootleggers, granted a monopoly on a booming market, commandeered everything from coffins to gasoline cans in wholesaling "Mr. Barleycorn" through an intricate network of coastal ingresses and offshore "Rum Row" rendezvous to the Crescent City.[32] "Poor but respectable wives and mothers" trying to make ends meet played a significant role in microproduction ("bathtub gin") and retailing, and clogged the courts with petty violations.[33] Department of Justice agents had a whole new criminality on their hands. Public intoxication arrests quintupled in New Orleans, to 12,511, just during the first three years of Prohibition, and the level of violence associated with illicit trade often proved shocking.[34] Suggested one Department of Justice agent, "Sherlock Holmes himself would be kept on his toes if assigned to the task of preventing bootleggers from smuggling whiskey [around] New Orleans"—and that was *before* the Eighteenth Amendment.[35] Famed undercover agent Izzy Einstein declared New Orleans to be the fastest place in America to get a drink when his taxi driver offered him a bottle thirty-five seconds from the train station. A study conducted in 1927 corroborated Einstein's claim; entitled "Does Prohibition Work," it found New Orleans to be the "wettest city in America," on account of rampant bootlegging on the supply side and general disregard for the law on the demand side.[36] Tourism thrived during Prohibition, as many visitors chose to visit New Orleans confident they could find a drink here, while others arrived to board ships for recreational forays to Havana. Prohibition created a new industry for New Orleans: alcohol tourism.[37]

Raids made daily news in the 1920s, and many had Bourbon Street addresses. During two days in March 1921, for example, forty cases of scotch whiskey were stolen from 735 Bourbon by men purporting to be police, while the next day "dry agents" raided a full-blown whiskey still, its pipes still hot, at 637 Bourbon.[38] Royal and Bourbon Streets, which had served up the most booze before the Eighteenth Amendment, logically got busted the most afterward; by one measure, these two streets averaged 33 percent more police raids between 1920 and 1933 than the average of all other main French Quarter streets.[39] Fines and jail time awaited those convicted, but worse was the possibility of "padlocking," the forced closure of the business. Among the speakeasies that suffered this costly fate were the Old Absinthe House and Turci's, located on either side of the second block of Bourbon. Royal saw more police action than Bourbon nearly by half, but that did not necessarily match the distribution of speakeasies. Recalled writer Robert Tallant, on "French Quarter streets there were as many as six drinking establishments to a block[,] and not all were speakeasies concealed from the public eye."[40] Among them were "the best restaurants, patronized by the best people . . . serving their fine wines . . . in teacups." What might explain the clustering was a little-known practice called "hot gas lining." Because delivery and storage represented the riskiest stages between production and consumption, some Quarter bars hired plumbers to install pipes through the sewer system to deliver illegal alcohol ("hot gas") directly from secret production facilities to the bar.[41] Booze could also be bought at soda fountains, confectionaries, and grocery stores, some of which were ingeniously configured to separate food and drink sales from living space. One such grocery/bar/home, established at 1243 Bourbon by Sicilian-born Atillo Pedone in the early 1900s, "had a bar room attached to the store with a swinging open door passage way to the grocery. We lived in the rear of the store and upstairs."[42] Just a few blocks upriver from this archetypal immigrant tableau, a new scene was emerging, and while it shared a Bourbon Street address with the Pedones, it could not have been any more different. It involved a new concept in the nocturnal social scene, one for which Bourbon Street would develop a particular forte: the nightclub.

How Bourbon Street Flourished
Late 1920s–Mid-1940s

In some ways, the "nightclub" represented the next in lineage after the concert saloons of the late 1800s. Both venues brought together entertainment and alcohol (legal or otherwise) in dark, stylized spaces scented with the possibility of sex. Unlike in concert saloons, however, an air of exclusivity circulated among nightclub patrons, constructed via fine attire, high prices, membership, a cover charge, a hat-and-coat check, and a velvet-curtain barrier. Restaurant service made nightclubs more of a total-evening experience rather than just a watering hole, and earned them the name "supper clubs" or "dinner clubs." Thematic décor, usually imaginative and sometimes garish, aimed to evoke swankiness or exoticism. Entertainment bookings were eclectic, including comedians, dance acts, contests, and novelty performances, but eschewing anything so vulgar as vaudeville. The cancans and all-girl revues of a few decades ago had given way to a single stylish dancer engaged suggestively but tastefully in "a *pas de deux* between her body and a spectator's gaze."[1] Music generally entailed bands with identities and soloists with personalities trying to "make it" in show business, rather than nameless house pianists churning out atmospheric melodies with their backs to the audience. Patrons danced, as most arrived as couples, quite different from the male-dominated scene of concert saloons. Nightclubs benefited from, indeed catered to, the liberated lifestyles to which women in the 1920s were laying claim. Whereas women were usually servants, performers, or prostitutes in concert saloons, in nightclubs they were patrons as well, participants in the emerging social trend of "dating," in which young men courted flappers with bobbed hair and cloche hats by treating them for a night on the town. The more dazzling the evening, the better the chance to score another new social dare: premarital sex, or something close to it. Nightclubs created classy and safe private-domain public spaces in which these newly permitted social interactions could take place.

The nocturnal appearance of "decent" middle-class women on Bourbon Street and the upper Quarter in the 1920s helped regender an urban space that for decades had been, at least at night, decidedly male and decidedly sketchy. Making such areas "commodious to women," as historian J. Mark Souther has pointed out, formed a key step in their conversion to safe modern mass commercial tourism; their presence took the dangerous edge off male-dominated spaces and replaced it with decorum.[2] These were also spaces where see-and-be-seen social networks could be woven, where social status could be upgraded through conspicuous consumption, and where new technologies such as electricity, amplified or recorded music, and air-conditioning made for a luxurious and novel escape from daytime drudgery. Upwardly mobile husbands and wives loved them as much as courting couples, and for the single man-about-town, nightclubs could also provide scintillating female entertainment akin to the cancan dancers of old—only with less petticoat and more sass.

The model for nightclubs emerged from France during the Belle Époque, and is best exemplified by the famous Maxim's on Rue Royale in Paris (1893), which would set European social trends into the twenty-first century. Similar venues appeared subsequently in other European and American cities, either diffusing as an innovation inspired by the Parisian original or independently arising from similar urban cultural milieus. While the Grunewald Hotel's "Cave" (1908) was probably the first modern nightclub in New Orleans, Bourbon Street offered the perfect environment for this new concept to take root, and it would soon cluster here more than in any other street in the city.

Nightclubs got an unintended helping hand from a Louisiana state law passed in 1908 known as Gay-Shattuck. This social reform measure is best known as the law that segregated whites and blacks to separate bars, prevented women from patronizing venues that served alcohol, and banned musical instruments and performances from alcohol-serving places. But the Gay-Shattuck Law did *not* prohibit women, alcohol, musicians, and performances from coexisting in establishments that also served meals, such as restaurants or hotels. Mixed company, cuisine, libations, musical entertainment: these were all the key ingredients to a "club." And because few people drink and dance during the daytime, the enterprise became a "night" club.[3]

What first brought nightclubs to Bourbon Street was the creative mind of Arnaud Cazenave, a colorful French-born wine and champagne merchant who, finding New Orleans to his fancy in 1902, decided to make it home. Cazenave established a French café in the Old Absinthe House and in 1918 expanded into a larger space diagonally across Bourbon on Bienville Street. A success, Arnaud's Restaurant played a key role, together with nearby Galatoire's (1905) and Antoine's (1840), in maintaining French taste and aesthetics in a neighborhood that exhibited less and less of either, particularly after the demise of the French Opera House. Ever the entrepreneur, "Count" Arnaud—the regal title reflected "his courtly manners and distinguished bearing"[4]—sought to expand his business into the nocturnal entertainment scene. Ever the Parisian, and contemptuously disdainful and brazenly dismissive of the American legal nuisance of Prohibition, Arnaud looked to the City of Lights to inspire the City That Care Forgot. He came up with an idea and shared it with singer Babe Carroll McTague, who recalled the conversation years later: "One night he called me over to his restaurant and told me of his plans to open a club on Bourbon and Bienville and call it 'Maxime's,' after the famous spot in Paris. He wanted me to sing."[5] Situated at 300 Bourbon (across from the Old Absinthe House) in a rather plain one-story building rented from the American Brewing Company, the Maxime Supper Club opened its doors in late 1925 but saved its formal inauguration for the new year. In retrospect, 300 Bourbon Street on the evening of January 13, 1926, can be considered the birthplace and birthday of modern Bourbon Street. And it was quite a night, with the Princeton Revelers' Orchestra providing "that dancy music" and featuring Joe Manne's Chicago blues, "Golden Voiced Tenor" Anthony Beleci, and Babe Carroll as "Cheer-up-odist."[6] Cheerful perhaps, but Babe initially had her doubts. "Rampart was the street in those days," she later explained, in reference to the Tango Belt, "and I wondered for a while if a night-club could really go on Bourbon." But the sheer force of Count Arnaud's "personality"—and his sixth sense as an entrepreneur—"could make a club go anywhere. And he did. Maxime's became a great success. . . . He was the real Columbus of Bourbon St."[7]

Carroll contended that Maxime's was, in the words of Thomas Sancton writing in 1949, "the first full-fledged Bourbon St. night club in the style that eventually made it one of the most famous streets in the country." What about Peter Casabonne's club in the Old Absinthe House? "In those days the entrance was on Bienville," explained Carroll. How about Turci's? And Toro's? "Those were restaurants. I'm talking about night clubs." Carroll's description of Maxime's serves as a checklist for what made a nightclub special. Opening night was by invitation only, fostering a sense of exclusivity. A hat check took patrons' garments. Alcohol was served in demitasse cups, grudgingly acknowledging Prohibition but otherwise ignoring it. The floor show included a master of ceremonies, and from behind a black velvet curtain emerged blues singers, triple pianos, comedians, jazz orchestras featuring names such as Max Fink, and dancers with "brief costumes" and "sex appeal" but absolutely no "sporting house" behavior. Patronage was "traveling men, salesmen, businessmen [as well as] wives and daughters [and] good decent kids" on dates. Babe Carroll McTague herself came to be viewed as "the first singing star of Bourbon Street" when she "walked out in the spotlight one night in 1925 and put it on the maps."[8] It helped that the Tango Belt, raided incessantly by police and losing ground to expanding warehouses behind Canal Street department stores, had been all but eliminated by the late 1920s. Prostitution survived there by going underground, while the bar and club scene shifted to, and blossomed on, Bourbon Street.

Count Arnaud's impact on Bourbon Street would last a long time, but Maxime's would not. It got "padlocked" in 1926, and Arnaud himself got arrested "for two automobile loads of assorted liquor" in 1927. By 1928 the former Maxime's was known as Frolics, and it would clash with the law repeatedly despite its classy aspirations. A few years later its biggest problem was not the law, but the marketplace: new nightclubs opened throughout the first three blocks of Bourbon, employing, by the early 1930s, 100 to 150 musicians catering to a mostly local crowd.[9] Arnaud remained a Bourbon entrepreneur and advocate until his death in 1948, having lived long enough to witness his street become famous for his innovation.

Our attention has been focused on the portion of Bourbon traversing the French Quarter. Technically, however, Bourbon Street entered the twentieth century measuring six miles long, starting at Canal, running down through the Quarter, elbowing at the Kerlerec intersection across Esplanade Avenue, and continuing straight northward into the marshes. As recently as 1920, there were actually two dairies on Bourbon Street! Licensed by the city for five dollars and addressed at 3325 and 4100 Bourbon Street, they were located in the sparsely populated areas north of the Gentilly Ridge, a topographic crest that had hosted truck farms since colonial times.[10] After the Sewerage and Water Board drained the backswamp, the city surveyed streets therein, developers constructed housing, and New Orleanians expanded lakeward. So too would the toponym "Bourbon Street" extend, nearly all the way to the Lake Pontchartrain shore. This ended in 1924, when a city ordinance that renamed a number of streets designated the long stretch north of the Kerlerec intersection as Pauger Street, in honor of the engineer who surveyed the original city.[11] Ever since, Bourbon Street has measured almost exactly 5,000 feet long, from Canal to Kerlerec, of which 92.6 percent is in the French Quarter, 85 percent is within the jurisdiction of the Vieux Carré Commission, 80 percent is within the original fortified colonial city, and 55 percent is commercial. The name change also gave Bourbon a new cartographic distinction: whereas all other French Quarter streets (excepting alleys like Exchange and fragments like Madison) extend dozens of blocks lakeward or downriver beyond the limits of the Quarter, Bourbon is almost entirely confined to the French Quarter. This gives a certain cachet to having a residential address on this world-famous street, and a pricey one at that.

In contemplating the origins of Bourbon Street, it becomes apparent that the dizzying, deafening strip of today spawned mostly from enterprises concentrated primarily on its first two blocks. Bourbon from Canal to Bienville, from the 1860s to the 1920s, came to host two imported innovations that proved to be popular—concert saloons and nightclubs—plus successful local creations such as the Old Absinthe House, Galatoire's, and Arnaud's. How did the success of the first two blocks expand to the nine blocks of today? One is tempted to point to the French Opera House as the magnet that pulled the action downriver, but the 1919 fire reduced that glorious amenity to an unsightly scrap yard. In fact, what gave Bourbon Street its modern-day commercial footprint was modern urban planning.

American cities had grown complex and contentious by the early 1900s. "In every large city of our country," lamented one urbanist in 1915, "a land owner could put up a building to any height, in any place, of any size and use it to any purpose, regardless of how much it hurt his neighbor."[12] Little more than a smattering of unenforced ordinances and neighborly ire prevented offensive operations setting up next door to families, and if property values suffered as a result, homeowners could only hope to recoup losses through a lawsuit. As a result, on Bourbon Street a hundred years ago could be found a horse stable near a family home, an undertaker neighboring a kitchen, an ironworker in a colonial mansion, and a vaudeville theater abutting a convent—all steps from a high-voltage electrical substation and an industrial-scale brewery. Similarly intermixed land uses abounded throughout the French Quarter, the city, and urban America, and while they certainly made for interesting cityscapes, they also put at risk homeowners' greatest source of equity: their property value.

Authorities intervened by introducing top-down expert planning and legal regulation into municipal management. New York set the vanguard when it passed its Zoning Resolution in 1916. Louisiana followed when in 1918 the state legislature passed Act 27, empowering municipalities with populations of more than fifty thousand to regulate construction within certain zones. It extended that power to all municipalities in 1922, and in 1923, New Orleans created its City Planning and Zoning Commission. That agency studied the cityscape over the next few years, producing in 1927 the informative *Major Street Report* while reviewing more than three hundred existing protective residential regulations, amendments, special laws, and setback ordinances that together had produced "an almost intolerable confusion" for developers and residents.[13] Out of this chaos, the commission devised New Orleans's first Comprehensive Zoning Ordinance, which was adopted on June 6, 1929.

In essence, zoning segregated residential, commercial, industrial, and transportation interests (particularly railroads, which crisscrossed the city to the great exasperation of motorists) in accordance with carefully delineated urban spaces. Where to draw those lines? Consultants surveyed existing land uses, analyzed them with respect to the commission's long-term vision for urban growth, and devised an intricate zoning map at a scale of 1 inch to 500 feet. The draft maps, which measured eight feet on each side, were reproduced and distributed to district meetings for public comment—the first full-scale coordinated public participation in urban planning in New Orleans's history.[14] In the final version, the commission generally delineated those areas that had naturally developed commercial clusters, through the mechanics of capitalism, to be "retail business" zones. Shipping, warehousing, and manufacturing areas got zoned as "industrial," and neighborhoods with homes officially became "residential" zones. Bourbon Street had by this time hosted mostly retail commerce and light industry from Canal Street to St. Ann Street, and mostly residences from St. Ann downriver. Exceptions existed: scores of residences (mostly second- and third-story apartments) could be found amid the commerce of the upper blocks, and a few businesses (mostly tiny corner stores) served residential populations in the lower blocks. But the larger pattern, a product of free-market forces playing out over two hundred years, was unmistakable, and it was driven by physical proximity to the Central Business District (CBD): blocks closer to the CBD were commercial; those farther, residential.[15]

What official urban planning and zoning did starting in 1929 was to lock that organic pattern in place legally, and turn its soft amorphousness into hard lines on maps. Bourbon Street blocks that had spontaneously attracted retail businesses prior to the formation of the City Planning Commission got officially zoned *for* retail businesses subsequently, thus establishing the maximum footprint into which the nighttime revelry trade would eventually grow. The rudimentary zoning of 1929 got an upgrade in 1951 via recommendations from consultant Harland Bartholomew, who in a report to the City Planning Commission defined and refined three Vieux Carré Zoning Districts: H-1 (residential, covering 74.39 acres); H-2 (commercial, 44.54 acres), and H-3 (industrial, 30 acres excluding railroads rights-of-way). The Vieux Carré Zoning Districts were legally adopted in 1953 as the Comprehensive Zoning Ordinance 18,565 C.C.S., and were modified in 1978 and again in the 2000s into a five-zone system (Vieux Carré Commercial, Residential, Entertainment, Park, and Service zones, with the first three zones subdivided into "1" and "2" designations indicating permitted densities and land uses). The legally binding zoning birthed in the 1920s would have a tremendous impact on the future of Bourbon Street because, starting in this era and lasting to century's end, ordinances explicitly permitted live entertainment in cocktail lounges and nightclubs on Bourbon Street, but either prohibited or remained silent about it elsewhere. Thus the law abetted the economic advantage of spatially agglomerating entertainment venues, and both legal and economic agency helped produce the Bourbon Street live-entertainment scene of today.

When tourists stroll down Bourbon Street today, they usually turn around just past the St. Ann intersection, ostensibly because that's where the action peters out. Why there? Because that's where the VCE (Vieux Carré Entertainment) zone changes to VCR (Vieux Carré Residential), and where, decades ago, the H-2 zone changed to H-1. The last gasps of commerce in the otherwise residential lower Bourbon—the Clover Grill, Lafitte's in Exile, Lafitte's Blacksmith Shop, a corner grocery, and a laundry (the last of so many on Bourbon)—all exist today because they too happened to host commercial uses historically, and were legally zoned as such starting in 1929. It's a reminder that what strikes the first-time visitor as spontaneous and organic urban fabric is, in fact, carefully woven and expertly patched.[16]

Perhaps the most far-reaching initiative undertaken by the nascent City Planning Commission was to heed the rising clamor for the architectural protection of the French Quarter. Activism for what preservationists preferred to call the Vieux Carré coalesced at a February 1920 meeting of history buffs, architecture aficionados, merchants, and residents which resulted in the formation of the Vieux Carré Restoration Society. The society's efforts gained momentum when writers and artists took up residence in the decaying old district, and through

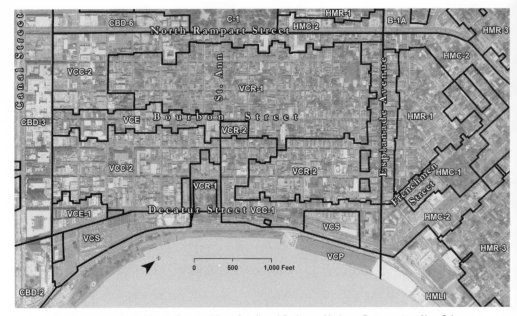

Land use zones in the French Quarter (Vieux Carré) and Faubourg Marigny. *Data courtesy New Orleans City Planning Commission.*

VCR—Vieux Carré Residential, subzones 1 and 2
VCC —Vieux Carré Commercial, 1–2
VCE—Vieux Carré Entertainment, 1–2
VCS—Vieux Carré Service
VCP—Vieux Carré Park
CBD—Central Business District, 1–3
HMC—Historic Marigny/Tremé Commercial, 1–2
HMR—Historic Marigny/Tremé Residential, 1–3
HMLI—Historic Marigny Light Industry/Industrial Park

their literature and art helped sway popular opinion on the specialness of this neighborhood. The efforts of six preservation societies, ladies' clubs such as Le Petit Salon, and support from the American Institute of Architects and the New Orleans Association of Commerce convinced Mayor Behrman's City Planning Commission to pass an ordinance in 1925 "to create a commission of seven members with authority to study the Vieux Carré with a view to determining what buildings were worthy of preservation." When the zoning ordinance came out in 1929, further regulations were established to limit the height, size, and use of buildings within the Special Vieux Carré District.[17] But exactly which area should be protected? Numerous blocks, particularly along the upper, riverfront, and rear edges of the original ca. 1722 grid, had lost their 1700s- and 1800s-era buildings and did not seem convincingly "historic" by the late 1920s. Seven different recommendations were traced onto maps during 1925–28: two by prior ordinances, one by the commission's consulting firm Bartholomew and Associates, one by a special committee, one by the Louisiana Historical Society, one by the Louisiana Chapter of the American Institute of Architecture (AIA), and a final one by the City Planning and Zoning Commission itself. All agreed that the blocks along the Rampart corridor should be excluded, as well as the 100 blocks between Canal and Iberville, most blocks along upper North Peters and Decatur, and most of the 200 blocks between Iberville and Bienville. Bourbon Street fared better; the AIA considered its streetscape to be worthy of architectural preservation from Iberville to Esplanade, more than any other Quarter street.[18]

Strangely, the very same entities that endeavored to save parts of the French Quarter schemed to alter its other parts—and radically. Bartholomew and Associates, the St. Louis–based engineering firm that consulted for the City Planning and Zoning Commission in the late 1920s, actually proposed demolishing eight solid blocks straddling Orleans Street for a civic center, complete with government office buildings, plazas, and a towering art deco–style City Hall. The project's positioning in the rear of the Quarter was no coincidence: since colonial times this was the socially marginalized fringe of the neighborhood, and by the 1920s it housed the scorned joints of the Tango Belt plus the lingering memory of nearby Storyville and Franklin Street. To unsentimental modernists, the area begged for a merciful razing and urban renewal. Bourbon Street would have been spared the Bartholomew plan, but the street's character would have been drastically altered because it would have found itself literally under the watchful eyes of city officials perched in their new high-rise office building. That the Municipal Auditorium, which formed a key part in the symmetrical design, was actually constructed (in 1929) suggests that the Bartholomew plan was not just a pie-in-the-sky vision.[19]

It's unclear whether that grandiose plan succumbed to the momentum of preservationist sentiment or merely petered out on practical grounds, but the very fact that it was seriously put forth as a possibility shows that the original Vieux Carré Commission lacked the authority (not to mention the boundaries) for bona fide protection. The razing of more architectural gems at the onset of the

Depression finally got the City Planning Commission to consider sanctioning the Vieux Carré Commission with real authority. With the civic leadership of Elizabeth Werlein plus field data collected by the federally funded Historic American Building Survey, preservationists came to realize that the proper legal tool for protection was a state constitutional amendment. Involving the State of Louisiana made the legal protection of the Vieux Carré that much more formidable because it brought to bear state interests, rather than capricious local attentiveness, if and when a controversy flared. Section 22A of the Louisiana constitution finally passed with overwhelming public support in 1936, followed by a new city ordinance establishing an empowered Vieux Carré Commission in early 1937. "Mrs. Werlein deserves the real credit for the constitutional amendment that set up the Vieux Carré Commission," said Mary Morrison, herself a major force in the effort, in an interview forty years later.[20]

Even then, incredibly, other branches of government concocted ambitious plans for the neighborhood. Tasked to site federally funded housing projects, Frederick D. Parham Architects proposed in 1938 constructing subsidized garden apartments on twelve blocks along the Orleans Street axis in the center-rear of the Quarter, including Bourbon Street from Toulouse to Dumaine. The project eventually found a new home two years later, on the footprint of old Storyville (today's Iberville Housing Project, built 1940–41), perhaps because the Quarter's new protected status had become clear, or because Mayor Robert Maestri owned land in old Storyville and stood to profit from its sale.[21] In any case, after that episode, the new reality of legally backed preservation began to sink in, and the Vieux Carré Commission found its stride. Demolitions would henceforth be curtailed, and all new construction, renovation, signage, color schemes, and street furniture would be regulated toward preserving what would later be described as the *tout ensemble* of the district. Fortunately, the erratic lines of the seven earlier recommendations gave way to simplified delineation that largely matched Pauger's original grid, although it did exclude all those between Canal and Iberville. Thus was born the jurisdiction of today's Vieux Carré Commission.[22]

Just as zoning legally locked in place age-old land-use patterns on Bourbon Street, codified preservation froze in time the street's ancient edifices. Never again would the latest architectural fashion gain an address on Bourbon or any other Quarter street. Quite the opposite: increasing sensitivity to the civic and touristic value of historicity led planners in this era to install nostalgic street furniture, anachronistic hitching posts, and lampposts made to look like nineteenth-century gas lights.[23] After the 1930s, Bourbon Street would look only backward in time for its architectural inspiration. That structural framework would form a perfect space from which the social memory of New Orleans's historical hedonism could be commoditized and sold.

Mardi Gras came twice in 1933. The first came predictably on Fat Tuesday. Then came April 13, at noon sharp—the moment an amendment in the Volstead Act went into effect to legalize beer. Rejuvenated breweries pumped out "500,000 gallons of the most welcome amber beer that ever passed through a cooling cellar," as throngs filled Canal Street and enjoyed legal brew.[24] When later that year the repeal of the Eighteenth Amendment ended the failed national experiment of Prohibition, it was all but anticlimactic; nightclubs and bars could now put aside all pretenses and flourish legally. Yet external circumstances once again prevented Bourbon Street from catapulting into the national limelight. Years earlier, Prohibition had robbed it of that big chance, squandering the golden opportunity formed by thousands of troops traipsing through town for the Great War, the elimination of Storyville as competition, the rise of leisure tourism, and the prosperity of what people were starting to remember as the Roaring Twenties. Now, in the 1930s, a severe global economic downturn intervened. Investments evaporated on Wall Street; jobs disappeared by the millions; disposable income dried up and so did tourism. But whereas New Orleans suffered as much as any American city during the Great Depression, Bourbon Street fared relatively well. Its nightclubs and bars offered affordable indulgences and refuges from misery, albeit ephemeral, and demand was on the rise for both. The clientele, however, was mostly local, and that sort of patronage does not parlay into fame or profitability.

Commercially, Bourbon Street during the Depression also benefited from an ethnic serendipity. A group of Chinese merchants, who since the 1870s formed a little Chinatown in the Third Ward, had lost the lease on their main building at South Rampart and Tulane Avenue. Forced to relocate, they pondered their options. Compatriots in the laundering business had long called Bourbon Street home, and the Quarter's rents and commerce roughly matched those around the old Chinatown. Back in 1924, for example, an industrious immigrant named Charles Tung, who, after learning English at the Chinese Mission and launching a tiny laundry at 240 Bourbon (in the Old Absinthe House) and 303 Bourbon (two doors down) in 1911, erected the first phase of his ambitious new enterprise in the 300 block of Bourbon. Economic success motivated its expansion two years later, resulting in the two-lot, three-story dry-cleaning operation known for decades as Oriental Laundry. The business, which at one point boasted five thousand customers, advertised itself as combining "the marvelous finish and minimized wear and tear of Chinese laundering . . . with the absolute hygienic cleanliness produced by American machinery and methods."[25] With this and other evidence of success, the homeless merchants realized where their future lay. On September 20, 1937, "Chinese merchants . . . started moving their pungent bales and barrels of stock, their Chinese clothes, nuts and herbs, dried fruit, firecrackers[,] noodles . . . chestnuts[,] mushrooms and bamboo shoots from their old headquarters . . . to the 500 and 600 blocks of Bourbon street."[26] Among the first to move was the old Chinatown's original merchant, On Yick & Company, which settled at 605 Bourbon Street next door to Tom Yuen's Chinese laundry, offering general merchandise and Chinese embroidery. The On Leong Association, which "closely [bound] the city's Chinese businessmen together and through its social activities [preserved] some Eastern customs,"[27] also made the move. Bourbon near Toulouse became home to up to a dozen notion shops, laundries, and eateries, and formed a favorite part of the midcentury Bourbon Street experience. That inexpensive Chinese dinners—America's original "ethnic food"—could be found abundantly here gave Bourbon Street a competitive advantage for the late-night cheap-eats crowd, including artists on shoestring budgets. One writer, a young man named Thomas Williams who moved to 722 Toulouse in 1939, regularly patronized the Chinese diners around the corner. "Thomas" later became "Tennessee" and, inspired by Quarter characters and the rattletrap streetcar that clanked down Bourbon and up Royal, gained worldwide fame after he penned *A Streetcar Named Desire* in 1947. When Blanche DuBois, a character in the play, symbolically shades the glare of a naked light bulb with a Chinese paper lantern, Williams has her explain that she purchased it "at a Chinese shop on Bourbon."[28]

Beyond the club scene and the Chinese shops, Bourbon Street had an unexpected mingling of businesses in the 1920s and 1930s. There was a place that fashioned wires and cables into curious sculptures. There was the Librairie Francaise and a church supply store. There was the Orleans Neighborhood Center Child Welfare Association Clinic and the Junior League of New Orleans adjoined by its thrift shop. Bourbon didn't have fancy antique stores; all twelve of the city's antiques dealers and bric-a-brac shops in 1920 operated on Royal Street, mostly on the 300–400 blocks, where some remain to this day. But it did have something special. "Huddled in Bourbon street, half-way between Canal street and the French Opera House, [are] the most fascinating shops of New Orleans," reported an observer, "—the old costume shops . . . which for more than a half a century have clothed the devotees of the Carnival with motley and tinsel."[29] In 1851 and probably earlier, one M. Sentenac operated a similar establishment ("kid gloves cleaned") at 200 Bourbon.[30] In 1863, next door to today's Galatoire's, a French immigrant opened a shop that specialized in the cleaning of elegant lace dresses and "fine kid gloves . . . worn everyday by well-dressed New Orleans ladies [particularly] when Carnival time draws near." It was called Madame Rapho's, and it remained in business until 1959. There were only three costume shops in New Orleans in 1920; all three were located between 200 and 400 Bourbon, and all three (the others being Madame Alabau's and Madame Snell's) had been operating since around the Civil War.[31] Royal Street's century-old proclivity for fancy antiques, contrasted with Bourbon's penchant for showy costumes, hints at these two streets' divergent modern-day personalities.

The interesting little costume cluster may have found a home here because of Bourbon's traditionally high population of skilled tradespeople, not to mention the nearby French Opera House. Those numbers, however, were dropping. City directories of the late 1930s indicate that what had historically been a street of traders and skilled trades had tilted toward a service economy. To be sure, a few cabinetmakers, dressmakers, tailors, and bakers remained, but many more locals were employed in and around the emerging nighttime entertainment economy. They worked and recreated in Bourbon Street in places like the Old Cobweb Bar, the Fox Bar, the Old Absinthe House and the Absinthe Bar, Hyp Guinle's Famous Door Bar, Steve Valenti's Paddock Lounge, the Four Forty Bar, and the Spot Light Bar—or in the New Silver Slipper Night Club, the Swing Club, the Yakine Social Club, and the Nut Club, featuring the Nut Club Ensemble. Then there were the Club Hotel, the Bourbon Hotel, and the Bourbon Inn. Restaurants employed even more, among them Manual's, the Vieux Carre, the Vanity Club, DeFranco's, Galatoire's, Bononolo, Turci's, the Columbia, Scibetta's, and La Lune Mexican Restaurant, featuring Don Ramon and his orchestra. Liquor stores, usually sole proprietorships, flourished on Bourbon Street in the late 1930s, among them Caltarero's, Borretto's, Lefevre's, Oldstein's, Villa's, Poche's, Mancuso's, and Tournier's Wine Cellar. Entertainment venues offered multiple floor shows starting as late as 3:30 a.m., and if they weren't open twenty-four hours a day, they often remained open to dawn.[32]

Bourbon Street by 1940 fell just short of national notoriety. A perusal of various visitor guides from this era reveals no special characterization of the street; one 1938 tourist map, for example, enumerated only six sites of interest on Bourbon compared to thirty-two on Royal. The influential 1938 *WPA Guide to New*

Orleans, meanwhile, attributed no particular salience to Bourbon.[33] But the night scene on Bourbon was rapidly approaching a critical mass, and religious and civic organizations were among the first to raise a red flag. In 1940 they complained to the mayor of what "by careful count" summed to "seventy-one bars in nine squares of the French Quarter [and] 131 bars in the sixty-six squares of the quarter, of which we are informed fifty-two are alleged night clubs. "Nobody has got around yet to counting the pianos," added an Associated Press journalist. "Most of them are on Bourbon Street, which once housed the old French opera, first in the United States. [It] would have a tough time getting in the groove on Bourbon Street today. It's gone blues, barrelhouse, and boogie-woogie. The tenors are all working night clubs, and Manon doesn't live here anymore."[34] That AP article, dated August 19, 1940, ranks as one of the earliest national news pieces to depict (albeit briefly) Bourbon Street as exceptional. Perhaps it was inevitable that a national journalist would pen the first article; the local press may have missed the story initially because gradual changes in one's own backyard often evade notice. The headline of a January 1940 *Times-Picayune* historical piece, for example, noted that "Opera [and] Jazz Music [Were] Just Four Blocks Apart in City"—a reference to the Old French Opera House and Congo Square—but completely missed that a new Bourbon Street music story was unfurling right before their ears.[35]

The AP article was right: Bourbon Street indeed managed to attract a concentration of upscale nighttime entertainment enterprises denser than in any other street in the city. Directories of the era show that Bourbon Street had nearly twice as many food, drink, and entertainment establishments as its nearest competing Quarter street, and four times more than most. Its ten listed restaurants, four nightclubs ("niteries," the cats called them), and nineteen bars, taverns, and liquor outlets—thirty-three total—dwarfed the nineteen that had addresses on Rampart and on Dauphine in the old Tango Belt. Royal Street, which had the most total businesses of any Quarter Street (191, compared to Bourbon's 112), nevertheless had only fourteen food, drink, and entertainment establishments.[36] Because censuses and directories generally tend to undercount—it's far more likely for compilers to miss an existing entity than to invent a nonexistent one—Bourbon probably had substantially more than those listed in the directories.

Now with Prohibition over, the Bourbon Street strip was growing, earning notoriety, and gaining traction. All it needed to catapult into national consciousness was a massive injection of transients with dollars in their pockets and a world of worries to forget.

Bourbon Street dawned gray and chilly one Sunday in the late autumn of 1941. Din from the previous eve had long since died down, and the last clubbers staggered into taxis. Old Glory was dutifully raised at the American Legion post at 819 Bourbon. Bells called the faithful to Mass at St. Louis Cathedral two blocks toward the river, and ten blocks uptown, the white cupola atop the Hibernia Bank Building glowed in Yuletide green and red. All was not well with the world, but rumors of diplomacy with Japan and hopes of evading embroilment in Europe's hostilities allowed New Orleanians to indulge in the warm, safe embrace of hometown normalcy.

Whatever normalcy existed in those dangerous times evaporated as reports of Japan's attack on Pearl Harbor aired shortly after 1:30 p.m. local time. Americans everywhere reeled from the news, but residents of port cities like New Orleans jumped into action because they saw themselves as possible next targets. A city-wide state of emergency was declared: hundreds of police officers and 1,500 Army soldiers locked down key municipal assets, guarded ingresses and egresses, and patrolled the sprawling shipbuilding industry, which had, since Hitler's invasion of Poland two years earlier, perked the city out of the Depression. Furloughs and leave were immediately suspended. Young civilians marched to the U.S. Customs House to enlist in the armed forces. Angry neighbors uptown gathered at the Japanese consulate at 4631 St. Charles and witnessed to their disbelief staffers burning documents in the backyard. The Japanese Society of New Orleans, for its part, declared itself nonexistent, and mortified Japanese students at Tulane made sure reporters knew their sympathies lay with the Americans. Italian-born New Orleanians—and there were plenty on Bourbon Street—felt compelled to declare their loyalty as well, while Filipino and Chinese, who also worked and lived around Bourbon, donned patriotic inscriptions clarifying their citizenship and assured their compatriots that their hatred of the Japanese ran very, very deep. Everyone knew that this afternoon's news meant a two-front world war, and if any port connected the American interior with both the European and Asian theaters, it was New Orleans.[37]

The task ahead at first did not bode well for Bourbon Street. The rationing of scarce items and patriotic plantings of Victory Gardens made the indulgences of a fancy dinner at a ritzy nitery seem unseemly. Mandatory blackouts and curfews wreaked havoc on entertainment, making an evening out more of a chore than a treat. Besides, most local folks would just as soon indulge in the comfort of domesticity while their families were still intact.

Bourbon Street's prospects soon changed as hard dollars and warm bodies started to pour into the city. The federal government invested $4.4 billion in southern war plants, including $1.77 billion into strategically positioned oil-rich Louisiana, more than into any southern state save Texas. What brought the action to New Orleans proper was the energy of one man, Andrew Jackson Higgins, a Nebraska-born boatbuilder who for years specialized in designing shallow-draft vessels capable of navigating Louisiana's bayous and swamps. Higgins had the answer to a tactical problem confounding American military planners: How do you land millions of troops on two overrun continents when the enemy controls all deep-draft harbors? By modifying his bayou boats, Higgins revolutionized warfare by dispersing amphibious invasions along sparsely defended beachfronts rather than dangerously concentrating them at a port which first had to be captured. With a mix of brilliant vision, dazzling managerial skills, and the type of arrogance that does not suffer fools, Higgins won over Navy bureaucrats and landed lucrative contracts to build assault craft and other vessels in his adopted hometown of New Orleans. For the next few years, New Orleans, long a mercantilist city, became a heavy manufacturing center as well, and while it paled in comparison to northern counterparts, its industrialization was rapid. By war's end, Higgins Industries had produced 20,094 boats—most of the Navy fleet—and employed thirty thousand people across seven gargantuan city plants. Thousands of rural southerners moved to New Orleans for the work, creating housing shortages and transforming Louisiana's bucolic population to one that was majority urban. Metro-area homeowners rented rooms to strangers, and historic mansions, including some just steps off Bourbon, were hurriedly renovated for "war-working families."[38] New Orleans's 1940 population of 494,537 swelled to an estimated 545,041 by mid-1943, "caused by worker migration to the city," and 559,000 by 1945.[39] The coastal and riverine region, meanwhile, shifted dramatically from a nineteenth-century fur, fisheries, and sugarcane economy to one of petroleum extraction and processing, forever changing isolated Acadian (Cajun), Creole, and Native American folk cultures.[40] Southern Louisiana became nationally important, and after years of poverty, Louisianians now had more work than they could handle, more cash than ever, and precious little free time. To downtown New Orleans they gravitated to blow off steam, and there they encountered other transients in a similar position, only in much greater numbers: military servicemen.

Men in the uniforms of the Army, Navy, Marines, Coast Guard, and merchant marine had become a common sight throughout Louisiana since the late 1930s. Many trained at installations near Alexandria, which dated to the Great War and ramped up in the summer of 1941 as four hundred thousand soldiers participated in the Louisiana Maneuvers. The South in general became the nation's training ground for the looming conflict, hosting eight of the nine largest Army camps, half of which were within a few hours' train ride of New Orleans. Of the 16 million Americans who served in World War II, well over half set foot in the South during the course of their experience, and roughly one-third were exposed to the keystone state of Louisiana and its largest city. Among them were more than 250,000 Louisianians, half of whom were from the metro area and nearly all of whom spent at least some time in New Orleans.[41] The vast circulation of humanity helped bring the states of the former Confederacy, which in recent years had been emerging from a poor agrarian order traceable to postbellum times, into the fold of a modern industrialized nation.[42]

What positioned New Orleans at the nexus of the circulation of southern servicemen was its upgrade in July 1941 from Army Quartermaster Supply Depot to Port of Embarkation, a status at the time shared only with New York, San Francisco, Seattle, and Charleston. Between Pearl Harbor and the war's end, 174,651 troops, many of whom were first staged at Camp Plauché in present-day Harahan, were processed through three gigantic buildings at Dauphine Street by the Industrial Canal. From there they embarked for the Panama Canal heading to Pacific bases, or to Latin America and the Caribbean, where German submarines threatened them as soon as they emerged from the mouth of the Mississippi. Additionally, 7,954,767 tons of cargo, requiring thousands of human hands, shipped from New Orleans to both the European and Pacific theaters.[43] Another million men trained at central Louisiana's Camp Claiborne and Camp Livingston, and hundreds of thousands more at Camp Beauregard, Camp Villere, and Fort Polk. On the West Bank of New Orleans proper was the Naval Station in Algiers, and along the Lakefront, which had been dredged out of Lake Pontchartrain just fifteen years earlier, were the Naval Reserve Air Station, Army Air Corps Base (Camp Leroy Johnson), two large wartime hospitals, the Consolidated Aircraft plant, and a POW camp. Thousands more trained at similar facilities in the nearby Mississippi Gulf Coast, Mobile, and the Florida Panhandle, not to mention Baton Rouge, whose own population swelled by 250 percent between 1940 and 1945. Bearing a world of worries, the troops longingly cast their eyes to the City That Care Forgot as soon as they earned some leave.

Indeed, New Orleans exhorted a nearly gravitational pull on young males away from home for the first time, and military authorities did little to fight it. "They gave you all of the . . . short leaves that they could," recalled veteran Ogden C.

Bacon Jr. "You didn't have to do watch hours and that sort of stuff, and so I got to see New Orleans. That was quite an experience."[44] Robert F. Moss, who was stationed at Camp Shelby in Mississippi, said that whenever "we had a weekend pass, we would go to New Orleans [by] train. . . . It would take three hours [and] we would get a hotel room over night." So strong was the demand that one "fellow . . . would . . . hire a bus and sell tickets to New Orleans on the side," he chuckled.[45] Others hitchhiked, rented or borrowed cars, took troop trains, shipped from upriver, or sailed in coastwise. Servicemen choose their leave destinations depending on the distance that could be traveled during the length of their "pass." A twelve-hour pass allowed a day trip to New Orleans from no farther than Gulfport or Baton Rouge. Two-day passes expanded the range to Mobile or Hattiesburg, whereas three-day leaves included Camp Claiborne in central Louisiana and four days went as far as Fort Benning in Georgia. Closer bases ran shuttle buses to downtown, which were so crowded that fights would sometimes break out "when we all wanted seats."[46] Roughly half the troops staged at Camp Plauché were African Americans, and many among them first experienced the less hospitable aspects of southern culture while busing into New Orleans. Once in New Orleans, uniformed Americans of all backgrounds brushed shoulders with locals and out-of-town plant workers as well as Canadian troopers; Brazilian air force cadets; Royal Air Force fliers from Britain, Australia, and New Zealand; and French and English sailors waiting for their battle-scarred vessels to be repaired in the city's boatyards.[47] They strolled the streets, toured the sites, attended religious services, patronized establishments, and relaxed in Jackson Square. In the words of one Coast Guard reserve woman, "New Orleans [during the war] was overrun with service people."[48] A local journalist described it as a "crowded city and new faces at every turn . . . Uniforms on all sides, too, with a general air of alertness. And so very much to be done."[49]

At various downtown train stations and bus stations they arrived, and at the United Service Organization headquarters at 119 Carondelet they registered— "soldiers, sailors, Marines, paratroopers, WAACs, and other service men and service women."[50] From there they sought a place to stay. Some found host families or registered at hotels like the Monteleone, one block from Bourbon. High demand and limited supply sent prices skyrocketing: even with federally mandated rent control in war-plant cities, a simple room that rented for one dollar in 1933 went for two dollars in 1941 and five dollars in 1944, while quality and service plummeted.[51] So tight were accommodations that the United Seamen's Service had to commandeer two hotels for the use of merchant seamen. (An attempt to use one to lodge African American seamen one block from Bourbon Street, however, was immediately and successfully resisted by local civic associations and politicians.)[52]

Once unpacked, servicemen ventured out and discovered quickly that Bourbon Street was no more than a couple of blocks away. It was almost impossible *not* to take a peek. You could see the rollicking strip; you could hear it; you could practically smell it. Bourbon vied for their business through advertisements, fliers, neon signage, and barkers, who appealed to their branch loyalty and promised the best value for their soldier's pay. The *Old French Quarter News* catered to newly arrived servicemen with a special section entitled "Guide to the French Quarter" ("What to See! Where to Go! What to Do!") and columns such as "At a Ringside Table" and "Quarter Sights and Sounds," which previewed Bourbon Street floorshows. One of its reporters described "wide-eyed servicemen trying out each bar as they would a box of chocolates."[53]

Veterans' memories are sprinkled with anecdotes of World War II–era Bourbon Street, and nearly all tell of a happy if brief respite in times of great anxiety and turmoil. Newark-born Ken Smith, who participated in the Louisiana Maneuvers and later shipped to Texas and Georgia before heading to the Pacific, recalled only one "thrill[ing]" part of his circuitous journey: when "we were laid over at a railhead in New Orleans." Their superiors had a treat for them, but, as Smith recalled with a laugh, they also had ulterior motives:

> [T]he officers were very nice. They told us they were going to take us into New Orleans, so [that] we could see Bourbon Street, and they did. They marched us down to Bourbon Street and showed us the buildings and turned us around and marched us back again, but, of course, the object was to make us exercise.[54]

Twenty-five-year-old northerner Arnold Spielberg thrilled to arrive in New Orleans as a Signal Corps enlistee in early 1942. Training was intense, but local hospitality and cuisine eased the strain. The "best time I had in New Orleans, recalled Spielberg, "was going on leave every weekend. I met a Jewish family at the USO[;] they invited me to their home every time I had a pass. They were wealthy people. They had black servants who wore white gloves and I sat down to dinner at a magnificent table." But even with that gratis extravagance, Spielberg's young eyes turned to Bourbon Street. "Every time I saved up any money," he said, "I'd go eat at Arnaud's or Antoine's [for] a good meal, yes, because Army chow isn't that great."[55] Veteran P. Richard Wexler sought similar refuge when he "stayed at the Roosevelt Hotel [and] ate myself sick at the best restaurants and returned with renewed energy."[56] Sailor Leon Canick became enamored with the city on two levels: "I thought very well of . . . New Orleans because I fell in love with a girl there . . . . I really remember her with a great deal of affection. New Orleans itself was a lovely city." He remained coy when pressed about what he and his buddies did upon arriving in port: "I went in to see my girlfriend [in New Orleans] all the time and almost never slept that few weeks that I was there. . . . What [we] did on land[?] [Well,] I'm not telling you either."[57] Private Joseph Lasker found that the French Quarter reminded him of images of Greenwich Village and Montmartre, particularly Lafitte's Blacksmith Shop on Bourbon—"a mellow, old, crumbling place, lit by candles, muskets on the wall, bare bricks show a fire in the old forge, [and] a pianist playing classical French tunes." Capped off with his hotel room, which looked like "a burlesque skit," Lasker recalled his wartime visit to New Orleans as "the best time I ever had on a pass."[58] Thousands of seamen who hung out at Bourbon and Conti befriended a little dog named Foxie, who patrolled the Spotlight Bar for more than ten years. "See you when I get back, Foxie," became the refrain of departing sailors—and if Foxie returned the affection, it was said to confirm that you were "all right."[59]

One morning in 1944, a local girl named Gloria Rose Simmons hitched a ride to work with her boss, the chief of staff at the Port of Embarkation. Seeing a young officer awaiting a streetcar on North Rampart, they stopped to offer him a ride. He was Lester Kabacoff, a lawyer from Brooklyn who had recently befriended the locally prominent Stern family. Lester and Gloria got to talking and made a date. Life churned with celerity in these turbulent times: the youths quickly fell in love and married in August. The Kabacoffs went on to become one of the most influential couples in local business and philanthropic circles for the next six decades; Lester himself became the principal force behind four major downtown hotels including the Royal Sonesta on Bourbon; the 1984 World's Fair; numerous civic, media, and charitable organizations; and the group that later became the New Orleans Convention and Visitors Bureau. He also founded a school at the University of New Orleans dedicated to researching and developing the hospitality industry. Lester Kabacoff did not invent modern New Orleans tourism, but he played a greater role than any other individual in its formation. His presence here from 1942 until his death in 2004 would not have happened were it not for

World War II—and were it not for an equally illustrious local girl. Gloria Kabacoff died in 2012.[60]

Kabacoff and Simmons might have crossed paths in 1944 with a young Navy man from Georgia named Richard Allen. Stationed in Gulfport and Mobile, Allen found himself gravitating to New Orleans whenever circumstances permitted. There he discovered jazz and befriended a drummer who introduced him to the local music scene. Allen eventually moved to New Orleans in 1949 and became an authority on jazz history, an advocate for live traditional jazz, a force behind the foundation of Jazz Fest, and first curator of what later became Tulane University's Hogan Jazz Archive—all unlikely outcomes had it not been for the war and New Orleans's role in it.[61]

Some servicemen got shown Bourbon Street as part of the standard tour that local hosts proudly offered newcomers. "I met a couple . . . at the USO," officer and northerner Crandon Clark recounted in a typical scenario, and "they took me around and showed me Bourbon Street, and it was very nice . . . very hospitable."[62] Most others found it on their own, guided there by locals who came to expect that any perambulating young man in uniform simply *had* to be seeking the strip. One day in the summer of 1944, John Tambasco and his buddy David Solomon took the train from their Navy electrician school in Gulfport to sightsee in New Orleans before shipping to the Pacific. Upon arriving, they approached a policeman and innocently asked where they could "have some fun." Seeing their uniforms and presuming what sort of "fun" they sought, the officer directed them to Bourbon Street. Hesitant but curious, Tambasco and Solomon "walked in [to the] honky-tonks," did not like what they saw, and promptly "walked out." They ended up riding the streetcar, pedaling ornamental boats at City Park, and getting invited to an uptown wedding—which was the sort of fun they had in mind when they naively queried the presumptuous policeman. The anecdote suggests that newly arrived servicemen beelined for Bourbon Street with such regularity that locals expected them to ask for directions to the neon strip, just as tourists do today. Bourbon Street had become famous.[63]

How many people passed through New Orleans for war-related reasons, and how many set foot on Bourbon Street? It's impossible to say precisely because how servicemen spent their leave went unrecorded. One potential source comes from a hospitality center established by New Orleanians as a home away from home for troops in transit. Civic centers welcomed troops citywide, but the Beauregard

House Center for Service Men stood alone for graciousness, hospitality—and good recordkeeping. Located in a ca. 1826 Chartres Street mansion on lower Chartres Street, the Beauregard House offered "billiards, ping pong, piano, radio, Victrola, stationery, and magazines" and the services of "coffee, tea, cakes, and doughnuts . . . plus a "pianist to play for guests when requested."[64] Hostess Nadia Moise explained the rationale for establishing the center:

> There were . . . young service men all over the place, [and] Mayor Robert Maestri was outraged to learn that the patriotic citizens of Bourbon Street were catching [these kids] from somewhere in the Midwest, [who] didn't know from nothing. First time away from home. And they were rolling them on Bourbon Street taking their money and leaving them knocked out, drugged or whatever in the street.

Maestri said that Bourbon Street would always be there for the ones that wanted Bourbon Street. . . . But he wanted those servicemen who didn't want Bourbon Street to have a clean, decent place to go where they would be properly treated. And that was the objective [of the Beauregard House].[65]

The Beauregard House was a hit. One grateful Texas lieutenant who visited along with ninety-six men under his command wrote that they "had never seen such a generous display of hospitality . . . what a morale builder. . . . Thanks a million."[66] For historical purposes, the Beauregard House is valuable because the ladies who managed it kept records of visitation, providing researchers with a crude metric for servicemen circulation in the French Quarter. The numbers are impressive: within weeks of opening, the Beauregard House welcomed 1,800 guests. Christmas 1943 saw its all-time-highest visitation, 864 in one day. Staff estimated an average of 3,000 sign-ins per month, and by early 1944, the total hit 85,341. This rate puts the total visitation by war's end in the 150,000 range, although one source stated that 750,000 "registered at the place [and] many never registered."[67] If for every one center-visiting serviceman there were ten who walked Bourbon Street—a conservative ratio—that puts a few million visitors from all over the world on a street that formerly catered to locals. Another source from the peak of the war estimated that "as many as 20,000 men of all branches [are] expected for some week-ends" in New Orleans.[68] When combined with plant workers, other visitors, and residents, we can safely estimate that well over 100,000 people set foot on Bourbon Street monthly for four years. Wartime visitation helped put New Orleans at the top of the list of America's ten "most interesting cities" compiled by a national tourism and convention magazine in 1944, edging out New York and San Francisco.[69]

Like today, most wartime visitors would have been clustered in the commercialized blocks of Bourbon closest to Canal, mostly during weekends. However they would not have strolled back and forth in promenade fashion because the action was indoors in the clubs, not in the public space as it is today. There were no to-go drinks; the whole idea of going to Bourbon Street in this era was to make an entry into a stylish club or restaurant and be treated like someone special. The artery itself was, well, just that. Parked cars lined at least one and sometimes both gutters, while streetcars plied the tracks in the center. Behind them were honking motorists, delivery trucks, mule-drawn garbage collectors, and ice trucks driven by the likes of one Harry Kelt, who had been "supplying the nite life hi-ball ice" to Bourbon Street since the First World War.[70] Pedestrians were thus limited mostly to the sidewalks. Even there, things were cluttered. Utilities had not yet been buried, and leaning poles and a tangle of electric and telephone wires crowded the streetscapes. A panoply of hanging signs protruded above the sidewalks, and neon blinked in windows. People littered with abandon. "They had garbage cans out on the streets and people would knock them over and nobody would clean it up," remembered one women.[71] More pollution came from above when ships at the port blew out their boiler tubes after a period of inactivity and blanketed downtown in greasy black soot.[72] It was a crowded, malodorous, smoky, and clamorous corridor, picturesque despite itself—until the midnight curfew, when by order of the War Manpower Commission all places of amusement had to close.

Club owners mitigated the "Cinderella curfew" by shifting show times into late afternoon. But the rule unquestionably cost the clubs money, and the city too, as it reduced the cabaret tax by two hundred dollars monthly to ease the pain. Owners complained, but authorities would not budge. Closing clubs at midnight, they said, increased productivity and decreased absenteeism in the war plants. A 1942 state law passed at the behest of the military additionally prohibited alcohol sales to servicemen after midnight. Enforcement, however, seemed to be as common as evasion: whereas one Bourbon barmaid was arrested for selling "two rum drinks for 80 cents" to two soldiers at 12:50 a.m.," at other times on Bourbon, an emcee would announce over the loudspeaker ways to evade the curfew. And everyone else figured out that "there is . . . nothing to prevent a girl friend from buying an extra drink to be consumed by her friend in uniform."[73]

Their jaunt through the city exposed servicemen from across the nation to New Orleans culture in an era when it deviated from the national norm far more than it does today. While the lollapalooza of cultural distinction, Mardi Gras, was not part of the wartime experience because all public celebrations had been cancelled starting in 1942, servicemen relished differences in realms such as food and music. Most Americans ate rather bland protein and starch staples in those days, and "government cooking" was that much worse. New Orleans offered a welcome respite from both. Servicemen found fresh seafood—a rarity in the interior, particularly oysters—cheap and abundant. Many treated themselves to fancy "French food" (as they called it) at Galatoire's, Arnaud's, or Antoine's, all on or near Bourbon Street, although, according to one commentator, some were "more interested in being able to say they ate at Antoine's or Arnaud's than in getting something to eat."[74] Most fellows, however, generally preferred simpler fare in homier settings. Hands-down, their favorite was southern fried chicken, which in the days before industrial cooking was a complex undertaking and a rarity outside certain regions and special days. Raved one trooper about his time in New Orleans: "That's some of the best food we ever had . . . That fried chicken! Those ducks! . . . It's worth going to war for[!]" Okra? Not so much. "It slips down before I can get a good grip on it long enough to taste it." "Rice cooked with gravy is an appreciated novelty," wrote one reporter. "But you can't be certain that shrimp or oysters will please Northern palates."[75] They certainly appealed to sailor Leon Canick, who also got to experience Louisiana country cooking. "Out in the bayous," he recalled, "you could go to a wooden bar-saloon [and] get a pile of shrimp this high for free and a beer or a crab meat sandwich with three . . . soft-shell crabs for 25 cents."[76] City prices were higher; food costs rose nearly as steeply as accommodations: "a scrambled egg, grits, biscuit, and a cup of good coffee [cost] 5 cents in a clean well-lighted restaurant" in 1933. By 1941, 35 cents; by 1944, 75 cents, by which time the restaurant was likely to be dirtier and the service poorer.[77] Labor shortages drove up the costs of anything requiring human handling. When the September oyster season opened in 1943, for example, supply was plentiful but prices were poised to rise nonetheless, from 50 to 60 to 75 cents a dozen, because of "man power shortage and high wages."[78] Beef grew scarce too, jacking up the price of hamburgers and leading to a local innovation: "'fishburgers,' and very good, too. Made out of fresh water fish with egg and seasoning added, fried in bread dust and served on a toasted soft roll just like a hamburger. Yum! Yum!"[79]

After dinner came entertainment, and servicemen wanted to hear live jazz. A so-called New Orleans Revival was afoot, and Bourbon Street happily obliged, mostly with Dixieland styles. Once they heard enough of the old stuff, servicemen, like Bourbon visitors today, opted for popular music. "Hill billy" or "cowboy" (country) music, barn dances, and jamborees were offered to appeal to rural folk, while other nightclubs played big band, swing, boogie-woogie, college fight songs, "jive" (black) music, and impromptu "jam sessions." Servicemen particularly enjoyed musicians who took requests, like the dueling pianists Mercedes and Sue at Pat O'Brien's, or Dixie Mills, "Bourbon Street's newest sensation . . . an artist on the keys [who] makes the ivories sing [and] also has a lovely set of pipes." Patriotic or folksy sing-alongs often ended up becoming the evening's entertainment, as servicemen and war workers gathered around pianos, drink in one hand and cigarette in the other. "Praise the Lord and Pass the Ammunition" drove the crowd wild. "Pistol Packin' Momma" and "I'm a Yankee Doodle Dandy" got them jolly. "The Boogie-Woogie Bugle Boy of Company B" had everyone on the dance floor. "When the Lights Go on Again All over the World" made them melancholic, and "Remember Pearl Harbor" got them dogged. The 1939 hit "You Are My Sunshine" was invariably crooned with an affected cowboy twang, and "Around Her Hair She Wears a Yellow Ribbon" inevitably became "Around Her Hair She Wears a Purple Garter." The Brits loved "Roll Out the Barrel," and if Frenchmen were around, so was "Marseillaise."[80]

When the band took a breather and the emcee addressed the crowd, out came wartime jokes and zingers. Overheard at Tugy's Famous Bar at 201 Bourbon (known for its nightly dart-throwing contests at a target of Hitler's face): "You must admit the German race / Is really not so super; Since the RAF blew up the place / And left 'em in a stupor."[81] And one block down Bourbon at the Famous Door Bar:

> The Rising Sun is not so hot
> And you will see quite soon, perhaps,
> Sufficient Yanks in air to blot
> It out completely from the Japs.[82]

Then there were the Berliners who passed the time huddled in an air raid shelter by swapping jokes, all too many of which were long-winded. "Don't you know any shorter jokes? one asked. "Sure . . . but I'll have to whisper it to you." "*We'll win the war.*"[83] One rhyme got the whole family into wartime service:

> Sleep, darling baby, let nothing annoy yuh
> Mom's welding upon a destroy-yuh
> Daddy is aiming to bring down a Jap
> While baby's enjoying his afternoon nap![84]

That was about the extent of poetic domesticity on Bourbon Street. Risqué revues proved more popular. For every three or four clubs that advertised bands and drinks, one billed eroticism. The acts and the lexicon shocked southern sensibilities at the time. The All Girl Show at the Three Deuces (222 Bourbon), for example, earned high praise for Doris's "cute chassis," Mavis's "torrid shake," Valerie's "swoon material," Mavis's "oriental routine," and Shirley's "Gypsy dance." At the Club Bali, Bonita Roesse sizzled "in a hot jungle dance" while "Boots O'Hara has the patrons yelling for more after her sleeve number." At the suggestive Kitten Club, "floorshow gals have talent and plenty of curves which add to everyone's enjoyment," while the Opera House Bar featured Anna Jane Wright's "hula number" and Patricia Lane's "curvaceous body [and] some A-1 exotic dancing."[85] Military edicts declared some places to be off-limits to servicemen, such as a dance hall where the girls "wear only a brassiere and skirt." Owners were keen to keep things legit—but that still left room for plenty of sass.[86]

Like Mardi Gras visitors today, some servicemen mistakenly assumed that the girls on Bourbon Street represented the women of New Orleans, whereas in fact most were transients, transplants, or visitors themselves. One soldier publicly accused New Orleans girls to be "cheap . . . man-chasing hussies," to which a more chivalrous airman responded that the soldier probably spent too much time in the "wrong places . . . hanging around bars and such" on Bourbon Street.[87] A certain moniker got dropped on newly arrived females who struck locals as free-spirited and presumably licentious: *gypsy*. Forerunner to "beatnik," "hippie," and "hipster," "gypsy" appears over and over in the gossipy *Old French Quarter News* and other sources. The term came to mean wastrel, vagabond, or slut. It also described Bourbon Street dancers who infused their performances with campy allusions to Bohemian or Oriental exoticism.[88]

Photographs of the Bourbon Street music scene in this era are uncommon, and newsreels and audio recordings scarcer still. But one beautiful depiction emerged from this era, a fine lithographic drawing made in 1942 by Caroline

Wogan Durieux, a New Orleans native and prominent member of the French Quarter arts scene. It features two stylish African American divas gracefully unleashing the blues to servicemen crowded in a dark smoky nightclub, with the New Orleans skyline visible through French doors. Durieux's *Bourbon Street, New Orleans* is arguably the finest piece of art inspired by the street. That the inspiration came in 1942 testifies to the sense of specialness of time and place that Bourbon Street generated during World War II.

An extreme scarcity of labor underscored home-front economic life during the war. Performers found demand for their talents so high on Bourbon Street that the local branch of the American Federation of Musicians set up shop conveniently at 1416 Bourbon Street.[89] Hoteliers in the French Quarter complained that their "main problems are too many wanting rooms and not enough people who want to work for us," and joked that guests ought to cater to the help.[90] Bars and clubs on Bourbon responded to the explosive demand by hiring people they would ordinarily reject. Like the city and region, Bourbon Street businessmen discriminated in who they served and who they hired; their want ads routinely specified the race and gender requirements of applicants. If anything, World War II ratcheted up local racism because it brought into town tens of thousands of rural white southerners ("Protestant hill-billies," according to one observer in 1944), who held stricter senses of racial separation than those practiced in the multicultural Crescent City. "The attitude of these newcomers toward the Negro" wrote the observer, "is different from that of the native New Orleanian."[91] Yet wartime employment on Bourbon Street outnumbered applicants by such a margin that relatively decent jobs opened up for African Americans, women, and others usually denied such opportunities. The Club Bali at 426 Bourbon, for example, advertised for a "five-piece Negro band," while the Eateria Restaurant two doors down sought "NEAT, light complexioned colored girls." A dance hall one block away reminded women "you can make $45 per week dancing with sailors and soldiers" if they applied within. So great was the demand and turnover that positions went begging daily. The sense of strike-while-the-iron-is-hot urgency exudes from one prototypical wartime ad: "WANTED—TWO FIRST CLASS BARTENDERS, GOOD PAY. APPLY AT ONCE. MARTY BURKE'S, 231 Bourbon." Competition among Bourbon Street clubs motivated businesses to expand their show times and spaces ("3 floor shows nightly [at the] Club Bali") and exoticize their content ("See the living mermaid in the fish bowl"). Competition among eateries led restaurateurs to offer live musical entertainment, juke boxes, pinball machines, slot machines, and modern high-volume equipment like walk-in refrigerators, deep freezers, meat grinders, mixing machines, slicers, and—to the relief of northern boys— air-conditioning. (What the boys may not have realized was that most of the jukeboxes, pinballs, and slot machines were controlled by organized crime, and those hired dance partners were probably B-girls suckering them for overpriced drinks.) No surprise, then, that the Vieux Carre Restaurant at 241 Bourbon did $75,000 of business in 1945, the equivalent of $1 million today.[92] Nor was it a surprise when Uncle Sam's man on Bourbon Street, Dennis S. Puneky, who collected the cabaret and nightclub tax for the U.S. Internal Revenue Service throughout the war years, switched sides and offered "night club tax specialist and counsellor" services, presumably for a lot more money.[93] Others did just as well, causing relentless turnover: every owner looking to cash out while the real estate market was hot found eager potential buyers motivated by equally hot demand. Even the Old Absinthe House went on the market in 1943, only to be promptly scooped up by Owen Brennan, of the savvy and soon-to-be-famous restaurateur family. Prototypical tourist-trap operations such as souvenir shops, wax historical figures, and photography studios with comic billboard props opened on Bourbon Street to tap into flow of money and attention. The fame also attracted the famous: Judy Garland, Bob Hope, Mickey Rooney, and Edward G. Robinson, among many others, paid visits to the rollicking wartime strip.[94] But what ultimately fueled the Bourbon boom was the young single male transient with a head full of fantasies and a pocket filled with cash. It's a market that New Orleans merchants have targeted since the days of The Swamp, Gallatin Street, concert saloons, Storyville, and the Tango Belt. Bourbon Street became the latest urban space where that same demographic could be sold the same wine-women-and-song pleasures that had imparted a risqué reputation to this city since colonial times.

Women on wartime Bourbon worked as retailers, entertainers, servers, and as bartenders—to the dismay of some, who later attempted to pass a city law to "forbid women to work behind a bar."[95] Some worked in the omnipresent but currently underground sex industry, which often budded in seemingly innocuous flirtation. Young ladies employed by the club would make themselves available for conversation or a dance, and then beguile their suitors into treating them to an overpriced drink. For reasons unclear, the ruse came to be known as "B-drinking," and it often culminated in sex for money. Women could also be found as customers, which gave men from across the nation a chance to meet Louisiana girls. Typical of them was Lena Porrier Legnon, a Cajun from New Iberia who joined her man in New Orleans to work as a Higgins welder. Legnon described riding the streetcar to enjoy a night of dancing and drinking in the French Quarter. A photograph taken at Marty Bourke's Bar on Bourbon Street in 1942 captures a classic wartime Bourbon Street night scene: three men and two women in their twenties and thirties, enjoying local brew and conversation, a world of worries checked at the door.[96] The broad smiles and stylish attire, however, betray a distant look in their eyes. The war permeated all discourse; the words "over there" began or ended everyone's sentences. Authorities worried that information on Allied troop movements or war production might spill from liquor-loosened tongues on Bourbon Street; "Don't Let Your Careless Words Become Weapons for the Enemy" became a common admonishment against "blaboteurs."[97] Just about everyone knew someone in or near the worst fighting, wounded, captured, or killed. Hundreds convalesced at the New Orleans Army Air Base Hospital and other local infirmaries; some patients were treated to motor tours of the French Quarter.[98] Casualties could even be found on Bourbon Street: Army Air Force staff sergeant Lloyd J. Brightman had his back shredded when, in 1944, German fighter planes machine-gunned his B-24, sending it hurtling to earth. Incredibly, he survived the 32,000-foot plunge—only to find himself, in January 1945, in the heart of the Bourbon Street strip. He recuperated in the same 327 Bourbon Street townhouse in which Confederate Treasurer Judah Benjamin and President Jefferson Davis had once lived.[99]

Most World War II–era visitors viewed Bourbon Street as a pleasurable respite from the nerve-wracking tensions of wartime. A notable exception was jazz critic and record collector Kenneth Hulsizer, who visited in 1944 and found much to his displeasure. Hulsizer may rank as the world's first Bourbon Street curmudgeon: the discerning purist who seeks undiscovered authenticity and carps contemptuously when displeased. Hulsizer found New Orleans "over-crowded," "uncomfortable," and "notorious for clipping suckers," and characterized its "cynical" service workers and "smirking waiter[s]" as dedicated to "extracting money from fools" as they served "mediocre . . . woop-de-do . . . food" for high prices to "hill billies" and "outlanders." On Bourbon Street he found "little more than a string of bars" with "dull, cheap shows" of "little gaiety and no sin," in which the desire to drink far outweighed an interest in music, let along good jazz. "Never again, I fear, will New Orleans be the pleasantly sinful place it once was," he prophesied. Like all curmudgeons, Hulsizer saw the past as superior and the future as dire:

For no valid reason, New Orleans is still the Mecca [for] the hot jazz enthusiast. . . . [M]ost of them must have gone away disappointed [because]
nowhere do you hear jazz, New Orleans jazz. Nowhere do you see any
prospects of jazz in the future. Jazz was born in New Orleans but it doesn't
live there any more. . . . It is my sad conclusion that things aren't likely to
be much better after the war. Instead of a revival, I see a decline of jazz in
the future of the Crescent City.[100]

Hulsizer proudly distanced himself from that which he judged to be fake. "I
seldom ate in these places," he sniffed, in reference to the old-line restaurants.
"I can't get my teeth in all this atmosphere and I want something more substantial than tradition; [besides,] the old Creole restaurants were never intended for
prosaic people anyway." (Hulsizer's "prosaic" is today's "authentic.") Where *did*
prosaic folk dine in ca. 1944 New Orleans? "I ate mostly in the big air-conditioned
cafeterias across Canal Street," *outside* the French Quarter. And music? He
grudgingly praised a few outlying jazz dives, particularly one "a mile out from
St. Claude"—the same area where modern-day Bourbon curmudgeons seek "authenticity."

Whether Hulsizer was accurate in his judgments is beside the point. Taste is
subjective, and as for authenticity, it's arbitrary: what Hulsizer deemed phony in
1944 comes across retrospectively in 2012 as genuine and real. What we can learn
from Hulsizer is that the vocalizing of cultural disdain for Bourbon is as old as
the street's fame. Loving Bourbon Street and hating Bourbon Street entered the
public discourse simultaneously, and they probably will forever coexist dualisti-
cally, with few people falling in between.[101]

"I was in New Orleans on V-J Day and they had a big celebration on Canal
Street[,] even greater . . . than the Mardi Gras. . . . Everybody was talking . . . service men all over . . . all the churches were chiming. It was such a delirious and
wonderful, wonderful time."[102] So recalled Cadet Nurse Corp Eula Lole MacPherson McMillan on that long-awaited day in August 1945 when Japan officially sur-
rendered. Bourbon Street had its own way of celebrating—and who else better to
do it than the denizens of Chinatown? For years the Chinese merchants of 500
Bourbon had been storing illegal pyrotechnics awaiting the Empire's defeat. Now,
granted a special police dispensation, two hundred Chinese Americans gathered
at the On Leong Assembly Hall and "shot more than $500 worth of firecrackers,
turning the block into a miniature battlefield."[103] A week later, authorities lifted

the Cinderella curfew, and Bourbon clubs reveled into the wee hours. "Lifting the midnight curfew," commented one journalist, "will evidently end the phenomenon of cabaret music drifting out into French Quarter streets at the dinner hour."[104]

Bourbon Street merchants had lots to celebrate. Their street had entered a period of efflorescence, having formed since the late 1920s enough of an entertainment agglomeration to reach, by 1945, a critical mass and *become its own attraction*. People before the war went to clubs that happened to be on Bourbon Street; now, they went *to* Bourbon Street. Millions of servicemen and plant workers passing through the city heard about Bourbon Street, found it, enjoyed it, and would now return home and spread its name. Veterans would return repeatedly to New Orleans for decades to come, drawing upon their wartime experience. Paul Rork, for example, fondly recalled eating "in Galatois" on Bourbon Street while in uniform. "Since then, I've been there several times. . . . Saw [a] football [game] in that big dome they have. We went down to Mardi Gras once. Oh, yeah, I like New Orleans. Love it."[105] Some local vets got into the act themselves. In 1946, a group of Quarter boys recently returned from overseas opened a bar at 427 Bourbon and named it "Kilroy's," after the "Kilroy Was Here" graffiti popular among American troops.[106] World War II vets would become pro bono advertising agents spreading The Street's reputation. Their generation's brains and brawn would soon render the United States the most powerful and affluent nation on earth, and their prolific issue would enjoy unprecedented disposable income in an era of jet travel and interstate motoring, both of which would further enrich tourist spaces like Bourbon.

The Street would get one final war-related boost from late 1945 to 1946, when an additional 59,842 happy troops disembarked at New Orleans and headed home—but not before celebrating on Bourbon Street.[107]

What the downtown tourism industry gained during the Great War, it lost because of Prohibition. What it gained during the Roaring Twenties, it lost again to the Great Depression. But what it gained during World War II finally won momentum and rolled forward—good news for Bourbon, but bad news for its residential neighbors. "We had no problems with Bourbon Street before the Second World War," rued Mary Morrison in 1977, reflecting back on her forty-plus years as a preservationist. "The Second World War just about created Bourbon Street as we know it now. There were maybe one or two clubs . . . but they were just incidental. . . . [It] was just another fine old street in the Quarter."[108]

Proof of the transformation came in the form of the first postwar Carnival. "Mardi Gras is revived—New Orleans to see first in 5 years" ran international headlines as March 5, 1946, approached. Visitors the weekend before "thronged the narrow streets of the famed French quarter or sought entertainment in the honky-tonk atmosphere of Bourbon street," while krewes such as the Bourbon Bounders met for their luncheon and elected a queen.[109] Elaborate parades returned to Quarter streets: the krewes of Comus and Hermes began near Lee Circle and headed down Royal, turning left at Orleans and gingerly stepping over Bourbon before beelining for their lavish ball at the Municipal Auditorium. More trash than ever was collected after the festivities, so much so that the city instituted an annual ritual of weighing the debris to gauge the size of Mardi Gras. Bourbon's Chinatown also did well after the war. A Cantonese-born Chinese American named Young M. Gee, recently returned from service in the Pacific, established Dan's International Restaurant at 600 Bourbon in 1946. The corner restaurant prospered, "helped to introduce Chinese cuisine to the city," and became a favorite late-night hangout for Bourbon Street characters ranging from literati to politicos to madams.[110]

What was remarkable about postwar Bourbon Street was that it boomed despite a slowing economy. The sudden contraction in federal spending spawned two recessions and an inflationary period in the late 1940s. Fewer people on the move, with less disposable income in their pockets, dealt a blow to entertainment districts nationwide. It didn't help that millions of young singles formerly in transit were now married and parenting infants at home. Nightclubs closed left and right in places like New York and Los Angles. But

> there was one important exception. It was New Orleans, where show people . . . were doing nothing but business. . . . [L]eading spots in New Orleans' teeming French Quarter were bulging at their cracked-plaster seams. Show people said they didn't know how come, frankly. But the transfer of 52nd street from New York to Rue Bourbon appeared almost complete. The parade of big names was staggering, [as were the] salary figures. . . . Hotels reported brisk business[;] one hotel even had five bands at one time.[111]

And all this was just four months after the Hurricane of 1947 disheveled the city.

The early postwar years were a key moment for Bourbon Street, a moment that had its counterpart in other cities. On Bourbon Street, though, the phenomenon didn't lose traction and peter out as it did elsewhere. Instead, it sprinted forward, in part because of the big-fish-in-a-small-pond nature of its entertainment scene, coupled with its relative isolation from other metropolises. New York and Los Angeles had vast entertainment industries competing for a shrinking pool of customers, while New Orleans had a small entertainer community, growing clientele, little regional competition, low overhead, inexpensive real estate, and no cover charges (which were "popularly taboo" on Bourbon, as they remain today). It helped that the Greater New Orleans, Inc., Association of Commerce, Dock Board, and other local entities poured hundreds of thousands of tourism-promotion dollars into what was described at the time as "the largest and most expensive advertising and publicity campaign on behalf of the City of New Orleans."[112] That the city's population continued to rise despite plant closures also fueled Bourbon's growth: estimated at 545,041 in mid-1943; 559,000 in 1945; and 565,000 in May 1946, the city's population hit 570,445 in the 1950 Census—15 percent more than 1940, and, in absolute numbers, the greatest single-decade population increase in New Orleans's history.[113] Most of all, as we shall see, postwar Bourbon Street benefited from a massive injection of profitability from organized criminal activity going on in the back of the bar.

The boom continued despite another recession in 1949. "Bars were packed" on Mardi Gras that year, which drew seven hundred thousand revelers, 10 percent of whom were estimated to have celebrated on Bourbon Street. "Night club operators hadn't seen such prosperity since V-J night," notwithstanding new anti-lewdness rules requiring strippers to wear brassieres and G-strings. That didn't stop one girl from going completely naked—save for a mask—in the middle of "garish Bourbon street," which a nationally syndicated article described as the "center of strip-teasing, bad whiskey and jazz music" which "a native will approach [only] having his pocketbook pinned to his undershirt."[114]

New Orleanians by the late 1940s were well aware that something in their midst had gained legs and started to swagger. They began referring to Bourbon as "The Street," and when they visited its clubs and restaurants, they "dressed like movie stars—men in pinstripes, women wearing strapless cocktail dresses and nylon stockings and thick four-inch heels," as one wide-eyed teenager from Mississippi recalled.[115] The press took note. When CBS recorded its nationwide *We the People* locally in May 1946, it selected Bourbon Street's iconic Old Absinthe House for the broadcast.[116] When Mary Bruns of the *New Orleans Item* investigated, she found that "all over the country other publications find topics of interest and color [on] this 'Street,' unique among others." Determined to see for herself, Bruns in August 1948 extensively toured "The Street" and interviewed owners and performers. She viewed the space not as a linear strip but rather a district that "includes several parallel streets on either side of the 'main drag.'" Bruns spoke with Carlo of Kilroy's at 427 Bourbon, who boasted about the stars he'd booked—"Lily St. Cyr, that stunning creature," among others—but bemoaned the competition from Texas, "willing to pay plenty for talent." Bruns also heard from Sarah and Elmo Baden of the Moulin Rouge, who pooh-poohed the alleged dangers of the strip and assured Bruns that "today it's progress, modernization[,] improvement everywhere you look. . . . Where else is it possible to stand at a bar . . . and see the entire show for the price of an ice cold bottle of beer?" Louis Prima, "leader of the night club owners," acknowledged that Bourbon Street had some "evils" but a whole lot more good. "Why, it's like having a big circus in town all the time. People look to us for what they have been led to expect [that] New Orleans can give them." Over at Sloppy Joe's Bar at 229 Bourbon, Joe Segreto explained that "New Orleans always has been a big Saturday night town, but we'd like week-day nights to pick up a little. It's the out-of-towners and visitors who make up the bulk of off-night businesses . . . and the season is just about to begin." The impending autumn motivated Mr. Ferrara across the street to convert his Puppy House to a swankier joint called The Show Bar, complete with a mezzanine, a raised floor, a five-piece band, and "the latest in professional spot lights." Bruns "came away with the viewpoint that Bourbon Street offers good entertainment as well as bad," but generally the journalist was delighted with her findings, and sprinkled her assessment with terms like "authentic," "charming," "appealing," "mellow," "atmosphere," and "renown[ed] all over the world." The *New Orleans Item* entitled the article "Bouquets for Vieux Carre's Bourbon Street."[117]

City directories, notwithstanding their propensity to undercount, allow us to quantify the change. The total number of Bourbon Street restaurants, nightclubs, bars, taverns, and liquor outlets remained in the 33 to 38 range amid the burgeoning business of the early 1940s, suggesting a wartime expansion of existing establishments rather than creation of new ones. Postwar fame, however, triggered new investment. Between 1937 and 1951, the number of nightclubs rose over 300 percent, to 13; bars, taverns, and trendy new "lounges" increased over 300 percent, to 17; and restaurants rose by 40 percent, to 14. Actual numbers were probably significantly higher: one count enumerated 22 bars on Bourbon Street just between Iberville and St. Louis in 1946, the same year that the city directory recorded only *half* that number for the *entire* street.[118] Midrange hotels and boardinghouses opened as well, as did a secondary economy of pizza parlors, hamburger joints, Chinese food, silly photo studios, gift shops, curio shops, and peddlers of everything from enchiladas to flowers to shoe shines to hot tamales. Above all, alcohol flowed liberally. Said one gimmick photographer stationed at 511 Bourbon in 1948, "no matter HOW drunk people get . . . they NEVER forget to come back and pick up their pictures."[119]

Names of clubs in this halcyon era reflected the thematic moods that the dons of Bourbon Street sought to produce. There was exoticism: El Morocco Lounge, Magic Lock Cocktails, La Lune, the Gunga Den. Edgy sexiness: Harlem Night Club, the Sho-Bar, Club Slipper. Frenchness: the Moulin Rouge, Café des Artistes, Le Rendezvous Night Club. Localism: Mardi Gras Lounge, the Sugar Bowl Night Club, Original Old Absinthe House, Café Lafitte, the Old Absinthe House Bar. Self-awareness: the Famous Door, the Spot Light Bar, the Torch Club. Quaint hominess: Le Petite Shoppe Gifts, Tony's Spaghetti House, the Puppy House. Irony: the Dunce Cap Bar. And rusticity: the Pig Pen and the Old Barn, the latter of which staged five bands playing "cowboy music" continuously twenty-four hours a day.[120]

The entertainment industry grew so big that the American Guild of Variety Artists set up an office in the heart of it all at 425 Bourbon, just as the American Federation of Musicians had done a few years earlier. Articles about Bourbon Street went to press nationwide. Between 1901 and 1950, newspapers in the rest of the country published only a handful of articles per year that mentioned New Orleans's Bourbon Street, and most of them involved the French Opera House or purely incidental news items. That pace doubled during the 1950s, doubled again during the 1960s, and nearly doubled once more in the 1970s—and most of those articles were about the fame and infamy of the Bourbon Street. Today they number in the thousands.

Bourbon Street's success emboldened it to adopt outside innovations, a propensity first seen in the days of Wenger's in the late 1800s. Bourbon clubs eagerly embraced air-conditioning in the late 1930s, recognizing it as a sure bet to lure in passersby for an overpriced drink. Ten years later, it pioneered the installation of televisions. Steve Valenti's Paddock Bar "became the first to establish entertainment behind the bar," as it was called at the time. Curly Lima reported in September that "the idea caught on to 'Joe Public,' [and] now most Bourbon bistros have [televisions]." Later in 1948, Lima predicted that "nearly every bar on Bourbon will have a television set and nearly every bar owner on Bourbon will have one in his home also, according to the sales reports."[121] He was proven right by year's end. The year 1948 also saw Bourbon Street bars adopt draft beer fed by pressurized containers. Competing local breweries took it upon themselves to install their taps in as many bars as they could. The new devices reduced the cost of beer, eased deliveries, and made overindulgence more affordable.[122]

That Bourbon Street had a major brewery on-site made the selling of beer all the more convenient and cheap. The American Brewing Company's Regal Beer brand became an integral part of local drinking culture, advertised with the jingle "Red beans and rice and Regal on ice." From the 1900s through the 1950s, the massive four-story Regal Brewery (similar in style and size to Jax Brewery), with its landmark tower and twin smokestacks, dominated the 700 block of Conti and the 300 block of Bourbon. Remarkably, some of the water for Regal's production process apparently came from the groundwater directly below Bourbon Street: the city in 1947 permitted American to dig and operate an underground well directly below the Bourbon Street sidewalk 77 feet from the Conti corner, for which the company paid the city a quarter of a million dollars over ten years.[123] "That oil-well looking object in the 300 block of Bourbon," explained a local writer to bewildered neighbors in 1948, "is there to drill for spring water [for] Regal Beer."[124] Beer making formed as much of the cityscape on Bourbon Street as beer drinking. The brewery's Bienville side featured a conveyor belt elevated above the street, on which hung a sign declaring to Bourbon pedestrians, "Home of REGAL since 1890: Genuine Lager Beer."[125] Its Bourbon flank, meanwhile, played host to an amalgam of brewery-related garages and sheds. Like other city beer makers such as Falstaff, Dixie, and Jax, Regal worked hand in hand with bar owners to develop retail outlets for their products; one Bourbon sage in 1948 went so far to say that "a brewery all but open[s] a bar for you." It is not coincidental that nearly two dozen bars, plus more on intersecting streets, clustered within two blocks of the Regal Brewery. The proximity kept transportation costs at rock-bottom and allowed delivery by dolly, giving Bourbon Street a competitive advantage over other night districts.[126]

How Bourbon Street Exploded
Late 1940s–Early 1960s

The 1940s boom changed public opinion about the French Quarter. Previously most New Orleanians viewed the neighborhood as a quaint but shabby encumbrance to a city that needed to sanitize and modernize. Now they saw its iconic streetscapes and packageable fame as a mother lode waiting to be mined. If a modest-sized joint on The Street grossed $200 daily in summer and $800 to $1,200 during Mardi Gras, imagine what larger establishments could yield![1] Property values rose, and the commercial real estate market heated up Quarter-wide.

A resolute few, however, begged to differ. Preservationists had long viewed the Quarter as an architectural gem, and they renovated their historic homes at great personal expense, for which they received little civic gratitude. Well-educated, often elitist if not patrician, and always outspoken, preservationists resented the opportunistic "vultures" circling over "their" beloved neighborhood. Many of them first arrived as artists, writers, intellectuals, and aesthetes in the 1920s and 1930s, and like urbanophilic transplants today, became more "local" than the locals. "There was one thing that these people seemed in have in common," recalled pioneer preservationist Mary Morrison. "They were not native New Orleanians. . . . They counted themselves expatriots of the United States."[2] They did, however, join forces with natives to win the legal protection of the French Quarter a few years before World War II. Now, together, they shifted their activism away from the prewar problems of apathy and decay, and recalibrated against the new postwar threat of crass commercialism. Nothing rallied preservationists more than Bourbon Street, which they viewed as a vulgar insult that lowered their property values, tarnished their quality of life, and demeaned the Queen City of the South. "Saturday night [on] Bourbon Street . . . can indeed be termed 'Running the Gauntlet Night,'" steamed one citizen. "The situation seems to have grown worse."[3] So had the din: a property-owners' association campaigned in August 1946 for an ordinance against excessive noise obtruding upon neighbors in the wee hours—a first for Bourbon Street. Stories of criminality on Bourbon, ranging from B-drinking, clip joints, and scam artists to pickpockets, lewdness, and murder, circulated with increasing regularity. At one point in 1946, the America Guild of Variety Artists threatened to "blackout" Bourbon nightclubs by withdrawing its unionized entertainers in protest of alleged forced participation in scams and the hiring of scab strippers at substandard wages. Rumors of organized crime made matters worse, as did the return of prostitution, which policing had driven underground during the war but resurfaced by late 1945.[4] A new witticism, "overheard in a Bourbon Street night spot," connected the new red-light district with its Storyville predecessor: "She went to an exclusive girl's school—Lulu White's Academy!!"[5]

All the fuss had Bourbonites like pugilist cum bar-owner Joe Herman rolling his eyes. Herman had lived on Bourbon Street for thirty years and claimed he could not sleep without the noise; the *quiet* woke him up. But his buddies rightfully fretted that Bourbon Street was in for a backlash. After an incident at the Pig Pen Bar, in which three servicemen got arrested for resisting overcharges, Bourbonites worried aloud that "the gouging of visitors and servicemen [might turn] 'America's Most Interesting City' [into] the 'City That Tourists Forgot.'" Explained bartender Curly Lima: "People put up with . . . third-rate places [previously] because there was a war on. [Club owners] went in for rude waiters, carelessly added checks, poor service, [cheap] whiskey . . . and food that was awful" because they knew that dozens more tolerant patrons were queued up outside. Now things were different, and owners, advised Lima, "better start trying to make customers happy like they use[d] to in the 1930's."[6]

Most did not take that advice, and instead pursued greater profits at the expense of quality and service. Postwar Bourbon Street started to earn something it never had before but retains to this day: neighborhood animus, civic disdain, and a nasty reputation. And in spring 1946, anti-Bourbon forces felt they gained a new friend: newly elected reformist Mayor deLesseps Story "Chep" Morrison.

Morrison vowed to fight vice and corruption citywide, namely on Bourbon Street. He also embraced the historical charm and architectural importance of the French Quarter, an enlightenment probably imparted by his sister-in-law, pioneer preservationist Mary Morrison. Denizens of the demimonde fretted.

"Everyone was scared to death that [Mayor] Morrison was going to eat them alive," recalled the grande dame of French Quarter madams, Norma Wallace.[7] An equally worried Curly Lima of the pro-business *Old French Quarter News* acknowledged that "a lot of guys are saying [that Mayor Morrison seeks to] close up the Vieux Carré." But he assured readers that "the mayor is a young man and likes a little Nite-Life once in a while. However, he does intend to have a clean French Quarter. By that he means 'Clip Joints' will not have a chance to operate."[8]

Lima was right. Morrison, like his peculiarly aristocratic and chummy sobriquets, straddled both sides of the French Quarter debate, wanting preservation *and* commerce *and* a whole lot more. In the words of historian J. Mark Souther, the mayor "wanted to clean up, not close up New Orleans."[9] A tidied metropolis would enable the chief executive to achieve his larger goal of throwing open the South's premier city through ambitious infrastructure upgrades and grandiose international trade initiatives. Toward this end he hired New York planning czar Robert Moses to sketch an arterial transportation plan, expanded airline service at the ample new Moisant International Airport, and endeavored to retain the heavy industry left over from the war. Most of all, Morrison oriented the city southward as the "Gateway to the Americas," a fixation so intense that his inaugural parade featured Central and South American officials sitting shoulder to shoulder with local authorities.[10] Young, sunny, and indefatigable, Mayor Morrison tipped his hat to tourism only to the extent that it abetted his core missions of metropolitan modernization, industrialization, and Pan-Americanism. A full-throttle attempt to close down venues and return Bourbon Street to its modest prewar demeanor was simply not forthcoming from Mayor Morrison's City Hall.

What did ensue were low-level crackdowns on B-drinking, clip joints, illegal bars, lewdness, bookmaking, and prostitution, with threats of further action if owners did not cooperate. Behind the effort was straight-laced Police Superintendent Adair Watters, who pressed for a full-scale crackdown on Bourbon Street but ended up sending mixed signals on account of Mayor Morrison's cheerfully lackadaisical attitude toward nonviolent vice.[11] Sensing that Morrison could be met halfway and that Watters ultimately deferred to Morrison, seventy bar managers in April 1948 voluntarily met with police in what Hyp Guinle of the Famous Door Bar described as a "friendly and stern discussion." The Bourbonites agreed to "see to it that dancers always are clad in panties, a fringe and a brassiere[; that they] bar suggestive dances[;] eliminate personal remarks from masters of ceremonies to patrons[;] do away with obscene or suggestive language[; and] forbid bartenders to sell drinks to persons who are intoxicated."[12]

Bourbon street scenes from the late 1930s (*left column*), paired with 2013 views (*right*). *Historic photographs by WPA, courtesy Library of Congress and Louisiana State Museum; modern photographs by author.*

Morrison's triangulating position sent the two opposing sides to hunker down on *their* positions. In one corner were the gruff and unctuous Bourbon Street club owners, managers, restaurateurs, and landlords, who pushed every envelope to maximize profit. Watching their back were taxi drivers, shopkeepers, bartenders, bouncers, employees, and entertainers, as well as secondary and tertiary service workers who benefited from the economic action. Bourbonites formed associations, curried local politicians, hired lawyers, and defended their interests.

In the other corner were residents, preservationists, writers, history buffs, old-line women's clubs, high-end tourism promoters, and other cultural hegemons (many from the same Franco-Anglo patrician society as Mayor Morrison), as well as an increasing numbers of educated newcomers who had made the Quarter their home. Through preservation societies and homeowners associations, principally the Vieux Carré Property Owners Association (VCPORA), they mobilized into political and legal action. "Bourbon Street, once . . . aristocratic[,] is now rows and rows of night clubs and 'honky-tonks,'" bemoaned one sympathizer in 1948; "It seems that the only way a historic building can be preserved now is to allow a barroom, night club, or honky-tonk to operate in them. . . .Wake up, New Orleans[!]" A kindred spirit questioned the taste of the "crazy snapshot [studios], epidermis artists, [and] corsage peddlers" joining Bourbon's entertainment scene, as well as dubious new clientele including "'local slummers,' 'misplaced hillbillies,' 'atmosfiends,' and 'Dixieland music lovers.'"[13] The permissiveness cultivated by the libidinous strip produced (or attracted) public behavior that would have been unthinkable elsewhere. Where else but Bourbon Street would one see, in 1940s America, an attractive young woman stroll publicly "without a stitch on her shapely form . . . and I mean not anything," and yet "no crowd gathered and nobody . . . tried to stop [her]"?[14] Even a Bourbonite like Tony Spargo (Sbarbaro), a New Orleans native and drummer for the Original Dixieland Band who made it big in New York, admonished his hometown peers about the direction of their district. "You've really got something here[;] all we hear in New York is about Bourbon st. . . . [B]ut it won't last long unless you clean up those Bourbon st. places." He rattled off a list of self-destructive ills: "'short drinks,' 'B' girls[,] petty thieves[,] waiters hovering over [patrons] shoving drinks under their noses and whisking [them] away half-finished[;] even the hat-check girls came in for a cut." He had seen it all before—on Fifty-Second Street in Manhattan—"and that ain't good."[15] Anti-Bourbon sentiment reached a crescendo in November 1948, when a *Picayune* magazine spread by Ray Samuel beseeched, "What's Happened to Bourbon Street?"

Look what they've done to one of the Vieux Carré's quiet thoroughfares! Bourbon's a bedlam, most of it, having replaced Basin street as the place where all kinds of folks meet. It's dirty, noisy and lusty. . . . Every day and night there's a Mardi Gras going on somewhere along Bourbon street. . . . If New Orleans is [the] "city care forgot," then this is [the] street where much forgetting took place.[16]

Samuel accurately traced the inflection point of The Street's recent history to the "Roaring Twenties, [when] the gaudy midway sparkle of signs . . . directed visitors into the new amusement places [and] they succeeded in turning Bourbon into a 24-hour carnival." But he failed to notice that the recent wartime bustle of the early 1940s had massively accelerated the transformations that had originated on a rather small scale in the 1920s. He also neglected to explain who "they" were. In fact, "they" were not one coordinated effort but scores of players, including restaurateurs, club impresarios, barkeepers, sole proprietors, managers, and landlords. Nearly all were locals, none were particularly powerful, zero could pass as patrician, and all acted more or less independently, keen to rise above their own plebian past. "They" were, essentially, the ethnic white working class of downtown New Orleans. Although salient players did emerge—popular club owner Gaspar Gulotta had been known as the "Little Mayor of Bourbon Street" at least since the war years, and he later headed the nightclub owners' association— The Street's operators otherwise had no consolidated administration, no president, no coordinator, no lobby, no marketers, and no corporate funding. Bourbon Street as we know it today effectively invented itself, locally, from the bottom up, with each constituent entity experimenting individually and adopting innovations laterally via competitive forces. It formed mostly during the second quarter of the twentieth century but rested upon cultural and structural substrate dating back to the eighteenth century. It succeeded by uniting an intimate pedestrian-scale framework of historic buildings with the tantalizing social memory of New Orleans's age-old gastronomical, musical, bibulous, and libidinous reputation. It worked well, and thus it rang true when, in 1949, a respected journalist called Bourbon Street "one of the most famous streets in the country."[17]

While the VCPORA crowd rejected any and all generous interpretations of Bourbon Street's success, it did see eye to eye with Bourbonites on some issues. Neither side liked the unsightly rail sheds and warehouses that separated the French Quarter from the Mississippi, and in 1946, VCPORA spearheaded a campaign to remove them. Both sides supported improvements in transportation, parking, congestion, sanitation, and garbage collection and worried about the postwar rise in Quarter crime. And after VCPORA argued for removing the Desire streetcar line going down Bourbon and Royal Streets, Bourbonites joined them in heralding "the removal of the clang and bang street cars [as] the greatest thing to happen to the French Quarter in 1948."[18] Both sides also curried the favor of the folks in the middle—working-class Quarter families, who had little interest in either nightclubs or preservation but whose property values, rent, and inner-city lifestyles were affected by both. After a new bar opened in 1949 at the corner St. Ann, within a few hundred feet of two schools, a convent, and St. Louis Cathedral, VCPORA investigated and discovered that prospective investors had been going door to door seeking places to rent for new liquor outlets. The association intervened with a program of its own, asking the same beleaguered locals to pledge *not* to rent to such businesses.[19] In other cases, VCPORA deployed a strategy of legal acumen, street smarts, political connections, and fierce resolve to contain the Bourbon scourge. Mary Morrison explained: "No one could get a liquor license . . . without the consent of seventy percent of the property owners who lived within three hundred feet of the proposed bar. But the whole ordinance was very loose, and so what we did [was get] it tightened up [such that] the person that proposed the bar had to first publish it in the paper three successive weeks [and] send registered letters to every property owner."[20] By that time, VCPORA would register its petition, contact the targeted neighbors, and lobby them to withhold their approval—usually successfully. Guerrilla tactics of this sort bred hostility between the well-connected white-collar cultural guardians of the French Quarter and the streetwise blue-collar businessmen of Bourbon Street. Remarkably, this tension would, over time, also generate a dynamic equilibrium capable of yielding the best of both worlds.

Disparities in social position—and a thinly veiled social animus—underscored the two sides' quotidian disputes. The uptown aristocracy generally looked down its nose at the crass servitude represented by the tourism economy, preferring instead the legacy industries of shipping, railroading, commodities trading, and, more recently, petroleum. Out-of-town French Quarter professionals, although excluded from blueblood society circles, nevertheless shared their class and cultural aspirations, and joined them in disdaining tourism and loathing Bourbon Street. This left the tourist trade to the descendants of southern and eastern European immigrants and working-class downtown Creoles. Sicilians formed at least a plurality and usually a majority among Bourbon and Quarter business and building owners, and more than any other group they deserve credit, or blame, for creating modern Bourbon Street. It was no coincidence that the reputed "Ambassador of Bourbon Street" was named Sal Palermo, that the "Mayor of Bourbon Street" was Gaspar Gulotta, and that Bourbon's most outspoken defender was Curly Lima, who penned a gossip column in the local press when he wasn't bartending for a Creole named Hyp Guinle at the Famous Door. (Incidentally, Bourbon Street also had an official chaplain. *His* name was Bob Harrington.)[21]

Those who reviled the Bourbonites used code words like "swarthy" and "greasers," or taunts like, "Who killa da chief," a relic of the 1890 purported mob hit which led to a mass lynching, to remind them of their social inferiority. The Sicilian-Creole alliance was later joined by eastern European Jews, many of them merchants from Canal, South Rampart, and Dryades Streets, who fulfilled the roles of investors and developers. Beneath many civic battles ostensibly about matters like "excessive" noise and "garish" signage were tensions between plebs and patricians, immigrant stock and charter groups, proletariat-bourgeois and bourgeois-elites, working-class natives and urbane transplants, and downtown and uptown. The tensions are detectable in Curly Lima's strident defense of Bourbon Street published in his "Vieux Carré Nite Life" column in the *Old French Quarter News*. "Special notice to the guardians of the historic French Quarter," he asserted sardonically:

> Stop . . . picking on the men [who] operate bars and clubs that pay heavy taxes. Bourbon Street has become the Broadway of New Orleans. . . . [Critics] should take a tour of . . . Dumaine and Burgundy [and] they'll see broken down property that is unhealthy for human beings to live in. . . . Gov. Earl K. Long [got] a tour of the hot spots last week [and] found every thing on Bourbon street in order and enjoyed himself very much.[22]

Lima pointedly defied elitist pretensions by saying that the "Broadway of New Orleans" (his relentlessly promulgated but ultimately unconvincing slogan for Bourbon Street) was "Yes sir . . . great. Chock full of good entertainment [at] *reasonable* prices that a *working man* can afford. . . . [A]ll bar and club owners are *proud* to present entertainment."[23] He cleverly played to preservationists' sympathies by pointing out the homier side of The Street. "Have you ever thought of how many different kinds of businesses we have on Bourbon St., 'Broadway of New Orleans[,]' from Canal to Esplanade?" He rattled them off:

Department store, D. H. Holmes . . . Kress' 5&10 . . . shoe repair . . . shoe shine parlor . . . ladies blouse shop . . . florist . . . hotels . . . apartments . . . brewery . . . religious store . . . dressmaker . . . tailor . . . laundry . . . barber shop . . . antique shop . . . jewelry store . . . Catholic convent . . . fruit stand . . . cabinet maker . . . printing shop . . . electrical shop . . . mechanic shop . . . doctor's clinic . . . wine cellar . . . beauty parlor . . . old folks home, Maison Hospitaliere . . . P.S. Also handbooks and lottery shops. S-h-h-h-h-h-h![24]

Lima also appropriated the scandalous Samuel piece by thanking the *Picayune* for publishing a "great ad for our Bourbon Street . . . the Broadway of the South. . . . It's talked about all over the States: our famous French Quarter." Rejoining Samuel's titular question "What's Happened to Bourbon Street?" Lima wrote, "We certainly could not expect Bourbon to stay as it was."[25]

While working-class white ethnics jeered the sneers of the elites, much of the cultural content they commodified for touristic consumption on Bourbon Street—jazz, blues, and foodways principally—derived from the city's Afro-Creole peoples. Yet blacks on Bourbon Street were excluded from the conversation, and physically banned from the bars and clubs. Their most prominent role on midcentury Bourbon Street was that of musician, hired from the Local 496 on North Claiborne Avenue to play traditional jazz in strictly segregated bands. Most others were relegated to the roles of the bowing doorman, devoted servant, obsequious entertainer, stereotyped prop, or sidewalk busker. The Famous Door Bar, for example, boasted in 1946 that it featured "the best small combo of Negroes in the entire state of Louisiana for entertaining, and special jive tunes." One block away, "Uncle Tom," described as an "aged Negro," entertained Old Absinthe House patrons with banjo music and guided them on tours of its secret mezzanine. When he fell ill in 1946, his boss, Owen Brennan, sought another "old Negro man" to play the Uncle Tom role—and if he could play the banjo, "so much the better."[26] A New York tourist that same year reported with delight "a little Negro . . . shuffling under the bell of [jazz musician Bill] Davidson's cornet [while] everybody was buying Sazeracs for everybody else," and marveled at the "wonderful pianist and singer at the Absinthe House, a Negro named Walter (Fats) Pichon, who refuses to leave New Orleans [despite that he] would make a fortune" in New York."[27] That same venue later featured "The Three Drips," caricaturing their inky black faces with an annulus of huge white lips and describing them as "three talented Negro boys who hail from way down yonder in New Orleans and please with their style of entertainment."[28] The Flamingo Bar at 405 Bourbon in 1948 presented, among other acts, a blackfaced Joe Glorioso impersonating Al Jolson impersonating a black person, while a few doors down, the exotic dance role of the Black Panther was played not by a sensual black woman but a white woman lathered in grease paint. (She had to quit because it made her skin break out.)[29] The most ubiquitous racially stereotyped act on Bourbon Street was that of the black tap dancers, who billed themselves with names like Po'k Chop, Kidney Stew, and Smoke Screen and worked both stage and sidewalk sporting "outrageous blue or purple or red coats, cleated shoes, muffler-type neckties and pork pie hats."[30]

White Bourbon managers dealt with black New Orleanians only to the extent that they provided entertainment content, cultural cachet, or cheap labor. Beyond that, segregation laws were strictly respected, indeed embraced. Black patrons at Bourbon Street hotels or nightclubs were absolutely out of the question. Even Ethiopian Emperor Haile Selassie, one of the most important figures in modern African history, had to suffer the indignity of his U.S. State Department hosts delicately negotiating a room for him at the whites-only Roosevelt Hotel during his 1954 visit, while local authorities tracked his delegation's moves to ensure the diplomats did not enter Bourbon Street clubs.[31] Black employees at those clubs, meanwhile, entered through separate entrances, and took subordinate positions for inferior pay. And if white showgirls were on the bill, black musicians had to be ensconced behind a curtain. Laws against interracial performance had the unintended effect of making Bourbon Street a highly localized or regionalized musical scene, as big-name bands from New York or California often declined gigs on moral grounds.[32]

By no means did segregation soften as the civil rights movement gained momentum in the 1950s. If anything, local authorities dug in their heels and heightened enforcement. In the past, white northern or European slummers who illicitly ventured into black musical hot spots were usually ignored by the police. No more. In 1952, for instance, nine white music buffs were arrested at the Dew Drop Inn on LaSalle for being white while drinking in a Negro establishment. By the late 1950s, whites had to attain special police permission to interact with blacks in black-only places, or else risk charges of disturbing the public order. Black patrons could gain no such permission to enter white establishments; there, the intensified animus took the form of an even more caustic exclusion.[33] "Whites

Only" signs were not posted on Bourbon Street club doors because it was all too well understood who could and could not enter (apartments and restaurants were a different matter). Additionally, the typical Bourbon venue of the 1920s–1960s, unlike today, sealed itself off from the street and employed a doorman, who could turn away any party on any grounds—age, attire, attitude, gender, or race. The streets themselves were open to all, but even there the racial order prevailed. An unrecognized black face that was not wearing a uniform or carrying an instrument was tracked suspiciously by the maintainers of Bourbon Street order. The sidewalks, meanwhile, featured—according to a 1953 American Automobile Association tour guide—"pickaninnies who will tap-dance for pennies."[34]

The efficacy of the April 1948 gentlemen's agreement between Bourbon managers and Morrison's people can be gauged by subsequent police blotters and crime reports. During the 1950s, stories of zany antics, lewdness, vulgarity, indulgence, illicit sex, gambling, violence, and organized crime became all the more intimately associated with Bourbon Street. Perhaps the stigma was unfair, given that immense numbers of visitors clustering into a single street upped the occurrences of *all* sorts of human behavior therein. But reputations develop and spread capriciously, and have a way of iterating, reifying, and validating themselves.

Zany antics on Bourbon Street? There was that night at the nasty Treasure Chest Club when a ferocious poodle, transfixed by the whirling tassels attached to Allouette LeBlanc's gyrating breasts, jumped on stage and bit into Miss LeBlanc's mammilla, necessitating a "a five minute intermission to carry out the wounded." Or that time comedian Lenny Gale hijacked a busload of unsuspecting tourists and drove them around town befuddled. Or that stunt that the proprietors of the Old Absinthe House would pull, escorting wide-eyed visitors up to the secret mezzanine to view a lifelike diorama of General Jackson and Governor Claiborne conferring with the pirate Lafitte, only to be startled as one of the costumed figures suddenly jumped to life.

Then there was that *Life* magazine story about Evangeline the Oyster Girl, whose act at the Casino Royale entailed emerging from a gigantic bivalve shell while peeling off her white negligée and leaving little more than her "flowing green hair" ("supposed to be seaweed," she later explained). One night, she lost top billing to a new act fresh from the Pacific Coast: Divena the Sensational Aquatease, who disrobed salaciously while submerged in a Plexiglas tank. In an obviously staged publicity stunt, the envious Oyster Girl grabbed a fire ax and cracked open the tank, sent 400 gallons rushing over the shag rug, yanked Divena out by the hair, and ended up at the cell block with a ten-dollar fine.[35] National coverage of such madcap capers left Bourbonites relishing the free advertising—and Quarter residents cringing.

Bourbon not only staged zany stunts, it attracted flighty characters and brought out the ribald in otherwise level-headed folks. The Street, like the city as a whole in historical times, exhorted a nearly gravitational pull on a certain type of male at a certain phase of his life. In most cases, he's the solitary transient relishing the exhilaration of anonymity amid a cornucopia of pleasures. Else he's the straight-laced Southern Baptist who was raised to recoil at mere mention of the strip or the city, only to find both utterly enticing and liberating. Husbands growing disillusioned with married life, closeted chaps seeking an outlet for gay fantasies, old codgers desiring a fountain of sexual youth: all are prime meat for the Bourbon Street grind. Case in point: Earl K. Long, the colorfully crotchety Louisiana governor who, after separating from his wife in 1959, behaved "like an eighteen-year-old [farm] boy who had just . . . discovered New Orleans for the first time[;] like a kid brought up by strict Baptist parents who had never seen a cigarette, a bottle of whiskey, or a loose woman in his life." Long would direct his state trooper to drive him nightly at breakneck speed from the Governor's Mansion to Bourbon Street, where he would ogle strippers into the wee hours and return to Baton Rouge by dawn to govern the state. His black limousine became a common sight parked in front of places like the Sho-Bar. That's where he fell head over heels in lust with the buxom Appalachian girl who went by the stage name Blaze Starr. The sensational story of the sixty-three-year-old governor and the twenty-three-year-old dancer helped made Long, Starr, Bourbon Street, and Louisiana all the more delectably notorious to the national consciousness.[36]

Lewdness on Bourbon Street? What got documented tended to be the tamest of the debauchery. There was the infamous Cat Girl, whose purring, slinking, panting act at Louis Prima's 500 Club got her in trouble in 1952 with the Louisiana Board of Alcoholic Beverage Control. What pushed authorities to file for indecency was an act in which the G-string-clad "Miss Christine" threw little pillows to men in the audience and, caressing a pillow of her own, crooned impishly, "Will you put your head on my pillow?" The board forced Miss Christine and her colleagues—women with stage names like Odessa, Hillary Dawn, and Galatea–The Statue That Came to Life—to cover their erogenous zones with four-inch-long fringes and something called "pantles."[37] Client demands and competition exerted constant pressure to show more. An undercover officer in 1953 investigating the Torch Club at 405 Bourbon described the last dance of the night, at 11:55 p.m.:

She was suggestive and her rear end was covered by black, wide netting that left nothing unseen. She momentarily pulled out the G-string front of costume at completion of her dance. . . . A blonde girl who had been seated near me at bar then slapped me on back and asked for a quarter for the juke box, which I refused.[38]

Once the glitzy performance concluded, the stars retreated to very different circumstances backstage. There, seediness and depressing anonymity prevailed. The misanthropic *Naked City* photographer Arthur Fellig (a.k.a. Weegee) delighted in the decadence of backstage Bourbon Street, crowing: "The strippers welcomed me . . . with open arms and open bras. One [even] gave me . . . her G-string"! But his ca. 1950 photograph "Dressing Room at a New Orleans Burly-Que" tells otherwise: three tough broads, one painfully world-weary, toiling in the glare of naked light bulbs amid cigarette smoke, peeling paint, and messily strewn costumes, undergarments, cosmetics, and bottles. Kent "Frenchy" Brouillette, who worked this scene in the mid-1950s, unflatteringly recalled the burlesque stars' loudly colored oversized wigs, "dragonfly" eyelashes, and "house paint" makeup. He called those "who sprung for Eisenhower-era breast implants . . . literally walking science experiments. . . . [T]he glamorous go-go bombshells of the 1950s," he concluded retrospectively, "resembled over-the-top trannies." It's not a pretty picture, and for all too many of Bourbon Street's showgirls, desperate lives filled with exploitive bosses and violent johns awaited beyond the illusory neon glow of Bourbon Street.[39]

Bibulous indulgence on Bourbon Street? Weegee's camera captured that too: "The drunks in New Orleans were so numerous," he recalled, "that the cops just swept them up and deposited them in the 'Country Club' (the drunk tank in the Bourbon Street police station). One tank was for gents; another for lady lushes. In the center was the common toilet bowl. [T]he cops and tourists walked by laughing."[40] One informant, a chaplain who closely monitored Bourbon Street in the 1960s, estimated that a midrange club with five hundred nightly customers would gross three thousand dollars a day and more than $1 million a year on drinks alone. "Alcohol lubricates Bourbon Street," he rued. "It is the oil that powers the engines of sin and makes millionaires of the smooth operators who own the honky-tonks."[41]

Sex on Bourbon? That could be found too, but more likely it was procured on The Street and delivered elsewhere. Along with B-drinking and handbook (bookmaking), solicitation for prostitution ranked tops among club and bar legal violations. A john—or "vidalia," as they were called in the Quarter—solicited sex for money in a number of ways.[42] He could seek a provocatively dressed coquette pouting alone in the corner of a bar: chances are she's a B-girl, and after she buttonholes you into a flirtatious conversation and suckers you into a couple of overpriced drinks (with a cut going to the house), there's a good chance she'll offer retail sex next (another cut). No B-girls? Drop a hint to a cabbie, barker, bartender, bell-hop, doorman, even the hot-dog vendors could help. Cabbies in particular acted as go-betweens between supply and demand in the sex trade; one undercover officer in 1953 didn't have to entrap one particular cabbie, who he described as "50 years old, fat faced and nose somewhat bulbous." Instead, the cabbie, stationed at Bourbon and Toulouse, proffered him a trip to the brothel, where he would earn a finder's fee from the house. The cabbie next offered to set him up with a B-girl, or "see a sex show between two girls."[43] Later that night, another cabbie cautioned the same undercover officer, at 1:15 a.m. at Bourbon and St. Louis, that he "was wasting both time and money here on the street, [and] that he could get me 'a good French'" (blow job) elsewhere. That usually meant one of two things: (1) a connection with any one of a number of pimps, who controlled the lowly carnal end of the sex trade involving streetwalkers, amateurs, B-girls, and strippers; or (2) a drive over to one of a handful of brothels, which were generally classier outfits run by "landladies" who sold a social as well as a sexual experience vis-à-vis top-shelf call girls. Queen of the landladies in his era was Norma Wallace, who ran well-appointed brothels at 328 Burgundy and 1026 Conti Streets.[44]

Getting a French was the least of the nontraditional sex purchasable on mid-century Bourbon Street. A vidalia could also arrange a "Greek" with another man (in which case he would be dubbed a "pansy"), or a "French Parisian" with a bunch of people. Prostitute and informant "Mrs. B" explained to a vice committee in 1953 how Norma Wallace handled gay requests:

[S]he had a male show boy that was working over there. . . . Whenever she had a French Parisian show to put on, if a man wanted a three way show, well, she called the boy [over]. He was a little blonde-haired fellow used to work down here at the Wonder Bar [on] the lakefront. It's a queer joint. [Else] she'd send down here to the Starlet Lounge . . . on Chartres St., that's another place where all the queers hang out. . . . A bunch of degenerate fellows. . . . [When a customer] wanted a date with a man[,] we'd send down to the Starlet Lounge to see whether one of the queers wanted to turn a date . . . and they'd split with the house just like one of the girls did. A lot of men wanted men instead of women. They had an intercourse with a man in his rectum. Greek date, in other words, you call it.[45]

When asked to describe a French Parisian, Mrs. B explained:

Well, that's 32 different positions[:] the Daisy Chain circle and the 69 . . . the lesbians, the dikes, the bull daggers [double penetration]. [They show] the men how the women have intercourse with their female lovers, and they up money with the vagina and smoke a cigarette with the vagina, it's done by muscle control, just little tricks, you know. The show lasts about 30 to 45 minutes [and costs] usually $100.[46]

This activity rarely took place on Bourbon proper—too many lights, too many eyes, and the rent was too high. Rather, the procurement took place on Bourbon, and the sex happened in the dark, quiet rear of the upper Quarter. That area had hosted the sex industry since it shifted out of Storyville between 1913 and 1917, and retained it even after the Tango Belt closed due to constant police pressure in the 1920s (which pushed the club scene into Bourbon Street). Now, in the 1940s and 1950s, Bourbon Street's relationship to the rear-Quarter brothel district was that of a vidalia hunting ground. All of Wallace's brothels, from the 1920s to the 1960s, were located in old Tango Belt area, while most of her clientele were drawn from Bourbon Street. Among those in on the racket was none other than popular bar owner and Bourbon "mayor" Gaspar Gulotta. "I was working for him, you know, B-drinks," recalled Mrs. B of a time in the early 1940s. "And if I wanted to take a guy out[,] I had to give [Gulotta] his cut." "Would he personally take his share of your prostitution earnings from you?" the investigator wanted to know. "Yes, indeed, he took it. . . . I gave it to him, himself."[47]

Vulgarity and tastelessness on Bourbon? Anti-Bourbonites pointed indignantly to The Street's billboards as evidence. Suggestive or obscene signage became a flashpoint throughout the 1950s because it externalized the outrages going on in private space into the public space, for all to see. It's what evangelist Billy Graham saw during his 1954 New Orleans crusade, and what prompted him to tell a vast throng in Tulane Stadium that Bourbon Street—"the middle of hell"—emitted "a stench in the nostrils of God."[48]

The ears of God would have burned from the vulgarity spewing from the overdressed, slick-haired masters of ceremony who presided over Bourbon burlesque performances. Emcees played a key role in the relationship between house and patron. They set the tone and wove the acts together with glib segues punctuated with drum-and-cymbal retorts from the collaborating band. Between the acts, emcees introduced stand-up comedians like Shecky Green, shticks like Phil D'Rey's Talking Ape ("Why are you in uniform? / I'm starting a gorilla war"), acrobats, jugglers, magicians, skating teams, and tap dancers like Po'k Chop and Kidney Stew.[49] They often wrote their own jokes and tested them on nightly audiences. One local emcee who worked The Street starting in the 1950s scribbled his ideas on index cards and saved them, providing an idea of the sardonic mirth that circulated in the smoky velvet interiors of a Bourbon nightclub. Typical were corny jokes like "Mexican ball game: *Jose, can you see . . .*" or "Cross a pygmy with a chef, get a short order cook." Then there were the thematic zingers, often at the expense of women: "She was so ugly . . . "

" . . . the tide went out & never did come back."
" . . . she had to hang a pork chop around her neck so the dog would play with her."
" . . . she was a perfect 36: 12–12–12."

Blacks, Jews, Arabs, Irish, and Italians served as punch lines, and if a celebrity could be thrown in, all the better: "I saw Sammy Davis Jr. in a nudie picture—I was disappointed; I really thought he was Jewish." Politics? Not so much. Why risk incensing an audience? You want their money, not their votes. Sex jokes worked much better in loosening up the crowd, and every conceivable aspect was fair game, from fat cocks, vaginas, and assholes to birth control, queers, sexchange operations, Spanish flies, and, of course, intercourse:

"Sign in a maternity shop: "you knock 'em, we frock 'em."
"A valentine is a card with a heart on."
"Sex is like a savings account . . . you lose interest at the moment of withdrawal."
"Honeymoon cocktail: Seven-Up in cider."
"Sure women live longer than men. Take a thousand screws out of a woman [and she's fine], but take two nuts out of a man & the ball game's over."[50]

Violence on Bourbon Street? There was that New Year's Day incident in 1950 at the iniquitous Latin Quarter Club, in which a Nashville contractor died when a B-drinking swindle involving a Mickey Finn—a drink laced with chloral hydrate—went awry. Bourbon folklore holds that the owners decided to hide his body in the dressing room and not notify authorities "until all that good business had come and gone." When the police finally arrived, the tourist was missing his wallet, shoes, and Sugar Bowl tickets.[51]

Then, a few months later, there was that predawn shoot-out following a wild Friday night. After seeing a show at the Treasure Chest, an ex-con named Donald Lee Wear took special interest in two dancers hanging out at the bar. The threesome shortly left for the girls' upstairs apartment at 335 Bourbon Street—"of their own accord," according to Wear, but, according to the girls, because Wear forced them at gunpoint. An hour later, startled pedestrians looked up to see one of the dancers plunge from a second-story window onto Bourbon Street. The commotion brought police to the scene, who learned from the injured girl that Wear had stabbed her friend in the chest and held her hostage upstairs. Nearly two dozen police surrounded the apartment and positioned themselves on the Regal Brewery across the street. Well-supplied with ammunition, Wear engaged his besiegers in a prolonged Bourbon Street gun battle. Reinforcements on the brewery roof lobbed tear gas and nausea bombs into the apartment. With two wounded and Wear arrested, the story ended up on page eighteen of the Sunday *Times-Picayune*—just another night on Bourbon Street. What landed it on the front page of the Monday papers was the revelation of the girls' involvement in an intricate B-drinking scam. Testimony in court later showed that Wear had previously conspired with the dancers to make their Bourbon Street apartment into a hideout for his nationwide crime spree. The dancers went from victims to coconspirators; even the police came out tainted, as Wear accused them of beating him in custody to extract a confession. What had started out as a story of a drifting sociopath ended up being about Bourbon Street's role as a magnet, incubator, and accomplice of that unsavory element.[52]

Gambling on Bourbon? Of The Street's sundry schemes, gambling in all its forms—lottery, keno, craps, cards, roulette, bingo, dice, slot machines, horse betting, and payoff pinball—generated by far the most money. Illegal betting in this era occurred all over town and spilled into outlying parishes, where undercover investigators would spy on clandestine casinos with binoculars and jot down license plates. Bourbon Street was the de facto capital of the racket, particularly for "handbook," or lotteries, which one local journalist said "means what it says—a gambling game with numbers. You pick out some numbers, just as in roulette. A secret drawing is held. If your numbers come up, you win."[53] The term "handbook" came from the ledgers kept for each game, as well as from the "dream books" that were kept on hand to aid clients with number selections. With titles like *Aunt Sally's Policy Player's Dream Book* and *The Three Wishes Dream Dictionary,* these strange encyclopedias listed imagery and themes that may have appeared in players' dreams, accompanied by the numbers they ought to bet on.[54] About five hundred handbook operations existed in New Orleans in the early 1950s, dominated by five major players and employing a few thousand people. It was all illegal and highly lucrative, and that meant organized crime.

Mobsters discovered Bourbon Street rather inexorably. Their ilk lived on or near it for as long as eighty years before it became famous. Their paisanos, notably the Matrangas clan, had immigrated to New Orleans starting in the 1860s and 1870s, leading some to view New Orleans as the cradle of the American Mafia. Gangsters comprised a tiny fraction of the thousands of Sicilians who settled in the sugar parishes and New Orleans around the turn of the twentieth century. Charles Matranga, who survived the 1891 lynching of the eleven Italians acquitted for the murder of Police Chief David Hennessy, controlled the so-called Black Hand in the city until he turned over power to Sylvestro "Silver Dollar Sam" Carollo during Prohibition. Organized moneymaking rackets—whether they can formally be attributed to "the Mafia" per se is a matter of definition—remained mostly local or regional until 1933, when Senator Huey P. Long befriended New York mob boss Frank Costello during a visit to his Sands Point home. In need of funding for his political machine, Long suggested that Costello bring his slot machine racket to Louisiana, with the assurance that state officials would look the other way so long as a percentage of the profits flowed into Long's coffers. It was a tempting deal, and what made it even sweeter from Costello's perspective was the fact that Mayor Fiorello LaGuardia's crackdown on gambling in New York City had Big Apple mobsters scrambling for a safer place to invest and launder their money. To facilitate the deal, Carollo traveled to New York in 1934 and coordinated with Costello and Philip "Dandy Phil" Kastel. The next year, slot machines started to appear in New Orleans bars and clubs, while full-scale casinos, all technically illegal, popped up just over the parish line in places like Southport in Jefferson and Arabi in St. Bernard. The symbiotic Long-Mafia deal survived Huey's assignation in 1935 as brother Earl K. Long took over matters, and by the late 1930s, the New York–New Orleans syndicate was running thousands of slot machines across Louisiana and generating millions of dollars. Bourbon Street, which by this time was well on its way to becoming a nighttime entertainment destination and had already garnered local mob interest vis-à-vis Prohibition, became the perfect nerve center and greenhouse for nurturing a criminal empire funded with out-of-town cash.

While Kastel controlled the Jefferson and St. Bernard operations, and Costello oversaw those in New Orleans proper, both needed local aiding and abetting. They got what they needed from the new mayor of New Orleans, Robert Maestri; hotelier Seymour Weiss; and a new name working his way up the local underworld ranks—Carlos Marcello, a Tunisian-born Sicilian with a familiar story of immigration into the Louisiana sugar parishes. [55] In typical mob fashion, Marcello ascended the syndicate by allying himself with the right people, in this case Quarter mobsters Frank Todaro and Baptiste Pecoraro, and even marrying Todaro's daughter. Proving himself highly competent, Marcello was appointed by Carollo to oversee operations throughout the Gulf South. For decades to come, Marcello would preside over illicit moneymaking endeavors regionwide while hiding in plain sight in his inconspicuous Town & Country Motel at 1225 Airline Highway in presuburban Jefferson Parish. During his and Carollo's reign, the New Orleans region grew into the premier money-laundering destination for mob earnings generated in the Northeast—"the Wall Street of the Mafia," according to one local journalist.[56] In part this was because of its large Old World Sicilian population from which potential accomplices could be recruited. More so, it was because the region had the same appealing traits, like corrupt politicians and purchasable police, that made certain foreign countries attractive sites for detaching the source of money from the stockpiling of money—without the hassle and danger of crossing borders.

Among Marcello's chief underlings was Sam Saia, who, from the backroom of Felix's Oyster House at the Bourbon/Iberville intersection, commanded all forms of sports betting far and wide. Under Saia were a legion of lieutenants who supervised specific handbook operations in clubs and bars, as well as tailor shops and corner grocers—the more inconspicuous, the better. They in turn commanded a team of runners and messengers zipping around Bourbon Street with envelopes stuffed with greenbacks, each one insured by threats of violence. Bribery in various forms, ranging from a cut of the pay to a piece of the action to flat-out fistfuls of cash, effectively kept police and politicians at bay. To get a sense of the sheer size of the local underworld economy, consider that unnamed forces guardedly offered Police Superintendent Adair Watters a bribe of $2,500 per *day*—the equivalent of $7.5 million annually in today's dollars—to allow a hundred handbooks to reopen in 1947. Unlike all too many of his underlings, Watters pointedly refused. A typical police sting on Bourbon Street's handbook scene went something like this 1953 operation, recorded by Confidential Investigator #8 of the Special Citizens Investigating Committee:

> While going to 11:00 o'clock court I observed PETER SCRAGGS, the former outside lookout man for the handbook that was located at 435 BOURBON STREET getting out of an automobile . . . and entering TORTORICH'S RESTAURANT. . . . Later in the day, I was informed by a former HORSEPLAYER that SAM SAIA has PETER SCAGGS [sic] and JAKE ROMANO walking in the streets, and picking up the bets and telephoning them in. They don't give tickets, however, and operate between TORTORICH'S RESTAURANT AT ST. LOUIS AND ROYAL STREETS to GASPER'S BAR [AT] FOUR-FORTY BOURBON, and go across the street to a bar in the rear of the CASINO ROYALE.[57]

As for Mayor Morrison, he accepted campaign contributions from the likes of Sam Saia, Gaspar Gulotta, and other Bourbon club owners affiliated with hand-booking.[58]

Gambling involvement spilled over into ancillary money streams, among them club ownership. The Sho-Bar, for example, was mob-owned and run by Carlos Marcello's brother Pete, while the 500 Club was operated by Carlos's crony Frank Caracci. Club ownership by the syndicate meant that all the B-drinking, prostitution solicitation, and narcotics sales transpiring therein were technically "mob run." It also meant that all the accomplices who participated in and earned money from these goings-on, from cabbies to runners to barkers and pimps, could be described as having "mob ties." Mob or Mafia influence was usually partial, piecemeal, or shadowy; many clubs and restaurants that were not outright mob-owned nevertheless played host, with or without coercion, to mob-administered handbook, slot machines, jukeboxes, cigarette machines, and the like. Small rackets were often stepping-stones to big ones. For instance, the "payoff pinball" racket, in which players paid a fee to the barkeep and received a cash prize in the rare times they exceeded a high score, had been set up through an alliance between New York gangster "Dandy Phil" Kastel and Bourbon Street's own "Diamond Jim" Bracato (a.k.a. Moran), so named for his penchant for bejeweled attire. That experience helped establish Diamond Jim as "one of the kingpins of organized criminal enterprises in New Orleans."[59] Bordellos such as the Green House on Conti Street, meanwhile, remained outside mob control—no gangster could handle Norma Wallace—but benefited nonetheless from diffuse mob criminality throughout Bourbon Street.

Murky documentation and tangled webs of evidence make it difficult to ascertain the degree to which Bourbon Street was invented or run by organized crime. It certainly was infiltrated, exploited, and bloated by it, with local oversight coming from Jefferson Parish and dollars coming from New York, Chicago, Las Vegas, and beyond. "Run" by organized crime, however, goes too far, and "invented" by it is not at all the case. Suffice it to say that midcentury Bourbon Street—starting during Prohibition, peaking from the mid-1930s through the 1960s, and petering out in the 1970s and 1980s—depended on illicit activity to generate the excesses for which it became famous, and the lion's share of that illicit activity, in that era, had indirect or direct ties to organized crime.[60]

Bourbon Street insiders were not blind to the self-harm their antics wrought, nor were they incapable of expressing dissent. One creative character who dubbed himself William Tell, "the Bard of Bourbon," riled up denizens of The Street in 1949 with the publication of his poetic polemic *The Beat of Bourbon Street*.

> There's a rowdy little skid row
> By the name of Bourbon Street,
> Where you'll find the man who's skidding,
> Though there's leather on his feet;
> It's a gateway in New Orl'ans
> To the ancient Vieux Carre,
> Where they're selling sex and history
> That border on decay.[61]

Sure there were other skid rows, Tell allowed—Boston's Scollay Square, the Bowery in New York; Chicago's State, West Madison, Clark; and those in San Francisco—"but the Bourbon slum's the only one," he wrote, "That's loudly ballyhooed." Thirty-two pages of wicked stanzas, illustrated with stylized woodcuts of strippers, bouncers, and an inexplicable recurrent baboon, poked fun at all that was deviant about The Street. Drunkards, Mickey Finn ploys, and the ruses of the B-drinking game all got their due:

> When a Bar Girl orders whiskey
> She gets whiskey, but it's weak,
> And she takes it like a gargle
> Or a tongue-swish, so to speak,

Then she trickles back the liquor
In a chase dark with coke,
Thus a girl can flip off B-drinks
Like a dip can lift a poke.

So too did the broads who staffed the B-drinking scams, who often moonlighted as whores:

When she learns the spit back method
Or the gargle or the spill,
When a girl's as queer as Sappho
Or a seven-dollar bill,
When the state grants her a pardon
Or she's turned out on parole,
She can always strip on Bourbon—
Even play a feature role.[62]

Players on Tell's Bourbon Street stage included gullible tourists, shady barkers, conspiring cabbies, corrupt cops, sadistic bouncers, dumb patsies, con men, marks, tramps, rapists, hookers, and pimps. No surprise that, according to Famous Door bartender and Bourbon defender Curly Lima, "most of the bar and club owners resent the book"—and probably not for its revelations, which hardly stopped the presses.[63] What they resented was the inside job, said to be the work of French Quarter press agent Bob Riley. If there's one type Bourbon Street did not like, it was the stoolie who snitched on its artifices, dispelled its illusion, and emerged looking savvy, smug, and sanctimonious.

For all the competition and criminality on midcentury Bourbon, veterans of The Street often spoke of a collegiality and solidarity among those of equal rank. Former dancer Mary Bromfield ("Kalantan, the Heavenly Body") conjured a close-knit community "where all the entertainers were family." They rendezvoused after their gigs for companionship and conversation, in a French Quarter she remembered as having a "slow, generous, compatible family feeling."[64] And despite all its vulgarity, cynicism, and violence, the commercial end of Bourbon Street still had room for a surprising degree of homey domesticity. It still retained a share of the aging immigrant tenement-dwellers, relics of the old Quarter, who spoke broken English and people-watched from upper-story windows. It participated in the Spring Fiesta and hosted evening courtyard tours. It celebrated

Christmas by stringing colored lights in front of bar and clubs.[65] Its workers saw themselves as comrades, looked after each other, and defended their dignity. Residences still exceeded businesses on many of the commercial upper blocks (midcentury photographs of nightclub exteriors often capture "Apartment for Rent" signs, a rarity today), and, by a wide margin, on all of the lower blocks. Even the heart of the nighttime district had a surprising door-to-door diversity of businesses catering to locals and tourists alike; in 1949, for example, Bourbon Alterations "cleaned, glazed, and repaired" fur coats and tailored your suit "while U wait," right next door to Zonia's Bar, Lounge, and Patio at 325 Bourbon.[66] And for decades, Bourbon was home to one Antoinette Forcelle, who cultivated an elaborate rooftop garden at 413 Bourbon, just steps from where the Wear shoot-out occurred. Tinged with a bit of the nuttiness emanating from The Street below, Miss Forcelle "mothers her plants[,] admonishes them when they do not grow, [and] send[s for] hospitalization when they are sick."[67] Indeed, the midcentury French Quarter still retained a large population of unaffected native folk—moms and dads, children playing in the streets—and the neighborhood provided everything they needed. The father of one typical Quarter family, which resided in a Bourbon Street shotgun house located between Café Lafitte's in Exile and Lafitte's Blacksmith Shop, waited tables at Galatoire's all his life, sent his four children to St. Louis School, and attended Mass at the Cathedral, all within six blocks of their home. The Quarter even provided some fresh-caught local meat for the Bourbon Street family: the children would toss a crab net over a covey of pigeons in Jackson Square and take the hapless creatures home to their mother. "She made pigeon gumbo," recalled the daughter years later, "and it was delicious."[68]

Who ran Bourbon Street? No one entity or individual oversaw the strip; it was a remarkably organic, bottom-up synergy of many constituent parts. A biologist might liken it to a beehive or ant colony; a systems theorist might describe it as a self-organizing network; a computer scientist as an open-source platform. An economist might view it as somewhere between monopolistic competition and perfect competition—except for one inconvenient factor: organized crime. The Mafia injected an unmeasured investment of out-of-town cash starting primarily in the 1930s, and its local tentacles touched many if not most Bourbon businesses and subeconomies over the next three to four decades. They ranged from the servicing of a tavern jukebox or pinball machine, to the highly lucrative administration of handbook, to the full ownership of a club and all its contents. But the out-of-town Mafia dons did not get involved in what the public saw and consumed on Bourbon Street; they did not create it, design it, manage its performers, or make it famous. That happened via hundreds of local players working independently in loose affiliation without any central planning. Some talented individuals, however, arose into ad-hoc leadership positions, and no one man was more archetypal of the captains of Bourbon Street during its midcentury zenith than Gaspar Gulotta.

Like so many of The Street's characters, Gaspar Gulotta came from poor Mediterranean stock, born in Italy in 1891. He arrived with his family in Houma, where demand for field laborers had run high since emancipation. It didn't take long for the Gulottas to see more opportunity in city life, and with baby brother Pete (born 1896) in tow, they migrated to New Orleans and settled in the lower French Quarter. No silver spoons in their mouths, Gaspar and Pete, like so "many poor New Orleans kids, claw[ed] for a living" in the only world they knew: the tough streets of Little Palermo. Pete became a pugilist at age sixteen, and gained fame as a champion bantamweight boxer. Gaspar tended bars on Bourbon Street and rose to the ranks of club owner, becoming, along with Count Arnaud, part of that key 1920s generation that transformed subdued saloons into glamorous clubs. During that stint he honed his skills in arbitrating among, and speaking on behalf of, the often contentious Bourbon Street cabaret community. By all accounts a convivial and generous man, Gaspar Gulotta emerged as the reasonable liaison in a world of aggressive, outspoken, self-important toughs. Some said it was the colloquial but shrewd Mayor Robert Maestri who first dubbed Gulotta the "Little Mayor of Bourbon Street"; others said it was future governor Jimmy Davis. Gulotta himself, when queried about the nickname, responded, "You know any udda guy on the street's gonna challenge?" The "Little" in the sobriquet came from the diminutive stature he shared with his 115-pound tough-as-nails kid brother, who himself ran a well-known Quarter club (Pete Herman's) and was briefly married to Quarter madam Norma Wallace. The "Mayor" in the nickname paid respect to Gaspar's ability to settle disputes, negotiate with authorities, connect problems with solutions, and communicate among stakeholders who hailed from very different positions in life. "You could call him a sort of mediator," an admirer recollected years later:

> Maybe one brings in a stripper with a name almost the same as another stripper who is better known. Maybe one guy is tryin' to hire away an act from another guy. Or maybe a joint is really puttin' the strong boost on the touristas. Things like that. Today, you'd have about eighty-eight lawyers

[involved, but] Gaspar [would] get 'em talkin'. He'd get things straightened out. Ya see, small as he was he was very big in every way. . . . [A]n' if you wanna know somepin', I think he prolly gave away a lotta loot to guys and dolls who had a little bad luck. Yeah, you could talk to Gaspar.[69]

Gulotta also knew when Bourbon Street was pushing its luck. When sketchy practices raised the ire of Bourbon's enemies, he pulled his buddies aside and got them to relent. Suspected of dabbling in plenty of sketchy business himself, Gulotta was called to testify at a number of inquests, including the 1953–54 Special Citizens Investigating Committee. When he didn't have his audience in stitches, he regularly outsmarted his erudite adversaries and "never lost a round" to them. He did, however, acknowledge participating in handbook at his 440 Bourbon Street bar, and was pressed about his connections to shady Bourbon Street characters with handles like Dutch, Lips, and Louie the Pimp. Others credibly accused Gulotta of hiring B-girls and taking a cut of their prostitution, of overseeing the movement of girls between cabarets and brothels, and of collecting graft for the cops and skimming a fee. Gulotta had an uncanny ability to resolve other people's problems and personally come out ahead: he gained popularity, for example, for helping build a gym for St. Mary's Italian Church, a facility from which he himself would benefit vis-à-vis his "unofficial job [as] the underworld's boxing boss."[70] He was the go-to man for any young woman hoping to see her name in lights, among them Abbie Jewel Slawson, who as a seventeen-year-old Mississippi girl, got herself introduced to Gulotta in 1947, and, one night later, brought down the house at his Bourbon bar.[71] Impulsive, prankish, dapper yet "sentimental, devout, and loyal," Gaspar Gulotta, with his trademark cigar, cut an almost cinematic figure.[72] His last establishment was the classy Club Pigalle, named after the Moulin Rouge cabaret district of Paris and located at 232 Bourbon, next door to his buddy Diamond Jim [Bracato] Moran's Old Absinthe House restaurant. Gulotta's death in late 1957—his pallbearers included his longtime emcee, the superintendent of police, a mobster buddy, and Mayor Chep Morrison—deprived Bourbon Street of a perspicacious peacemaker and a charming defender just five years before a time when it would desperately need such a mediating figure. The Little Mayor of Bourbon Street rests today in Greenwood Cemetery next to his wife, Mae.

Each job on Bourbon Street drew from a particular social realm. The owner/manager class mostly comprised New Orleans natives, if not Quarterites. All were white, save for the Chinese of the 500 block's Chinatown; black owners were nonexistent.[73] White staffers at restaurants and bars comprised locals as well as transplants, many of the latter from the rural South. Some had come originally for wartime opportunities; others came because the same magnetism that attracted writers and artists to New Orleans also drew performers, adventurers, vagabonds, hell-raisers, and crooks. African American employees were almost all local or regional because extremely few blacks migrated into the segregated South. Most bar owners were male; Mabel Persson (1946) was among the few female owners, along with Dixie Fasnacht (1949), who was probably also the first lesbian owner. In a fair number of cases, the level-headed wives of impetuous male club owners ended up running the joints. Hypolite Guinle's wife, Genevieve, played that role at the Famous Door, as did Steve Valenti's spouse at the Paddock Lounge—situations in which the hapless husbands inexorably came to be called "pussy-whipped" by snickering guidos.[74]

Barkers, who had the worst reputations of all Bourbonites, came from wherever there was a wrong side of the tracks. Glib and slick, with index fingers jabbing and handheld signs a-twirling, barkers did whatever it took to route the flow of pedestrians into the club. "*Come one and all to see the incredible, the glamorous, the exotic . . . !*" Barkers specialized in making aggressive eye and verbal contact, particularly with solitary males, and always seemed to be at the brink of violence: "*the world-renowned . . . the internationally famous . . . the femme fatale of the French Quarter! . . . no cover no minimum no cover no minimum . . .*" If a couple approached, the tactic changed. "As the couple walked past, the barker would open the door a little bit, just enough for the two to get a peek. . . . Then he'd close it, and address the man, "Would you and your lady care to see a risqué show tonight?"[75] Aggressive barkers drew the ire of vice squads repeatedly throughout the 1950s and 1960s, on grounds of disturbing the peace and other charges. "*A full night's slate of entertainment, from hilarious comedy to stupefying magic. . . . Why waste your time with all these other low-class joints? . . . no cover no cover no cover . . .*" Many barkers also served as nodes in gambling, B-drinking, and solicitation rings. Cabbies, who ranked only slightly above barkers in the strip's pecking order, participated in similar rackets. Some would receive payments for suggesting to their fares certain clubs, hotels, and restaurants, a practice known as "diverting." The scam came to the attention of the Better Business Bureau in 1962, when tourists complained of lousy accommodations proffered by pushy cabbies.[76]

Burlesque dancers came to Bourbon Street from farthest and widest. Their specialized skill set put them in short supply and high demand, which translated to opportunities coast to coast, sometimes on a syndicate. An example was Amber of the Mardi Gras Lounge, described in 1948 as "sex feet sex inches of SEX" who had "out of town agents and night club owners . . . bidding high for [her]."[77] The strip's most famous dancer, Blaze Starr, earned her place in history for her affair with Louisiana Governor Earl Long, but her humble origins (born in rural West Virginia) and cross-country treks (via Baltimore's "The Block") made her typical of midcentury Bourbon burlesque stars. Abbie Jewel Slawson (a.k.a. Kitty West, a.k.a. Evangeline the Oyster Girl) had similarly poor rural roots in Shuqualock, Mississippi, and parlayed her Bourbon Street fame into headliner acts in Texas, Indiana, and at the Kentucky Derby. She performed for the likes of Frank Sina-tra, Don Ameche, and Ceasar Romero and sometimes earned upward of $1,500 weekly.[78] Chaplain Bob Harrington, who ministered to Bourbon's fallen souls in the 1960s, found the strippers to come from a particularly broad cross-section of society in terms of class, education, geography, profession, and life experi-ence. Their reasons for entering the world of Bourbon burlesque fell into three main categories: some saw it as a springboard into show business; others as a statement of resistance or independence against parents, boyfriends, or husbands; and the rest simply because it was a paying job. Whatever her reason, a new bur-lesque dancer found herself in a ferociously competitive marketplace and strove to develop a distinguishing act. They are a lost art on modern Bourbon Street, acts such as that of Ruth Corwin (a.k.a. Alouette LeBlanc, the Tassel Spinner), who defied physics by twirling in opposing directions four tassels attached to her breasts and buttocks; "Champagne Girl" Rita Alexander, who toasted the evening with glasses of bubbly balanced on her bosom; Yvette Dare, whose par-rot was trained to steal her sarong (the secret was a tomato slice entwined in the knot); Von Ray, the Texas Tornado, who donned a cowgirl outfit and galloped on a pony down Bourbon Street; Miss Amazon and her "6 Feet of Gorgeous Body" at the 5 O'Clock Club; schoolteacher-turned-stripper Patty Wite, "The Schoolboys' Delight"; Evelyn West, "The Treasure Chest," whose frontal assets were suppos-edly insured for $50,000 by Lloyds of London (against what? some pondered); Redi Flame, "The Fire Ball of New Orleans," who cashed in on her fiery red hair; Baby Doll, who weighed 300 pounds; Shalomar, who had "the face of Liz Taylor and the body of Frankenstein"; Fatima, whose persona as "the Glorious Goddess of the Gaza Strip" came from the fact that she was from Cairo—in Illinois; and Suzanne "Jezebel" Robbins, who entertained audiences with five shows nightly complete with emcee, comedians, a band, and a pack of fluffy poodles dyed hot pink and powder blue.[79] Acts fell on the stylish side of sexy, and on the campy side of creative. Kitty West's nightly performance was prototypical of the era. It commenced upon a darkened stage, clarinet or piano playing mystically in the distance, whereupon the emcee would dramatically intone, "We take you on a mythical trip to the bayous of Louisiana, where deep in the mist is . . . Evangeline THE OYSTER GIRL!" The curtains would draw to reveal a slowly opening bathtub-sized oyster shell. From within a pedicured foot would emerge, followed by a long graceful leg, then a scantily clad body. The music would pick up, and after fully extricated, the Oyster Girl would cradle a gigantic pearl within her bosom and dance sultrily—part "Afro-Cuban," part ballet, with splits and slides and swirls, for the better part of eight minutes. Finally a net was tossed over her body, leaving her writhing pleasurably on the floor as the music climaxed: for this was, explained the emcee to the audience, mating season in the bayous. Rarely did the sensual become sexual in Bourbon Street acts, and never was the body fully bared.[80]

Acts grew progressively more sexual as the burlesque era of the 1940s and 1950s evolved into the striptease routines of the 1960s—"less choreography, more gynecology," in the words of one commentator.[81] By the mid-1960s, a typical Bourbon Street stripper worked three or four shows of ten to twenty minutes each nightly, and usually disrobed down to her G-strip and pasties in the first five minutes. Legally, she could not bare her nipples, vagina, or anus, nor sit down, touch herself or customers, or let customers touch her. But she could "gyrate, shake, wiggle, bump, grind, tell off-color jokes and bring her body within inches of customers." For this she would be paid anywhere from seventy-five to five hundred dollars a week, depending on her notoriety. Once the curtains closed, a second set of opportunities were offered to the stripper, which could easily double or triple her income. Chaplain Harrington disapprovingly described them as "hustling customers for drinks, prostitution, drug addiction, lesbianism, posing for pornographic photographs, and performing unspeakable acts of perversion in stag movies."[82]

Emcees, comedians, ventriloquists, contortionists, crooners, and other professional entertainers also operated on a wide circuit because, like the showgirls', theirs were talent jobs that required stage style and demeanor. An example is Larry Fontaine, born David C. Oliveira-Amaral in Massachusetts in 1923, who, after fighting in World War II, emceed on Bourbon Street as well as on Clark and West Madison streets (Chicago's Bourbon counterparts) in 1948; in Baltimore in 1952 (where he worked with Blaze Starr); in nearby Biloxi, Mississippi; and in scores of other clubs across twelve states, on cruise ships, on television, and in

Vietnam. His home base, however, was New Orleans, where the singer-pianist-comedian worked nine different Quarter clubs. He lived one block away, at 626 Dauphine, and died in 1985, by which time jobs for old-school peripatetic emcees had grown nearly as scarce nationwide as they had on Bourbon Street.[83]

Musicians on Bourbon operated within their own local subculture and hierarchy. True, some national bands played The Street, but they were the exception. Only one club "follow[ed] a policy of bringing in out-of-town jazz talent"; it simply cost too much. Besides, tourists wanted to hear traditional jazz, and Jim Crow restrictions against interracial performances kept some out-of-town entertainers away on legal or moral grounds.[84] This left most Bourbon gigs to a pool of musicians that usually had deep local roots. Like Storyville a half century earlier, Bourbon Street, for all its flaws, provided musicians something that the Bourbon-hating purists and progressives could not: decent, steady, reasonably paying jobs.

At the zenith of this employment sector were well-known employer-musicians like Pete Fountain and Al Hirt, who owned and headlined their eponymous clubs and hired their own sidemen. At the nadir were neophyte or vagabond musicians, who drifted in and out of the scene either for adventure or desperation. In the middle—the vast majority—were serious professional musicians who, starting at the dawn of the nightclub era, organized themselves into two unions under the auspices of the American Federation of Musicians: Local 496 for blacks, and Local 174 for whites. Unions served as mediators between the members' desire for better pay, stable work, steady hours, reasonable work conditions, and fringe benefits, and the employers' demand for prompt, talented, and presentable performers—all under arrangements of contractual clarity and professionalism. The union had the effect of formalizing, stabilizing, and equalizing resources and opportunities within its membership. Under a leadership that was elected for two-year terms with staggered annual turnover, "the Local" also served as a clearinghouse for gig opportunities, a mediator for disputes, a settler of grievances, and a leveler of the playing field against charges of favoritism or preferential treatment. Whenever possible, the union offered access to credit and health benefits. The racialized separation was more a product of state law and the Federation's nationwide policy than it was of racial animus among the musicians themselves; by most accounts, members of either group knew and respected each other, grew up together, and generally got along. Sociologist Jack V. Buerkle, who worked closely with jazzman Danny Barker and other Local 496 members, described them as "Bourbon Street Black"—"a semicommunity . . . of musicians, their

relatives, peers, friends, and general supporters, whose style of life is built around
. . . the production and nurture of music." Buerkle estimated that about four to
five hundred people made up the "core" of Bourbon Street Black; they included
the main Local 496 black musicians and their administrative apparatus, plus their
families, mentors, and protégés. Another 1,500 to 2,000 operated in the "periphery"; among them were open-minded Local 174 white musicians plus families
and friends who circulated in or near the live-music industry. Access to the core
was easy: all a "young jazzman . . . has to do to gain entry is to show same talent
and interest," and he would get in return "a very responsive, supportive social
group."[85] But getting a paying gig meant joining the Local 496. With its office
on North Claiborne Avenue, Local 496 oversaw a membership numbering in the
low to mid-hundreds, of which just fewer than half were classified as full-time
musicians. Of the full-timers, some worked two gigs that each ran three nights a
week, one on weekdays and one weekends; others had steady jobs with predictable hours in house bands at hotels, clubs, cabarets, or lounges. This was the case
for lots of Bourbon Street musicians from the 1930s through the 1950s, when
live music prevailed and bands had up to fifteen members (it was called "big-
band music" for a reason). But during the late 1950s to early 1970s, jazz bands
declined, and those that persisted comprised fewer players, around five. Their
work increasingly took the form of one-time gigs at conventions or parties, or of
rotating band memberships in various nightly venues. With the help of the union,
both full-timers and part-timers cobbled together gigs at conventions, dances,
weddings, private parties, or at special appearances at casinos or bars.

If a club owner needed a band, he would contact either Local 496 or Local
174 and request, or be appointed, a band leader and his players. "The band leader
agrees to provide music . . . at a designated place [and] times. . . . The employer
agrees to provide certain working conditions including playing time and intermission terms," and payment at union scales.[86] When the contract was signed, the
employer was billed for an additional 17 percent for social security and the union's
pension fund. The leader was then paid, after which the fringe benefit percentage was deducted and the remainder was split among the sidemen. The leader,
who would usually earn double pay for his extra responsibilities, set the rules for
sidemen's musicianship, behavior, appearance, and for policies on matters such
as drinking on the job. Most sidemen themselves played the role of leaders now
and again—over 90 percent, by one survey. All union members were instructed to
work only with union musicians, only at places that hired union musicians, and
never for less than union pay scales. They were also strongly discouraged from

"jamming" freely in public, as it cultivated the expectation that live music could be enjoyed gratis, and gave wing to potential scabs.

The Local 496 experience produced a midcentury New Orleans musician whose lifestyle was decidedly more professional and conventional than his counterpart from 1900, and far less capricious and spontaneous than the progressive artist of Jazz Age mythology. Those who worked Bourbon Street in particular, according to the 1973 Buerkle study, took "what can be described as a 'moderate' approach to racial matters in music." They were cognizant of their white audiences, and hardly radicals themselves.[87] Racial integration further regularized the Bourbon Street musicians' experience in 1971, when the black Local 496 and the white Local 174 merged and became the Musicians Mutual Protective Union, Local Number 174–496, and shortly thereafter, musicians playing Bourbon Street were roughly fifty-fifty black and white. Today the twin organizations comprise the American Federation of Musicians Local 174–496, based at 2401 Esplanade Avenue ever since integration.[88] Most Bourbon Street musicians today are white.

Musicians on midcentury Bourbon Street were not musically confined to jazz. They also played big band (a gentrification of jazz), barrelhouse (urbanized blues), boogie-woogie (danceable blues), hillbilly (country), and burlesque accompaniment, and generally tried to put on classy acts. Sometimes they fell short: one earwitness described the resulting heterophony as "an orgy of overlapping rackets, sleazy, burlesque-striptease music full of braying trumpets, raucous, coked-up, drum-thrashing 'party' jazz, badly amplified crooner ballads, smoky pimp and switchblade electric blues."[89]

Nor were Bourbon musicians confined to city limits. They often found secondary or off-season employment at the beach resorts of Biloxi, which bore the same relation to New Orleans as Atlantic City had to New York, or Ocean City to Baltimore and Washington. Adjacent Jefferson and St. Bernard Parishes offered gigs as well, some more debauched than their downtown counterparts, on account of their isolation and lively illicit gambling scenes. Highways 90, 61, and 51 put Bourbon Street within a few hours' drive of places like Pensacola, Mobile, the entire Mississippi Gulf Coast, Jackson, Baton Rouge, Lafayette, and Houston. Because weekend leisure tourists drove these modern motel-lined arteries into downtown New Orleans, Bourbon Street clubs, as they do today, positioned giant billboards along major ingresses and egresses advertising the likes of "Al Hirt and his Swingin' Dixie" at 501 Bourbon, or "Pete Fountain and his Jazz Group" at 600 Bourbon. "Even before you get to New Orleans," reported one 1959 recollection, "you can already tell . . . that . . . Bourbon Street [billed itself] as "the so-called 'Main Street of jazz.'"[90]

On The Street proper, venues that portrayed themselves as inheritors of the old-school jazz tradition arranged reverent bay-window displays of antique coronets, stained drums, yellowed newspaper clippings, and iconic album covers. Other clubs maintained glass cases with photographs of the jazz luminaries featured that night: "You've Seen Them on T.V., Heard Them on Radio . . . in movies . . . Here They Are in Person! No Minimum! No Cover!" The equestrian-themed Paddock Lounge was not alone when it indulged in two favorite Bourbon Street hyperboles, by declaring itself to be "Famous" (capital "F") as well as being "The Spot Where 'Jazz' Originated."[91]

But everyone except Bourbonites themselves seemed to realize that the strip's commercial success came at the expense of its artistic creativity. Striptease clubs outnumbered jazz venues by a twenty-to-five ratio in 1959, a predomination lessened only somewhat by the fact that strip clubs backed the dancers with live bands. Progressive jazz (bebop) aficionados found Bourbon's brand of jazz "second-rate" at best, and hackneyed at worst.[92] The reason: a clientele arriving with the specific aim of consuming a preconceived product can only be satisfied with the delivery of exactly that. "There are in New Orleans virtually no full-time gigs where the modern jazzman can develop his talent unfettered by commercial considerations," wrote a disappointed purist in 1961. "The tourist trade demands Dixieland bands and strip shows." Creative musicians, he continued, must "brave the anarchy of the neo-Dixie groups . . . in order to make a living. So it is that musicians like the bassist Oliver Felix turn up in Al Hirt's hell-bent-for-leather Dixie group, and talents like those of the alto saxophonist Don Lasday provide backgrounds for the bump-and-grind queens of Bourbon Street."[93] From this creativity-punishing, conformity-rewarding environment arose the musical stigma of modern Bourbon Street: the same acts in the same spaces reciting the same chestnuts to ever-changing audiences. "You have to play what the people want," lamented one jazzman, "or you're just not gonna get gigs."[94] The problem aired nationally in 1962 when *David Brinkley's Journal* devoted a full half-hour to the demise of jazz in the city of its birth. Positioned after a nostalgic opening piece on the last of the old-time dance halls, Brinkley's Bourbon coverage made The Street look like exactly what its detractors said it was: greedy, tacky, sleazy, and dumb. Viewers cringed at seeing aging black gentlemen employed by the Paddock Lounge succumbing to Uncle Tom antics for "bus loads" of frivolous white tourists, and playing "When the Saints Come Marching In" every hour on the hour while marching ridiculously out of the club and into the street. Worse, the ebulliently clueless owner used the nightly tableau to evidence to Mr. Brinkley that, in fact, "authentic" jazz was alive and well, right here in her club. Later in the program, a more sympathetic Bourbon club owner recounted how he reluctantly had to lay off his jazz band in favor of striptease because, overwhelmingly, the tourist dollar demanded it. Cut with B-roll shots of the Cat Girl, the Gunga Den, and sketchy barkers rattling come-ons to tipsy club hoppers, the broadcast had Bourbon-haters cheering, and Bourbonites shrugging it off as free advertising.[95]

Free advertising: Bourbon Street loved it, especially when it fell into its lap unbidden. National media representations of Bourbon mounted as The Street gained notoriety during World War II. Scenes from Paramount's *Swamp Fire* (1945) were filmed in the iconic Old Absinthe House, the same setting where the *We the People* radio show broadcast an installment in 1946. Director Elia Kazan shot Bourbon Street and other local scenes for his 1950 film noir *Panic in the Streets*. A year later he used the strip's musical din as an audio backdrop to his film version of *A Streetcar Named Desire*, which itself contained Bourbon references drawn from Tennessee Williams's time living a block from the strip. Musically, local jazzman Adolphe Paul Barbarin's "Bourbon Street Parade" (1949) portrayed The Street as a cheerful historic playground for out-of-towners flying and driving in, its lyrics seemingly torn out of the Chamber of Commerce's playbook.

At the opposite end of the media spectrum was *Naughty New Orleans*, a 1954 Rebel Pictures production that, despite its rank amateurism and one-sentence story line, rates as a valuable document of midcentury Bourbon Street. Filmed entirely on location, the adult feature (PG by modern standards) is structured weakly around the plot of a New Yorker visiting his New Orleans girlfriend whom he believes works as a secretary. In fact, she's Julianne, the Baby Doll of Bourbon Street, which he discovers inadvertently while taking in a burlesque show at the Moulin Rouge. What makes the film valuable is its use of real Bourbon Street characters performing their actual nightly shows for the camera, including a joke-cracking emcee; a slapstick comedy duo performing skits laced with double-entendres; famous striptease artists like the tassel-spinning Alouette LeBlanc, the Arabian-themed Lili St. Cyr, and buxom Tempest Storm; and black tap dancers Po'k Chop and Kidney Stew, who showcased their bulgy-eyed, lip-quivering vaudevillian antics. *Naughty New Orleans*'s low budget was its saving grace; it

Classic Bourbon Street burlesque acts, as depicted in Rebel Pictures' *Naughty New Orleans* (1954).

forced producers to document a piece of cultural history with minimal editorial interference. Watching it today is a reminder of just how much American society, as reflected by Bourbon Street, has changed since the 1950s.

Later that decade, the Elvis Presley musical *King Creole* (1958) told the story of a troubled French Quarter youth who got caught in the web of a "coarse, vulgar, very powerful" Bourbon Street kingpin. Filmed throughout the French Quarter, the movie showed the actual strip only fleetingly because, according to one local editorialist, they "took one look at [Bourbon Street's] neon and strip joints and rejected it as being just like *that* kind of street in every city in the nation." The movie's trailer, however, gave both Elvis and Bourbon their due: "They've Crowned a New King . . . On the Street Where Jazz Was Born!"[96] Indeed, *King Creole* probably did more to associate not jazz, but rock-and-roll with Bourbon, and within a few months of the movie's release, that genre would first gain a toehold on The Street. Rock remains the most-played musical style on Bourbon Street today.

The makers of *Bourbon Street Shadows* (1958) saw the neon strip very differently than *King Creole*'s scouts, relishing it with sweeping, on-location pans. An ominous voice boomed over the trailer, "Bourbon Street, a street like no other in the world. . . . A street that lives in the light, AND . . . *in the shadows.* Anything can happen—and does—on Bourbon Street, like: Strip time. Sex crime. MURDER. AND EVEN A LATIN AMERICAN REVOLUTION!" Bourbon Street fared better in a 1958 nationally televised program about jazz, which gave the Paddock Lounge favorable coverage despite The Street's nasty stigma. The relieved owner admitted she had been disturbed by all the recent bad press. "I don't have B-girls and I don't knowingly serve deviates," she remonstrated, "but I am feeling the pinch just like everyone else."[97] CBS's short-lived *Yancy Derringer* (1958–59), a Southern done in the style of a Western in the years after the Civil War, featured episodes such as "Nightmare on Bourbon Street."[98]

Yancy Derringer's two-year lifespan overlapped that of ABC's police detective series *Bourbon Street Beat*. Although it mostly filmed the show in California, the network nonetheless purchased a half interest in the Brennan family's Absinthe House restaurant in order to create a detective agency scene in the building's famous hidden floor. Opening with a grating theme song ("*Bourbon Street . . . BEAT!*") and a sequence of animated antique-lamppost cuts, the drama featured one of the very few African American characters on television at the time, musician Ed Cole (elder sibling of Nat King Cole), who played a pianist at the Absinthe bar.[99] *Bourbon Street Beat,* too, petered out after a couple of years, but not before millions more Americans gained exposure to this alluring and exotic street. Then came a sour note, that critical *David Brinkley's Journal* piece in 1962, which demonstrated that Bourbon Street, unsurprisingly, fared better in the hands of entertainment media than news media.

Bourbon Street's rising profile on film paralleled its musical enshrinement. Around the same time as the TV series, local jazzman Gaston Olivier penned "Crazy Mixed-Up Bourbon Street," a song described as "real two-beat hot stuff" designed to "'un-mix' the crazy mixed-up street [with a] 'dog scratching fleas' jazz tempo." The Dixieland tune was performed in 1959 by Joyce Mayo, recorded at Bourbon Street Records, and advertised to "bopsters, hopsters, jumpsters, humpsters, flipsters, and hipsters" as "the song that immortalized New Orleans' entertainment strip and strip entertainment."[100] The catchphrase "crazy mixed-up" became something of a slogan for Bourbon Street in the 1960s, appearing on postcards, brochures, and Mardi Gras doubloons. This era also saw the Bourbon Street image and name diffuse nationally, from a Bourbon Street nightclub in New York City to a theme park at Disneyland—free advertising all.[101]

Back in New Orleans, the notoriety garnered by the real Bourbon Street attracted national celebrities to its door, and that gave locals an opportunity to become famous themselves. A phone call from Lawrence Welk, who in 1957 sought a Dixieland musician for his weekly variety show, ended up making a part-time exterminator named Pete Fountain the nation's best-known clarinetist. Things didn't work out with Welk—"champagne and bourbon [Bourbon?] don't mix," he explained later—so he returned to New Orleans and leveraged his national exposure into a successful club career at the corner of Bourbon and St. Ann. "Bourbon Street is my love," he told an interviewer. "I went through the Conservatory of Bourbon Street."[102] Al Hirt, Fountain's friendly rival, gained comparable fame as a trumpeter which he similarly parlayed into sustained local success.[103] Together the twosome anchored the Bourbon Street jazz scene from the 1960s through the 1980s, and while they never pleased the purists and their national recognition waned over time, they always enjoyed celebrity status at home. Fountain and Hirt also illustrate the role that Bourbon Street has played repeatedly as a launching pad, base camp, or landing strip for broader fame.

Congestion in the postwar French Quarter inspired a number of proposals seeking to balance public access and public safety on Bourbon Street. Trucking companies boldly recommended widening the streets by narrowing the sidewalks, which was anathema to preservationists. The fire department proposed staggering deliveries to one side of the street at a time, which would have been difficult to administer. Others sought to ban oversized trucks from certain streets at certain times.[104] The problem diminished when the Desire streetcar line tracks and overhead wires were removed from Royal and Bourbon in 1948, and when neighborhood industries such as beer brewing, food processing, and warehousing closed or relocated. When mass tourism revived the congestion in the 1950s through the 1970s, authorities and civic groups experimented variously with parking by meter or resident pass, proscribing parking on commercial blocks, regulating truck deliveries, and instituting daytime and/or nighttime pedestrian malls.

Beyond traffic, a nocturnal stroll "down the Line" of midcentury Bourbon Street was quite an experience. Club signage would command the attention: oversized, over-the-top, winking, unctuous, chummy, and patronizing, its copy abounded in "incongruity, double entendre, and the well-turned phrase" in an era before irony.[105] The strip had a lot more neon lighting than today—it was in vogue, not yet retro—and it blinked, crawled, and pulsated colorfully. Unlike today, all the action was inside the clubs and along their interface with the sidewalk; no one walked in the street sipping drinks, and no revelers hung out on the balconies and galleries above. Upper floors at the time were well-utilized as residential space; "Rooms to Rent" signs were a common sight between clubs entrances, this being an era when living "above the store" was the norm for urban Americans. Nearly every club featured a locked glass display case posting the floor show schedules along with glib copy and girlie graphics, some of them dramatically "CENSORED" with strategically placed stickers. Famous buildings like the Old Absinthe House and the Judah Benjamin House extolled their historicity by hanging various historical Louisiana flags off the balcony. The Confederate battle flag was a particularly common sight in gift shops, on balconies, or at clubs like the Famous Door, which used it to emphasize the "Dixie" in Dixieland jazz.

Bourbon Street smelled of garbage in the 1950s but not nearly so much as it does today, because people walked the street destined for a club and not as a destination per se. One major change since the strip's halcyon days of the 1920s was the removal of the unsightly yet picturesque tangle of electrical and telephone wires overhead, strung from wooden poles amid shepherd's crook lampposts and streetcar cables. New Orleans had been ahead of the curve in burying its downtown utilities; the New Orleans Public Service, Inc. (NOPSI) started the costly

Mardi Gras on Bourbon Street, 1963–1965. These photographs, taken by pioneer news cameraman Del Hall, capture carnival revelry at a time when American cultural norms in everything from race and gender relations to public sexuality and behavior were rapidly transforming. Note the neat-casual attire of mostly uncostumed carousers, something that would disappear within a few years, as well as the intoxicated woman in the bottom photo, whose button reads, "Play with My Dog But Leave My Pussy Alone"—a sight that would have been deemed rather scandalous just a few years earlier. *Photographs by Del Hall; used with permission.*

More Mardi Gras scenes on Bourbon Street, 1963–1965. Note the absence of beads, balcony revelers, and litter, compared to similar scenes today, as well as the overwhelmingly white faces in these last years of *de jure* segregation. At bottom is Pete Fountain's Half-Fast Walking Club (with Fountain visible at lower center) making its way down Bourbon Street to the famed clarinetist's lounge at the St. Ann intersection. *Photographs by Del Hall; used with permission.*

project on Camp, St. Charles, Carondelet, and Baronne, from Canal to Lafayette Streets, in the 1920s and 1930s, and proceeded with the French Quarter, street by street, throughout the 1940s and 1950s.[106]

For all its frenetic energy, Bourbon Street operated in a bubble seemingly insulated from the social changes swirling around it. Citywide in the 1950s and 1960s, the white middle class decamped for the suburbs and took their tax dollars with them, even as gentry moved into the French Quarter. Regionally, new bridges were built across the Mississippi River and Lake Pontchartrain, enabling the centrifugal transfer of resources from core to periphery. Oil money fueled the growth of coastal Texas at south Louisiana's expense, initiating an intense and often reckless rivalry with Houston that would eventually transform New Orleans's skyline with towering office buildings, a widened Poydras Street, and the world-class domed stadium. Plans were also being laid for new federal interstates to crisscross through downtown, including a controversial riverfront expressway that would be visible, and perhaps audible, from Bourbon's cross streets.

The infrastructural changes were matched by social turmoil throughout the South, where blacks were taking to the streets demanding equality. Bourbonites and Quarterites had an unusual perch from which to witness this era, because preservation, tourism, gentrification, and an expatriated ethos had positioned them as somewhat detached spectators to change. No major organized protests, for instance, took place on or near Bourbon during the civil rights movement, despite The Street's national notoriety. One historian pointed out that "the city's dependence on tourism made white businesses in New Orleans peculiarly sensitive to the threat of disruption." Activists, for their part, prioritized for attaining basic rights in voting, education, and public accommodations; needlessly endangering their moral high ground by demanding equal access to overpriced booze and extravagant entertainment was unthinkable, particularly since the churchgoers who peopled the movement universally condemned such dens of iniquity regardless of race. And when getting inside a club meant black men ogling scantily clad white women, all the more toxic became the idea of a Bourbon Street protest. It's no coincidence that when protestors did stage a sit-in at a segregated national-chain Canal Street lunch counter, they choose not the Woolworth's at the corner of Bourbon, but the other one at Canal and Rampart. Resistance on the part of black New Orleanians instead came in subtle forms, such as progressive young black bebop musicians refusing to play the Dixieland jazz demanded by Bourbon clubs, which they viewed as Uncle Tom music.[107]

Resistance to segregation by whites was a different matter. Entertainer Chris Owens, who remains active on Bourbon Street today, recalled when her customers threatened "never [to] come back to my club" after she hired four African American girls to dance a watusi routine Owens had learned in Havana. She reluctantly had to let them go.[108] Black visitors who dared challenge Jim Crow, for their part, were met with racial rebukes and refusals of service citywide, particularly on Bourbon. The taunts mostly went unreported—until January 1965, when the American Football League's all-star team arrived at Moisant Airport for a marquee matchup at Tulane Stadium. Black players encountered discrimination as soon as they attempted to hail cabs; others were insulted and denied entry to hotels, French Quarter restaurants, and Bourbon Street clubs. There were exceptions: some black players received polite applause at Pete Fountain's and Al Hirt's Bourbon Street clubs, and, two weeks earlier, their counterparts on the Syracuse team competing in the Sugar Bowl reported no such problems. But when the twenty-one all-stars compared notes and found corroborating evidence of widespread racial hostility, they boycotted and forced the AFL to relocate the game at the last minute to Houston. The white establishment salted the wound by shrugging off the incident as a misinformed overreaction. "We are a very cosmopolitan and tolerant city," Mayor Victor Schiro explained, adding darkly, "but we are also a Southern city." Others accused the black boycotters of hurting their own cause by "humiliating a city that had come much more than halfway in friendship and acceptance." The nationally reported incident was an embarrassment to New Orleans, a victory for Houston, a setback for the New Orleans Sports and Cultural Activities Foundation's efforts to land an AFL or NFL franchise, and a costly loss for Bourbon Street.[109]

To say that white Bourbonites looked askance at the civil rights movement would be an understatement. Most were working-class second-generation immigrants who took no part in slavery, felt like they owed blacks nothing, and begrudged the competition for "their" jobs. Most sought to distance themselves socially from blacks, while declaring racial solidarity with old-line whites by almost hysterically advocating maintaining the segregationist order. Though too proud to acknowledge it, downtown white ethnics themselves had suffered certain indignities of stereotyping and discrimination, and, in the words of historian Edward Haas, "relied heavily upon their belief in white supremacy for solace."[110] Most Bourbonites supported segregation as much as anyone in the white community, particularly in schools. Bourbon Street's elite were generally more progressive, but not much, and not always. Literary couple Patrick and Deane Settoon Mernagh of 411-A Bourbon gained local notoriety penning poetic polemics with titles like *Mammy Liza's Appeal to Her People; The Pope Approves Segregation;* and *Uncle Ned Warns His People of the Dangers of Integration in Southern Schools.* These pamphlets were distributed far and wide by White Citizens Councils after *Brown v. Board of Education* in 1954. Printed by what the two white Bourbon-based authors described as "a wise and far-sighted Negro" publisher from Newark, *Mammy Liza* featured verse like "You's seen de ugly mongrel pup? Well, dat's what comes from mixin' up," and compared the idea of a black child in a white school to "a weevil in de white cornmeal."[111] Deane Mernagh often dressed up as a mammy in blackface and gave anti-integration lectures to local civic groups. Poets, writers, bons vivants, and archsegregationists, the Mernaghs hosted Spring Fiesta "Patio by Candlelight" groups in their Bourbon Street courtyard—a favored literati rendezvous at the time—where Deane gave tours of the slave quarters in her Mammy Liza character, complete with affected Negro dialect.[112] The *Times-Picayune* heralded the Mernaghs as "nationally regarded poets" and suggested that the *Mammy Liza* pamphlet was "helping to solve the segregation question."[113]

There was, however, one major snag to the Bourbonites' embrace of segregation, and that was when Jim Crow cost them money. New Orleans in the early 1960s remained one of the few major southern cities to enforce segregated lodging, a practice that came under increasing scrutiny as more professional and fraternal organizations had themselves integrated and looked for a host city to book their conventions. After a number of major events cancelled for fear of humiliating their black delegates, Famous Door club owner Hyp Guinle and Roosevelt Hotel owner Seymour Weiss conferred with the City Council. "When conventions with 1200 to 1400 people cancel out," Guinle confided, "we know it on Bourbon Street. We live on conventions." The tourism industry gnashed its teeth again in 1963 when 60,000 fun-loving American Legionnaires transferred their convention to Miami explicitly because of segregation, and took with them $6 million-plus in spending power. That same year, a race-based refusal of a guest at the Royal Orleans Hotel, one block off Bourbon, produced a lawsuit that landed in the docket of the New Orleans–based U.S. Fifth Circuit Court of Appeals.

Yet tourism stalwarts, who were deeply conflicted over this issue, hesitated to alienate their white friends and neighbors by speaking out for change. Weiss, for instance, clarified incomprehensibly to the City Council that he was not actually asking to repeal the segregation laws, but just observing that they threaten New Orleans's status as a major convention city. Two years later, his own Roosevelt

Hotel made national news when it refused a room to a black Puerto Rican Army colonel and hero of two wars, causing an infuriated Department of Defense to relocate its Adjutant General Association convention to the integrated Jung Hotel. That the Roosevelt incident occurred eleven months *after* federal judges ruled in the Royal Orleans case that segregated hotels were unconstitutional illustrates how southern establishments took their sweet time in complying with federal law. Even when the Civil Rights Act of 1964 outlawed de jure discrimination in restaurants, bars, clubs, and hotels, and went further by burdening proprietors with proof regarding accusations of de facto discrimination, it still took another six years of rulings before the message finally sunk in among white New Orleanians. After a federal court in 1967 struck down the old city ordinance segregating establishments selling alcohol for on-premise consumption, enterprises circumvented the law by suddenly declaring themselves to be members-only private clubs whenever unwanted patrons approached. Black visitors who got the private-club treatment on Bourbon Street lodged their complaints with the city's Human Relations Committee in July 1969, renewing concerns about boycotts and conference cancellations. Finally, the City Council itself banned racial discrimination in bars and public transportation with an ordinance in late December 1969.

Yet segregationists would still not let the turbulent decade end without one final fight. Eighty bar owners, including some on Bourbon Street, filed suit against the city on the grounds that the ordinance would produce civic strife and disorder, and that their "businesses will be ruined by loss of white customers."[114] A judge restrained enforcement of the ordinance pending a hearing in the new year. That last segregationist victory proved to be short-lived, as the Civil District Court judge who heard the case swiftly upheld the ordinance. Undeterred, lawyers for the bar owners took the case to the Louisiana Fourth Circuit Court of Appeal, which also upheld. Next they appealed to the Louisiana Supreme Court, which upheld as well. Then the lawyers went to federal court, arguing audaciously that it was *their* clients who had actually suffered discrimination because the ordinance targeted bars but unfairly exempted barber shops and beauty salons, and was therefore unconstitutional. Federal judge Herbert W. Christenberry rejected that argument absolutely on January 15, 1970, but the mentality behind it persisted.[115] Into the early 1970s, Bourbon Street venues advertised for "white dancers—no experience necessary, will teach," or for a "colored, light complexion, neat hatcheck,"[116] and the *Times-Picayune* continued to print racialized want ads (at a rate of about fifteen per day in 1972) because of a loophole in the 1964 Civil Rights Act exempting smaller firms from employment discrimination.[117] Even-

Carnival exuberance at the climactic intersection of Bourbon and St. Peter, Mardi Gras, 1963. Note the Bourbon Orleans Hotel under construction in the background, and Dixie's Bar of Music at lower left (now the Cat's Meow karaoke club), one of Bourbon's premier gay-friendly businesses at the time. Note also how the crowds begin to peter out past the Orleans and St. Ann intersection in the distance, as they do today. This area, since at least the 1950s, has marked the transition of Bourbon Street from straight to gay space, a sexual geography very much alive today. *Photographs by Del Hall; used with permission.*

tually the newspaper dropped the practice, owners ostensibly conformed, and racism went underground. Discriminatory incidents would continue on Bourbon Street to the present, but no longer would they have an explicit or indifferent law on their side.

Demographically Bourbon Street's environs were transforming as well. Sicilian immigrants, who had replaced French Creole families from the 1870s to the 1910s, were by the 1930s and 1940s climbing the economic ladder themselves and casting their eyes toward the new whites-only subdivisions by the lake. By mid-century, they had emulated their affluent antecedents and decamped the cramped old Quarter for those trendier environs, places like Lakeview and Gentilly, or left Orleans Parish altogether for St. Bernard or Jefferson. Most French Creole families had departed by the late 1910s, and the few remaining finally left around World War II. One combat veteran encouraged his French Quarter family to sell their ancestral house "because it's more quiet on the battlefield!"[118] In their stead came not a new wave of immigrants, nor poor locals, but prosperous professionals from out of town.

Census statistics capture the Quarter's transformation from a rustic old neighborhood of working-class folk visited by thousands, to a famous historic district with a gentrified population visited by millions.[119] Between 1920 and 1930, when nightclubs were first opening on Bourbon Street, the central and lower Quarter lost 23–25 percent of its population while the tract nearest the commercial end of Bourbon lost 48 percent. By 1940, a total of 11,053 people remained in the French Quarter: 880 in the most mostly commercial upper tract, and 5,426 and 4,747 in the mostly residential central and lower tracts, respectively. Those figures changed by -24, -13, and +33 percent by 1950, when 9,530 people lived in the Quarter. By 1960, tract populations declined by -20, -16, and -32 percent, leaving 7,669 denizens. Over the next ten years they declined further by -27, -30, and -53 percent, such that by 1970, only 5,257 residents remained.[120]

A closer look at the figures shows deeper social change: fewer children, fewer blacks, fewer ethnic whites, more transplants, higher housing prices, and higher incomes—a social transformation that would later be termed "gentrification." The French Quarter in the first half of the twentieth century was home to multigenerational families with children; in 1940, for example, more than 1 out of every 7 residents was below age fourteen, and more than 1 out of 4 was below age twenty-four. By 1990, those figures were, incredibly, 1 out of 50, and 1 out of 11, respectively. At least five schools operated in the Quarter in the 1940s, educating local children; by the 1970s, there were only two, and most of their students were bussed in. The early-1900s Quarter also exhibited much of the door-to-door racial and ethnic diversity of historical times: in 1940, 20 percent of Quarterites were black, not too far off from the 30-percent citywide figure. Fifty years later, however, the Quarter was less than 5 percent black, although the city by then was 62 percent black. Housing values in the Quarter went from roughly the same as the rest of the city in 1940 to two to three times more than the citywide median in 1990. Incomes rose similarly, from markedly below the city median in 1950 to well above it in 1990, and in one tract, nearly double.

Gender proportions also shifted. New Orleans has long been majority-female, by a ratio of around 53 to 47. But in the French Quarter, men outnumber women, and by a widening gap. In 1940, the French Quarter was 53.7 male, whereas the city was 47.4 male; in 1990, the Quarter was 61.9 percent male in a city that was only 46.5 percent male. Behind this change was another brewing societal revolution, the uncloseting of homosexuality.

Like most big port cities, New Orleans long harbored an underground gay population, if not a community. The same factors that made this city and this neighborhood tolerant of heterosexuality in overdrive—transience, diversity, cosmopolitanism, anonymity, festivity, escapism—spilled over into same-sex relationships, and made everyday life here less alienating for gays than elsewhere. Their gravitation to the French Quarter occurred as a component of the same 1920s–1930s in-migration of creative people that brought in the likes of Lyle Saxon and Tennessee Williams. Spatially clustering in the Quarter minimized exposure to intolerance and maximized access to social capital and economic opportunity. The district's architecture and ambience certainly played a role: gay males have long found historic neighborhoods appealing and excelled at restoring them, perhaps on the grounds of the aestheticism, romanticism, domesticity, and culture-keeping associated with this population (and also with straight society women, who costarted the preservation movement).[121] A psychological connection may be involved as well, as New Orleans, with its marginalization, splendor, decadence, and cultural renaissance, seems to have characteristics typical of classic gay icons. Might the world wars have played a role? Soldiers "undesirably discharged" (the term at the time) for homosexual activity, finding themselves unceremoniously dumped at the port from which they departed and unable to return home, accelerated the growth of San Francisco's gay community in the 1940s, and it's possible that the same thing happened in New Orleans. Whatever their reason for coming, once the charter generation of gay Quarterites reached a threshold, their community solidarity and opportunities attracted additional migrants.

That threshold was passed in the French Quarter during the 1930s and 1940s. The 1940 Census suggests that the Quarter had roughly 700 more males than if it had the same gender ratio as the rest of the city. Of course, not all these men were gay, but when we adjust for undercounting of roommates and transients, and add in outside residents who utilized the Quarter's gay-friendly social spaces, a midcentury community of more than a thousand comes into focus. That demographic was sufficiently large and cohesive by the mid-1930s for Café Lafitte's Bar, operating in the old blacksmith shop on Bourbon corner St. Philip, to become the most popular of a smattering of clandestine gay-friendly hangouts. It had enough members by 1949 to warrant the founding of the Fat Monday Luncheon Club, a gay men's association that has been marching every Lundi Gras since. Homosexuality had become sufficiently visible by that time for the poetically inclined Bourbon Street cynic known as William Tell to jab the "gay boys," as he called them, in his 1949 *Beat of Bourbon Street*:

> For you'll find up there in the Twilight Set—
> The kind that swish and swosh:
> Where the ones who swish say "Goodness,"
> And the ones who swosh say "Gosh . . ."
> For the sex is all confusing—
> It's like picking posh from pish;
> So we'll call them neuter gender
> And away from there we'll swish.[122]

Swoshing and swishing aside, gay expression remained socially suppressed and legally penalized, except during Carnival, and that drove it into scattered and furtive spaces. Meeting places could be found in certain Pontalba buildings, at Victor's Café on Chartres, at James' Beer Parlor on Royal at Toulouse, or along the dark, narrow Exchange Alley and the adjacent "monkey wrench corner" of lower Royal and Chartres Streets.[123] Nearly all gay bars erected some sort of barrier blocking curious outsiders from peering inside, or else they directed same-sex interactions to an upper floor or rear room. Fear of humiliating police raids and a public outing in the local newspaper drove gay spatialities in this era.

Tourism and more in-migration brought a bit more cohesiveness to gay geography after World War II. For one, Dixie's Bar of Music, founded in 1939 by Irma and Dixie Fasnacht—"Miss Dixie," a musician who was lesbian—on St. Charles Avenue, relocated in 1949 to 701 Bourbon, where the likes of Truman Capote, Tennessee Williams, and Helen Hayes paid visits. A few years later, Café Lafitte lost its lease on the old blacksmith shop, and when the new business operating therein proved unwelcoming, the old business decamped to the next corner up-river, 901 Bourbon, and dubbed itself Café Lafitte's in Exile (1953).[124] Together, Dixie's and Lafitte's in Exile "became the twin hubs of gay life, with exclusively gay patronage."[125] The two bars made homosexuality visible, particularly during Mardi Gras, and rendered this stretch of Bourbon Street New Orleans's first best example of what today would be called "queer space." Evidence comes in the forms of jokes of the era. Mayor Morrison, for example, once toasted, "Here's to Bourbon Street, where men are men—at least 9 times out of ten." Columnist Howard Jacobs wrote about a lisping Bourbon Street barker enticing "swish hitters" by paraphrasing Huey Long: "Here every man is a king except for a few queens."[126] Evidence also comes from police blotters, because the clustering of gay bars gave police a convenient target to enforce Louisiana's laws on obscenity, sodomy, and crimes against nature. Records from the 1954 Special Citizens Investigating Committee describe the Driftwood, Dan's International, and Tony Bacino's (all near Bourbon and Toulouse), Dixie's, Eric's Bar & Restaurant, and Lafitte's in Exile, among others, as "pervert hangouts," and documented evidence of "juves" (juveniles), lewd behavior, criticism or jokes about the police department—even questionable drink names like the "Fairy Flip" (sixty cents).[127] The clustering also made this area vulnerable to violent homophobes. In 1958, for example, three Tulane students targeted Café Lafitte's in Exile with the stated intention of "rolling a queer," the old phrase for gay bashing. The trio ended up bludgeoning to death one Fernando Rios, a Mexican national who worked as a tour guide. When the case went to court, the Mexican government retained the services of an up-and-coming attorney named James C. Garrison to aid the prosecution, but to no avail. The Tulanians were quickly acquitted by a twelve-man jury, which had been pointedly informed by the defense that silk panties had been found on Rios's person.[128]

At the nexus of the emerging gay space was the St. Ann Street intersection, and for this reason the so-called "lavender line" exists along St. Ann today, dividing straight and gay Bourbon with remarkable exactitude. Why here? The proximate reason was the ca. 1950s gay patronage of a handful of bars sprinkled between the 500 and 900 blocks, particularly Dixie's and Lafitte's in Exile. The

Mardi Gras was the one day each year when homosexuality came out of the closet and, dressed to the nines, made a grand appearance in the public space. Police raids of gay hang-outs would resume the next day, and the sort of eroticism and cross-dressing seen in these 1962–1965 photographs would go back underground. *Photographs by Del Hall; used with permission.*

ultimate reason was because Bourbon at St. Ann formed the point at which the seven-block-long line of predominantly straight tourist-oriented commercial blocks of upper Bourbon intersected the increasingly gay residential neighborhood of the lower Quarter. That community would later play an influential role in Bourbon Street society.

Meanwhile, other gay-tolerant bars operated surreptitiously off Bourbon in their historically scattered pattern. Arrests in 1954–55 were made on legal grounds such as "Solicitation for unnatural acts by homos" at Cy's Lounge at 435 Esplanade, Mack's Villa Court at 111 Chartres, the Midship Bar at 606 Iberville, at the Village Bar at 608 Iberville (charge: "indecent solicitation by homosexuals in presence of owner"), and at Retreat Bar at 1334 Magazine. Men seeking men who wanted to avoid the facial identification of the bar scene took their risks cruising places like Cabrini Park in the lower Quarter. There, gay men knew they could meet gay men, but so did gay bashers and hostile policemen.[129]

The captains of Bourbon Street had long worked City Hall to their advantage, a task that made them inherently conservative and wary of political change. Chep Morrison was their kind of mayor: he talked the talk of reform, placating the shrill old dames bellyaching about preserving this and prohibiting that. But when it got down to business, Morrison met the Bourbonites more than halfway, generally letting them master their own domain, and even hanging out with them. That cozy relationship started to change, however, when Morrison's political fortunes declined in the late 1950s. His eyes fixed on the national horizon, Morrison parlayed his Latin American predilection into an appointment by President Kennedy as ambassador to the Organization of American States. New Orleans would be getting a new mayoral administration, and that made Bourbon Street nervous.

Councilman Victor Schiro finished Morrison's term and campaigned for his own mayoral election in the March 1962 primary, running heavily on a segregationist stance. Of working-class Italian stock, Schiro seemed like someone the Bourbonites could handle. But the election was fraught with unknowns, premier among them the Office of District Attorney primary contest. That race pitted incumbent Richard Dowling against the towering and outspoken but little-known Jim Garrison, the same attorney who had prosecuted the Tulane "queer rolling" four years earlier. Bourbon crime and vice had long been a rallying cry for reformers; Garrison knew it played well among voters, and he went out of his way to shine light on it during his campaign. A few days before the election, he went public with documents purporting to show fourteen Bourbon Street club owners contributing to Dowling's campaign—clubs that had previously been charged with "possession of narcotics, B-drinking, theft, obscenity and lewdness." The charges were ironic because Dowling had spearheaded a crackdown on these activities back in 1958, pinching so many strippers that one club held a benefit to raise funds for their bail.[130] No matter: Garrison, who was prone to hurling incendiary charges, had been pressing this accusation in televised debates, using his six-foot-six frame and acerbic bearing to his advantage. "Can you blame Mr. Dowling for wanting to obscure these facts?" Garrison asked incredulously. "And yet he is asking you, the voters, to put him in office for four more years."[131] They didn't, by a slim margin, sending Garrison into an April runoff against Republican Carroll Montet. Garrison upped the ante on his anti-Bourbon platform when, in an interview, he drew a direct financial link between syndicated crime activity and Bourbon Street club ownership. "Prosecution in this area will need special attention, [but] the first step toward a change," he reminded voters, "will be the selection of personnel—D.A.'s and investigators."[132]

On April 3, 1962, voters selected both Garrison and Schiro over their Republican opponents by ratios of roughly six to one.[133] Now District Attorney Jim Garrison, who shook his fist at Bourbon Street publicly but partook of its erotic pleasures privately, had anti-Bourbon supporters who needed to be thanked, pro-Bourbon enemies who needed to be punished, and a golden opportunity to become a rising star in a brand-new city government.[134]

Garrison took some months to staff up and strategize. He calculated that burlesque clubs were costly operations with big staffs, and could only turn a handsome profit if they ran illicit moneymaking schemes on the side. *Knock out those schemes, and the clubs close; Bourbon Street is cleaned up, and Jim Garrison is a hero.* In August, an ultimatum went out against a litany of violations, among them insufficient lighting, aggressive barkers, illegal nudity, serving juveniles, handbook, narcotics, prostitution, and homosexuality. But Garrison had to choose his battles carefully. Carlos Marcello and his mobsters controlled handbook more than any other racket, so better not to kick that beehive. And prostitution? Garrison had some of his own skeletons in that closet, in more ways than one. That left B-drinking as a target, and a worthy target it was. B-drinking had developed into an elaborate and lucrative racket—Venus Fly Traps, they called them—since the old days of flirting for cocktails. Now it involved B-girls coyly enticing a "mark" to treat for costly liquor, starting with overpriced mixed drinks and working incrementally up to hundred-dollar bottles of champagne. The more "lush" he became, the more the potations would come unsolicited, and the less likely it became that he would get his change. This continued until either the mark's money ran out or his interest shifted to sex, in which case, if he were lucky, the conspiring Salomé would guide him to an off-site crib to make the transaction. Else he would get escorted to a backroom, "rolled" by an in-house thug, robbed of whatever cash remained, and jettisoned into an alley. A mark who refused to drink or otherwise managed to maintain his faculties was prone to be knocked flat with a Mickey Finn and subsequently rolled. One mark could easily bring in hundreds of dollars in a well-oiled B-drinking racket.[135]

Clubs reacted warily to the sting rumors, and, hoping to stave off a full-blown crackdown, toned things down and policed themselves. The Bourbon Street Association of Nightclubs issued a set of standards, and owner-members passed the marching orders down to their employees.[136] In one club, a foul-mouthed stripper got a tongue-lashing from a nervous bartender worried about an obscenity violation. In another, suspected undercover cops were pressed to dance the Twist in the hope of revealing their affiliation.[137] As Garrison's agents furtively infiltrated the clubs, it became apparent that this was going to be a costly operation: to maintain credibility while undercover, agents had to spent enormous sums on alcohol as they gathered their evidence. Three agents who targeted six clubs for five nights in November, for example, spent $1,850 on B-girl prostitutes with names like Cookie, Candy, Sexy Debbie, and Tempest Storm. That was nearly half of what a typical blue-collar New Orleans household earned in a year, and it raised eyebrows inside and outside of city government. But the expenditures got Garrison the goods, and he demanded continued budgetary support from the criminal district court judges. Continued funding became a flashpoint between the old-line judges and the brash young maverick, who made sure the press knew that he had to borrow thousands of dollars under his own name to keep the sweep going.[138]

The arrests mounted. On August 22, twelve people were arrested at three Bourbon clubs on B-drinking charges, followed by another twenty by month's end. Garrison's high-profile tactics incited a feud with Superintendent of Police Joe Giarrusso, who, fearing that the public might sense he was not doing his job, pointed out that *his* men had made 326 vice arrests within the First District (French Quarter) since Garrison took office, including 144 for gambling, 79 for prostitution, 59 for B-drinking, 14 barkers, 13 for alcohol violations, and 57 for "crime against nature," while Garrison's people had made only 59.

It made no difference to the Bourbon clubs who was arresting whom; the crackdowns were affecting their bottom line fundamentally. Garrison's strategy was dead-on: without a stream of illicit income, a typically lavish burlesque operation with ornate décor and a staff of dozens struggled to survive. It *had* to rip off patrons. By September, some Bourbon clubs were reluctantly considering downgrading their format, while others were "sweating it out." Garrison pounced on the symbiotic relationship between B-drinking and striptease: kill one and you kill the other. He thrilled a VCPORA audience by predicting on September 19, "I don't think there is going to be a single strip joint left by early spring."[139] After a busy Saturday night that brought in desperately little cash, fifteen Bourbon strip clubs shuttered in protest. Days and weeks went by and most remained closed. Others had their doors "padlocked," a term not heard on The Street since the days of Prohibition.

Bourbon Street was in trouble. It could no longer bring to bear the likes of "Little Mayor" Gaspar Gulotta to smooth things over with the politicos. And, given its history of prioritizing for short-term individual gain over the long-term betterment of the commons, Bourbon Street proved incapable of speaking with a united voice, failed to cultivate public sympathy, and neglected to hire top guns to defend its interests. But it did not take the attacks lying down. From his headquarters at 522 Bourbon, vice president of the Bourbon Street Association of Night Clubs and Gunga Den owner Lawrence J. "Larry" LaMarca complained bitterly to Councilman-at-Large Joseph V. DiRosa about the "wild charges" by "headline hunting" Jim Garrison. He offered physical evidence of undercover operations against his own Gunga Den and the Club Hotsy Totsy, which yielded zero violations yet ended up hectoring his employees with spurious profanity arrests. The association professed legal and moral indignation and, rather naively, offered a deal: "Any time the authorities agree to enforce the law *totally* and *impartially* and not try to use Bourbon Street as a convenient method of making spectacular headlines for themselves, Bourbon Street clubs will reopen."[140] LaMarca also suggested to Councilman DiRosa a more permanent solution: Why not simply legalize employee-customer mingling, let them solicit all the drinks they want, and tax any clubs that were so licensed? Las Vegas, after all, had legalized gambling, and Mississippi had figured out a way to tax black-market liquor. Insurance salesmen solicited coverage; car dealers solicited automobiles; why not showgirls drinks? As if confiding in a buddy, LaMarca explained to DiRosa the facts of life, Bourbon Street style:

Scenes from Larry LaMarca's famous Gunga Den Night Club in the early 1960s, showing star Linda Brigette and other dancers, with club rules ("No Mingling with Customers") posted on the dressing room wall. These photographs were captured by New Orleans native and WWL-TV journalist Del Hall, who later became a Chicago-based cameraman for CBS News. *Photographs by Del Hall; used with permission.*

New Orleans has always been known as a convention town, Joe, and to call a spade a spade, nothing draws conventioneers as much as girls. [Most] are not seeking sex per se; [rather,] they are curiosity seekers. In many instances, this is their first exotic show. They have a desire to talk, not to just any girl, but a show girl. They want to ask (almost invariably), how did she happen to get into this business[?][141]

LaMarca also fought back by co-opting the other side's methods. He instructed association members to require customers to sign paperwork before buying a girl a drink—proof positive, he thought, that B-drinking was not occurring. Madame Francine's at 440 Bourbon printed up slips that read, "I have personally requested this entertainer, ———, to join me for a drink," followed by a signature and date. It was enough to douse anyone's fires, but it yielded results: Two undercover cops casually signed the slips (realizing that not doing so would have blown their cover) as they treated "Kathy" and "Laurie" to drinks—and then unceremoniously arrested them for B-drinking. A breathlessly outraged Larry LaMarca sent the evidence straight to Mayor Schiro, berating the Alcohol Beverage Ordinance and plaintively asking the mayor: "How long does anyone expect the businessmen on Bourbon Street, who have large investments and who are sincerely trying to improve relations [toward] making the Quarter a bigger and better tourist attraction, to remain in business if they are ceaselessly subjected to his type of harassment?"[142] The threats, the drink slips, the pleading: all failed to compel nervous council members to relent, much less Mayor Schiro or District Attorney Garrison. The public and the press were watching, and siding with the Bourbon Street dons nowadays would produce more costs and fewer benefits than in times past. So the raids intensified and the closures increased. By year's end, El Morocco at 200 Bourbon, Jazz Limited at 201 Bourbon, and Guys and Dolls at 418 Bourbon were ordered padlocked for a year, while the Flamingo Club and Club Sultana at 405 and 423 Bourbon were next on the lawsuit list. Most were not literally padlocked and could remain open pending appeals, but because they had to behave impeccably, many decided to cut their losses and close up anyway. Two additional joints had their liquor license renewals declined, which is the kiss of death on Bourbon Street. In all, twenty-four downtown clubs had closed, and a single night in December yielded an additional twenty-two prostitution arrests. Bourbon-haters in organizations like VCPORA heralded Garrison as a hero, while those dependent on Bourbon income, from cabbies to clubbers, loathed him and bitterly reminded anyone who would listen about Garrison's own carousing. One proprietor estimated that Bourbon business had dropped by 40 percent since the raids, and he was probably underestimating to hide his under-the-table losses. Strippers and prostitutes, who endured degradation and risk for their incomes, found themselves in jail, out of work, or hitting the road. Even madam Norma Wallace, who had overseen the delivery end of the French Quarter sex industry since Prohibition, finally met her match in Garrison. The press generally cheered the crackdown, but occasionally betrayed a sentiment that a colorful era was coming to an end. One newspaper editorialist pondered, "Final chapters in the Bourbon Street fantasy—Is this strip necessary?"[143]

The Bourbon Street crackdown, costly as it was financially and priceless as it was politically, introduced tensions to competing branches of government. As Garrison battled the Criminal District Court judges over funding, the New Orleans Police Department tried to beat the district attorney at his own game by intensifying its own vice raids. One sting in May 1963 netted more than forty arrests (including Tempest Storm) in just one night, in full public view. Mayor Schiro also wanted a piece of the politically rewarding action, proposing ordinances "aimed at toning down the strippers' routines and stopping their mingling with male customers"—laws that, incidentally, would undercut Garrison's costly but high-profile undercover sting operations.[144] The antimingling laws were quickly judged unconstitutional but not before more clubs shuttered under the growing cloud of uncertainty. The so-called Chaplain of Bourbon Street, Reverend Bob Harrison, got closed down himself when the Circus Club, where he had been ministering, got busted.[145]

Garrison, meanwhile, was not about to hand over his great crusade to his competition. He fought back using his penchant for eviscerating enemies with allegations that were usually questionable and sometimes libelous. After he accused his budget-withholding nemeses at the Orleans Parish Criminal District Court of laziness and racketeering in late 1962, eight judges sued Garrison and got him convicted in a state court of violating the Louisiana Criminal Defamation Statute. Garrison appealed to the Louisiana Supreme Court, but it, too, rejected his contention that the law and the conviction violated his First Amendment rights. He appealed to the highest court in the land, and in November 1964, he emerged victorious when the U.S. Supreme Court unanimously found that Garrison's criticism of public officials was not only constitutional, but essential to a democracy. *Garrison v. Louisiana* started in the striptease joints of Bourbon Street and ended up making legal history by clarifying and strengthening Americans' right to freedom of speech. It also sent the triumphant Jim Garrison, having whipped

Bourbon Street, the judges, *and* the Louisiana Supreme Court, in search of a new crusade.[146]

Demoralized Bourbon club owners licked their wounds and looked for new lines of work. As if to add injury to insult, a fire broke out one night in 1964 at 223–225 Bourbon, causing $20,000 damage nearly to the point of structural collapse. A charred ruin in a key gateway block seemed to both symbolize and exacerbate the degeneration of the strip.[147] The tragic death in an airplane crash of former mayor Chep Morrison, a longtime friend of The Street, deepened the malaise. Tourists noticed the changes on Bourbon, and many were not happy. "About ten years ago I visited New Orleans and found it to be one of the few charming cities in the United States," wrote a man from Miami in December 1964, after the raids had noticeably lobotomized the strip:

> Bourbon [Street] was delightfully different, beautifully old, tingling with electric excitement, fine food and adult sensuality. I returned a month ago and was shocked to find [that] most of the old places are closed, the excitement is largely gone, and modern hotels, like bulls in a China shop, are being built in the heart of the Quarter. . . . Crusaders "cleaned up" Miami Beach a few years ago the same way you are cleaning up your French Quarter, and [it] subsequently opened up its first retirement home.[148]

The passage of time tempts us to view Jim Garrison's 1962–64 vice raids as the death knell of the colorful, sexy, edgy, glory days of postwar Bourbon Street. New Orleanians love to wax nostalgic about the "golden age" of this and the "halcyon days" of that, and Bourbon Street is no exception. Just as the notion of authenticity requires something else to be inauthentic, romanticized revisions of the past legitimize our bemoaning the dreary present. Problems exist, however, in the "good ol' days" interpretation. For one, few people thought of Bourbon Street in its midcentury days as glorious, golden, or good. Conservatives hated The Street on religious grounds, liberals hated it on social grounds, preservationists hated it visually, jazz buffs musically, and neighbors civically. Women were regularly exploited for money on Bourbon Street, as were a wide range of human vulnerabilities, from loneliness to desire, from escapism to wagering. The few people who might have viewed midcentury Bourbon Street as glorious were either smart patrons who knew to evade the strip's predators, or the predators who devoured the strip's fools.

And that's how Jim Garrison really did change Bourbon Street: he understood that predatory activities were imperative to the financial viability of burlesque venues: the bigger and fancier the club, the slimmer the profit margin, and the greater the need to subsidize the enterprise with illicit side projects. Indeed, some venues could be better described as vice mills hiding behind entertainment rather than entertainment venues that dabbled in vice. By cracking down on the illegal but lucrative side shows, Garrison made the legal but costly main attraction untenable. So the Cat Girl strayed, the Oyster Girl withdrew into her shell, the Tassel Spinner stilled her swirls, the emcees bowed out, the doorman became a bouncer, and the old-school, over-the-top, colorfully corrupt nightclubs clicked off the neon and vacated the premises. In their space, inevitably, opened businesses that were, yes, legal, but also cheap—cheap to run, cheap in appearance, and cheap in spirit. They had to be. If the new venues could still be called nightclubs, they were bare-bones, and in short time they devolved to tawdry strip joints with a trinket shop on either side.

Garrison's timing had been good. His raids took place shortly after the Bourbon Street establishment of the 1920s to the 1950s had lost its ringleaders. "Little Mayor" Gaspar Gulotta, who would have resolved this tiff with a few strategically placed phone calls and a back-slapping round of drinks, had died in 1957. He was followed in death by Diamond Jim Moran, Sam Saia, and Dutch Kraut, who, as career gangsters who made an awful lot of money on Bourbon Street, had long kept the strip's potentially riotous ne'er-do-wells on their best behavior, while keeping the politicians and the police on pay and at bay. Their passing deprived Bourbon Street of its arsenal of political skullduggery—a decades-old memory bank of who's on the dole, who owes whom a favor, who's got a skeleton in his closet—and the diplomatic skills to deliver it with style. The ringleader deaths of the late 1950s and the vice raids of the early 1960s made Bourbon Street less appealing as a destination for dirty New York and Chicago money in need of laundering. Las Vegas, which lagged behind Bourbon Street in the 1940s and competed with it in the 1950s, became the new municipal magnet for mobsters, and it pulled ahead of Bourbon Street and New Orleans in the 1960s—way ahead—and never looked back. "Wiseguys stopped coming to the Quarter for pleasure or business," recalled one crony. "Burlesque clubs, bars, and lounges began to close, and the ones that didn't close became less extravagant, less clean, and less profitable."[149] Old-line organized crime continued to dabble with Bourbon Street into the 1970s and 1980s, but it became less organized, more fragmented, increasingly geriatric, and ultimately incapacitated.

Bohemian Bourbon Street took a beating as well in this era. One of the favorite hangouts of the Quarter's connoisseurs and eccentrics was the Bourbon House Bar and Restaurant, which opened in 1936. Among patrons such as William Faulkner, Tennessee Williams, and Lyle Saxon were artists, musicians, and actors, "strippers, doctors, lawyers . . . judges, a district attorney and some members of the City Council," as well as neighborhood characters with names like Hank the Man, Pete the Hat, the Big E, the legless Mr. Jimmy, and Banjo Annie, who once gave Burl Ives strumming lessons. For years its upper gallery was screened in, West Indian style, as if reflecting the expatriated sentiments of its occupants. The Bourbon House closed in 1964 ostensibly because it lost its lease, but the underlying reason was the crowding out of local clientele, local ownership, locally relevant commerce, and locally sensitive pricing by Bourbon Street tourism. Pondering the end of an era, the Bourbon House's longtime manager described the joint as a "cultural landmark . . . that gained a national reputation because it maintained its neighborhood atmosphere on a street that [otherwise] went commercial." Hundreds of people came out to witness the Bourbon House's jazz funeral on September 30, 1964.[150] The procession might well have mourned all of Bourbon, so much had changed on The Street.

As for Jim Garrison, he succeeded in finding his next crusade all too well. It involved not the peccadilloes of Bourbon Street, but the crime of the century. Motivated by his craving for heroism and burdened by his propensity for reckless dot-connecting and wild accusations, Garrison began investigating rumors about local connections to the assassination of President John F. Kennedy. After concocting a preposterous conspiracy and convincing himself of its veracity, Garrison arrested and prosecuted a local man named Clay Shaw—civic luminary, preservationist, and a member of the lower French Quarter closeted gay community who socialized in Bourbon Street bars. The 1969 trial, which garnered national attention, ended abruptly when an astute jury speedily found Shaw not guilty—but not before the case shined blinding light on the French Quarter's two worst-kept secrets: its gay population and its Mafia connections. Both would feature prominently in countless Kennedy conspiracy books, and in Oliver Stone's 1991 film *JFK*. Garrison's malicious and ultimately futile pursuit of Clay Shaw, whose subsequent financial and physical decline led to a premature death in 1974, ended up putting his own career on trial, and when it fizzled, his career flatlined. Garrison turned himself into his own victim, just as, in the words of writer Christine Wiltz, he "turned the French Quarter into the very thing he said he despised."[151]

Mardi Gras on Bourbon Street, 1964–1965. *Photograph by Del Hall; used with permission.*

How Bourbon Street Degenerated
Late 1960s–1970s

Bourbon Street delocalized on a number of levels in the mid-1960s. Garrison's raids flushed out the old-school nightclubs and Old World shenanigans, and a fair portion of the locals behind them. Federal civil rights legislation trumped local public accommodations laws, leading to the de jure desegregation of The Street. Working-class white neighbors fled for the suburbs, and in their stead came out-of-town gentry. Containerization zapped thousands of local port jobs, and authorities looked to tourism to fill the gap. What they saw was untapped potential but also much work to be done, on both the demand and supply sides.

On the demand side of the tourism market, transformations in American society had to be taken into account. The dinner-and-a-show scene had grown musty and square. Seersucker suits got tossed for T-shirts and dungarees, and crew cuts grew shaggy. Jazz succumbed to scruffy rock-and-roll cover bands. The tuxedoed emcee stepped down for someone called a deejay; the door-man, for a bouncer. Show-sex became sexier and sleazier, as it competed with new pornographic movies; the restrained titillation of choreographed strip-tease yielded to stilted onstage "love acts." Modern jet travel, interstate connectivity, credit cards, and corporate expense accounts promised to deliver the new mass tourism to Bourbon, but only if The Street accommodated it.

On the supply side, the spacious new Rivergate Exposition Hall at the foot of Canal, coupled with the end of segregation in public accommodations, green-lighted the expansion of the convention trade. Developers, many of them out-of-town corporations, eyed the French Quarter and Bourbon Street for potential lodging sites and, partnering with local real estate experts, found them in abundance. A new abbreviation appeared in the paperwork of Bourbon Street—*Inc.*—and the postmarks came from places like Dallas, Houston, and Memphis. New faces and surnames came as well, and they were less likely to be Sicilian or Creole and more likely to be Jewish or Anglo.

The idea of a major new French Quarter hotel first surfaced in 1946 from the agency tasked to preserve the neighborhood. The Vieux Carré Commission, which at the time worked closely with commercial interests, deemed that there were "numerous potential sites and places where buildings could be torn down without any great loss to [the] historic character of the quarter."[1] One site was the empty lot on St. Louis Street where once stood the old St. Louis Exchange. Owner Edgar B. Stern envisioned a major hotel for his property in 1957, and with assistance from Lester B. Kabacoff and collaboration with chairman of the Hotel Corporation of America Roger Sonnabend, the massive Royal Orleans arose and opened in 1960. According to pioneer preservationist Mary Morrison, the Royal Orleans "exceeded everyone's expectations [and] became, overnight practically, a very, very popular hotel."[2]

Stern and Kabacoff, a rising civic and business star who played key roles in professionalizing and promoting modern tourism in New Orleans, had concurrently introduced Sonnabend to the 300 block of Bourbon Street. That site hosted the rambling American (Regal) Brewery, a relic of the downtown food-processing industry which, with Quarter property values now soaring and Bourbon retooling for tourism, made ever less economic sense. The brewery finally closed in 1961, and two years later, the development team of Sonnabend, Stern, Kabacoff, and their architects proposed a 543-room luxury hotel for the site, under the working name Vieux Carré Hotel and later the Chateau Louisianne. The commission, seeing little historical or architectural significance in the gritty complex and fearing that it might become blighted, permitted its demolition, and contemplated designs put forth by the reputable local architectural firms Koch and Wilson, and Curtis and Davis. That's when the trouble started.

Preservationists, disinclined to concede anything to Bourbon Street, protested the "'enormous, monumental design' inappropriate for the area" and the demolition of three remaining historical structures deemed "worthy of preservation," among them a Greek Revival storehouse.[3] Out-of-state investors worked with Councilman-at-Large Joseph V. DiRosa to persuade the Board of Zoning Adjustments at the Department of Safety and Permits to allow their hotel to exceed the fifty-foot Vieux Carré height limit by as much as eighteen feet. After all approvals were secured in September 1963, letters of gratitude with Texas and Mississippi postmarks arrived in DiRosa's City Hall mailbox. "Your splendid and outstanding action . . . is greatly appreciated," wrote investor Oliver W. Hammonds of Dallas;

"[Now we can] go ahead full steam on what I know will be a great development for the City of New Orleans."[4] The preservationists' victory in Garrison's vice war was short-lived, as Bourbon Street had just won a major battle of its own: for the first time since the days of the Cosmopolitan (Astor) Hotel, hundreds of guests would be lodging in the absolute heart of the neon strip.

After all structures had been cleared away in 1964, workers for the Diversa construction company began excavating the underground garage. And that is when, in the words of one attorney, "evidence of something strange going on" started to appear.[5] The enormous ditch began draining groundwater from surrounding soils, causing them to subside vertically and, worse, slough horizontally into the abyss. Vertical benchmarks on Bourbon Street ranging around 8.8 to 9.3 feet above sea level had dropped, within a single month, to 8.5 to 9.28 feet, while horizontal benchmarks measured at sites such as the Famous Door Bar and the Gunga Den nightclub widened by 3/16 of an inch.[6] Buildings moved along with the soils: cracks appeared on 323–325 Bourbon; the façade of the Judah Benjamin mansion at 327 Bourbon fractured while its base separated from the sidewalk; a courtyard wall between 315 and 319 Royal partially collapsed; and other Royal Street rear quarters leaned so badly that emergency permits were issued for their demolition.[7] The crisis made headlines throughout August and September 1966, as leaders intervened to halt the project and lawyers filed suits under the case name "Diversa Bourbon Street Hole." Preservationists, who had long battled Bourbon Street's cultural offenses, now had its geological problems on their hands—at the same time they were also battling the bitterly controversial Riverfront Expressway. They distributed a flier entitled "The Requiem of the Vieux Carré," which read in part:

> Almost a square on Bourbon Street
> Is now a gaping hole;
> The fine old buildings on its edge
> Are sagging and we're told
> The damage is beyond repair—
> They're doomed to demolition,
> And brand new replicas will fill
> These sites of planned attrition.
>
> Since engineers and planners
> Have learned our strange terrain,

> It seems to us they might beware
> A plan far more insane.
> To build a huge expressway
> Along the riverside,
> With pilings sunk in fickle mud
> Would cause this earth to slide.[8]

Preservationists also hired a decidedly less poetic attorney, who tallied numerous code violations on the part of Diversa and lectured Mayor Victor Schiro about them:

> The Mayor and the Council must understand that this Hole is acting as a cancer drawing out . . . imperceptibly but constantly, the moisture from the surrounding sub-soil. . . . [S]top the spread of this cancer!! . . . [T] he City has ample authority . . . to safeguard the public and surrounding property owners against the Diversa holocaust in the Vieux Carre.[9]

What to do? A construction freeze would only allow soils to continue to slide inward. Sealing the hole and reintroducing groundwater were advocated by preservationists-turned-geologists, but the hoteliers resisted such a radical alteration to their plan. Authorities decided that the best way to solve the problem *and* save the project was to fill the hole with the intended garage and weigh it down with the edifice as quickly as possible.[10] Construction work finally began in 1968 after local financiers found an operator for the lodge, the Hotel Corporation of America. The complex, designed as ca. 1840s American-style common-wall townhouses inspired by the Miltenberger Buildings at 900 Royal, arose speedily and resolved the subsidence problem—and imparted a lesson to future Quarter developers about the dangers of excavating an old urbanized delta.

Opened in August 1969 and named the Royal Sonesta ("Son" coming from the surname of the chain's founder, A. M. Sonnabend, and "esta" from his wife, Esther), the enterprise garnered commercial success similar to that of the Royal Orleans. It ratcheted up the flow of tourists visiting, lodging, and spending money on Bourbon, and simultaneously validated and augmented The Street's economic importance. It also added a number of storefronts and hundreds of feet of spacious balconies and galleries from which guests could enjoy a perch and interact with club-hoppers below. The Royal Sonesta Hotel today ranks as the single-largest privately owned parcel of the French Quarter's 1,739 pieces of property.[11]

The Requiem
of the Vieux Carré

Almost a square on Bourbon Street
    Is now a gaping hole;
The fine old buildings on its edge
    Are sagging and we're told
The damage is beyond repair -
    They're doomed to demolition,
And brand new replicas will fill
    These sites of planned attrition.

Since engineers and planners
    Have learned our strange terrain,
It seems to us they might beware
    A plan far more insane,
To build a huge expressway
    Along the riverside,
With pilings sunk in fickle mud
    Would cause this earth to slide.

The Mint would be the first to go -
    Cracked by the shifting soil.
The Old French Market would be doomed
    Unless this plan we foil.
The elegant Pontalbas
    Would crumble into dust
And break the heart of the Vieux Carre,
    So foil this plan we must!

Even Jax might not escape
    And beer would bathe Decatur;
Jackson Square, by the greed of men,
    Would become a yawning crater,
And when the dust had settled
    The trucks would still be there -
Grinding through the lonely streets
    of "The City That Didn't Care."

Louisiana Council for the Vieux Carré
Martha G. Robinson, President

Pamphlet (*left*) circulated by the Louisiana Council for the Vieux Carré in the mid-1960s to bring attention to multiple threats to the neighborhood, including the "Bourbon Street hole," site of today's Royal Sonesta Hotel (*above;* photographed by author during Mardi Gras 2012). *Courtesy Tulane University Southeastern Architectural Archive.*

In the seven years it took for the Royal Sonesta drama to play out, a parallel controversy unfolded at the other end of the strip. As a reminder of the incongruous land uses of historic Bourbon Street, this site did not involve industry or residential or retail but rather the compound of the Society of the Holy Family, an order of African American nuns founded locally in 1842. The society had purchased an old ballroom-turned-courtroom (the famed Quadroon Ballroom) at present-day 717 Orleans and expanded onto Bourbon Street when an adjacent theater burned down in 1889. There, in 1892, they created the St. John Berchmans' Orphan Asylum, which later became a high school.[12] For seven decades, the sisters resided on Orleans Street and fulfilled their mission to educate young black girls at St. Mary's Academy on the corner of Bourbon. By midcentury, that corner had been all but engulfed by adult entertainment. Needing more space and beleaguered with high maintenance costs, the Sisters of the Holy Family were ready to decamp, arguing that "none of the students in the school come from the Quarter and the location . . . is definitely not desireable [sic]. There is a hesitancy of the part of parents to send their girls in that area."[13] The only way they could fund their relocation was to sell to a developer who had for-profit plans for the site, which required a zoning change from the City Council. The sisters' attorney heard no retort from council members when he said, "I don't believe you gentlemen would want your daughters going to a high school on Bourbon Street."[14]

Bad enough that Quarter homeowners could not convince their tranquil neighbors to stay. Worse was the new neighbor's plan. Baton Rouge real estate developer Wilson P. Abraham and his affiliates proposed to construct a sixty-five-foot-high hotel modeled on the recent success of Royal Orleans. The envisioned Bourbon Orleans, as it would eventually be called, was controversial on a number of levels. First and foremost was the fate of the Holy Family Convent complex, which was not only historically and architecturally valuable but downright famous, on account of quadroon balls held in the building under a prior owner. The story of the balls was a part of local lore, and the edifice was a fixture on the walking-tour circuit. An equally contentious matter was the requested zoning downgrade from H-1 (Vieux Carré Residential) to H-2 (Vieux Carré Commercial), which could set a dangerous precedent in the ongoing war between Quarter residents and businesses. The City Planning and Vieux Carré Commissions supported the change, but the City Council shot it down. The developers regrouped and instead proposed an apartment-hotel, which cleverly circumvented the zoning change by making the project both residential and commercial. Quarter homeowners, who pumped immense sums into restoring their old houses and did not want to see their property values decline, worried that "hotel" meant transients, and that while "apartment" meant residents, it also meant guests visiting at all times. Who could distinguish a guest of a transient from that of a tenant? Opponents invoked images of johns, prostitutes, and late-night parties. Tenants also needed parking, yet another Quarter flashpoint. And what of those conference rooms, restaurant, and bars mentioned in the plan? Preservationists feared that the out-of-scale, out-of-zone proposal could, in the words of one opponent, "open the flood gates directly bringing Bourbon Street into the age-old heart of the Quarter." A colleague went farther, describing the Catholic girls' school at Bourbon and Orleans as a critical "bulwark [against] the extension of the Bourbon Street influence."[15]

The situation smacked of irony. Here, wealthy white homeowners and historical preservationists, who pointedly eschewed modern suburbs, protested the plans of a pious local black clergy to sell its historic property to white developers—on a street that appropriated and caricatured black culture while denying black people hotel service—so that a hotel could be built for white merrymakers while black nuns fled with their schoolchildren to the white suburbs! Opponents of the plan mocked the disingenuous attempts by investors to portray their project as "a humanitarian gesture calculated to rescue young girls from attending school on [Bourbon Street, despite that] the fate of these young people never bothered anyone until the motel idea came along."[16]

Abraham countered by offering to donate the Quadroon Ballroom–turned-convent to the city in exchange for permission to proceed with the full-scale Bourbon Street hotel, sans apartments. That overcame a major sticking point, but preservationist spokeswoman Mary Morrison demanded further that Abraham scale down the structural height to fifty feet and create off-street parking, while stipulating that the city utilize the former ballroom only for nonprofit or civic affairs. A compromise was finally reached in late 1963 in which zoning changes would be limited, concessions would be made on the hotel's size and design, apartments would be eliminated in favor of hotel rooms, and the ballroom on Orleans would be preserved.

In early 1964, the sisters moved to their new home on Chef Menteur Highway; the ca. 1892 orphanage-turned-school on the Bourbon corner was demolished; and work commenced on the Bourbon Orleans Hotel. As would happen later with the Royal Sonesta, the pile-driving and excavation destabilized nearby historic buildings, including some ballroom walls, and necessitated their razing. But, unlike the Sonesta, the Bourbon Orleans did not include a geologically risky underground parking garage.

After the 241-room hotel opened in July 1966, it seemed to validate preservationist arguments. For one, entrances were placed on St. Ann and Orleans, which was good because it shifted taxi congestion off Bourbon. But it also left the Bourbon frontage unusually spacious and overscaled, with sky-high galleries supported by colossal steel posts. Altogether the structure interrupted the block-to-block *tout ensemble* that the Vieux Carré Commission endeavored to preserve, yet extended the buzz of Bourbon Street entertainment activity up to the St. Ann intersection. The project was at best a vinegar victory for preservationists, more like a mitigated defeat. They exacted structural concessions and saved the ballroom's exterior, but they lost the residential zoning, the nuns, the schoolchildren, the apartment, the ballroom interior, and adjacent historical structures. For the merchants of the Bourbon strip, however, the Bourbon Orleans and its hundreds of nightly guests were happy news.[17]

The simultaneous commotions of the Royal Sonesta and the Bourbon Orleans in the 300 and 700 blocks overshadowed a third major Bourbon hotel project situated precisely between. At the corner of Toulouse lay a weedy eyesore where once stood the Old French Opera House. The lot, which had fallen into the unlikely possession of Tulane University, hosted such unbefitting land uses as the base camp for the Samuel House Wrecking Company. Ironically, this and other Quarter wrecking yards became Meccas for first-generation restorers, who would go "nosing around the sidewalks[,] beachcombing[,] swapping hardware. . . . You'd buy some beautiful particular fine wood or something, and you'd just drag it home!"[18] But as Bourbon Street grew more popular and valuable, entrepreneurial eyes saw better uses for the weedy lot. In 1964, investor Winthrop Rockefeller of Arkansas teamed with corporations based in Memphis and Houston and received permission from the Vieux Carré Commission to erect on the site a $3 million, five-story hotel with 186 rooms.[19] Because no demolition was involved and few could argue that a wrecking yard benefited the French Quarter, the project drew little attention from preservationists, and its architects did not have to wrangle over design disputes. When the Downtowner Motor Inn (later Le Downtowner Du Vieux Carre) opened on December 4, 1965, forty-six years to the day since the Opera House had burned, architectural historians were appalled to see that the dormers, shutters, and other details were as ersatz as the hotel's name.[20] For all the fist shaking over the Royal Sonesta and Bourbon Orleans, the fact that the warring parties were forced to listen to each other ended up producing better architecture than the uncontested Downtowner project. Bourbon merchants, meanwhile, were hitting three for three. A thousand new hotel rooms within steps of their cash registers! Guests were nearly assured of spending much of their money on the strip, if not nearly all of it.

Old-line hoteliers, meanwhile, scowled at their new competition. The new lodges opened their doors at a time when pioneers from the early days of tourism, such as the Roosevelt, Monteleone, DeSoto, Pontchartrain, Jung, and St. Charles Hotels, had all been running at half capacity during the slow summer months and barely three-quarters in peak Carnival season. They would tolerate no more, and neither would Quarter residents. Ten years later, Mary Morrison reflected that the Royal Orleans's success "opened the way for . . . a spate of hotels" and demolitions. "These hotel people would demolish anything that stood in the way."[21] The decade that saw the opening of the Royal Orleans in 1960, the Downtowner in 1965, Le Richelieu on lower Chartres in 1965, the Bourbon Orleans in 1966, the Bienville House Motor Hotel on Decatur in 1967, La Dauphine Motor Hotel at Dauphine and Conti in 1968, and the Royal Sonesta in 1969 ended with a city moratorium on any further hotels in the French Quarter. By then the neighborhood had 2,655 rooms, and in the next decade it would add nearly 900 more rooms in "guest houses," which exploited a loophole in the moratorium. For the first time, tourism began to eclipse the port as the city's premier economic sector; data from 1972–73 conservatively estimated that the metro area's 3,888,389 visitors (80 percent leisure and 20 percent business) spent at least $324 million, while the port generated only $227 million and fewer and fewer jobs, on account of containerization. Industrial-scale tourism had arrived, and it brought to "Crazy, Mixed-up Bourbon Street" something not anticipated: all-out nightly carnivals.[22]

Entertainment spaces do a remarkable job of separating locals and visitors. Locals enter such spaces with the awareness that social and professional peers may be present, making a night out a potential opportunity for advancement as well as a time for pleasure and relaxation. Because the evening may be "on the record," locals tend to dress up, turn on, and behave properly. The specter of stigma is very real to them, and the importance of restraint is not to be forgotten. Encountering a peer, after all, might have long-term consequences, and meeting a stranger might mean a lasting relationship. Similarly, restaurants and clubs that cater to locals keep prices modest, standards high, and service courteous because they, too, are operating on the record. Recreating in one's own primary social space has a remarkable way of civilizing human behavior. *Don't defecate in your own backyard.*

Visitors, on the other hand, are more inclined to let their guard down, confident that their peers are unlikely to see and pass judgment on them. Liberated by anonymity, they dress down, turn off, overindulge, and behave in ways they themselves might condemn elsewhere, particularly at home. They are egged on by the managers of that space, in our case Bourbonites, who instruct newcomers of the special social rules in effect here by means of props such as soft-porn imagery plastered on windows, inebriation quips imprinted on T-shirts, and flirtatious strippers positioned in doorways. Visitors are also encouraged by the behavior of other visitors, which green-lights their own abandonment of restraint through a mix of peer pressure and peer permission. The most visitors could hope for in an encounter with a stranger is a one-night stand; everything else is off the record. The oft-observed aphrodisiacal power of travel, and the wickedly effective slogan "What happens in Vegas, stays in Vegas," are predicated on the tantalizing possibilities created when one immerses oneself in a foreign social ambit in which the very notion of stigma is taken offline.

Such antithetical interests flush locals out of entertainment spaces once a tourist tipping point is passed. The turnover becomes complete when operators raise prices and lower quality, knowing that tourists come carrying cash, generally settle for less, and will probably never return. Musicians Union president David Winstein, who played Bourbon Street starting in the 1930s for mostly local patrons, explained in a 1997 interview the economic reason for the incompatibility of locals and out-of-towners: "When the War came along, it changed everything, because [Bourbon businesses] were using the troops as a money-making deal. They didn't want any local people there because the local people always spent just the minimum. And that's when the whole of Bourbon Street changed."[23]

As visitor-dependent as Bourbon had become during and after World War II, The Street did not permanently tip past the threshold until the late 1960s. Jets and cars brought tourists in, and the three big new corporate hotels lodged them right on Bourbon Street. A steady stream of strangers numbering in the millions annually came to dominate a Bourbon streetscape that by now had been mostly cleared of the outrageously corrupt shenanigans of the pre-Garrison era. Their ubiquity brought an unsettling night-after-night, season-to-season regularity to Bourbon Street, despite the door-to-door, block-to-block, round-the-clock assault on the senses. So too did the ban on parking on the main commercial blocks in 1966, followed by the nightly barricading of the strip from 7:00 p.m. to 3:00 a.m. to form a pedestrian mall starting in 1971, both of which made Bourbon Street that much harder for locals to reach and easier for tourists to perambulate. A study by a Chicago firm in the late 1960s found that the new megahotels and supercharged tourism industry, "designed to capitalize on the outpouring of humanity that nightly thronged Bourbon Street[,] threatened to eliminate what it came to exploit."[24] Augmenting the tourist brigades was a vast national pool of baby boomers who by this time were gaining independence, getting wheels, breaking from college, and seeking a place to let their long hair down. The French Quarter in the late 1960s became the South's Haight-Ashbury, and Bourbon Street, while never truly embraced by politically conscious countercultural types, nevertheless appealed to enough of their fellow-travelers to make it a hippie haven.

With jet-setting tourists and jalopy-driving hippies now convening on Bourbon Street, the last of the local tie-and-jacket dinner-date squares ended their love affair with the neon strip and never returned. Cash-strapped youth and wide-eyed tourists eschewed those few clubs that remained open, sensing that they risked a shakedown, and instead strolled up and down the street *past* the clubs. Whereas from the 1920s to the early 1960s the action on Bourbon occurred behind closed doors, now it shifted to the street. Club owners desperately tried to cajole strollers indoors by deploying their shifty-eyed barkers to offer two-for-one drinks specials and assure that there were no cover charges or drink minimums. But some time during 1967, one unremembered enterprise came up with a better idea: instead of convincing people outside to buy drinks *inside*, why not sell inside drinks to people *outside*? One by one, bars, clubs, and restaurants on Bourbon opened tiny retail outlets in interstitial spaces such as carriageways, windows, and unused doorways, from which they sold beer, drinks, hot dogs, corn dogs, and snacks directly to pedestrians. So many opened that they competed among themselves, some by lowering their prices and others by offering increasingly large and colorful concoctions in creative crucibles. "Window hawking," it was called, and it led to the new phenomenon of "drink-carrying," not to mention widespread ambulatory inebriation. The go-cup was born, and in a few years, it would completely rewire the social and economic dynamics of Bourbon Street.

Everyone seemed to come out ahead with window hawking. On the supply side, it enabled owners to tap into the outdoor money stream with a minimum of capital improvements. It put less emphasis on décor, facilities, bathrooms, air-conditioning, heating, and other costly overhead. It reduced the need for labor, particularly live entertainment. On the demand side, window hawking allowed tourists to stroll noncommittally amid all the eye candy and people-watching, while drinking and eating at a fraction of the cost had they patronized a club or restaurant. And it eliminated the unknowns of a pricey floor show or musical set, not to mention a bartender with an attitude and an expectation of a generous tip. Young people particularly loved buying booze from windows because the hawkers rarely asked for proof of age, knowing that once the youths staggered away, their purchases were all but untraceable. Gift and novelty shops benefited as well because drink-carrying pedestrians were more inclined to meander into their shops and buy souvenirs than were clubbers, and the tipsier they were, the more likely they'd make a dumb purchase. Retail stores opened left and right to tap into

Vending drinks directly to pedestrians through windows, secondary doorways, carriageways, and other interstitial spaces (*top*) first began in the late 1960s and forever changed Bourbon Street, as it shifted the action from indoors to outdoors. All venues except strip clubs now throw open all their doors (*lower scene*), blurring the line between private and public space as they cater to the passing parade. Quite different was the scene prior to the 1960s, when the action was in the nightclubs, behind closed doors and velvet curtains. *Photographs by author, 2012.*

the new foot traffic, and their best-selling merchandise was the favored garb of the hippie generation: T-shirts. Retailers threw open all their doors to divert the passing parade inside, flooded their shelf space with blinding white light, cranked up the atmospheric music, and blasted frigid air into the hot summer night, or warmth into those rare freezing winter eves—all of which further blurred the line between indoor and outdoor space.

Not everyone came out ahead with window hawking, however. Traditional musicians lost their audiences. Businesses that could not structurally adapt lost out, and hoteliers fielded complaints from guests kept awake by the all-night racket. The city lost tax revenue in the often off-the-books window transactions, and taxpayers got stuck with picking up the unholy mess of discarded go-cups and wrappers each morning. The pedestrian parade also attracted panhandlers, pickpockets, purse snatchers, and con men with treacherous entrapments aimed at gullible newcomers, not to mention Hare Krishnas and adherents of the Process, a splinter group of Scientologists headquartered in New Orleans. The smell of spilled beer, formerly unknown on Bourbon, became the least offensive ingredient of a malodorous new sensory-scape. "There are [also] latrine smells and disinfectant smells and booze smells and people smells and horse smells along with kitchen odors," the *Atlanta Constitution* reported, "as if everything and body on Bourbon Street were being cooked in one grotesque bouillabaisse." Add to this what one writer described as "enough rock-and-roll to send [a tourist] back to Minerva, Ohio," and Bourbon-haters added a new word to their lexicon of loathing: *disgusting*.[25] A place that was once famous, fashionable, and pertinent to local lives had become infamous, embarrassing, and irrelevant. Locals stopped calling Bourbon "The Street," an affectionate term that arose in the 1940s, because they expunged it from their daily lives and had little reason to speak of it at all.

Bourbon's new outdoor drinking and littering problem came to public attention during Mardi Gras 1969. Shortly afterward, Mayor Schiro formed a committee of prominent club owners—including Pete Fountain and Al Hirt, who had become de facto spokesmen—to discuss an ordinance on window hawking, which the mayor said "demoralizes our city and cheapens the charm of Bourbon Street."[26] The *States-Item* agreed in a September 1969 editorial:

Bourbon Street has taken on a cheap carnival atmosphere more in keeping with a back-country road show than with a storied street. . . . Up until two years ago "the strip" seemed to be improving steadily. "B-drink" joints gave way to legitimate business [like] Fountain and Al Hirt. . . . But then somebody discovered that you could make a buck by selling beer and buttered corn (don't trip over the wet, slippery cobs) through an open window on the street. Such low-overhead enterprises multiplied and flourished until, today—instant Coney Island. As might be expected, the "coat and tie trade" is . . . going elsewhere, [and] legitimate businessmen, such as Fountain, are talking about doing the same.[27]

States-Item cartoonist Ralph Vinson accompanied the editorial with a caricature of what late-1960s Bourbon Street had become. It showed tippling youths with shaggy manes and ragged clothing crowded around Ye Window Bar, from which a tattooed arm shoved a sloshy cocktail into the face of a lush tourist toting a camera. Ads for liquor, beer, and snacks marred the façades, and ankle-deep refuse littered the street. "And I thought it was named for French kings!" exclaims the weary tourist. The days of tuxedoed emcees and glamorous burlesque stars were indeed over. Hippies themselves poked fun at the decadence of it all, and co-opted the accusation that they were to blame. Some formed a gag "Rent-a-Hippy" business that, among other things, held a sweep-in on Bourbon Street. "Dirty *hippies*? Well, how about those dirty *streets*?" The stunt got national press attention. So did Bourbon's demise.[28]

The City Council, which saw no humor in Bourbon's filth, gave Mayor Schiro his ordinance within days of the committee meeting. Banning any "sell[ing of] food or beverages from a window, door, or other aperture facing the street or other public way within the Vieux Carre," the law was later modified to prohibit all sales within six feet of the street. Two years later, the nightly pedestrian mall policy went into effect. More pedestrians upped the economic ante for bartenders to hawk through windows, and they did—by evading code enforcers, finding loopholes in the ordinance, or, in the case of bars, throwing open their doors and meeting the pedestrians halfway. Illegal hawking persisted throughout the salacious 1970s, a time when the petroleum boom pumped new money into the city and hippies gave way to disco kings and queens. Enforcement was erratic, and well worth the risk vis-à-vis low overheard and high gross.

When Latin song-and-dance entertainer Chris Owens tried doing the same from a doorway of her eponymous club at the corner of St. Louis, however, police busted her. Owens, who had worked on or near the strip since 1958 and had emerged as a Bourbon leader on par with her friends Fountain and Hirt, promptly filed suit. The case fell into the Civil District Court docket of Judge S. Sanford

Levy, who in May 1981 ruled the ordinance unconstitutional on account of its vague and imprecise wording. "Does the ordinance prohibit the display of jewelry from windows?" Levy asked. "Does the ordinance disallow a cashier to exchange a crystal chandelier for money within six feet of the doorway of antique shop on Royal Street?"[29]

The ruling cleared the way for the open and legal sale of alcohol from apertures affiliated or unaffiliated with the adjoining establishments throughout the Bourbon strip. Old bars adopted the new strategy and opened all their bays. Clubs did the same, and through their open doors flowed not just tourists and drinks but amped-up decibels of rock cover bands and deejays spinning vinyl. New bars developed in the late 1980s and 1990s went further, with completely open designs and a bare minimum of seating, in the expectation that people would swoop in, purchase drinks and a slice of pizza, and promptly depart. No waitresses, no bathrooms, no social interaction, no live entertainment, just a pit stop on the passing parade. Drinks were modified to meet the transient nature of the purchase: the "go-cup," an unadorned translucent plastic cup sized from twelve to thirty-six ounces (later dubbed the Huge Ass Beer) became ubiquitous every night, and in the gutter every dawn. Spiked beverages became increasingly gaudy, colorful, beachy, tropicalized, oversized, and extra-powerful—enter the daiquiri—while the containers grew ever more outlandish, molded in the form of hand grenades, penises, fish bowls, and footballs, some equipped with neck straps. By the 2010s, fourteen open-format, minimum-seating daiquiri bars operated between the 200 and 700 blocks of Bourbon Street, in addition to eleven window, doorway, or a carriageway hawkers. All are products of late-1960s sociospatial changes on the strip.

The successful perforation of the wall between private profit-making interiors and free public exterior space forever changed Bourbon Street. The passing procession of Rabelaisians had become its own attraction, as much a part of the Bourbon experience as the old buildings, the blur of neon sex, and the reverberating decibels. The new Bourbon Street perpetual motion machine had, among other effects, finally flushed out the last of the apartment dwellers upstairs, leaving the upper stories of most commercial buildings dark and foreboding. The strip was now a place where thousands of people worked, and tens of thousands meandered, but for the first time in history, it was no longer a place where people lived.

Curious as it is, the spectator-as-spectacle phenomenon is not all that uncommon in the geographies of tourism. Consider the beachgoers who are more interested in showcasing or ogling bodies than in swimming, or the tourists who pull their lawn chairs up to the bustling Pigeon Forge commercial strip to watch traffic heading to and from Great Smoky Mountain National Park. Similar scenarios transpire at the Eiffel Tower, in Times Square, and at festival marketplaces. Bourbon Street's structural environment, however, adds unusual dimensions to spectator spectating. The balconies and galleries encroaching the narrow artery provide revelers with picturesque perches close enough to make visual and verbal contact with strangers, yet far enough to insulate them from the dangers of face-to-face encounters. A flirtatious proffering that could prove humiliating or violent at street level becomes emboldened and buffered by vertical distance when shouted from a balcony. The lofty position also imparts an empowering sense of exclusivity to balcony dwellers as they banter with the masses below. Mixed with copious quantities of alcohol and the mirth of the moment, street-balcony interactions are inclined to become contagiously frisky. When set within the context of Carnival—that annual citywide truce on selected social mores—Bourbon's street-balcony social topography becomes downright sexual. That change seems to have started in the early 1970s.

Bourbon first became a Mardi Gras hotspot when krewes held their Carnival balls at the French Opera House. Revelers during the 1920s and 1930s gravitated to Bourbon because that's where the bars and nightclubs were, and that's where booze could be had. But who wants to remain inside a dark smoky club on this public fete? Mardi Gras, if nothing else, is an outdoor bacchanal. Better to bask in the subtropical winter sun of Canal Street, or in the French Quarter twilight, and catch the splendid parades as they roll down Royal Street and cross Bourbon on Orleans. So it was for generations—until the early 1970s. With the opening of the new megahotels from 1960 to 1968, and the introduction in 1969 of the "super krewe" Bacchus with its megafloats and celebrity royalty, authorities began to grow concerned about public safety. Should a fire break out, the multitudes packing the narrow streets of the French Quarter would impede emergency response, and possibly become victims themselves. To the ire of some and the disappointment of all, authorities decided to ban large-scale float parades from the French Quarter starting with the 1973 Carnival season.

The new regulation transformed Mardi Gras in a number of ways. It ended the spectacle of thunderous marching bands and dazzling floats shimmying down narrow French Quarter streets. Second, as parade activity relocated uptown to St. Charles Avenue, it took with it all the local families whose lives revolved around the annual ritual. That left the city's most famous tourist attraction—the French Quarter—with a surplus of randy out-of-towners and a deficit of scheduled activities to keep them occupied. Idle, intoxicated, sexually liberated youth—this was the era in which "streaking" became a national fad—invented their own spectacle by cajoling each other to bare flesh. That women comprised an increasing segment of the Bourbon reveler population was a factor as well; a photographic analysis indicates that while only one in four people on Bourbon were female on Fat Tuesday 1965, that proportion would nearly double by century's end.[30] It also helped that the three big new Bourbon hotels all featured ample galleries and balconies connecting to bedrooms: the perfect space to blur the line between private and public sexuality. Anecdotal evidence suggests that Mardi Gras exhibitionism may have also been catalyzed, if not instigated, by men "weenie wagging" on Bourbon at the St. Ann intersection in the early 1970s, and by nudists sharing a second-story apartment during the 1975 Mardi Gras, who regaled crowds below and exhorted them to "Show Your Penis" or "Show Your Tits" in return. The 1979 police strike, which led to the cancellation of all parades and left Mardi Gras completely unstructured, also incited what the *New York Times* described as "a noticeable quickening of activity on Bourbon Street, [with] more tourists peeping through open doors to stare at nude dancers, and crowding into the bars and lounges."[31] Whatever its origins, public nudity on Bourbon Street was rare in the late 1960s and ubiquitous by the 1980s. It gave reason for religious conservatives to hate Bourbon for its heathen carnality, for progressives to hate The Street for its affected bourgeois indulgences, and for everyone else to absolutely love the place.[32]

The conversion of Bourbon into a campy cavalcade of crocked carnies had earned the strip a new cadre of critics. But unlike traditional Bourbon-haters—that is, residents, preservationists, and the cultural commentariat—the new decriers had a soft spot for the "crazy, mixed-up" strip. They waxed nostalgic about its past, lamented its demise, and offered proposals to save it. Many of them had a professional stake in the outcome. "I can remember when the streets were empty and the clubs were packed," said a bartender in a fine restaurant who needed Bourbon Street to work. "Now [in 1973] it's the other way around. And the clubs? Shells of what they used to be." A respected Bourbon restaurateur concurred, calling the 1971 enacting of the pedestrian mall "the death blow; [afterward] the excitement became the traffic itself, and the Mall has created an atmosphere conducive to loitering and 'bumming around.'"[33] Entertainer Chris Owens, who had lived and worked on Bourbon since 1958, said unequivocally that her beloved street "was going downhill [in the] early '70s. . . . [I]t was like a carnival," and not in a good way.[34]

Owens prided herself in offering a classy act, but some of her colleagues, egged on by heightened expectations from the sexual revolution and competition from the triple-X porn industry, found that they could regain audiences by doffing all their scanty attire. Roughly half of all erotic dancers, according to former striptease artist Lee Fox, went further by moonlighting in prostitution. ("If you were a stripper," she told an interviewer in 1975, "would you turn down a guy who plopped down $500 in cash?")[35] Total nudity undermined Bourbon Street's little remaining decency, but at least it pulled the crowds indoors and the cash out of men's pockets. That gain, however limited, was lost when the Supreme Court ruled that community standards would be used to define obscenity. Local authorities shortly thereafter banned bottomlessness and required pasties, but that did little to reverse the sleaziness.[36] The twenty or so classy burlesque clubs that once operated on The Street had dwindled by the mid-1970s to at most "four worth talking about," according to Lee Fox. She offered one of the reasons behind the change. "Why go to a nightclub that requires a minimum of two drinks at anywhere from $2.85 to $3.85 plus cover charge to see nothing but a chick going down to a G-string and pasties when they can see it all in a porno movie, and in color yet?" Worse, she said, the music was canned, the managers refused to pay union scale, and the dancers had a "peculiar . . . dislike for men," wore "boyish haircuts, masculine clothes . . . smok[ed] cigars [and] talk[ed] rougher and tougher than the jailhouse slang you hear in the Parish Prison."[37] Musically, too, Bourbon Street in the early 1970s won little praise. According to one journalist, one could, after a struggle, still "hear the competing wails of clarinets from several clubs." But that sound was overwhelmed by country music, Latin (disco), and most of all, by rock, which had turned Bourbon Street "into an amplified echo chamber."[38] The sole city-owned open space on Bourbon Street—the mothballed electric substation which NOPSI donated to the city in 1970—also went downhill. Renamed Edison Place Park, the green space had the potential to breathe new life into the heart of Bourbon Street, "as a landscaped park which will be attractively lighted at night."[39] But the city failed to maintain it, and vagrants moved in. Instead of an amenity, the pocket park became a barricaded eyesore that drove down the whole block.

The national media noticed Bourbon's decline. An Associated Press article pondering the titular question, "Mardi Gras in New Orleans: Is It Worth It?" described the "constant nightroar of the kids of Bourbon St., pierced by rebel yells in the city they call 'The Big Easy,' swilling Boone's Farm [and] grabbing

"It was like a carnival"—Bourbon Street in the scruffy 1970s, at its absolute nadir, just prior to the formation of Mayor Landrieu's reformist task force. *Courtesy City of New Orleans, Vieux Carré Commission.*

flesh," and made Bourbon Street sound debauched to the point of degeneracy.[40] What especially hurt was a scathing 1973 article by Maurice Kowalewski in *New Orleans Magazine,* a metropolitan monthly that usually tried to see the brighter side of all things local. Entitled "Flies in the Bourbon," the piece evoked the Ray Samuel exposé that first riled up New Orleanians back in 1948. Kowalewski took readers on a guided tour—"Why? [Because] if you're the average New Orleanian, you probably haven't seen Bourbon Street in a long, long time." He went on to describe the strip with words like "sickness," "disease," "cheap," "trap," "pigsty," "con," and "huckster," and likened it to "a strident slut that would repulse a college boy *before* he slept with her." His inspections and interviews yielded an inventory of failings: Oversized signs overflowing with overstatement. Unposted and predatory pricing. Unbelievable filth. Drugs. Crime. And the dregs of society in ever-growing numbers—that's what every beleaguered business owner told Kowalewski. Said one bar manager: "This street is a haven for scum. Get rid of the GD bums and crums on Bourbon and we'd be a helluva lot better off. They hurt my business. They hurt it like hell." A boutique owner at wit's end confided: "Some of the hippies—I swear this is true—buy Purina Dog Chow and eat it for dinner. They're animals." Bourbonites agreed: "GET THE HIPPIES OFF THE STREET!"[41]

An attempt to do just that instead brought more hippie attention to Bourbon Street. In the wee hours of January 31, 1970, members of the folk-rock band the Grateful Dead filed back to their Bourbon Street hotel after a Friday-night gig. To their surprise, they found their room doors wide open and strange men rifling through their suitcases. It was a joint NOPD-federal narcotics bust, and it yielded nineteen arrests of band members, managers, roadies, hangers-on with monikers like the King of Acid and "spiritual advisor" Summer Wind, plus some hapless Bourbonites in the wrong place at the wrong time. The bust, which made front-page news locally and coursed through the Deadhead grapevine nationally, would have been forgotten had the musicians not later recalled the incident lyrically. First performed in August and released in January 1971, "Truckin'" would become the Grateful Dead's signature road song, a vagabond anthem, and an official Library of Congress–designated national musical treasure. It also introduced millions of youth, in an appealingly unflappable and world-weary way, to a place called Bourbon Street. Despite the run-in with the local constabulary, that street sounded, to a young Deadhead marooned in mundane suburbia, like a deliciously interesting place. The Dead went ahead and played their second gig at the Warehouse that night, but avoided New Orleans for the remainder of the decade, purportedly on account of getting "busted, down on Bourbon Street."[42]

If only they took the hippies with them! More than ever long-haired dropouts filled the French Quarter, and their brand of cashless grunginess—witness the 1969 cult classic *Easy Rider*, which featured ragged Bourbon Street scenes— drove out the old dashing, cash-carrying crowd. A sentiment began to prevail that something had gone terribly awry. Vieux Carré Commission director Lynda C. Friedmann wrote to a colleague about that feeling in the understated tones of an appointed government professional:

Local people don't visit the street as often as they used to; Pete Fountain moved to the Hilton and other night clubs have closed. People's fear of crime in general increased [and] the Supreme Court decision allowed greater flexibility for those promoting pornography. T-shirt shops and take out food establishments seemed to blossom all of a sudden. Bourbon Street seemed to be changing, but no one really knew how or why.[43]

Not all assessments of Bourbon Street were derogatory. While the music, bars, shops, crowds, drunks, hippies, and litter got a universal thumbs-down, one local critic, after enjoying more than 90 good meals out of 103 visits to Bourbon Street restaurants in 1975, came away calling Bourbon "the best restaurant street in New Orleans" and "maybe . . . the best Eating Street in America." Sheer numbers helped make it so: it boasted 35 sit-down eateries from Canal to Dumaine, and close to 70 if one went fifty feet beyond each intersection. Every major cuisine except Greek and Jewish could be found on The Street. The critic ranked seven restaurants near the top of their respective classes, and only two as rip-offs. As if expecting incredulous responses, he preemptively asked, "Why can we not give this most famous part of New Orleans its due?" The plaintive tone suggested that, at best, perhaps restaurants formed Bourbon's sole bright spot and kept alive the hope that things could be turned around. More likely it suggested that the critic was pulling for the place, not wanting to kick it when it was down—the kindness of strangers, as Tennessee Williams might say.[44]

How Bourbon Street Stabilized
1980s–Present

The 1970s crisis, which everyone agreed marked The Street's nadir, did not go unnoticed by New Orleans's new chief executive. A progressive reformer with a strong civil rights record and a knack for modern urban planning, Mayor Moon Landrieu realized that the past administrations' complicity with or insouciance toward the strip could not continue. Bourbon Street's chronic problems had become acute, and something had to be done. But he also recognized that Bourbon Street required special treatment. Investing too many scarce resources into that sin pit seemed to enrage one half of local society, while cutting it loose had the other half up in arms. So Mayor Landrieu did what most politicians would do: he formed a task force.

To Landrieu's credit, the Bourbon Street Task Force was not just another bunch of overtasked and underfinanced civil servants cobbled together to placate indignant voters. Chaired by former city chief administration officer Richard Kernion and funded at thirty thousand dollars, the task force united key agencies with local planning-design firm Marks Lewis Torre Associates to study Bourbon Street's history, conditions, and communities; survey stakeholders; analyze results; and propose improvements. Landrieu made it clear in the opening press conference that the stakes were high. Bourbon Street, he declared, was "an institution that makes New Orleans famous throughout the world." This wasn't about just any street, he explained; it was about a signature street, one that spoke on behalf of the whole city to the nation and world. If Bourbon Street went, so went the city.[1]

The six leaders of the Task Force got started with a tour of the adult-entertainment districts in Boston, New York, and Atlanta—a potentially scandalous junket if ever there was one. But the participants took their work seriously. They met with counterparts; toured Boston's "Combat Zone," New York's Times Square and Little Italy, and Atlanta's Peachtree Walk and the Underground; and came away with new understandings. They also discovered that Bourbon Street, "with its particular problems, was not typical of the usual adult entertainment districts throughout the country."[2]

Next the task force met with Bourbonites on their home turf. Landrieu himself opened the initial meeting at Al Hirt's nightclub on February 24, 1977. The good news was that, nationwide, Americans still felt there was no place quite like Bourbon Street, and no one wanted to sterilize the strip. Rather, the task force sought to identify problems and remedy them with the full backing of local government, so long as merchants were equally committed. The bad news was that Bourbon could no longer continue the status quo. Worse, it no longer held a monopoly. Competing spaces for the nighttime entertainment dollar were popping up locally and nationwide.

After Councilman Mike Early, Chairman Richard Kernion, and Vieux Carré Commission Director Lynda C. Friedmann had their say, the Bourbon merchants and commercial property owners stepped to the microphone. They were mostly male and middle-aged, with a mix of Sicilian, Creole, Irish, Anglo, and Chinese surnames, and they did not see eye to eye on everything. Hoteliers, for example, were at odds with club owners about noise abatement. And feelings were mixed about the pedestrian mall: those who adapted to it via window hawking wanted to keep it, while traditional club owners smarted at the promenade's impact on their nightly attendance. Nearly everyone wanted to "get rid of," in their words, litter, congestion, prostitutes, loiterers, bums, panhandlers, pot smokers, kids, and Hare Krishnas—and not necessarily in that order. Some added flower peddlers, shoe-shine boys, barkers, false advertising, and obscene language. One attendee noted that the hosing down of sidewalks created stagnant pools of filthy water. Everyone wanted leniency on the issues of signage, open-door policies, and amplified music. Some tacitly acknowledged that The Street had an excess of massage parlors and cheap strip joints and a deficit of classy entertainment, but they let the officials know that "good burlesque doesn't exist on the Street because clubs can't afford to pay the cost," evidence that the Garrison raids remained a sore subject even fifteen years later. The attendees offered some suggestions: to encourage everyone present to join the Vieux Carre Action Association; to designate a portion of the hotel/motel tax for police and sanitation, and—among the more creative—to install an arch over the entrance of Bourbon Street at the Canal intersection, like the one in San Francisco's Chinatown. (That suggestion came from Frank Hara, owner of Takee Outee and one of the few remaining Chinatown denizens.) The meeting concluded with a promise of new funding, projects, regulations, and ordinances toward an improved Bourbon Street—the first of which Landrieu was ready to announce: $250,000 for the long-overdue renovation of Edison Place into a pocket park. Other changes would depend on what the task force learned from the other half of the Bourbon Street equation: the visitors.[3]

In mid-June 1977, six researchers interviewed 638 Bourbon Street "users" over eight days and analyzed the results on a mainframe computer. The survey, designed by data analyst Allen Rosenzweig, found that out-of-towners ("visitors"), unsurprisingly, outnumbered New Orleans–area residents ("natives") on The Street, but not overwhelmingly, comprising 58 percent of those interviewed. Roughly two-thirds of the users on the main commercial blocks were between ages eighteen and thirty-five, while 10 to 20 percent were over age fifty-five. Two-thirds also appeared to be white-collar professionals, while 70 percent were male and 87 percent were white. Roughly 40 percent of the groups interviewed comprised dyads; a quarter to a third were solitary, and the remainder were triads or larger groups. Why did they visit Bourbon Street? "Listening to jazz" and "fine dining" were the top reasons, but the researchers had to pencil in an additional choice because interviewees proffered it so frequently: simply walking, browsing, and witnessing—in other words, participating in the passing parade. Both visitors and natives agreed that Bourbon Street was "unique" and "fascinating," but visitors held that sentiment more passionately. Both groups also concurred that Bourbon Street was "dirty," "smelly," "cheap," and "tacky," natives more so than visitors. Both groups disagreed that Bourbon was too "loud," "unsafe," and "offensive," but natives disagreed to lesser degrees. The only true difference of opinion regarded whether Bourbon Street could be described as "quaint and picturesque": visitors agreed; natives did not. In all, visitors and natives in 1977 generally viewed Bourbon Street similarly, differing mostly in intensity. They wanted nuisances controlled, not pleasures.[4]

The task force presented its findings at the Blue Angel Club at 225 Bourbon on October 19, 1977. Its recommendations came in the form of a series of remedies that would be promulgated into new laws and policies.

To remedy the shady maneuvering involved in spot zoning and nonconforming uses, the task force worked with the City Council in passing a new Vieux Carré Entertainment (VCE) zone, which "set up the mechanisms by which other [task force] recommendations can be implanted and enforced."[5] The VCE zone, a modification of earlier Bourbon commercial zones dating from 1929 and 1951, included all parcels fronting Bourbon from Iberville to St. Ann, and permitted only places of amusement; theaters; restaurants (but not fast-food or drive-ins); museums; flower shops; artist studios; residences; retail shops smaller than 2,000 square feet; and certain utility apparatus.[6]

To remedy complaints about unsightly signage, the Task Force forged a formula in which a business was allowed a two-faced sign sized at no greater than 8 percent of the square footage of the business's public space frontage. A bar with a 30' x 10' façade on Bourbon Street, for example, would be permitted one 3' x 4' hanging sign with graphics on both sides, or a single-faced sign twice that size mounted flush with the façade.

To remedy the low grades users gave to shopping on Bourbon Street, Councilman Early got the City Council to approve a resolution for the removal of outdoor T-shirt displays throughout the French Quarter, under the threat of a law with penalties if merchants did not comply.

To remedy complaints about rough streets and puddles, the task force coordinated its design recommendations with the Department of Street's resurfacing project, resulting in the stripping and repaving of the asphalt, with Bomanite-pattern brick detailing along the gutters, in 1977.

To remedy cheating on taxes and codes, the task force clarified and enforced which enterprises were "bars" as opposed to "restaurants."

To remedy the awkward nightly transition to a pedestrian mall, authorities designed a system of portable bollards—heavy, hollow cast-iron cylinders, forty inches high, that mounted snugly into circular collars set six inches into the asphalt. The devices would keep out cars but not people, resisted jostling, and could be immediately extracted for emergency response.[7]

To remedy the littering problem, the task force dramatically increased the number of trash receptacles, shifted garbage collection from dusk to morning, and synchronized street cleaning and sidewalk washing with trash collection, such that the opening wave of midday visitors would encounter an uncluttered, puddle-free, litter-free street.[8]

To remedy the lack of organizational cohesion among managers, business owners, and building owners, the task force formed the Bourbon Merchants Association, which, among other things, produced a newspaper, *Bourbon Street Sights & Sounds*. The association was housed not on Bourbon Street but at 108 Royal Street. And ironically, the newspaper's publisher was, of all people, Jim Garrison.[9]

Perhaps the task force's wisest decision concerned what *not* to remedy. Notes taken during an early brainstorming session listed various flashpoints that the task force might want to tackle. Among them were cracking down on Mardi Gras revelry, padlocking clubs for obscenity, aggressively nabbing prostitutes, rethinking the pedestrian mall, banning barkers from sidewalks, and implementing a closed-door policy on all places serving alcohol. It sounded a little like another Garrison-style crackdown. Someone at the meeting spoke out against such a heavy-handed approach because, the anonymous note-taker jotted down, "Don't want to sanitize the street."[10] It was advice well taken: very few stakeholders indicated that heavy-handed interventions were necessary. And none were enacted: the pedestrian mall was maintained; doors of nonstrip establishments could remain open; drinks could be sold directly to pedestrians; and no one would mess with the constitutionally protected rights of what the official Bourbon Street Revitalization Plan publication described as "countless beggars, shoe shiners, tap dancers, religious fanatics, and weirdos." The task force succeeded because it knew just when to let Bourbon Street be Bourbon Street, and just when to not.[11]

In November 1977, the task force marked the completion of their work with a black-tie party at Edison Place for seven hundred invited guests, with the adjoining 300 block of Bourbon Street intentionally left open so visitors could mingle. Between musical sets performed by a group named the Las Vegas Connection, organizer Ruth Ann Menutis of the Bourbon Merchants Association delivered an inspiring speech on the history and importance of the famous street, and the hope she now had in its future. Vieux Carré Commission Director Lynda Friedmann, who like most preservationists spent more time fighting Bourbon Street than loving it, later confided to Menutis, "I've personally come a long way in understanding and appreciating both the people and the street and feel that I've found some friends there in the process."[12]

Her sentiments echoed those of most participants. The task force had been a model of public/private sector collaboration and conflict resolution. Its data collection, analysis, problem identification, and crafting of solutions had all been thorough, fair, inclusive, and informative. It evidenced that cooperation among parties of differing views, if done properly, can solve more problems than litigation. Most important, the task force's momentum throughout 1977 parlayed into an equally successful implementation phase in 1978. That year saw a suite of task force recommendations—many of them spearheaded by District C councilman Mike Early, who came to be known as "the councilman of Bourbon Street"—become rules, policies, and ordinances.[13]

While the legal implementation of Mayor Landrieu's Bourbon Street Task Force helped halt The Street's free fall in the 1970s, it was a series of fortuitous changes nationwide that catalyzed a Bourbon Street renaissance—or at least a stabilization—in the 1980s.

Americans were reassessing themselves in the new decade. Voters jettisoned President Jimmy Carter and his "national malaise" in favor of the sunny confidence of Ronald Reagan. The economy revived in 1983 and hummed for the remainder of the decade, creating more disposable income for leisure travel, more reasons for business travel, and fattened expense accounts. A worldwide oil bust wreaked havoc on the Gulf Coast but had the opposite effect nationwide, delighting Americans with a windfall of fuel savings which often got rebudgeted for vacations. The devastating plummet of New Orleans's white-collar petroleum sector shifted attention to the sole bright spot in the local economy, tourism, which was about to benefit from a massive infrastructure investment in preparation for the 1984 World's Fair. Bourbon Street's sidewalks were completely rebuilt from Canal to St. Ann, while every intersecting street was repaved, as were Royal and Chartres.[14] To compensate for the disruption of business, the city held a neighborhood-wide party that evolved into today's popular French Quarter Festival, yet another annual windfall for Bourbon Street. Investors came away ruing the world's fair, which cost $350 million and ended up bankrupt before it even opened. But Bourbon Street not only didn't lose a dime on the event, it gained from the free marketing and profited from the 7 million visitors drawn to town by the fair.

The fair also provided a concession license to a Mississippian named Earl Bernhardt and his associates to sell fruity cocktails at a stand they called the Tropical Paradise. Its success emboldened Bernhardt and partner Pam Fortner to invest in a bar on Toulouse just off Bourbon, which they named the Tropical Isle. The brisk business at the fair, however, did not parlay into Bourbon Street success until Bernhardt and Fortner made two innovative adjustments. First, they heard a new sound, "trop-rock," coming from an auditioning band led by Al Miller. The easygoing Caribbean melodies inspired by the music of Jimmy Buffett (who got his own start on Bourbon Street) complemented the theme of the Tropical Isle and appealed to the spring-break beach culture popular among youth at the time. Miller's "Late as Usual" band—so-named for their tardiness—"became a real hit with the college students," recalled Bernhardt. "It got so crowded . . . we put a speaker over the door and they'd dance out in the street." Second, Bernhardt and

Earl Bernhardt, the modern-day "mayor" of
Bourbon Street. Note the hand-grenade jewelry
and attire. *Photograph by author.*

Fortner noticed the dynamics of the Bourbon Street crowd. "The party [was]
in the street," he recollected. "They'd come in the bars, get themselves a drink,
listen to the music for a while, and then they'd kind of go from bar to bar to
bar." The duo also noticed what was in the peripatetic partiers' hands. "We'd
look out on a Friday or Saturday and see nothing but Hurricanes, people carrying Hurricane [drinks from Pat O'Brien's]. We had to tap into that market."[15] So
they invented a powerful and brightly colored tropical-flavored drink, designed a
transparent to-go container shaped like a hand-thrown bomb, and trademarked
it as the Hand Grenade. Most important, Bernhardt, who cut his teeth in radio
advertising during the civil rights movement in rural Mississippi, marketed the
Hand Grenade creatively and relentlessly, including on local television. Today
the fruity cocktail sells by the millions annually, entirely in portable containers
and exclusively from Bernhardt and Fortner's empire of six bars, clubs, and restaurants on or near Bourbon. In the process, the duo reconstrued the prevailing
Bourbon Street thematic motif from one of nocturnal jazziness to beachy tropicality and Caribbean escapism. Bernhardt himself has become a leader, spokes-
man, defender, and constructive critic of The Street, following in the tradition of
Henry Wenger, Arnaud Cazenave, and Gaspar Gulotta.

The cultural changes of the 1980s bode well for Bourbon Street. College youth rejected the dour political activism of the previous generation and focused instead on their lives, their careers, and their pleasures. Rock music became synthesized, and musicians swapped message for style, grit for glam, and acoustic chords for dance beats. Hippies went out along with their long hair, tie-dyes, and cutoffs; yuppies came in with their feathered bouffants, preppy polo shirts, and designer jeans. The shift from the penny-pinching barefoot decadence of the Flower Children to the stylish credit-card-wielding swagger of the MTV generation made the burgeoning youth market on Bourbon Street attractive and lucrative. Campy historicity disappeared from the streetscape: Confederate flags came down and "Dixie" grew rare; steamboats and Huck Finn caricatures disappeared from signage and restaurant themes; hostesses changed from hoopskirts to miniskirts. Grungy bars with shaggy bands became pulsating dance clubs with brash deejays. Every night was Saturday night, and Carnival lasted all year. "Bourbon Street came back in the Eighties," recalled one eyewitness to decades of The Street's ups and downs. "Word got out to the kids, hey, you know, Bourbon Street's back; we're gonna hang in the Quarter now."[16]

Rigor returned to Bourbon Street to such a degree that no less an authority than Al Hirt decided in 1991 it was time to reopen. Eight years earlier, Hirt had made national news—and enemies—by shuttering his Bourbon club and declaring the Quarter unvisitable "without an armed guard." His 501 Bourbon corner became a Ripley's Believe It or Not, the type of enterprise even Bourbonites did not want, and they were relieved when it closed and Hirt returned. "We're seeing definite signs that jazz and the music of New Orleans are returning to the French Quarter," Hirt reported. "This is good for New Orleans and for the many, many visitors . . . who want to experience firsthand the best of music on Bourbon Street."[17] Bourbon Street also discovered the Cajuns in the 1980s, not because of a newfound appreciation for its neighboring folk culture but because local chef Paul Prudhomme had introduced the rest of the country to Cajun cooking. He precipitated a nationwide craze for spicy Louisiana country food, along with the associated music and swamp scenography. Bourbon Street jumped on the Cajun bandwagon at roughly the same time that New York, Hollywood, and corporate chain restaurants did. To Bourbonites, Cajuns meant good food, good music, and good times—a match made in heaven which peaked on Bourbon Street in the 1990s and endures today.

Even Edison Place, the 44' x 128' substation cum pocket park cum homeless hangout, came back to life. The city in 1983 agreed to lease the space at lowered rates to a restaurateur in exchange for maintenance expenses—"a good example," said the official who stewarded the arrangement, "of how a city can improve a public park through a cooperative effort with private industry."[18] In 1999, the space was renamed New Orleans Music Legends Park and was later adorned with statues of Fats Domino, Ronnie Kole, Al Hirt, Pete Fountain, Chris Owens, and Irma Thomas. Today traditional jazz bands play for free for patrons who purchase drinks from a concession in the rear, continuing the private-public arrangement established in the 1980s. Because it is public space, no one can be shooed away for not ordering, and because of stipulations in NOPSI's donation, the park will forever remain open to the sky.[19]

In sum, Bourbon Street reinvented itself in the 1980s with a free-spending party-animal zeitgeist modeled after the frat-boy/sorority-girl spring-break culture in vogue on campus and in cinema at the time. Ever savvy to where the money was, Bourbon Street also reattuned itself to the new business-class patronage that megagatherings (which could now be hosted in the brand-new convention center built for the 1984 World's Fair) brought to the city. In response, Bourbon Street, said the executive director of the Greater New Orleans Marketing Committee in 1989, "has become more sedate, more family oriented, more middle-class."[20] The socially progressive sensibilities of the 1960s and 1970s, which never gelled well with Bourbon, became a bad memory for The Street. The cheerfully unapologetic consumerism of the 1980s, on the other hand, suited Bourbonites just fine, and they prospered commensurately.

The Bourbon Street of the 1980s to the 2010s settled into a remarkable level of night-to-night consistency. Aside from stylistic changes and particular enterprises, a walk down Bourbon Street today could be swapped for any evening twenty-five years ago with no great noticeable difference, something that cannot be said about any prior era since the antebellum. In 1988 and in 2013, you could buy a "Huge Ass Beer" in a thirty-two-ounce translucent go-cup for a few dollars. You could fall for the huckster betting he can "tell you where you got dem shoes." You could steal a glance at the strippers leaning in doorways, or the faded amateur orgy photographs in the Topless-Bottomless place (they may even be the same photos). You could visit Chris Owens, who pretty much looks the same, and see her pretty similar Latin dance show. You could buy plastic tchotchkes, boorish T-shirts, outlandish Mardi Gras beads, or spectacularly overpriced hot sauces. You could walk past St. Ann Street in 1988 and 2013 and cross from straight to gay space: the line hasn't moved. The musical repertoire has also stabilized: you'll hear "Mustang Sally," "Margaritaville," "Sweet Home Alabama," and other rock standards, despite that American musical tastes have since fragmented. Even "the problems we have today," according to one Bourbon Street luminary speaking in 2012, "are the same problems we had 25 years ago"—not acute crises, but merely chronic civic disputes. After centuries of urban churn, Bourbon Street by the turn of the millennium had exhaustedly stumbled into stability.[21]

Behind that stasis was Bourbon Street's retooling for industrial-scale tourism. Souvenir, gift, and other retail shops increased in number from twenty-six to fifty-six between the early 1960s and the early 1980s. Bars and restaurants increased from thirty-four to forty-nine. Hotel rooms increased from a few score scattered across six locally owned boardinghouses to thousands in three corporate complexes. These megahotels did not turn a profit until they surpassed 60–70 percent occupancy rate, thus they required ever more promotion to attract more tourists, which in turn incentivized new competition, which edged up the break-even point, which called for more promotion, more tourists, more, more, more.[22] Residences, too, increased on Bourbon Street, from 133 to 156, despite that the French Quarter's population had declined from 7,669 to 5,596 between 1960 and 1980. The paradoxical rise of residences amid a decline of residents reflected the increasing number of townhouses, cottages, and shotgun doubles that were being carved into condominiums and sold to wealthy out-of-towners who craved a pied-à-terre with a Bourbon address for their occasional forays to New Orleans. That booming market drove down vacancies on Bourbon Street from forty-four to twenty between 1962 and 1982, yet those new living spaces were vacant most of the year. The only active land use that declined in this period was clubs, which dropped in number from nineteen to thirteen. Rents by 1990 averaged five thousand dollars per month for a typical ground-floor commercial space on Bourbon Street, 250 percent more than on Decatur.[23] Throughout the Quarter, there were 3,544 hotel and guest rooms in 1984, plus numerous illegal ones. There were also 23 new condo units with a total of 206 rooms that year, up from one unit of ten condos in 1972. Time-shares were attempted in the French Quarter but banned by a zoning change in 1981, which led them to cluster right up against the Quarter, in the 100 blocks or in the CBD.[24]

Disputes and discontents continued on the new Bourbon Street, but rarely were they unprecedented. Instead they represented replicating microperturbations within the stabilizing new order.

Disputes over street entertainers? Any distractions that diverted dollars into unlicensed, untaxed hands have long incensed Bourbon club and bar owners, who never have made peace with the public space of the street. When buskers used that space to earn tips from tourists, that was money denied the owners. Councilman Mike Early sided with them in passing a 1980 ordinance banning "musical performances, dances, mime, juggling, sword swallowing, magic shows, card tricks and shell games . . . during the busy night hours and only along Bourbon Street."[25] Buskers today work The Street right up to the ordained 8:00 p.m. endpoint, but with erratic enforcement, many continue afterward, particularly tap dancers. Tourists are often startled by the anachronistic and stereotyped sight of young black boys putting on impromptu tap-dance performances, and stare in ambivalence when shopkeepers or police chase them away.

Disagreements over the pedestrian mall? Bourbon merchants in 1988 got the City Council to change the motorized-traffic closure to 8:00 p.m. to 6:00 a.m. weekdays, based on their suspicion that strictures on taxi, truck, and bus traffic (which discharged tourists directly into targeted clubs) put The Street at a competitive disadvantage. Limiting this traffic, argued the merchants, had contributed to the closure of twenty businesses in the previous five years.[26] Worse, traffic closures also opened up space for street entertainers to perform. The nightly mall is now here to stay, but the timing and manner of the traffic blockage is tweaked and adjusted variously according to need. The method has also changed: instead of the three iron bollards and matching collars specially designed for this purpose in response to the task force recommendations, police now drag standard crowd barricades into place, which create slow-moving people jams preyed upon by pitchmen and pickpockets. Cross-street auto traffic continues to flow freely except for the drunken throngs, leading to sometimes comical, sometimes contentious interactions between impish crowds and irritable motorists.

Dismay over the decline of localism? "I'm one of the minute few (club owners) that's local," said Texas-born Chris Owens, after a wave of out-of-town, out-of-state, and in some cases out-of-country investors scooped up Bourbon properties during the peak tourism years at the turn of the millennium. Rents rose by at least 50 percent between 1997 and 2002, and in some cases doubled to the range of $250 per square foot. In other cases, purchasers got into bidding wars to buy out longtime property owners of what the *Times-Picayune* called "New Orleans' most valuable commercial real estate." "New money, new club owners": it seemed like the end of the era of localism. In fact, it had all happened before. Sicilians, most of them foreign-born, purchased Bourbon properties from Creole owners eighty and a hundred years earlier, which many locals viewed at the time as the end of the Old Quarter. Rents skyrocketed after World War II and again between the 1990s and 2009, each time flushing out older residents and bringing in new ones. Out-of-state corporations bought parcels to build huge hotels in the 1960s, and again the end-of-an-era dirge was sung. Each established group bemoans the newly arrived, forgetting that they too once held that status.[27]

Questions of cultural authenticity? That old Bourbon Street discourse found new cases in point as well. One involved the Absinthe Bar at Bourbon and Conti, a ca. 1840 storehouse that housed a Prohibition-era watering hole started by the same Pierre Cazebonne who ran the speakeasy inside the original Old Absinthe House at 240 Bourbon. Both establishments survived into modern times as Old World relics, with dark, mysterious interiors and an ornate bar. Patrons at both saloons tucked their calling cards into wall crevices, as if to personalize the exuding sense of time and place. The Absinthe Bar also featured a graceful old bar-top dripping fountain and an early example of an interior-lit protruding street sign. Blues musicians, playing in punch-clock shifts daily from noon to the wee hours, made the so-called "A-Bar" a favorite for local music lovers who otherwise hated Bourbon Street, as well as for luminaries such as B.B. King, Eric Clapton, Bruce Springsteen, Jimmy Page, and Robert Plant. By the late 1990s, however, fewer and fewer Bourbon patrons appreciated such quaint charms; college students in particular gravitated to wide-open grab-and-go alcohol outlets bathed in colored lights and pulsating with dance rhythms. The city's 5 percent amusement tax on live music, the hassle of scheduling gigs and dealing with insouciant musicians, and the relative frugality of local blues aficionados compared to tourists, all undermined the viability of the A-Bar. Owner Joe Sinatra opted to change course, and in late 1997 the tavern underwent a complete redesign—to a tropical-themed pizza-and-daiquiri bar. It was all perfectly legal because the Vieux Carré Commission retains no jurisdiction over building interiors. "Certain places are a tradition and you'd think they'll be here for ever and ever, but it's not always the case," explained the commission chairman. "We're in a market-driven economy, and businessmen go where the money is."[28] Coming amid the closing of Maylie's, Godchaux's, D. H. Holmes, Kolb's, Krauss, K&B's, Maison Blanche, and numerous other downtown institutions, plus the arrival of national chains such as the House of Blues, Starbucks, Hard Rock Café, and Bubba Gump, the A-Bar's closure came to be viewed as a requiem for New Orleans culture in general and Bourbon Street in particular. All that remained of the old motif was the antique protruding sign—until Hurricane Katrina's winds swept it into the hands of a pilferer.

But all this, too, had happened before, and Bourbon Street and New Orleans culture survived. When the Bourbon House, a favored watering hole of the literati since the 1930s, had closed in 1964, bohemians mourned the loss with a jazz funeral and lamented the decline of old French Quarter culture. When the old-school nightclubs disappeared a few years later, nostalgic souls once again decried the end of old Bourbon Street. And fifty years before all of this, when the Old French Opera House burned down, many predicted it would "sound the death knell of that entire quarter of the city, with its odd customs that charm the stranger."[29] All were wrong. Change had plenty of precedent on this centuries-old street. If anything, it was *stabilization* that was unprecedented!

Innovations on Bourbon Street? The Street has long served as a local laboratory for testing the viability of external fads and trends. Concert saloons, Turkish baths, orchestrons, melodeons, gas-jet illumination, and electrical lights and fans came to Bourbon Street in the late 1800s before they could be found elsewhere in the region. Fancy leisure-travel hotels like the Cosmopolitan (1892) arrived on or near Bourbon Street first, as did nightclubs and speakeasies in the 1920s. Bourbon bars were the first commercial spaces to adopt air conditioners in the 1930s, and televisions and pressurized draft beer in 1948. As the social scene moved outdoors in the 1970s, Bourbon innovators invented "window hawking" and developed whimsical receptacles for the crowd to carry their drinks to-go. When wine bars and smoothies became all the rage, a Bourbon entrepreneur established the NOLA Tropical Wine Smoothie Bar in 2012. Bourbon Street also hosted New Orleans's first and best example of a gay bar in the 1950s, and of gay public space starting a few years later—a space that is now headquarters of the Gulf South's oldest and largest gay weekly, *Ambush*. Musically, too, Bourbon has a history of innovation. Entertainer Chris Owens brought Latin music and dance from Havana to Bourbon Street decades before the *Buena Vista Social Club* introduced it to the rest of the nation. Owens also "incorporated the latest dance innovations she'd picked up in Paris and Las Vegas."[30] Veteran jazz trumpeter Wallace Davenport adapted his repertoire to changing musical tastes in the late 1980s with "probably the world's only rap version of 'Muskrat Ramble.'"[31] Starting in 1989, the Cat's Meow on Bourbon introduced the Japanese innovation of karaoke to New Orleans, and a few years later, Bourbon clubs were among the first

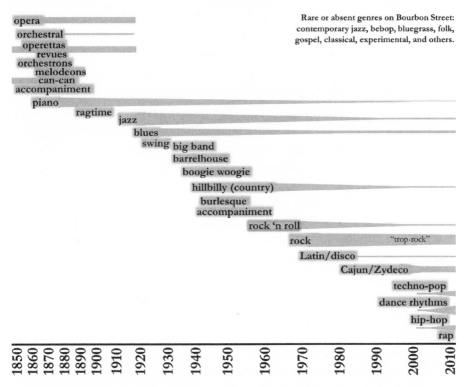

Musical genres performed on Bourbon Street, from the 1850s to the 2010s. *Interpretation by author.*

to install webcams broadcasting street scenes over the Internet. Today, Bourbon Street changes personalities late on Fridays and Saturday nights by tossing out the classic rock for the latest hip-hop, rap, and bounce—a musical transformation that may be unique in the city. Bourbon also served as a launch pad, base camp, or landing strip for the careers of Louis Prima, Oscar "Papa" Celestin, Freddy Fender, Clarence "Frogman" Henry, Albert "Papa" French, Jimmy Buffett, Al Hirt, Pete Fountain, James Booker, Mac Rebennack (Dr. John), the Meters, and Chocolate Milk, among others. "A lot of people don't realize the number of people who graduated from Bourbon Street," said singer Ernie Cosse in 1988; "As an educational tool, I think the street is invaluable. . . . [The] 'University of Bourbon Street[:] When people ask me where I learn my music, that's what I tell them."[32]

Debates over din? Neighborly conflict over clamor has a legal history in New Orleans dating to at least 1831, when a city ordinance forbade "cries, songs, noise or . . . disturbing . . . the peace and tranquility of the neighbourhood."[33] It height-

ened during World War II, when a "distressed citizen" complained of the "singing and shouting all night" to "juke boxes and other noisy music" on Bourbon
Street, which kept up those "who have come here to work in war industries."
VCPORA campaigned in 1946 for a law specifically targeting Bourbon Street
racket.[34] Noise ordinances soon went on the books, but most suffered from legal
chinks. To begin, sound waves vary constantly, defy reliable measurement, and
are difficult to trace to a point source in a legally airtight way. Clubs accused of
violations in an agglomerated environment like Bourbon Street often successfully
argued that they were being singled out amid an ambient cacophony. Why not go
after the revved motorcycle engines on St. Peter Street, they asked, or the howls
of delirious carousers? With the attendant controversies of the pedestrian mall
and window hawking, a music club could argue for the necessity of clamoring for
the cavalcade as convincingly as an angry homeowner could complain about its
intolerability. Fines at one point were imposed when sounds surpassed 85 decibels (the equivalent of a dishwasher, or a passing motorcycle); later, the nighttime
limit was set at 60 decibels in residentially zoned areas, and 10 decibels above
ambient levels in the Vieux Carré Entertainment zone including Bourbon Street.
Club owners and musicians wrestled with the regulations and resented their irregular enforcement, which put the law-abiding ones at a competitive disadvantage. Even longtime Orleans Parish coroner and jazz musician Frank Minyard,
who does not hesitate to opine on the affairs of the living, denounced his NOPD
colleagues for cracking down on noise. "Police should keep Bourbon Street safe,
not silent," he said in 1977, mocking their "running around the street with a
decibel meter in their hands" while criminals roamed freely.[35] Spurred by angry
neighbors who did not see the matter as trivial at all, the city established a Noise
Control Program in its Health Department and introduced computers and digital
decibel meters for enforcement. The hullabaloo nevertheless erupted regularly
into the 2000s. After the 2005 flood, the city generally gave Bourbon Street and
other entertainment hot spots leeway to compensate for weak post-Katrina tourism. According to preservationists, bars and dance clubs on Bourbon exploited
the leniency and entered the 2010s louder than ever—the chief reason why the
Louisiana Landmarks Society put Bourbon Street ("threatened by excessive noise
and pounding vibrations") on its 2012 list of most endangered historic sites.[36]

The latest noise-control controversy produced strange bedfellows. Bourbonites found themselves befriended by their own detractors, namely the denizens
of Frenchmen Street, who universally snubbed Bourbon Street but also resented
attempts to muffle local musical culture. Together they found themselves on

the defensive against preservationists and homeowner groups like VCPORA and the Faubourg Marigny Neighborhood Improvement Association. Likewise, those groups, whose members tend to wax eloquent about New Orleans music, found themselves pitted against musicians, who generally love historical neighborhoods. Aware of the sensitive situation, music-loving preservationists tried to defuse the tension by emphatically distinguishing between "music" and "noise," going so far as to name their activist group "Hear the Music, Stop the Noise." Addressing the matter fell into the hands of District C councilwoman Kristin Palmer, who, recognizing the technical shortfalls of audio enforcement and after consulting with Bourbonites and neighbors, crafted a new approach. In 2012, Palmer amended the existing noise ordinance to stipulate that loudspeakers had to be oriented inward and mounted at least ten feet inside exterior doors in the case of alcohol-serving bars and restaurants, and twenty feet for retailers. The amendment was easily enforceable, required no special equipment, used indisputable quantitative measurements, and cleverly forced perpetrators to endure their own mayhem. But it did not ultimately prevent the production of excessive noise. The 10-decibel-above-ambient limit, despite its problems, remains the premier metric for legally curtailing Bourbon Street din. The city is currently consulting with an acoustician on how to simplify, standardize, and enforce the balance between the commercial need to make noise and the residential right to have peace.[37]

Resistance to "junk" retailers? Authorities in the early 1980s tinkered with zoning ordinances in an attempt to curtail the sort of shops that, when concentrated, blighted The Street and neighborhood. These included T-shirt and novelty shops (eleven of which operated just on the 400 block of Bourbon in 1981), massage and tattoo parlors, and triple-X bookstores. Preservationists had complained about such places at least since the 1950s. Some felt the marketplace would solve the problem; the recession of 1981–82, for example, cost some Bourbon merchants 20 to 50 percent of their business, leading Bourbon Street Merchants Association founder Ruth Ann Menutis to predict that low-end retailers "with poor volume [and] poor operators" would be purged from The Street. Others wanted to try the zoning concept of "spacing," in which a certain land use is permitted so long as a certain distance separates the permitted entities. Instead, a moratorium on new businesses offering the offending goods or services went into effect in August 1981. But because demand persisted, the supply crept back into the marketplace. Councilman Mike Early, who walked a tightrope between his Bourbon-hating and Bourbon-dependent District C constituents, proposed in 1987 that businesses would have to renew their permits annually subject to a review of their inventory. The proposal pleased residents but enraged merchants. The latter heckled a hapless City Council representative who attempted to explain the proposal at a raucous public meeting, and later took their protest to Bourbon Street with a three-hour "blackout" that left half the neon strip dark and all its visitors bewildered. The inventory-inspection proposal raised constitutional questions as well, about whether "government [should] have the arbitrary authority to 'tell you what you can buy and where you can buy it. Where does it stop?'" Early struggled to convince a majority of the council to enact the tough new law, and it went down to defeat in 1988—thus the proliferation of trinket and T-shirt shops on Bourbon Street today. Nevertheless, restraints do exist on the supply side of the Bourbon Street marketplace; the City Planning Commission, the Vieux Carré Commission, and other city agencies, not to mention VCPORA and preservationists, remain actively involved in opining what businesses can open where and in what numbers. Crafty entrepreneurs, meanwhile, have developed skills to evade them, because, in the end, they are supplying what visitors demand at the price they want to pay.

Bourbon Street is anything but the seemingly spontaneous spasm of ecstasy it schemes to be, and the days of free-market perfect competition are over. That *did* change.[38]

Nudity in private space? Baring of flesh in Bourbon clubs had been a target of social reformers ever since the "tease" went out of the "strip" fifty years ago. Interactions between dancers and patrons, suspected to lead to B-drinking and prostitution, have been regulated since the Garrison crackdowns. Both issues resurfaced in the early 2000s, when state legislators proposed imposing a six-foot buffer between strippers and customers. Bourbon clubs protested the legislation vehemently because it would have thwarted a major source of income: lap dances and private-room showings.[39] They won.

A burlesque revival on Bourbon Street? The late 1990s and 2000s heralded a certain nostalgia for Old Bourbon. Retro was in; young women got a kick out of donning vintage threads and fire-engine-red lipstick, and guys wanted to look and act like the Rat Pack. A revival of burlesque ensued on and off Bourbon Street, and attempts to bring back over-the-top headliners and campy fabulousness were met with great enthusiasm—but limited commercial success. If anything, Old

Bourbon became something of a show itself. Playwright and longtime *Times-Picayune* theater critic David Cuthbert cowrote and staged a theatrical production in 1998 entitled *At the Club Toot Sweet,* based on an incident in 1958 when a Bourbon venue held a benefit to raise bail for busted strippers. Cuthbert was uniquely qualified for the task; as the son of ventriloquist Phil D'Rey, he spent much of his boyhood in and around club dressing rooms and grew up with the stars. The Street struck him as "the most glamorous, magical place in the world," and provided him with his first job as the spotlighter for Evelyn West. By then the days of emceed nightclub entertainment were waning. "They were variety shows with tits," he chuckled, recalling the last days of Old Bourbon. "It was like where vaudeville went to die."[40] Vaudeville has been long dead on Bourbon, and burlesque never quite revived, largely because the people who now find it retro-chic and ironic-cool generally shun modern Bourbon Street and are not prone to dropping eight hundred dollars at a nudie joint. Today the burlesque revival in New Orleans is a self-aware, glammed-up parody of itself, in which performers perform past performances in an annual festival attended mostly by retrophiliacs. And it isn't held on Bourbon Street.

Mardi Gras on Bourbon Street? Here too we see forms recognizable today. A collection of photographs taken during Mardi Gras 1965 provide clues as to how. We see revelers who, judging from the 285 discernible faces in the images, are 100 percent white, 75 percent male, overwhelmingly middle class in appearance, and mostly in their twenties to forties, with a few in their middle years and only one child and one senior. The statistics today are much more diverse but still predominantly white, male, middle-class, and similarly aged. A small portion of the 1965 revelers wore costumes; some were simply stylized hats and garments while others were elaborate: court jesters, an Aztec warrior, a vaquero, Jesus, plus a fair number of men in drag. One woman had phony inflated breasts beneath her shirt and a pin saying, "I Like Sex." All of these trappings are immediately recognizable today—times a hundred. Some revelers in 1965 wore a strand or two of pearl necklaces from Mardi Gras parades; today most revelers sport dozens of pairs of colorful and elaborate beads. About 10 to 15 percent of the photographed revelers had drinks in their hands, mostly twelve-ounce tin cans of beer (which sold for thirty-five cents, the same price as a Lucky Dog with chili) or draft beers in paper cups (forty cents). Today at least three-quarters of Bourbon carousers, by midafternoon on Mardi Gras, bear libations a lot bigger than twelve ounces and

priced commensurately. There are some differences: almost no one stood on balconies or galleries in 1965; litter was very light; parked cars lined the street; and
crowd density appeared to be at most one-quarter of that of Fat Tuesday today.[41]

Nudity in public space? Flashing on Bourbon Street during Mardi Gras, which
started in the mid-1970s when the cessation of French Quarter parades opened
up opportunities for alternate diversions, grew increasingly popular in the 1980s.
By then, bead manufacturing had shifted to China; prices dropped, demand increased, and the sizes, styles, and quantities of the plastic jewelry grew annually,
as each Carnival krewe competed for the favor of the public. Beads thrown liberally from parade floats had become a major Mardi Gras attraction, and the catches
that revelers carted back to Bourbon Street became a coveted form of currency
to negotiate a flash with a stranger. Typically, males in the street identify a sufficiently buxom young female on a balcony and pressure her with chants of "Show
Your Tits." Beads are displayed as enticement—and like her breasts, the bigger
the better. More often than not, she acquiesces, yanks up her blouse, catches her
remuneration, and retreats. The mob howls its drunken approval and seeks the
next victim. So widespread had the flashing phenomenon grown that Louisiana
State University sociologists Wesley Shrum and John Kilburn designed a scholarly
investigation of the practice. Using more than a thousand videotaped flashing
exchanges captured during the 1991 Carnival season, the researchers found that
Bourbon Street hosted immensely more flashing that Royal Street, that women
flashed far more than men despite male numerical predomination, and that the
activity mostly occurred during daytime and in spatial and temporal clusters,
flaring up sporadically on certain balconies. The research posited that a "market
paradigm" existed in the flesh-for-beads exchanges, such that the accumulation
and public display of beads legitimized an activity that would otherwise be considered deviant. It also showed that women up on balconies were more likely to
disrobe for sheer public veneration, uncompensated by beads, than when they
were down in the street. The researchers concluded that Mardi Gras flashing "is
not simply unstructured hedonism but a ritualized enactment of the economic
markets that characterize contemporary society," something that can be said
about Bourbon Street in general.[42]

Fueling the flashing phenomenon was the burgeoning popularity among college students of spring-break jaunts to Fort Lauderdale and other sunny warm
spots, where alcohol-drenched exhibitionist beach parties became the central

attraction. Because New Orleans was en route to these destinations, and because Mardi Gras often coincided with university spring breaks, youth flocked to Bourbon Street and found a perfectly conducive cultural ambit for balmy springtime escapism. Bourbonites met them halfway by theming their joints with a tropical flare complete with fruity daiquiris and Jimmy Buffett music. The social *tout ensemble* seemed to embrace and encourage public sexuality. Middle-class white college students from the South came to dominate the scene, and many young men, invariably dubbed "frat boys," patronized Bourbon Street during Mardi Gras expressly for the flashing action. (One researcher who interviewed 150 Bourbon revelers who participated in public "lewd behavior," ranging from flashing to penetrative sex, found that 79 percent were white; 83 percent had been to college; and 44 percent had bachelor's, master's, Ph.D., law, or medical degrees.)[43] The flashing craze created a subeconomy on The Street: shops sold "Show Your Tits" T-shirts and obscenely huge beads as specie for the exchanges; building owners cleaned out upper floors and rented out balconies; and an entrepreneur who compiled footage of the disrobings made millions off his *Girls Gone Wild* videos—more free advertising for Bourbon Street. By the late 1990s, flashing had spread from Carnival season to most weekend nights, and according to the Mayor's Mardi Gras Advisory Committee, diffused beyond Bourbon Street "up St. Charles Avenue and Canal Street—[Carnival] turf usually considered safe for the family set."[44] Increasingly the spectacle came to define Bourbon Street, Mardi Gras, and New Orleans in general to people worldwide, who did not realize that it was visitors and not locals disrobing. Crackdowns on the illegal practice occurred periodically; in 1999, police arrested 360 Bourbon flashers—mostly males who exposed their genitals, because breast baring had become so commonplace that snaring a specific woman bordered on arbitrary. The Bourbon Street Merchants Association, concerned that revelers might go home with police records, posted warnings in windows, but they knew all too well that the unpaid voluntary strippers boosted their bottom line.

What tossed a bucket of cold water on the practice was not the crackdown but the unholy union of digital video and Internet connectivity. A smartphone in every hand upped the chances that a single moment of impetuous exuberance might become permanently enshrined in cyberspace. That possibility made young women with professional aspirations think twice before succumbing to the barbaric chants of a gaggle of drunken lads. In effect, digital recording and distribution undermined that liberating sense of anonymity which, since historic times, made a cosmopolitan crossroads like New Orleans conducive to debauched dabblings. Nudity on Bourbon continues today, but it has largely retreated to Carnival season, and it tends to involve fewer well-bred college girls.[45]

Organized crime on Bourbon Street? The syndicate—whether one calls it the mob or the Mafia is a matter of terminology—that controlled illicit moneymaking activities on The Street from the 1930s through the 1960s petered out in the 1970s and 1980s. Said one owner interviewed in 2012: "When we first came [to Bourbon in 1984], we rented from [these guys who] were at the time the Jewish Mafia down here. They kind of ruled the street." But organized crime's reign was waning by then. Legalization of gambling ("gaming") in Louisiana in the 1990s robbed the mob of its racket, even as their ilk aged and died off. Of those that held on, "most . . . have gone into the video poker business now," said the informant. "They kind of legitimized what they do."[46] The Mafia's status regionwide today is often described as "unknown," probably because of the difficulty of proving nonexistence.

Occasionally, however, a relic of Bourbon Street's bad old days surfaces. In 2004, a man named Mitchell Schwartz Sr. was arrested for hustling tourists in the back of a Bourbon Street souvenir shop. Not an uncommon thing—except this huckster was ninety-two years old and had a criminal record going back generations: a burglary in Minnesota in 1930, bootlegging in Chicago during the Depression, a sodomy offense during World War II, a Thompson machine gun charge in 1946, a French Quarter racket in the 1960s and 1970s, and drug charges in 1976. Bourbon-loving Governor Edwin Edwards pardoned him in 1984 because of his age, after which Schwartz promptly opened a souvenir shop at 335 Bourbon and worked clean day and night. But he eventually drifted back to his Bourbon ways, scamming visitors with illegal backroom gambling games such as Razzle Dazzle and bribing police for protection. He was arrested and convicted, but he died on the day of his sentencing in 2005. "I used to be a gangster. So what?" he told an interviewer. "I did what I wanted to do."[47]

Is Bourbon Street dangerous? Those who answer affirmatively fail to account for the fact that, while scams, pickpockets, drug sales, prostitution, muggings, and gunplay occur here with seeming regularity, their frequency is dwarfed by the tens of thousands of people who pack themselves nightly into this space. Normalized by this huge denominator, the high absolute number of crimes on Bourbon Street sinks to a very low per-capita rate. Indeed, when measured in this manner, Bourbon Street may well be one of the safest places in New Orleans. Particularly now that Mr. Schwartz is gone.

Bigotry on Bourbon Street? While racial tensions have persisted on the strip since integration, no longer are they overt like times past. But traces of that era have persisted. The image of the Confederate battle flag abounded in gift shops and on balconies as recently as the 1990s, but disappeared shortly thereafter when a number of high-profile protests elsewhere infused the symbol with racial tension. So too went black mammies and pickaninny dolls, although they still may be found (made in China) in some novelty shops.

Beyond material culture, racialized moments occur stealthily on Bourbon Street today, such as when businesses suddenly decide to board their windows and take a vacation precisely as thousands of African American Louisianians arrive for the Bayou Classic football game. Or when bouncers allow entry to a white man dressed in gang attire but block a similarly dressed black youth, directing his attention to a sign that reads:

NO BACKWARD/SIDEWAYS HATS/NO EXCESSIVE BAGGY CLOTHING/[No] Over Sized Shirts and Pants past the Butt/NO HOODS OR DO-RAGS/NO PLAIN WHITE OR COLORED T-Shirts that are Oversized.[48]

Such obliquely racial stratagems usually evaded public attention. That changed on New Year's Eve 2004, when a black college student named Levon Jones clashed with white bouncers over a dress-code dispute and ended up suffocating to death at their hands. Murky details aside, the incident brought to light the differing treatments that blacks and whites often encounter on Bourbon Street. To investigate, an advocacy group teamed with the city in 2005 and dispatched pairs of similarly dressed young white and black men to various Bourbon Street bars and compared their experiences. Black testers, the activists reported, were overcharged or hassled at fifteen of the twenty-nine bars visited. The findings recalled the American Football League incident of 1965, when black players endured egregious and widespread discriminatory experiences on Bourbon Street and boycotted the All-Star game in response. "Man, it's like New Orleans was stuck in the 1950s and 1960s," pronounced Mayor C. Ray Nagin upon hearing the results of the 2005 investigation. "We all know Bourbon Street is a hustle, and nothing is wrong with that, as long as you're hustling everyone equally," said a member of the Nagin administration. "But [the Bourbon bartenders] got caught hustling African-American men." As in 1965, the incident made international news; the London Independent, for instance, headlined "Old South Racism Lives on in Big Easy's Bourbon Street." Unlike in the 1960s, when civil rights activists assiduously avoided bawdy Bourbon, this time the NAACP staged a "March on Bourbon Street" and advertised widely. The event, which took place on a hot summer Saturday, suffered from reports of black marchers ejecting sympathetic whites from their ranks, and drew commentaries by unfriendly skeptics who cast the black travails on Bourbon Street as trivial compared to the violence and poverty of black neighborhoods. Two months later, Hurricane Katrina struck and made everything seem trivial in comparison. But racial tensions resumed only six weeks later, when white policemen were videotaped beating a sixty-four-year-old African American former teacher alleged to be intoxicated and resisting arrest.[49] Bouncers today must seek certification through the state's Office of Alcohol and Tobacco control, and the program includes plenty of "sensitivity training."

Recent years have seen a new social trend with racial implications on Bourbon Street. As weary tourists stumble back to their hotels after a long Friday or Saturday evening, youths arrive around midnight and congregate in certain clubs, which musically accommodate them by switching from classic rock to hip-hop, rap, and bounce. Unlike the evening crowd, the wee-hour revelers are mostly local, young, black, and poor. "It started a little bit after Katrina, when so many of the African American bars were destroyed," recollected one Bourbon businessman. Other predominantly black bars "had issues with the Alcohol Beverage [Control] Board; several had been closed down for shootings, fights, and stabbings." So young black patrons started to come to Bourbon Street, and because many are underage, "they congregate out in the street and sometimes fights erupt. . . . Unfortunately I think a lot of these kids are packing guns, [and] that's when the trouble starts."[50] Late-night shoot-outs on Bourbon Street occurred every few months in the post-Katrina years, sometimes making the national news. The new development worried Bourbonites, but they spoke carefully about it to the press, using nonracial descriptors such as "gangster-type individuals," "juveniles," or "thugs [with] convictions for felonies." Others used musical metaphors. "We've never played a hip-hop song and never will," said one club owner, clarifying: "It's not about the money. It's all about the quality of the music."[51] Some owners enacted internal policies toward keeping the unwanted guests at bay, at times flouting public-accommodations laws. It's fair to say that some Bourbonites are as oblivious to the discriminatory effects of their door policies as some civil rights activists are to Bourbon Street's late-night "thug problem." When in 2011 a black employee at Pat O'Brien's was murdered by young black males who had a row with him on Bourbon Street, civil rights activists remained silent. And when a white stripper was abducted in 2012 by a white couple and horribly dismembered, her head and legs washing up on Mississippi beaches, no one talked about Bourbon Street's white-thug problem. As for the Bourbonites, it's not the first time they've griped about undesirable "invasions." They excoriated the white hippies of the late 1960s just as they do the late-night black youths of the 2010s—even more, because the hippies had no money to spend and took all day not spending it.

Ethnic composition among Bourbonites changed as well, but those changes, too, had familiar historical antecedents. The last of the Chinese merchants decamped in the 1980s, and today there is only one reminder of the former Chinatown, the painted On Leong Merchants Association sign at 532 Bourbon. Yet now there is a new Asian presence—South Asian. It arrived as part of remarkable economic specialization on the part of immigrants from Gujarat, an industrialized state in western India whose population, many of whom bear the surname Patel, is known for its entrepreneurial acumen. In seeking opportunities for self-employment, Gujaratis found budget motels to offer a decent fit, as they provided living space and jobs for the whole family. They shared their success, which mounted in the 1970s, with compatriots who invested similarly. Largely unnoticed by the national media, Indian Americans, who comprise barely 1 percent of the population, today control 40 percent of the United States' total lodging supply, and most of its economy units (dubbed "Patel motels"). Because hotels and motels are clustered in hospitality hubs, Gujarati hotelier success spilled over into the related sector of souvenir and trinket retailing. For this reason, an American family vacation to the Great Smoky Mountains or the Alamo or Niagara Falls probably involves a visit to a Gujarati-owned hotel or souvenir shop. So too Bourbon Street and the French Quarter, where most trinket shops are staffed by Indian Americans and owned by Kishore "Mike" Motwani, the so-called "T-shirt kingpin." Motwani's retail spaces have a certain look: white pegboard walls and drop ceilings, blinding white florescent lighting, shelves packed with tchotchkes, racks overloaded with feathered boas and T-shirts, with incongruous Cajun accordions grinding over the CD speakers. Proprietor of dozens of T-shirt shops, ATM niches, and other cut-rate enterprises throughout downtown New Orleans, Motwani has for more than two decades locked horns with preservationists, city agencies, and former employees, who have accused him of everything from misrepresenting his merchandise during the permitting process, to demolition by neglect, to denying overtime pay. His detractors love to hate him, and his own colleagues tell him to his face that he's "not a good person." It's not the first time that an immigrant population capitalized on an economic niche and raised the ire of the establishment. Chinatown was criticized as an opium den; Sicilian-owned clubs and bars were viewed as Mafia joints; Jewish merchants on Dryades Street were accused of profiting from blacks but not hiring them; and throughout poor neighborhoods today, Arab and Vietnamese corner grocers are viewed as exploitive by some African Americans. As for Bourbon, most merchandise purchased on The Street today is made by East Asians and sold by South Asian Americans to visitors seeking to remember their trip to quaint New Orleans. Their souvenir, however, is mostly a tribute to globalization.[52]

Queer space on Bourbon Street? The St. Ann "lavender line," traceable to the late 1950s and well established by the 1970s, now benefits from a massive annual reinforcement every Labor Day weekend in the form of Southern Decadence. Like Bourbon Street itself, the loosely organized festival has no president, no Inc., no headquarters, and a rather prosaic origin—a 1972 house party in Tremé in which "a handful of bored college students" asked attendees to dress as their favorite decadent southern literary, historical, or cinematic character.[53] The party's success warranted a repeat the next year, and soon it developed a parade, a grand marshal, and a spontaneous route linking favorite gay bars, most of them around Bourbon and St. Ann. Early Decadence revelers were mostly gay and mostly local, drawn from a metro-area population (1980) estimated at around fifty thousand.[54] The AIDS epidemic took a terrible toll on that population, as well as on the festival. The event recovered in the 1990s when gays nationwide, informed by Internet sources, reinvigorated attendance. By mid-decade, it had grown to fifty thousand strong and was responsible for $25 million in spending; by the 2010s, it had nearly tripled in attendance, while spending increased over sixfold. Southern Decadence solidified the St. Ann–Dumaine stretch of Bourbon Street as the epicenter of the gay geography of the city, region, and Gulf South— even as gays are increasingly departing decades-old gay residential enclaves and integrating with the general population. Today, this space has four major gay bars and clubs, two restaurants, two gift shops, a gay tabloid publisher, and additional gay-oriented enterprises within a one-block radius. The area developed its own cityscape, marked with rainbow flags and bunting and multicolored neon. It re-

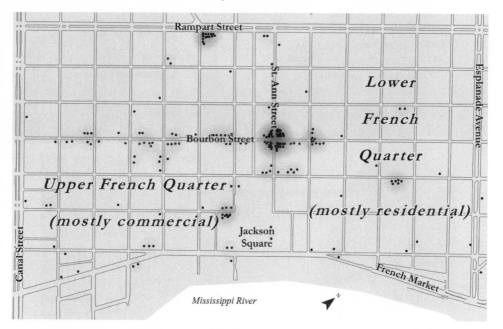

Gay spaces during the 2010 Southern Decadence Festival: each dot represents one rainbow flag visible in the public space, as surveyed and mapped by the author.

mains, however, almost exclusively male. The few lesbian bars in the city tend to be dispersed, and the closest New Orleans comes to having a lesbian neighborhood is Bayou St. John.

Contentiousness on Bourbon Street? Veteran bar tycoon Earl Bernhardt is philosophical on the inevitability of Bourbon battles: "The problems we had [in the 1980s and 1990s] are the same problems we have today. . . . There's always been a constant fight[;] the residents hate the businesses and the businesses don't like the residents. . . . I don't know of any city in the country that doesn't have the same problems." He allowed that "VCPORA is not as vicious today . . . as they have been in the past," and compared it and the Vieux Carré Commission to "a thorn in your side; pretty soon you get used to the pain. I've learned to deal with them. I used to really get upset over the things they'd do; I don't anymore. . . . They'd love for the Quarter to be a little quiet community with no activity, but that's never going to happen. It all kind of balances out."[55] Bernhardt's words of 2012 echo those of Bourbon defender Curly Lima, who in 1948 wrote: "To the guardians of the historic French Quarter: Stop . . . picking on the men [who]

Bourbon Street at the St. Ann intersection (*top*, Mardi Gras 2012) has formed the premier gay spot for decades, and for this reason is often the site for pro- and antigay confrontations. This dispute (*bottom*) took place on Mardi Gras morning of 2013. *Photographs by author.*

operate bars and clubs that pay heavy taxes." To those who decried the changes on The Street, Lima pointed out its surging economic activity: "We certainly could not expect Bourbon to stay as it was."[56] Bernhardt and Lima would have also agreed on The Street's internal ungovernability, and on how order somehow seemed to emerge from disorder. Merchants associations, said Bernhardt, "work for a while, and then they don't. Bourbon Street's probably the biggest disorganized street in the whole country. . . . I was once president of the Bourbon Street Merchants Association, for five years. That was probably the worst five years of my life," he said, laughing ruefully. "It got so time-consuming; you get tired of just fighting, fighting, fighting."[57]

Bernhardt had better things to do on Bourbon Street, and his record proves it. He is half owner of five bustling bars on Bourbon and a restaurant on Royal. He is also the creator of the tropical Caribbean theme that has since diffused throughout Bourbon Street, the employer of 130 full-time staff positions and 65 musicians, and the inventor of the trademarked Hand Grenade—"the number-one drink in the French Quarter; we sell well over a million of them a year." Musically, too, Bernhardt and partner Pam Fortner have won over critics, bringing trop-rock and blues to a place better known for covering hair bands; in 2013 they were recognized for "providing quality music and entertainment on Bourbon Street" by *OffBeat Magazine,* a local music monthly otherwise more inclined to criticize the strip. Brains, creativity, marketing skills honed as a radio station manager in civil rights–era Mississippi, and relentless hard work brought Bernhardt his success. "We never let up. We advertise all the time," he says. "We didn't take a vacation for the first ten years." And Bourbon Street provided just the right entrepreneurial environment for an enterprising spirit like Bernhardt to prosper. "It's fun. Where else can you walk into your business and meet people from four or five different countries around the world, all sitting at your bar? It's work, but it's pleasant work. I'll be [on Bourbon Street] as long as the good Lord allows me." More so than any other street in the city, economic success has found a home on Bourbon Street.[58]

In sum, nearly everything that transpires on Bourbon Street today has happened yesterday. Newcomers overestimate the spontaneity and abandon of what they see, and old-timers underestimate how resilient, stable, and important this cultural-economic engine has become. Those who love Bourbon Street find in it harmless fantasy and pleasure, and worry that it might someday lose its charm;

those who hate it view it as tasteless, inauthentic, and immoral, and worry that it stigmatizes the city—all echoes of what was said in the 2000s, the 1980s, the 1960s, the 1940s, and the 1920s. For all its din and mayhem, Bourbon Street will enter its fourth century as the single most stable social and economic space within the least predictable city on the continent.

III
BOURBON STREET AS
A SOCIAL ARTIFACT

Locating Bourbon Street
Why Here?

To all men whose desire [is] to live a short life but a merry one, I have no hesitation in recommending New Orleans.

— HENRY BRADSHAW FEARON, *Sketches of* America (1819)

Bourbon Street happened when New Orleanians realized that their city's "merry life," as reported regularly in the nineteenth century by the likes of Henry Fearon, could be sold in the twentieth century to the traveling leisure class. It was forged into the marvelously lucrative perpetual gratification machine it is today through an ongoing civic wrestling match between enterprising plebian proprietors who figured out how to monetize merriment, and educated professionals and patricians who wanted peace, order, and preservation. Bourbon Street succeeded because it supplied the demanded indulgences within a walkable space amid an intimate historic setting, making it maximally appealing and consumable by pleasure pilgrims from places like Peoria.

Which begs the question, why did that spatial concentration of bars, nightclubs, and restaurants end up on Bourbon and not some other street? After all, its predecessors were located as far down as Gallatin Street, as far up as Girod, and as far back as the swamp, Franklin Street, and Storyville.

Why did Bourbon the Phenomenon not end up on, for example, St. Charles Avenue, Camp, Carondelet, Baronne, Magazine, or other streets in the Central Business District? A handful of nighttime entertainment venues did exist here, and do to this day, but high-priced office space, white-collar jobs, and incompatible zoning would have prevented a critical mass from forming, let alone along a single street. Additionally, the district's arteries are multilaned, its buildings scrape the sky, and its urban granularity is hardly intimate. And, except for South

Rampart Street, it was never home to the intrepid immigrants who populated the French Quarter and gave rise to the real Bourbon.

Returning to the Quarter, why not Decatur or North Peters? Fronting the river, these arteries bustled with light industry and retail, and had up to four lanes of traffic. Lower Decatur in particular was "Little Palermo"—poor, elemental, and Old World, while upper Decatur had warehouses, trucks, and trains serving the nearby sugar-processing district. Would you want to take your date to a nightclub here? It was simply too commercial, industrial, and arterial to exude the right twilight aura.

Likewise Rampart Street, which, from colonial times to today, always had a sketchy feel, not to mention four lanes of traffic and a working-class residential neighborhood on the other side. As Decatur and North Peters were too close to the river and its industrial nuisances, Rampart was too close to the urban and demographic echoes of the former backswamp.

What about Dauphine or Burgundy? Readers will recall that Bourbon Street's predecessor as a rowdy drinking and dancing district was the Tango Belt, centered on upper Dauphine and Burgundy. Could either of these streets have snared the club trade? Unlikely, because beyond the first few blocks, these streets were mostly residential. Cottages and shotgun houses do not make good nightclubs and restaurants. Dauphine and Burgundy simply did not have the right architecture to host Bourbon the Phenomenon, and subsequent land-use zoning made sure of that.

Chartres and Royal are different stories. Replete with storehouses and townhouses, these elegant streets, famous in their own right, had since the 1860s laid claim to their share of nighttime entertainment, much like Bourbon. Royal in particular boasted the ca. 1892 Cosmopolitan Hotel, and still has the ca. 1912 Monteleone. Why they did not draw the nightclub economy may well be because they did not want it. The high-end antiquarian trade had come to characterize Royal (and, to a lesser extent, Chartres), and it both reflected and produced an aristocratic ladies'-club atmosphere that was more inclined to sniff at Bourbon Street than to emulate it.

Antiques have dominated Royal Street for decades longer than nightclubs have been on Bourbon. Old-line antiquarians were not inclined to sell out to barkeeps and impresarios, and the proprietors of the pricey buildings were decidedly not the working-class Sicilians who owned much of Bourbon Street and the lower Quarter.[1] The resulting contrast between Bourbon and Royal became an oft-observed dualism. Walt Disney, who so admired the French Quarter that he reproduced it at Disneyland, is said to have mused, "Where else can you find iniquity and antiquity so close together?"[2] Travel writing about the Quarter regularly juxtaposes the two streets in a manner like this 1989 example: "If Bourbon Street is an outdoor nightclub, then Royal is a street of great treasures and pleasures, though of a quieter, more tasteful kind."[3] Or this, from twenty years later: "Royal . . . has always been the most patrician of the Quarter's main thoroughfares. Lined with antiques and art galleries, [it] is the prestige address of the Vieux Carré. One block walking takes you from the grand and sophisticated to the carnal and crass: you have arrived at Bourbon Street."[4] Royal Street in the early 2000s retained twenty-eight antique shops, or 13 percent of all those regionally. Chartres Street had a comparably sophisticated milieu, though not quite like Royal's, and also deflected a nightclub agglomeration. To the extent that social spaces are imbued with gendered identity, Royal is feminine and Bourbon is masculine. To the extent they have class, Royal represents upward mobility whereas Bourbon stands for downward decadence. To the extent they reflect time, Royal is broad daylight and Bourbon is the dark of night.

Structural factors also contributed to nightclub avoidance on Royal and Chartres. After 1906, both streets found the Louisiana Supreme Court on their flanks, which, needless to say, worked against an adult-entertainment atmosphere, and Chartres additionally had the traffic interruption of Jackson Square and the ecclesiastic presence of St. Louis Cathedral. Royal Street's traffic flow also presented problems: its upriver directionality meant that downtown streetcar, truck, and taxi traffic could not proceed onto it without awkwardly looping around congested upper-Quarter streets. This leaves Iberville as the best contender for Bourbon the Phenomenon. Indeed, it used to have it: formerly known as Customhouse, this street had an ill repute going back to antebellum times. It had concert saloons in the day of Henry Wenger; it penetrated into Storyville between 1897 and 1917; it intersected the extraordinarily wild Franklin Street at what was probably the city's most notorious intersection; it ran through the Tango Belt in the 1910s and 1920s; and even today, its stretch from Decatur to Dauphine is probably the closest surviving example of those edgy spaces. And perhaps that's the reason why Iberville never succeeded in attracting a critical mass of fancy nightclubs: it was a little *too* edgy.

So then, why Bourbon Street? Broadly speaking, the thoroughfare benefited from being far enough from the riverfront to be buffered from its industrial nuisances, and equally far from the back-of-town to be insulated from its déclassé denizens. Bourbon did not have the pricey real estate and establishment antiquarians of Royal and Chartres, nor the humble hovels of Dauphine and Burgundy. It *did* have a rather good mix of architectural typologies at reasonable prices, with lots of old commercial storehouses with alleyways and courtyards, all of which fostered an intimate sense of anonymity amid a streetscape replete with antiquity and mystery. Most important, Bourbon Street was disproportionately owned by the ambitiously creative working-class immigrants to whom was left open the entertainment and tourism niche that the bluebloods did not want. It had a streetcar line connecting it with all points uptown, where many club patrons lived, and with all points downtown, where many employees lived. Bourbon Street, in sum, comprised fertile ground. It had a good liminal geography for an entertainment industry to flourish, proximate to favorable factors and distant from detrimental ones.

Fertile ground does not bear fruit unless it is seeded. For entertainment, Bourbon Street's seeding came in the form of the French Opera House and its countless performances and galas from 1859 to 1919, and from Wenger's concert saloon from 1868 to 1892. For libations, it came from places like the Old Absinthe House and Lafitte's Blacksmith Shop, whose citywide fame as archetypal aged saloons dates to the late 1800s. For gastronomy, it came from Victor's, Galatoire's, nearby Antoine's, and other restaurants boasting a classy Old World flair. For lodging, it came from the fancy Cosmopolitan, which opened up directly onto Bourbon starting in 1892. Most of all, it came from Count Arnaud's Maxime's Supper Club, which, coupled with the adjacent Absinthe House, found success in the late 1920s and attracted kindred enterprises in the 1930s. Bourbon Street was the first vice space in the city's history to "feminize" its otherwise assertively male-dominated gender identity and thus render it safe for middle-class tourism—and thus appealing for tourism investors. This was something the Tango Belt, Storyville, Gallatin Street, Customhouse Street, and earlier vice districts never pulled off. Once World War II catapulted patronage into the stratosphere, Bourbon Street's propinquity of adult entertainment passed the tipping point and became its own reason for attracting new bars and clubs—because it was world-famous Bourbon Street.

The relationship between World War II and Bourbon Street was not a unique one. Millions of young men in transit catalyzed entertainment districts in many great port cities; activity at the Brooklyn Navy Yard, for example, invigorated the adjacent Sands Street prostitution strip, while Times-Square, Forty-Second Street, and the jazz scene on Fifty-Second Street in Manhattan all profited massively from pleasure-seeking servicemen. So did Scollay Square in Boston and The Block in Baltimore. Those embarking for the Pacific energized the Chinese nightclubs and restaurants in San Francisco, quadrupling the size of its Chinatown.

Washington, D.C., Charleston, Mobile, not to mention London, Paris, Honolulu, Manila, and other major and minor wartime nodes, all saw their entertainment districts boom. What makes Bourbon Street unique is the steepness of its rise from local to national fame, and its ability to sustain and parlay that renown into a multimillion-dollar nightly commercial engine at the forefront of a metropolis's premier economic sector—for three-quarters of a century with no signs of slowing. It has survived Prohibition, the Depression, wars, recessions, fires, hurricanes, floods, mobsters, raids, crackdowns, segregation, integration, white flight, hippies, rappers, evangelists, the oil bust, the dot-com bust, and relentless cycles of cultural tastes. Apparently it found the right soil.

A jurisprudential reason also played a key role in answering the "why here?" question for the Bourbon Street Phenomenon: land-use zoning ordinances. As an official with the City Planning Commission explained, New Orleans "had one ordinance in 1929, revised in 1953, then in 1970, and each time we said we will not have live entertainment in cocktail lounges, but [we] allowed it in bars and strip joints [on Bourbon Street]. Technically nothing is legal [off Bourbon Street]." Live music venues sprouted elsewhere but operated in legal limbo, prone to litigious neighbors and code-enforcement raids. Ordinances have since changed in recognition of live music's importance to the cultural economy, but venues off Bourbon Street, particularly in avant-garde spaces like St. Claude Avenue, still regularly find themselves at odds with City Hall over proper permitting—an uncertainty that Bourbon Street legally settled generations ago. Zoning by no means created Bourbon the Phenomenon, but it aided and abetted it while frustrating the competition.[5]

Bourbon Street also benefited from a number of obscure factors that, while neither intentional nor particularly weighty, were nevertheless propitious. For one, Bourbon Street made its own beer. That the gigantic American (Regal) Brewery sat at the heart of The Street from the 1890s to the 1960s made local brew conveniently deliverable to neighboring outlets—this in an era when competing breweries worked closely with bar owners in establishing and maintaining brand loyalty. Bourbon's directionality helped as well: trucks delivering daily resupplies of food, liquor, kegs, and ice could enter The Street smoothly from Canal Street and the urban core, whereas Royal and Dauphine had inconvenient contrary directionalities. Then there is the name: that America's most famous locale for libations shares a sobriquet with America's most famous distilled spirit was pure serendipity. Bourbon the street and bourbon the whiskey do, however, have a common origin: both salute the royal House of Bourbon, the former in the

1720s and the latter in the 1780s, when a county in Kentucky was so named to honor King Louis XVI's aid to the American Revolution. That region would later specialize in the distilling of a fine American whiskey and lend its name to it. It would also send a steady stream of flatboats and steamboats loaded with whiskey and other commodities down the Ohio and Mississippi to New Orleans in the nineteenth century, and it's fair to say that bourbon whiskey has been flowing on Bourbon Street for the better part of two centuries. The coincidence by no means explains the latter's fame, but it certainly didn't inhibit it.

One final spatial question begs: Why did Bourbon's clubs not spread beyond The Street? In fact, they did: into each intersecting street from Iberville to Orleans, particularly along St. Peter. Consequently, the Bourbon entertainment space today is not so much linear as it is shaped like a fish bone. Why the clubs did not spread even farther can be explained by their owners' wrestling match with preservationists and residents, who ensured that the Bourbon scourge, while incurable, would at least be quarantined. Because of the proliferation of bars on Bourbon Street after the Second World War," explained preservationist Mary Morrison, "we organized a nuisance abatement committee and did everything we could to contain Bourbon Street as we know it now between Canal and St. Peter and just on Bourbon . . . There was a tendency for it to go out on the sides and different areas, and to come on down [the street]."[6] They succeeded partially, as the Vieux Carré Entertainment land-use zone now extends two blocks past St. Peter and a number of parcels laterally—but no farther. It and a host of related ordinances empower French Quarter homeowners and preservationists to keep Bourbon Street in line, figuratively and literally.

Working Bourbon Street
How the Machine Runs

More than 10 million people visited New Orleans in 2004. The numbers tumbled after Katrina but steadily recovered, and in 2012, 9 million visitors spent a record $6 billion despite a lingering recession. Roughly four-fifths of that transient humanity visits Bourbon Street; adding in local patronage, this equates to roughly 100 million people-hours and billions of potential dollars arriving into the Bourbon Street machine annually. That activity is spatially clustered on the commercialized upper half of The Street, particularly the 200 through 500 blocks. Temporally it is concentrated at night, particularly on Fridays and Saturdays, and from midwinter through late spring, by a roughly two-to-one ratio over summer and fall.[1]

On the supply side, an enormous cast of characters has kept the Bourbon machine humming—right this minute, day and night, year-round, for the better part of a century. They distribute themselves to match when and where the demand for pleasure exists, and vice versa. Where the two sides meet, there are dollars, and where there are dollars, there are jobs. Information filed by employers in 2008 shows that the twenty square blocks straddling either side of Bourbon from Canal to St. Philip contained 6,832 jobs.[2] This statistic may be adjusted upward for subsequent years because it was gathered at a time when the Katrina recovery was still in progress, and both the tourist base and city population were at barely three-quarters their prediluvian levels. Even without adjustment, the 2008 data show that one out of every twenty jobs in the city of New Orleans (6,832 of 146,530) was located within Bourbon's one-twelfth-of-a-square-mile footprint. Orleans Parish covers 170 square miles, which means that while the city produced 862 jobs per square mile, Bourbon Street produced 81,984. If economic rigor is measured solely by job density, then Bourbon Street is 95 times more productive than New Orleans. Apart from skyscrapers and institutions like universities and hospitals, Bourbon Street accounts for the highest spatial concentration of employment in the city. It also claims some of the most valuable real estate. The Orleans Parish Assessor's Office estimated Bourbon Street's land to be worth over $47 million and its buildings $144 million, with nearly three-quarters of that value coming from the commercial half of the street. These are conservative estimates because appraisals generally fall below what the market would command (owners only protest overestimates), and some records are missing or outdated.[3] Accounting for these shortfalls, the total real estate value of Bourbon Street ranges around a quarter to a third of a billion dollars. And that's not including the lucrative businesses.[4]

Bourbon workers are fairly young; 36 percent in 2008 were thirty years of age or younger (compared to 26 percent of employees citywide), and barely 12 percent were over fifty-five (18 percent citywide). Inclusion of independent contractors such as shot girls would likely lower the average age. According to one informant, Bourbon bar or club staffers are typically twenty-five years old, while band members are usually in their thirties or forties and seniors in any capacity are rare. In terms of wage-based income, 26 percent of Bourbon employees make $1,250 per month or less (compared to 20 percent citywide); 50 percent earn between $1,251 and $3,333 monthly (41 percent citywide); and the rest earn higher. Incomes on Bourbon Street have been fairly stable over the years. In the late 1970s, for example, a full-time cocktail waitress earned in lieu of a salary a commission of forty dollars per week, plus tips ranging from thirty dollars daily and one hundred dollars on Fridays and Saturdays. Occasional generous tips (a "score") raised her annual income to around $14,000 a year. Adjusted for inflation, this figure is comparable to what the same position earns today.[5]

Music, sexuality, and alcohol are the unholy trinity of the Bourbon Street economy. Music creates a mood of pulsating energy; sexuality transforms it into libidinous anticipation; and alcohol converts all of the above into revenue—while, by upping the appetite for music and sex, priming the whole system. While strip clubs monetize overt sexuality, most other venues focus on music and alcohol and rely on lusty customers and provocatively dressed staff for the sex appeal. Evidence for the importance of the music-booze pairing comes from the fact that, of the 104 legally licensed Alcohol Beverage Outlets on Bourbon Street in 2012 (one of every twenty citywide), fifty-five are bars (one of every four in the Quarter), and roughly half of the bars feature live entertainment. The rest always play recorded music.[6] Evidence also comes from employment: more than eighteen out of every twenty jobs are officially categorized as "Accommodation and Food Services" (that is, bars, restaurants, and hotels, 56 percent) or "Arts, Entertainment, and Recreation" (mostly musicians, 35 percent). Using conservative assumptions, Bourbon Street puts roughly $200 million in the pockets of local workers every year, and that's just legally reported wages paid to official employees.[7] The unmeasured gratuity and under-the-table economy—everyone loves cash on Bourbon—would inflate this figure substantially, perhaps massively. Bourbon Street's economic activity is particularly valuable to the city because it is "basic"—that is, it brings outside money into city limits. Magazine Street, by contrast, is a "nonbasic" economy, in that it mostly circulates local money.

However, like most service employment, Bourbon jobs generally lack health insurance and go nowhere professionally. One informant estimated that during the school year, when college students are in town, at most one-third of a typical club staff comprises folks who likely have educated, professional futures; the remaining two-thirds are service-industry lifers. During the summer, when the universities empty out, that latter figure is more like 90 percent.[8] Working on Bourbon Street also entails risks, particularly for women, who in addition to tolerating flirtatious and pushy patrons, sometimes find themselves threatened while returning to cars late at night. And for all Bourbonites, the every-night-is-Mardi-Gras intensity, where every stranger is presumed to have the worst of intentions and all too many actually do, generally does not make for a healthy work environment.

Owners encounter risks all their own. Complacency and a lack of creativity top the list. "A lot of people think if you come to Bourbon Street and open the doors, the money's going to roll in, but it's *not*," said bar owner Earl Bernhardt. "If you don't have something to offer the public and you don't know how to market it, you're going to fall flat on your face." Case in point: a few years earlier, some employees of Bernhardt's Tropical Isle jumped ship and competed for their former employer's customers. They opened a similarly themed joint (its décor "a half-hearted attempt at a beach hut vibe"), launched a novelty drink that aped Bernhardt's Hand Grenade, failed to orient itself to the passing parade—and found itself hemorrhaging four thousand dollars a month and a half million dollars in debt.[9] Likewise, inattentive management is a prescription for failure. Absentee ownership, said Bernhardt, is "the problem with a lot of things that happen on Bourbon Street. . . . They really don't watch what's going on and sometimes their clubs get a little out of line, too loud, or too rowdy." Greed is another business killer. "Some bars have the mentality, 'well, you only get one shot at them; charge the hell out of them.'" That may work in the short run, but eventually it's detrimental. "Instead of getting [your customers] angry over . . . an excessive amount for a drink," Bernhardt advised, "make the prices reasonable and [he'll] sit there and have three or four!" Astronomical rent deals the fatal blow to subpar businesses—thus the high turnover of mediocre enterprises. Businesses on Bourbon at any given moment tend to fall into two categories: the "mainstays, like Pat O'Brien's, [which always] stay the same," and "all these other places [that] come and go." Reflected Bernhardt after twenty-eight years and six successful businesses on the strip: "Bourbon Street is kind of an evolving thing; it never stays the same. Sometimes you've got too many T-shirt shops, the next thing you know you've got too many daiquiri shops; now we've got too many strip clubs."[10]

A new day on Bourbon never clearly commences because the preceding eve never entirely ends. Bars throughout New Orleans may remain open twenty-four hours a day, but doing so may not be profitable. "It depends on what's in town," explained Bernhardt. "If it's a Saints game, we'll open at ten o'clock; [otherwise] we'll open at twelve." Closing times are equally adjustable. "If everything dies at four o'clock in the morning, why stay open any later?"[11] Venues from St. Ann to Dumaine spill music into the street on weekday mornings even at the depths of the subtropical summer, when the rest of Bourbon shutters around 2:00 to 3:00 a.m., because their mostly gay patrons tend to be locals who can walk home. It's a different story on weekends, when scores of venues do not shutter until the sun rises and the sanitation trucks scrub last night's sins from the gutters.

The commercial end of Bourbon Street is notoriously unsightly in the light of day. Columnist Howard Jacobs, writing in 1970, compared it to "a lady of the evening in curlers, face cream, and sleazy housecoat [who] mopes frumpy and nondescript."[12] Daytime Bourbon is unpleasant on account of the impatient taxis, rumbling beer trucks disgorging their kegs, club hands hosing down sidewalks (a responsibility of the business, not the city), puddles of loathsome fluids, and manure deposited by the mounted police's undiapered horses.

By early afternoon, Madame Bourbon has fixed up her hair, painted her face, donned her sequins, and is readying for business. Pedestrian traffic picks up as the shadows grow long, and when policemen barricade (most of) the vehicular traffic, street entertainers swiftly claim space and start their routines, which in turn draw more pedestrians. Busking has made something of a comeback in recent years, and Saturday afternoons in particular feature an assortment of weird

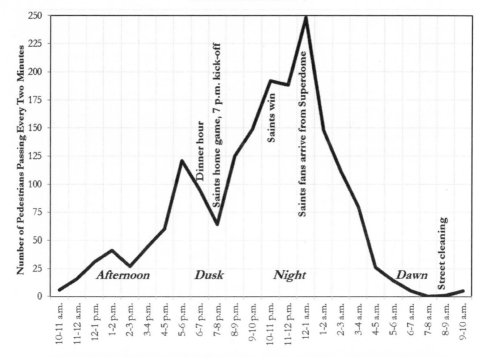

Twenty-four-hour cycle of Bourbon Street pedestrian traffic on a typical Saturday on which the New Orleans Saints football team played an exhibition game at home. Figures represent the number of pedestrians crossing the St. Peter intersection, measured hourly starting at 10 a.m. Saturday, August 25, 2012, through the subsequent morning. *Data analyses by author using EarthCam—New OrleansCam online video from Cat's Meow.*

goons and creepy carnies offering their shticks to the passersby. The scene turns Bourbon Street from a figurative to a literal stage, with performers and audiences intermingling in an ephemeral marketplace of amusements and gratuities. Competition is intense, leading to innovation: the Man-Baby tucks himself into a box made out to look like a crib, and, protruding only his hands, feet, and freaky bonneted head, gurgles like an infant at astonished tourists. A futuristic Creature from the Black Lagoon lurks around in a striking skin-hugging monster costume. A fellow in a Homer Simpson outfit unsheathes a gigantic boner, and—punch line—it's a gigantic bone. Colorful Mardi Gras Indians, who earn the opprobrium of their Seventh Ward tribes for figuring out there's more money on Bourbon than in Tremé, pose for pictures and tips. The Silver Guy, the Construction Worker, the Dog-Walking Patriot, and the Gold Guy Giving the Finger to Roger Goodell all do versions of the living-statue act. Drummers pound on baker's buckets with

Buskers compete with retailers and clubs for space, time, attention, and dollars. What appears to be spontaneous festivity to a first-time Bourbon Street visitor is in fact constantly contested, negotiated, and regulated. *Photograph by author.*

impressive dexterity, and magicians and jugglers put on one-man variety shows. Break-dancing troupes, which draw big crowds and earn decent tips, have learned to evade the wrath of shopkeepers by instructing spectators not to block sidewalks and store fronts, going so far as to draw a chalk outline on the asphalt and remind folks constantly to draw close to it. Their cautions speak to the underlying competition for public space and patron attention on Bourbon Street. Both bring with them the potential of money; every Bourbonite wants a piece of it, and the more taxes they pay, the more they see their share as fair and the others' as an outrage. Those business owners who are legally licensed and heavily taxed know damn well that the buskers pay nothing, which fuels the animus. Tourists are oblivious to this tension, and some, particularly first-time visitors, believe what they are seeing is spontaneous joie de vivre special to this day. They particularly startle to the sight of pretty young women walking around completely topless, their breasts painted to skirt indecent-exposure laws. It's a new sales gimmick: the girls work for clubs, distributing promotional flyers and coupons in the hopes of stoking tonight's action. Male visitors take to them like flies to honey, which is exactly why the clubs hire them. Couples are a different matter.

Finally, darkness settles in. Restaurants shake out their diners and guests emerge from their hotels for an evening on the town. Some are dressed nattily;

most are not. Overwhelmingly they gravitate to Bourbon Street. "Cinderella-like Bourbon springs to glittering life by nightfall," wrote Jacobs in 1970, "neon-bejewelled and throbbing to the rhythmic beat of drums and the wail of trumpet and clarinet."[13] His words recall those of Thomas Ashe, who in 1806 described a similar scene in New Orleans: "the instant the [sun] sets, animation begins to rise, the public walks are crowded[,] the inhabitants promenade[,] the billiard rooms resound, music strikes up, and life and activity resume their joyous career."[14]

As the busking window closes at nightfall, pedestrians effectively replace the street performers as the free entertainment; for the rest of the evening, the spectators are the spectacle. This is also the time when licensed venders position themselves along the human river. The iconic Lucky Dog carts emerge from their Gravier Street cupboard and set up at the busiest corners; rose peddlers come out of their St. Philip Street den and stake out key spots; and caricature artists and tarot card readers gather in front of Legends Park, which is city-owned and therefore safe from angry merchants. The promenade also attracts a shadow force of predators. Pickpockets and prostitutes circulate surreptitiously in unknown numbers. Beggars and hucksters are easier to spot. "'Scuse me. Ex*cuse* me!" A black man in his forties, who has been studying passersby as if fitting them to a profile, badgers a young couple. He jabs his finger at the fellow's feet, and with aggressive affability, declares, "Bet I can tell you where you got 'em shoes!" It's a common scam throughout the upper Quarter, and the first block of Bourbon, replete with the naïve and the disoriented, is prime hunting grounds. Suckers who accept the bet soon hear the huckster retort, "You got yo' shoes *on your feet, on* Bourbon Street, *in* New Or-leens, Louisiana!" followed by a payment demand. Another variation proffers a "free" shoe shine, then a call for a tip. An angry exchange usually ensues, and, more in an effort to stave off the embarrassing spectacle, a few dollars usually change hands. It's a humiliating welcome to Bourbon Street for many visitors, and has been going on since World War II. Journalist and local historian Mel Leavitt fell for the "shoes" trap when he first arrived to Bourbon Street in 1950.[15]

The flow of humanity onto Bourbon materializes at the Canal Street intersection. Here, on most evenings, black men in African attire vend jewelry, ointments, CDs, incense, or pipes, to the multiple channels of perambulating pedestrians. Over half are visitors, and typically three-quarters of them are on leisure travel: middle-age couples from the Midwest, a gaggle of giggling co-eds from a regional college, a hesitant husband and wife with two wide-eyed teenagers. Other visitors are here on business, at least ostensibly: a cadre of corporate muckety-mucks in sports coats, three mismatched colleagues from a scientific conference, a shifty-eyed conventioneer relishing his anonymity. Most, but by no means all, are American in ethnicity, white in race, and middle in class. Then there are the locals, mostly nonwhite, who generally fall into three groups: (1) those destined for work or home, who pace with pointed indifference; (2) those destined for this space, who loiter, beg, bicker, and settle scores among each other; and (3) those for whom this space represents work. Members of this last group survey the scene from doorways and taxis, their arms folded, their gaze distant: the Slavic electronics merchant, the Indian souvenir retailer, the Asian foot-masseuse, the Pakistani driver, the African doorman.

Most locals continue on Canal Street; most visitors turn onto Bourbon. Greeting them is the To Be Continued brass band, a group of young black men who deliver a spirited performance of jazz or hip-hop melodies—much to the displeasure of the merchants, who don't want the distraction, and the residents, who resent the cacophony. Despite its illegality—ordinances ban the unlicensed playing of musical instruments on public rights-of-way from 8:00 a.m. to 9:00 p.m., and any outdoor performances on Bourbon from 8:00 p.m. through 6:00 a.m.—To Be Continued's act is one of the few lauded by local music aficionados, who otherwise dismiss any and all tunes emanating from The Street. After enjoying a song or two, visitors slip out of the crowd, evading the tip bucket, and head into the neon-lit multitudes of the pedestrian mall.

A moveable police barricade at the Iberville intersection diverts pedestrians laterally, like a brook around a boulder. There to exploit the slowed current are sketchy characters with a melodramatic pitch: "I'm sorry, we've been informed by the Party Patrol that you've been spotted not enjoying yourself—," at which point they proffer a cap and aggressively solicit a donation for a local charity. They are Hare Krishnas, and whether their nightly take actually ends up doing good is of little concern to Bourbon merchants, who successfully lobbied City Hall for an ordinance against "aggressive panhandling."[16] Behind the Party Patrol is an aged woman perched behind a wooden handcart, vending roses to would-be Romeos trying to charm their dates the old-fashioned way. Between and among buildings, in side doorways and windows, hawkers sell drinks directly into the public space via tiny "go-bars," a controversial practice that forever changed Bourbon Street forty years earlier. The other end of the drinking business—bathrooms—remains in private space. There is only one public restroom on Bourbon, and tucked in the rear mezzanine of Music Legends Park, it's one of The Street's best-kept secrets. Many tourist dollars are spent to gain access to restrooms in restaurants or bars

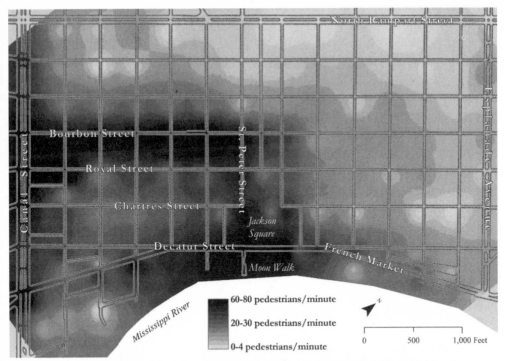

Pedestrian circulation in the French Quarter, showing how most foot traffic emanates from the CBD across Canal Street (*left*); strolls down Bourbon Street as well as Royal, Decatur, and Chartres; streams through Jackson Square to the French Market (*lower right*); and returns the same way. Shadings reflect the number of pedestrians per minute as they crossed Quarter intersections, based on a survey conducted by the author on February 3, 2002 (Super Bowl Sunday, hosted locally).

posting "Restrooms for Customers Only" signs. It's one of the ways the Bourbon machine works.

Human circulation patterns on Bourbon Street reveal how, where, and when The Street operates. To measure them, the author counted the number of pedestrians who crossed an invisible line in the middle of each of the thirteen blocks from Canal to Esplanade for a period of exactly 120 seconds. The survey was conducted between 9:00 and 11:00 p.m. every ten days for one year, an interval designed to yield weeknight (Tuesdays and Wednesdays, usually fairly quiet) and Friday/ Saturday (usually very busy) patterns. Special events such as Southern Decadence and Mardi Gras were also included. In all, more than forty surveys were conducted during 2010–11.

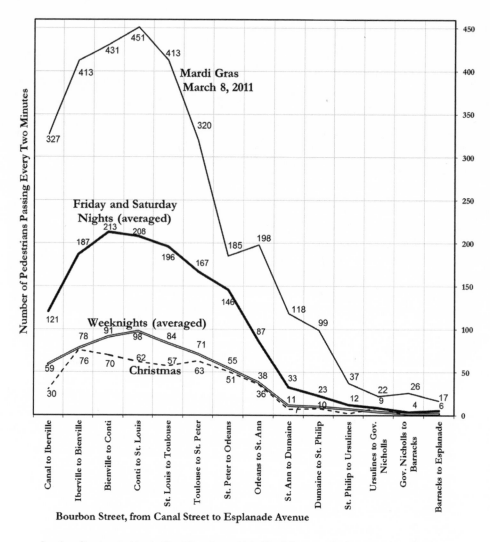

Number of Pedestrians Passing Every Two Minutes

Mardi Gras March 8, 2011

451
431
413
413
320
327

Friday and Saturday Nights (averaged)
213 208
187 196 167
198 185
121
146 118
99
87
37
33 22 26
23 17
11 10 12 9 4 6

Weeknights (averaged)
91 98 84
78 76 70 71 62 57 63
59 55 51
36
38
30

Christmas

Bourbon Street, from Canal Street to Esplanade Avenue

Canal to Iberville · Iberville to Bienville · Bienville to Conti · Conti to St. Louis · St. Louis to Toulouse · Toulouse to St. Peter · St. Peter to Orleans · Orleans to St. Ann · St. Ann to Dumaine · Dumaine to St. Philip · St. Philip to Ursulines · Ursulines to Gov. Nicholls · Gov. Nicholls to Barracks · Barracks to Esplanade

Bourbon Street pedestrian traffic at its extreme high (Mardi Gras, top line), extreme low (Christmas, bottom line), and typical weekend and weeknight averages (lines in between). Figures represent number of people passing a given spot every two minutes, between 9 p.m. and 11 p.m., surveyed every ten days from August 2010 to August 2011. *Data collection and analyses by author; assistance from Julie Hernandez.*

What the data show are amazingly smooth and structured patterns—order, once again, emerging from apparent chaos. The passing parade enters from Canal Street, steadily increases and peaks in the heart of the strip, then smoothly diminishes and peters out after Lafitte's Blacksmith Shop at the St. Phillip intersection. This general pattern remained true 100 percent of the time, varying only in magnitude, and evidences that the Bourbon Street parade is truly a linear movement of people. To be sure, it has tributaries and distributaries on side streets, and it eddies and accelerates sporadically, but it is primarily a two-way human river. Where are the people flowing to? "Almost nobody goes . . . to hit a specific venue," realized a business-makeover specialist upon assessing The Street; "they go there for the bacchanalia."[17] So central is the rolling bacchanal to Bourbon's functioning that even Rick's Cabaret, the fancy strip club featuring naked women on the inside, recently installed a streetside bar so that patrons may gaze *outside* and "watch the action on Bourbon from the comfort of a barstool."[18] On weeknights, the river flows at a fairly steady pace of 30 people per minute on the 100 block between Canal and Iberville, increases to 39 per minute on the 200 block, peaks at 46–49 per minute in the 300 and 400 blocks, then diminishes to 42, 36, 27, 19, 6, 5, 4, 2, and 1 per minute for the remaining blocks, ending at the quiet Esplanade intersection. Unsurprisingly, the geography of din generally correlates to this pedestrian curve; blocks from Music Legends Park to the St. Peter intersection typically generate 85–100-decibel noise levels, about 10 percent higher than on adjacent blocks.[19] On Friday and Saturday nights, the pedestrian traffic streetwide runs 2.33 times higher than on weeknights; its spatial structure, however, remains the same. No wonder bars and clubs staff-up and beer-up for weekends: those days make up one-third of the week but see two-thirds of the traffic. Money, however, is not necessarily spent commensurately. Weekday visitors tend to be conventioneers with professional salaries and expense accounts; weekenders are more likely leisure tourists and penny-pinching day-trippers.

Seasonally, springtime walking traffic on Bourbon Street is higher than in autumn, but, contrary to expectations, the surveys show that summers were actually higher than winters as a whole. Seasonal variations, however, were dwarfed by weekday-weekend fluctuations. That is, a Saturday night during the worst season was always more crowded than a Wednesday night during the best season.

The slowest day? Christmas. A survey conducted on Thursday, December 23, 2010, yielded the lowest pedestrian rates, averaging 27 percent less than a typical weeknight and 68 percent less than a weekend. The busiest day, needless to say, was Mardi Gras, which saw throngs so tightly packed that people ceased to move—a problem for our breakline methodology, which depends on movement. Adjusted through a statistical technique, the data revealed that Mardi Gras 2011 saw crowds on Bourbon Street that were eight times higher than a typical Tuesday night and four times higher than a normal weekend. The third and fourth blocks of Bourbon saw rates of 215 to 225 people moving across a theoretical line per minute—if they could move at all. None of these numbers measure crowd size in bar and club interior spaces, nor do they measure the spillover traffic on side streets.

How many people pack Bourbon Street on Mardi Gras? Consider the arithmetic: a block measures 320 feet long and 22 feet wide, plus two four-foot-wide sidewalks. Eliminating street appurtenances, this amounts to about 9,000 square feet per block. If we assume each human occupies a three-foot-by-three-foot space at or near the height of Mardi Gras (substantiated by field observations), then this area would hold a crowd of 1,000. Another 100 or so stand on the balconies, roughly 200 to 300 are indoors, and more mill about the intersections, summing to roughly 1,500 people per block. Fitting this figure to our pedestrian-distribution curve, this equates to more than 12,000 to 13,000 people on Bourbon Street. Often the multitudes grow so dense that individuals are forced into claustrophobic and potentially dangerous one-foot-by-two-feet spaces; when this happens, crowds within a certain block may swell to 2,000, and the total street to 15,000 to 20,000. And of course crowd composition churns constantly; some spend all day on Bourbon while others come and go. By the time the police flush out The Street at the stroke of midnight, the aggregated population of Bourbon Street sums to more than 100,000—and that's just on Fat Tuesday. All that remains of them by dawn on Ash Wednesday is 16 million pounds of trash scattered throughout downtown.

Balconies and galleries form a privileged position in the social geography of Bourbon Street. Usually you need money or connections, or at least an attitude, to attain these scarce perches, and those who do relish them. They are gendered spaces that exude public sexuality: buxom women thrill to their power (should they wish to use it) to enthrall hundreds of strangers below with a body flash, in exchange for adulation and beads.[20] Nevertheless, men outnumber women consistently on these perches, by a margin of half on weeknights and nearly two-thirds on weekends. In the gay space from St. Ann to Dumaine, men outnumber women by 400 percent, but only on weekends; it is largely empty during the week. On the Saturday night of one particular Southern Decadence (2010), men

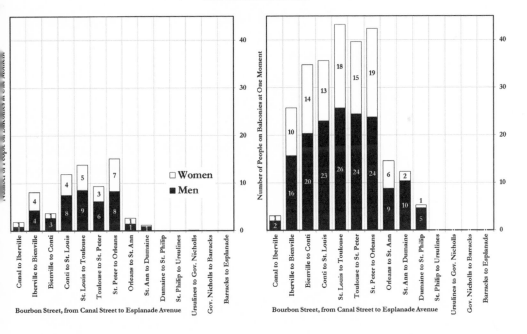

Numbers of women and men standing on Bourbon Street balconies, on Tuesday/Wednesday nights (*left*), and on Friday/Saturday nights (*right*), at a given moment between 9:30 p.m. and 11:30 p.m. *Figures represent averages over 35 evenings during 2010–2011; data collection and analysis by author; assistance from Julie Hernandez.*

predominated on balconies at the St. Ann intersection 84 to 0, and at the Dumaine intersection 27 to 2. Interestingly, that same night, the balconies in the "straight space" from Toulouse to Orleans saw women outnumbering men, 41 to 16 and 40 to 27—a rarity on Bourbon Street. Whether this bore any relation to the overwhelming gay male presence a block down the street is difficult to ascertain, but possible.

Racial patterns in the Bourbon Street pedestrian parade show that whites, Hispanics, and Asians predominate by a four-to-one ratio over people of apparent African ancestry.[21] Interestingly, while the white flow pattern limned the standard peak in the heart of the strip, the black trendline peaked earlier, in the 100 block between Canal and Iberville. Reason: many of the African Americans walking this end of Bourbon Street are locals, spilling over from the Canal Street shopping district and adjacent housing developments. They may be employees traveling to and from jobs, residents running errands, or youths drawn to the action (the NOPD nabs more curfew violators—unaccompanied youth under six-

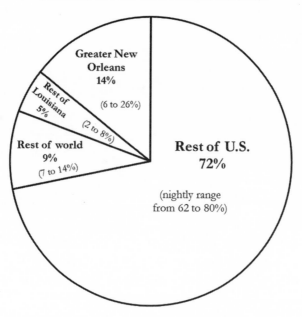

Origins of Bourbon Street pedestrians, based on 423 individuals queried throughout Bourbon Street on four typical evenings during 2010–2011. *Survey and analysis by author; assistance from Julie Hernandez.*

teen out after 8:00 p.m.—here than anywhere else in the city).[22] Higher numbers of black tourists may be found here as well. A survey conducted during the 2011 Essence Music Festival weekend, which is geared toward African American audiences, found that black visitors outnumbered whites on the 100 and 200 blocks by nearly a three-to-one ratio.

Where are the pedestrians from? Research by the author assisted by Julie Hernandez, who conducted the street inquiries, found that, of 423 pedestrians queried throughout Bourbon Street on four typical nights, 72 percent were from the United States outside Louisiana; 5 percent were from Louisiana outside the Greater New Orleans metropolitan area; 14 percent were from Greater New Orleans; and 9 percent were from outside the United States.

Researchers in the summer of 1977 found that out-of-towners outnumbered New Orleans–area residents on Bourbon Street by a roughly 3-to-2 ratio. To the extent that the surveys are comparable, the native patronage of Bourbon Street has decreased in the past generation.[23] However, these figures fluctuate spatially and temporally. Nativity tends to be higher in the 100 block, due to its proximity to Canal, and below St. Ann, due to its residential nature, whereas out-of-towners predominate overwhelmingly in between. Some clubs draw natives and outsiders in different ratios; an informant who worked at Fat Catz and the Funky 544 estimated that about 10 to 15 percent of patronage is from metro New Orleans, and 20 to 25 percent hails from Louisiana or Mississippi. An owner of five Bourbon Street bars who advertises on local television estimated a 60/40 ratio between tourists and local/regional customers.[24] A big convention or a festival augments the number of out-of-towners, while Friday nights (said to be "date night") and Sunday nights (dubbed "ghetto night" by some Bourbonites because local black patronage goes up as tourists leave town) inflate the number of natives. Winters and springs generally bring more tourists, while summer sees lots of drive-in patronage from Louisiana and Mississippi. Christmas draws a disproportionate number of foreign nationals living in the United States, particularly East Asian and South Asian professionals who use the time off as an opportunity to see America.

The biggest driver of native patronage of Bourbon Street is football, particularly a Saints home game. Bourbon Street's association with football goes deep. The very presence of the strip, as well as the French Quarter, is intrinsic to the argument for New Orleans being *the* Super Bowl city because unlike most metropolises, its downtown stadium is only one mile from its flagship night spot. National sports media return the favor by featuring B-roll vignettes of Bourbon Street in on-air segues, providing free advertising to exactly the right demographic: beer-drinking sports guys who enjoy a good time. Bourbon Street traditionally plays host to fans the night before the game, and it's the first place to which they beeline immediately afterward.

When football suffers, so does Bourbon Street. The 1982 NFL players strike cost it millions of dollars from thousands of Saints fans; the owner of one club, the Famous Door, estimated that fully 40 percent of his income was "football business." And when football carries the day, so does Bourbon Street. A game at the Superdome brings in tens of thousands of regional boosters in a festive spirit, plus thousands of rival fans on "football weekends"—essentially sports tourism.[25] One of the most memorable moments in Bourbon Street's history came on the night of January 24, 2010, when mostly local crowds packed Bourbon bars to watch the New Orleans Saints vie for a first-time-ever trip to the Super Bowl, leaving the street eerily empty. Once a Saints overtime field goal cinched victory, people by the thousands exploded from indoor to outdoor space, filling Bourbon Street to Mardi Gras capacity in a matter of seconds. It was a remarkable and possibly unique moment, testimony to Bourbon Street's status as a sort of cultural agora for spontaneous public celebration, akin to Times Square in Manhattan or Trafalgar Square in London.

The thousands of staffers who run the Bourbon Street machine perform roughly a dozen tasks. They serve alcohol, prepare and serve food, entertain, sell merchandise or services, maintain lodging, and clean up, restock, secure, guard, manage, or promote. None are simple, and each has a story to tell.

A typical club's personnel comprises an owner, manager, bartenders, "bar backs" (who keep the bar stocked), "shot girls," bouncers or "door guys," and a band, which plays until 10:00 or 11:00 p.m. Afterward, a highly energized emcee tag-teams with a deejay in an ongoing volley of repartee and dance numbers, keeping the crowd spirited and buying drinks. A certain camaraderie exists among staffers—and for good reason: interdependence. The clubs that survive are well-oiled machines, and the pistons that turn the cash crankshaft are the bartenders.

Bartending on Bourbon Street, according to informant Evan, is "very strict, very by-the-book," requiring special training and a host of rules. Aged eighteen at the time he tended bar on Bourbon (too young to drink but old enough to serve), the Kenner native later tended bar uptown and found that, despite the wild reputation of Bourbon Street and the staid image of uptown, the exact opposite is the case. Bartenders at his Bourbon joint—and this is typical—must weigh each bottle when they clock in, keep track of empties, and reweigh unfinished bottles when they close out their shift, so that the managers can match quantities to receipts (minus the five hundred dollars used to start the register). "Owners don't really trust anybody," said Evan, "much less the bartenders," and they often make themselves visible overseeing the workplace. Everything must be recorded and tracked, even spills, and discrepancies must be paid by the bartender. It's the ultimate incentive to handle the commodity with great care—nozzles ("jiggers") are used to allot ounces and half ounces—but if the careful handling takes too much time, the bartender is again penalized because tips depend on being "very, very fast." Evan sensed that bartending on Bourbon Street is tougher for men than women because male customers tend to be more forgiving and generous with female bartenders. "I guess it's because sex sells," he reflected.

Gratuities make up most of the take-home pay for bartenders and others staffers, and while the tips originate from customers, they flow laterally as well. Bartenders tip bar backs; shot girls tip bartenders; emcees tip deejays and vice versa; and the house tips the band. Whenever one person's efforts affect another's, a gratuity is expected, and giving one now means getting one later. Wages are usually nominal, and this is why official government data on the Bourbon Street economy tell only a fraction of the story. Evan got paid only twenty dollars for working the first weekend shift from 7:00 p.m. to 4:00 or 5:00 a.m.; the second shift comes in around 9:00 to 10:00 p.m., ends when the bar closes around 6:00 or 7:00 a.m., and gets paid about the same. Utter dependence on tips makes Bourbonites notoriously acerbic in reading a crowd and scheduling around those stereotyped as cheap. For example, staffers hold that tips go down as the percentage of African Americans goes up. Shifts on Sunday night (so-called "ghetto night") are particularly avoided, as is Essence Festival and Bayou Classic, when informants have commented that they've "never seen the bar so full but the tips so low."[26]

There are, however, other ways to pad income. Bartenders might "upsell" a customer by serving a medium or large when a small or medium was requested. Bouncers may impose illicit cover charges, or let in underage women, because women bring in men, and men bring in money. Some clubs also run an elaborate incentivized sales system involving "tooters." Slang for cocaine-snorting tubes, tooters are clear plastic vials filled with (at most) a one-ounce shot of colorful watered-down alcohol which are prepared during the daytime and refrigerated in special racks. When the action starts, tooters are peddled by provocatively dressed "shot girls"—usually independent operators as opposed to official club staffers— who meander-dance throughout the club, joisting the "tooter rack" above the head. So mobilized, tooters are a way to sell a tiny amount of alcohol for a high per-ounce price but a low total cost (three dollars, higher in strip clubs), while increasing staff/patron interaction (more tips) and keeping the crowd randy and inebriated (more sales). Most important, shot girls proffering tooter racks bring the bar to the patron, instead of waiting for the patron to approach the bar. They can earn upward of five hundred dollars a night, but, according to Evan, must "sell their soul to the devil" for it, lending their sexuality to the product and enduring gropes and advances in return. Shot girls are the latest incarnation of a 150-year-old Bourbon Street ploy of mobilizing and sexualizing the selling of alcohol via perambulating young women. In the 1860s, the girls were called beer jerks; in the 1890s, beer slingers or waiter girls; in the 1940s, B-girls; in the 2000s, shot girls.

Sold separately from those peddled by the shot girls, tooters also form a kind of currency for bartenders to earn *lagniappe*. Evan explains:

> The way the tooter system works is that a rack of fifty empty tooters are
> stacked behind the bar. When a bartender upsells[,] he or she will take one

of the empty tooters from the rack and fill it with the liquor and pour it into the drink. The bartender will throw away the empty tooter after it is used. After a full rack of 50 is emptied out, the bartender would receive a $10 bonus.[27]

Bartenders are allowed to drink on the job, but only in the form of tooters that are fully paid by a treating customer, no more than two per shift, and with explicit permission from management. That's how carefully business is regulated on the seemingly wild and rowdy Bourbon Street. Bars are also humorlessly authoritarian on the matter of "outside drinks." You can purchase an obscenely huge florescent cocktail "to go" and stroll about with it all night on The Street, but try taking it one step into another bar and you will be stopped in your tracks. Outside drinks are among the gravest of common offenses on Bourbon Street because they fundamentally short-circuit the financial wiring of the machine, sending profits and tips into the competition's pocket while denying the victimized bar its ability to recover overhead costs.

Barkers man the front lines of club rivalries. Their favorite tactic to snare customers is glib banter attuned to the characteristics of the passersby—coquettish charm, for example, if it's a dance-club barker enticing a gaggle of coeds, or dirty guy talk if it's a strip-club barker coaxing a lone male. Cover charges are all but nonexistent on Bourbon Street, but that does not stop barkers from rattling "*no cover no cover no cover.*" When crowds are thin and competition fierce, staffers agree among themselves to offer two-for-one or three-for-one drinks. The bartender records the decision so he or she does not get stuck with the bill, and the barkers are deployed to hold up signs outside. Drink prices are notoriously variable, but the special deal is usually legit; buyers really do get twice the quantity for the high price that one ordinarily costs. The two drinks, however, are served at the same time. Machines, after all, need to be efficient.

Bourbon Street strip clubs share many commonalities with music clubs and bars. Quality ranges widely, from the dirty dives around the corner on Iberville, to fancy places like Rick's Cabaret, to national chains like the four owned by Larry Flynt's Hustler empire. They employ a similar cast of characters as other entertainment enterprises, have comparable regulations on alcohol, operate stages with sound and lighting systems, and deploy shot girls, only more of them and with higher-priced tooters. The main difference, of course, is their constant demand for shapely young women. Larger clubs employ scores of them, and staff-up to well over a hundred during big events. Limited supply of qualified applicants means managers must draw heavily from out-of-town labor pools, often from markets with more liberal laws; nervous about crackdowns, the higher-end establishments contractually spell out to newly hired girls what is not permitted on stage, and that includes bottomlessness. (Those clubs that claim otherwise usually split the difference between obscenity ordinances and truth-in-advertising laws by using specially designed G-strings.) There are other differences: unlike music clubs and bars, doors on strip joints by law must remain shut, although barkers allow for enticing peeks. Covers are charged on all nights except the slowest. There are no distracting bands, and recorded music is selected to drive the bump-and-grind. Stripping may be one of the most racially and ethnically diverse jobs on Bourbon Street; whereas bartenders are mostly white and bouncers often black, exotic dancers are hired across the spectrum, so long as they are sufficiently attractive, young, shapely, and willing to bare it. A top dancer at the biggest clubs can go home with a few hundred dollars on a good night, and from one to two thousand dollars on the best nights; most others settle for half or a quarter of those sums. Some strippers, like shot girls, are independent contractors, and actually pay the club to appear on its stage, in exchange for tips and pricey lap dances. This puts the performer in control of her own business, but it also puts her at risk of losing more than she earns on slow nights—or, worse, on what Bourbonites call "bad busy"—times when a large crowd is demanding but frugal.

While flesh commands the attention of the customers, it's the wildly overpriced drinks at the bar that pad the club's bottom line. Some strip clubs indulge in variations of Bourbon Street's bad old habit of B-drinking. When the stripper finishes her performance, for example, she circulates among patrons soliciting dances or companionship. Whenever a pairing forms, a shot girl materializes and pressures the hapless male, usually easily, into treating the disingenuously doe-eyed stripper to a tooter. Those revenues pale in comparison to what clubs earn from table dances, lap dances, and especially from VIP service in upper or rear "champagne rooms," which can cost from five hundred to one thousand dollars per hour or a whole lot more. In gearing up for Super Bowl 2013, one Bourbon strip club offered a "party package" for twenty thousand dollars, including top-shelf champagne and a veritable harem, but not including tips.[28] The more exclusive the service, the higher the price, the more touching is permitted, and the more privacy (curtains and watchful floormen) is granted. Reports vary regarding the degree to which Bourbon Street VIP rooms are really velvety prostitution cribs; likely, sex acts happen in inverse proportion to how much the clubs risk losing if they are caught: lots at high-end clubs, little at shabby ones. More

Nearly every business on Bourbon affects a theme or brand, among them (1) flamboyant musicality, (2) eroticism, (3) mischievous macabre, (4) nostalgic historicity, (5) beachy tropicality, (6) pleasurable excess, (7) New Orleans localism, and (8) regional rusticity/Cajun-ness. Bourbon Street theming sends messages to millions of visitors that drive, for better or worse, notions of locally acceptable behavior and perceptions of Louisiana culture. *Photographs by author, 2012.*

often, sex for money is arranged in Bourbon clubs and delivered elsewhere—a risky proposition for the strippers, as more than a few have been murdered under such circumstances in recent years. Nearly all informants agree that you can get anything you want on Bourbon Street, so long as you find the right contacts and pay the right price.

Nearly every business on Bourbon affects a theme or brand. Signage, décor, and programming appear chaotic en masse, but in fact, their theming falls into eight clear categories, each speaking volumes about place making and image construction on Bourbon Street. They include beachy tropicality (Mango Mango, Tropical Isle, the Beach); eroticism (Lipstixx, Temptations, World Famous Love Acts); flamboyant musicality (Boogie Woogie, Blues Company, Rhythm and

Soul); New Orleans localism (Court Tavern Po-Boy, Mardi Gras Mayhem, Big Easy); regional rusticity (Fais Deaux Deaux, Cajun Cabin, the Swamp); nostalgic historicity (Court of Two Sisters, Yesteryear's, Maison Bourbon); mischievous macabre (Jazz Funeral, Voodoo Blues, Marie Laveau's House of Voodoo); and pleasurable excess (Desire, Fat Catz, Huge Ass Beers). Theming is particularly critical to bars and clubs, and the line between the two often blurs. Big clubs have full-blown stages and lighting but may downsize to bar service only if the crowds are thin. Bars often have little stages tucked in corners and can scale up with live entertainment when crowds are big and feisty. The main difference between the two is the presence of live music and a dance floor.

Live music on Bourbon Street today accounts for about half the decibel level on a typical night; recorded music and crowd noise makes up the rest. Dominant genres are classic rock and pop from the standard American and English commercial songbook of the past fifty years, with an emphasis on the 1970s and 1980s ("I must have heard Journey's *Don't Stop Believing* four times one night," rued one bartender) plus a recent late-night infusion of rap. A number of venues play recorded dance-pop, electropop, or hip-hop and overlay it with live singing or rapping from an emcee.[29]

Most live music on Bourbon is "covered" from other artists who made the melodies famous; original composition is rare. The reason is simple: patrons hate it. People do not go to Bourbon Street to seek intellectual challenge or to expand their cultural horizons; they go there to unwind. True, Bourbon Street has a history of introducing innovations, but only those previously tested elsewhere—and for no other motivation than profit. Evidence is ample. Bourbon Street offered rollicking piano and cancan dancing in the late 1800s, but only when concert saloons had proven successful in other American cities. It featured orchestrons and melodeons at places like Wenger's Garden in the 1880s, but only after these musical technologies became a nationwide fad. It drew upon local jazz and regional blues at places like Maxime's in the 1920s, but only after the nascent popular music industry had nationalized these sounds via commercial records and radio. It featured big band, barrelhouse, and boogie-woogie when these styles became the sound track—literally, through the movies—of World War II–era America. It offered hillbilly (country) music in the 1940s and 1950s, but only after rural southerners settled into the city for war-plant jobs and longed for the sounds of home. It featured its first rock-and-roll band right around the time when this new commercial fusion of white hillbilly and black blues enraptured American youth—and Elvis Presley himself cinematically brought rock to Bourbon in *King*

Creole. Bourbon Street abandoned lounge music and burlesque accompaniment when it realized the rest of the nation had lost interest, and has since embraced rhythm and blues, hard rock, and pop. Likewise it hosted the quirky banjo supper club Your Father's Mustache when rustic folk-style music became popular in the 1960s, only to dump it in the 1970s in favor of Latin (disco), which itself gave way to the synthesized glam rock of the 1980s. It eagerly adopted the Japanese invention of karaoke starting at the Cat's Meow in 1989—a perfect fit for Bourbon Street in that it turns paying patrons into unpaid entertainers and keeps the crowds amused regardless of talent. And Bourbon Street has embraced Louisiana's own Cajun and zydeco music—but, once again, only after the Cajun cultural revival of the 1980s went national with gastronomic help from Paul Prudhomme and cinematic assistance from Hollywood's *The Big Easy*. Today Bourbon Street dabbles increasingly with rap for the same reasons: that's where the demand is going. It happily leaves creative musical experimentation—and the risk, and the low pay—to Frenchmen Street or St. Claude Avenue. Music on Bourbon has always reflected national culture, not driven it. It's the main reason why music mavens snub the place, and one of the reasons why investors adore it.

A typical Bourbon Street cover band comprises mostly white males in their twenties to forties, sometimes with a female vocalist or other member. Generally nonunionized, they often live in the suburbs and work a circuit of venues, getting their gigs through connections and networks. Classic rock and blues-rock cover bands make up one-third to two-thirds of the live music reaching the ears of the passing parade; the rest is Cajun and zydeco, traditional jazz (usually limited to the Maison Bourbon, Fritzel's, Bourbon Saloon, and Music Legends Park), country, contemporary R&B, and a few solo acoustic artists and pianists. Recorded music, with or without live vocal overlays, is usually dance-pop, electro-pop, hip-hop, rap, or bounce. Some places mix and blend to suit the crowd, a flexibility that Bourbon Street has long honed. Back in 1949, for example, Ciro's at 331 Bourbon offered everything "from boogie to Bach," not to mention "Risque Songs." Today, the Tropical Isle features what its owner calls "'trop-rock,' music that combines Jimmy Buffett–style music, rock, island music and a little reggae."[30] The Inn on Bourbon has recently taken to hiring opera singers to capitalize on its location on the site of the Old French Opera House.

Career musicians who play Bourbon Street, who are more likely to be unionized, grapple with a professional dilemma. On the plus side, The Street is among the few places where they can earn a decent income at a steady gig with predictable hours. Payments, which range from fifteen to thirty dollars for a one-hour set to $125 per band member for feature acts playing a full evening, are guaranteed regardless of turnout. This explains why bands play to empty barrooms on sunny afternoons: it all pays the same. Clubs on Frenchmen and elsewhere, in contrast, pay musicians based on a percentage of the bar (not much, because drinks are cheaper than on Bourbon), a cover charge (if any, and it's shared if more than one band plays), and/or the proceeds in the tip jar. Thus, low turnout means low pay.

But Bourbon Street's stability can also lull performers into a flat-lined career track of endlessly repeating tired old chestnuts. "Once you're in it, you're really tied to it, and it's hard to do outside performances," said Idaho-born Amy Trail, who has played Pat O'Brien's piano bar since 2004. Performing solo gigs intellectually liberates musicians and increases the chances of being discovered, but at the cost of a reduced income and a fragmented schedule. "Maybe I'll eventually get off Bourbon Street, maybe not," she said in 2010. "Who knows?"[31]

Bourbon musicians are sensitive about the stigma they bear. Music writer John Swensen described it as "the lack of critical credibility that comes with playing the commercial strip." Blues singer Big Al Carson sportingly shrugged it off, although he did confide that "sometimes I truly believe that I'm the best-kept secret in New Orleans." Trumpeter Irvin Mayfield, who enjoys a sterling reputation among most Bourbon-hating music connoisseurs, raised their eyebrows when he opened a jazz venue in Bourbon Street's Royal Sonesta in 2009. As if to assuage their anxiety, Mayfield made peace with an outspoken critic, seventy-one-year-old Bob French Sr., by offering the veteran jazzman gigs at Mayfield's Bourbon digs. French readily accepted, saying: "I love playing music, and I love money. And I get both of them [on Bourbon Street]."[32] Such sentiments unsettled the authenticity crowd, who didn't know what to make of either Mayfield or French so long as they had a Bourbon Street address. Mayfield assured them that "the Royal Sonesta's core values are authentic experiences," and vowed that his playhouse would, in Swensen's paraphrase, "change the nature of Bourbon Street."[33]

Musically, Bourbon Street may have to change. Tonight on Bourbon Street, one is more likely to hear forty-year-old songs than forty-day-old songs—at a time when American musical tastes are increasingly experimenting and fragmenting. Perhaps what we are hearing today represents The Street's attempt to adapt to the complex new soundscape, by musically offering a little bit of everything to everyone and seeing what resonates.

Millions of people and a drink in every hand can spell danger, and danger and pleasure don't mix. Hence the task of policing is critical to the functioning of the

Bourbon Street machine. It falls to the Eighth District of the New Orleans Police Department, whose officers, stationed in a ca. 1826 former bank on Royal, keep an eye on The Street in proportion to its diurnal, weekly, and seasonal visitation cycles. They are aided by colleagues from the Mounted Division, who provide the ideal platform for policing Bourbon's potentially volatile throngs. A smartly uniformed officer towering atop a formidable yet placid steed works wonders in quelling mayhem and establishing rapport between civilians and the law. Visitors are fascinated by the majestic beasts and take time to admire them; mounted officers enjoy the empowered perch and occasionally thrill the crowd with displays of horsemanship, or by playfully poking their animals' heads into crowded bars. From a policing standpoint, visibility is the goal: patrons' seeing the police makes it clear that the police can see the patrons, and that reduces anonymity and increases accountability. Toward this end, the Eighth District, during the biggest events, also rolls in police towers with spotlights and cameras, positions cops at key intersections, deploys undercover officers and personnel from neighboring jurisdictions, and sometimes adds helicopters to the mix. And for good reason: Bourbon keeps the NOPD busy. Action on The Street produces an average of 34 complaints per day to the police, of anything from suspicious persons to shootings; the number during 2012 ranged as low as 16 on Christmas Day to as high as 160 on Mardi Gras. The spatial clustering is intensive: Of the 503,968 citywide service calls fielded by the NOPD during 2012, fully 12,227 of the complaints emanated from tiny Bourbon Street. For comparison, 5,652 were filed on the same thirteen blocks of Royal, and across the parish, a typical residential street of the same length filed from 300 to 600 complaints while commercial arteries registered from 1,300 to 1,600. Judging from this metric, Bourbon Street as an urban space sees ten times more deviancy than the rest of the city, and Mardi Gras on Bourbon yields ten times more than on its slowest day. Complaints about underage drinking were twelve times more prevalent on Bourbon than Royal; drug violations were eleven times more common; pickpockets, ten times; illegal possession of firearms, eight times; curfew and truancy, six times; and fights, five times.[34] The figures attest not so much to the perils of Bourbon Street as to its popularity: humanity, after all, populates this street at least ten times more than Royal, and well over a hundred times more than the quietest thoroughfares. The NOPD, admired nationwide for its crowd-control acumen, hones its skills nightly on Bourbon, and it is a testimony to their success that riots and stampedes are all but unknown on The Street.

Challenging Bourbon Street
The Rise of the Anti-Bourbons

In true capitalistic fashion, creative niches overlooked or underserved by Bourbon Street enticed entrepreneurs to compete with and drink from Bourbon's beer. They gave rise to new places and spaces borne of the cultural negative space around Bourbon Street: the anti-Bourbons.

Jazz buffs who bristled at the nightly repertoire of tired standards, for example, found an alternative in a smattering of clubs that encouraged the one thing Bourbonites forbid, and that was musical experimentation. All too often, unfortunately, the insurgent venues took the form of "a depressing bar usually owned by a well-meaning hipster, [with] morbid pseudo-modern paintings on the wall," as one frustrated jazz enthusiast put it. "Such places [have been] in tenuous existence somewhere in the Quarter since time immemorial." The Canadian-born owner of Cosimo's Lounge—transplants abound at such places—drew a direct line between his claim to musical creativity and the shortfalls of the neon strip: "Bourbon St. has gone commercial," he said in 1961. "Even the tourists are looking for a place off the beaten track where they can hear good jazz."[1] Places like Cosimo's, the Playboy, Mambo Joe's, the Pendulum, the Joy Tavern, Joe Burton's, and the Hidden Door (a counterpoint to the Famous Door Bar) similarly challenged Bourbon Street musically. Of particular note was Lu and Charlie's on North Rampart at Ursulines, which during the 1970s formed the city's premier, and probably the only, black-owned contemporary jazz club—something that was doubly nonexistent on Bourbon Street.

The decline of traditional jazz presented another anti-Bourbon toehold. It inspired Larry Borenstein, an art dealer from Wisconsin who became one of the Quarter's biggest property owners, to hold recording sessions for old-time jazz bands in his St. Peter Street gallery steps off Bourbon. Tourists sat in to listen, among them a couple from Pennsylvania named Allan and Sandra Jaffe. Contributions were collected to keep the musicians going in what some called "Authenticity Hall," but popularity soon called for more formal management. The Jaffes rose to the challenge in 1966 and took the reins of what had been renamed the New Orleans Society for the Preservation of Traditional Jazz. Aware of the slick and sleazy reputation of Bourbon Street clubs, the Jaffes crafted their "Preservation Hall" as the antithesis: a simple old building where aging gentlemen played traditional jazz for appreciative audiences who sat on wooden benches with no air-conditioning, no food, no drinks, and a spartan interior designed for verisimilitude. Within a couple of years, local music aficionados identified it as "most popular tourist Mecca of the French Quarter, [where] visitors flock in droves to hear the old-timers 'speak the idiom as she should be spoke.'"[2] Designed against Bourbon Street but benefiting from its throngs, Preservation Hall soon became a nationally recognized brand, and its musicians would play Carnegie Hall and tour the world. Never one to pass up a good idea, Bourbon itself got into the anti-Bourbon act, as Dixieland Hall, Maison Bourbon, and Fritzel's adopted Preservation Hall's approach, only with nostalgicized interiors and plenty of drinks. Similar experimentalist and traditionalist venues soldier on today in pointed defiance of Bourbon Street, which they perceive as having abandoned its roots and aimed for the wallet over the heart, soul, and mind.

Early anti-Bourbons did not spatially cluster; rather they scattered hither and yon seeking cheap rent. What gave them an opportunity for propinquity was a transforming Decatur Street. Into the 1960s, lower Decatur was still the domain of the old Sicilian families, and the nearby French Market continued to serve neighborhood housewives seeking fresh fish and local vegetables. Their departure, and the impending conversion of the French Market into a festival marketplace, left lower Decatur in the early 1970s, particularly the 1100 block, "one of the darkest, dirtiest blocks in the French Quarter," filled with "winos and bums. . . . [I]t was the slums."[3] Rents were so cheap that the French Quarter's only health dispensary, run by hippies for hippies, could afford to set up shop there—until it got raided by the police.[4] But one person's slum is another's opportunity. Consider lower Decatur's attributes: it was zoned commercial for its proximity to the market. It had liquor licenses galore. It was convenient to downtown residents yet also close to the tourist circuit, and its rents were 60 percent below Bourbon's.

The Pied Piper of Decatur Street was Jim Monaghan, who closed down his bar on Toulouse near Bourbon ("a fool," friends called him) and in 1973 opened Molly's at the Market at 1107 Decatur. He brought with him the Bourbon Street technique of throwing open the façade such that patrons inside and outside the bar intermingled freely, and the sidewalk became moneymaking space. He tapped into the new procession of tourists to the renovated French Market, just as Bourbon Street tapped into its passing parade. He also retained just enough grunginess and funkiness to keep cagey cognoscenti convinced Molly's was cool—so much so that the bar counted a number of local literati among its regulars, something Bourbon Street could no longer claim. Monaghan's success helped lower Decatur flourish in the late 1970s and 1980s with self-consciously scruffy bars, respectable restaurants, noteworthy musical venues, and the sort of antique flea markets that had disappeared from the rest of the Quarter. By 1990, it boasted eighteen vintage clothing and bric-a-brac shops, thirteen bars and eateries, three record stores, two grocers, a smattering of other retailers, and a new streetcar line nearby linking it with the Moonwalk, Aquarium of the Americas, Riverwalk, and upper Decatur Street—which itself was undergoing a Bourbon-like transformation. "Decatur is going to be the Bourbon Street of the 1990s," predicted one new restaurateur. Property values increased; Monaghan saw his building rise in value from the $175,000 he paid for it in 1973 to nearly $1 million by 1991, by which time he headed the Decatur Street Merchants Association.

Upper Decatur did indeed come close to replicating the Bourbon scene, with door-to-door bars catering to tourists and T-shirt shops spilling Cajun music into the streets. It even garnered the same Vieux Carré Entertainment (VCE) land-use zone from the City Planning Commission, courtesy of lobbying by the House of Blues. But lower Decatur opted for a different destiny. Its denizens cultivated a progressive, underground aura, and rejected gaudiness and pizzazz as much as Bourbon Street embraced them. It offered an alternative to visitors who had a certain notion of how authenticity should look, and found it lacking on Bourbon Street. Since the 1990s, the 1100–1300 blocks have stabilized with a fairly even mix of local and tourist patronage, a rarity in downtown New Orleans. It's a street where morbid Goths commiserate at the Abbey right across the street from Jimmy Buffett's blissfully Bourbon-ish Margaritaville Restaurant, and where retro-edgy musicians can get a gig at the Balcony Music Club a block away from the traditional jazz at the Palm Court Café. Lower Decatur is one of the few places where hipsters and gutter punks brush shoulders with yuppies and tourists.[5]

While Bourbon Street looked askance at the new Decatur Street, more threatening competition arose ten miles away. As thousands of New Orleanians decamped to Jefferson Parish in the 1960s, the demand for nightlife shifted westward with them. Starting around 1970, a few restaurants and lounges opened around the Edenborn and Hessmer Avenue intersections with Eighteenth Street in Metairie. They prospered and, abetted by zoning laws, attracted similar clubs—which drew more patrons and lured further investment. The spontaneously formed district benefited from the adjacent Lakeside Shopping Center to the east, a number of apartment complexes catering to young singles to the north, the auto culture of the surrounding Metairie suburbs, and a white middle-class clientele that had turned its back on downtown New Orleans. People started to call the new suburban nightspot "Little Bourbon Street," but Roy Anselmo, who owned six of its lounges and whose family ran a number of Bourbon joints, wanted to brand this up-and-coming area against that musty old image. He opted for a very different name gleaned from a local snowball stand: Fat City. It stuck, and Jefferson Parish later officially renamed Eighteenth Street "Fat City Boulevard."

Fat City peaked in the mid- to late 1970s with more than seventy nighttime drinking, eating, music, and entertainment venues, all within walking distance. The new suburban anti-Bourbon had the old urban Bourbonites worried, and helped motivate them to support Mayor Landrieu's 1977 effort to reverse Bourbon's downslide. Fat City itself started declining in the mid-1980s when Bourbon Street became cool again, and when the young swinging singles living in the nearby apartment complexes were no longer young, swinging, or single. Fat City became cheap and seedy in the 1990s and was hit hard in the 2000s with new parish zoning regulations and—perish the thought—mandatory closing hours. Today, the downsized "surreally suburban Bourbon Street"[6] caters to an aging demographic with musical tastes ranging from hair bands to the Yat Pack. As if taking a page from the Bourbon Street Task Force's playbook, Jefferson Parish authorities in 2012 looked to New York City to learn how to breathe life into a dying entertainment district. Advised the president of the Times Square Alliance, "create a 'cluster of cool'" in the heart of Fat City, "where you can really make it look and feel different."[7]

Bourbon Street itself might have benefited from that advice. As Bourbon gained back ground lost to Fat City, it began to lose ground in the 1990s to a new cluster of cool developing on nearby Frenchmen Street. Like Decatur, Frenchmen had organically formed commercial uses of its land throughout the nineteenth century, which became legally reified when the City Planning and Zoning Commission delineated and regulated land use starting in 1929. Midcentury Frenchmen sported a handful of functional shops and unpretentious spots which served local working-class folks in the same way lower Decatur did; one place, the Frenchmen Street Social Club, was raided by police in 1969 for illicit gambling.

The surrounding neighborhood was "pocketed with 'chop shops' and dilapidated housing," and Quarter tourists were routinely warned "Don't cross Esplanade" in the same manner they are now advised against crossing Rampart.[8] That the first bar to greet those who ventured across was named Check Point Charlie evidenced the sense of social division.

Frenchmen's blue-collar scene began to change when the same forces precipitating the transformation of lower Decatur—the seeking of financial refuge from high Quarter rents and cultural refuge from Bourbon Street abominations—made lower Frenchmen attractive as well; the two streets, after all, join at a doglegged intersection. Proximity to the Quarter aided Frenchmen's growth, as did the gentrification of its surrounding neighborhood, which had revived its historic moniker "Faubourg Marigny." "The Marigny," as residents would call it, attracted a sophisticated and moneyed demographic with an epicurean flair, a penchant for historic renovation, and an outspoken pedantry regarding cultural authenticity—in other words, anti-Bourbonism.[9]

As occurred in the French Quarter a generation earlier, artists and gay men predominated among the newcomers. Among the first new businesses on Frenchmen were the Dream Palace (1976) at 534 Frenchmen, the Vis-à-Vis Art Gallery, and the Faubourg Marigny Bookstore, said to be the first gay bookshop in the South. By 1980, the Dream Palace regularly featured musical guests ranging from jazz orchestras to the Radiators; the Theater Marigny at 616 Frenchmen hosted avant-garde productions; and the Faubourg, a seafood restaurant two doors up, booked well-regarded local jazz bands like the Astral Project for all-night jams. That year a local journalist noted that Frenchmen was "becoming a haven for those yearning for music in the wee hours."[10] Snug Harbor opened shortly thereafter and soon developed a national reputation for critically acclaimed jazz acts like Ellis Marsalis and Allen Toussaint. Restaurants followed, including the Santa Fe (1985) and Praline Connection (1990). Because zoning ordinances implicitly viewed live music as a neighborhood nuisance that should be limited to Bourbon Street, venues on Frenchmen Street constantly struggled with permitting issues. "If it's not permitted, it's prohibited," said attorney Mary Howell in explaining Café Brasil's frustrations over trying to stage live acts on Frenchmen in 1992. "You can have a tape playing of Dylan Thomas" under the present law, she pointed out, "but he couldn't appear in person."[11]

Changes to the ordinance helped Frenchmen gain momentum. Musical and culinary eclecticism, something Bourbon Street had long rejected in favor of catering to mass tastes, also proved to be the key to its success. By the late 1990s,

Frenchmen offered "everything from jazz and blues to brass band, punk, salsa, samba, rock, reggae, zydeco and Cajun sounds," to which could be added, in the 2000s, klezmer, bluegrass, folk, performance art, and pure experimentation. Food-wise, Latin American to Lebanese to Creole, Indian, Japanese, Italian, Louisianian, vegetarian and soul food could be found, all within a thousand feet.

Like Bourbon Street, the social action on Frenchmen today occurs largely in the public space; midnight on a typical Saturday sees hundreds of people milling about outside, dipping periodically in and out of clubs. Also like Bourbon, Frenchmen now finds itself at loggerheads with neighboring homeowners, who file noise and traffic complaints with city government. The Faubourg Marigny Improvement Association (FMIA), meanwhile, wrestles with Frenchmen owners and managers as VCPORA does Bourbon's. The same noise ordinances created to control Bourbon Street also apply to Frenchmen Street.

Unlike Bourbon Street, however, the Frenchmen crowd does not flow like a river, drinks in hand, but rather eddies and pools in conversation clusters. Local jam and brass bands entertain people for tips without getting chased away by agitated club owners. Pop-up vendors, usually unlicensed, sell foodie-style tapas and appetizers, and are generally left alone. Lucky Dog vendors? Never, nor the flower peddlers nor the bet-I-can-tell-you-where-you-got-dem-shoes guys. Instead, hipsters vend handmade jewelry and dog-eared radical paperbacks, or pound out poetry on manual typewriters for tips, things never seen on Bourbon.[12] Everyone on both streets seems to have a shtick to hustle or an image to affect; they're just different shticks and different images.

Officially, Frenchmen contrasts markedly from Bourbon. It exists today because the city in 2004 designated it an Arts and Cultural Overlay District, a master-planning tool that allows a certain land use—live music, in this case—in a zone where it would otherwise not be permitted. The designation turned technically illegal operations into legal ones, and signified an emerging appreciation for the value that the cultural economy, and specifically live music, brought to the city. In exchange for that authorization, however, came rules and limits. Clubs must not surpass 4,000 square feet in size, cannot vend drinks directly to the street, are supposed to keep their doors closed during performances, and are permitted for live entertainment only, not recorded music. Overlay-district regulations also limit live-music venues to comprise no more than 20 percent of the district's total businesses, and if restaurants hire bands, they must be acoustical with no more than three members. Frenchmen's popularity, however, has inspired the same sort of envelope pushing seen on Bourbon Street decades ago. Prospective investors today increasingly eye opportunities on Frenchmen for bigger and flashier venues. In 2012, for example, a proposal floated to convert the old Laborde print shop (a relic of pre-cool Frenchmen) into a two-story 7,000-square-foot club with three bars, two stages, and a kitchen—the likes of which could be found, at least structurally, up and down Bourbon. And that 20 percent cap? The city calculated in 2013 that 38 percent of the thirty-four properties on the three-block strip offered live music, while neighbors put it closer to 50 percent. The boom had the keep-it-funky crowd and FMIA members worried that Frenchmen Street "may finally be nearing its tipping point" and "will soon begin to feel more like Bourbon Street."[13] Their trepidation sheds light on another distinction between the two situations. Frenchmen's clubbers and its neighborhood critics are generally cut from the same cultural cloth; most residents are also patrons, and many Frenchmen owners and workers live in the neighborhood. Bourbonites and *their* critics, on the other hand, occupy decidedly different socioeconomic realms, and generally view each other contemptuously. Very few Bourbonites live in the French Quarter, and most Quarterites, particularly homeowners, shun Bourbon Street.

Financially, music making on Frenchmen falls short of Bourbon. Frenchmen clubs regularly charge cover fees and pass around tip jars to pay the musicians, a financial arrangement that, on the one hand, selects for patrons who really want to listen to the music, but on the other, pegs musicians' compensation to turnout. A slow night means low pay. One Frenchmen musician complained of grossing only ten dollars one night and netting barely one dollar after expenses. Others gripe that the illegal street bands make more than they do.[14] On Bourbon Street, where music is mostly atmospheric (meant to be heard more than listened to) and money is made from alcohol, payments to musicians are preset regardless of turnout. Alternatively, some Frenchmen clubs pay musicians 10 to 20 percent of the bar's gross, but again they find themselves at a disadvantage because drinks are cheaper on Frenchmen.

The crowd on Frenchmen, which one out-of-town journalist described in 1997 as "a multicultured mix of yuppies, hippies, retirees and college kids bouncing from one venue to the next, black and green stamps smudged on their wrists,"[15] is worlds away from that which Bourbon draws, except that the majority in both spaces is middle-class and white. Except during Carnival, there's nary a pair of Mardi Gras beads in sight on Frenchmen, nor are there any vulgar T-shirts, public-nudity eruptions, black tap dancers, or bright-colored tropical drinks in novelty containers. Instead, one sees drowned-rat hairdos, facial hardware,

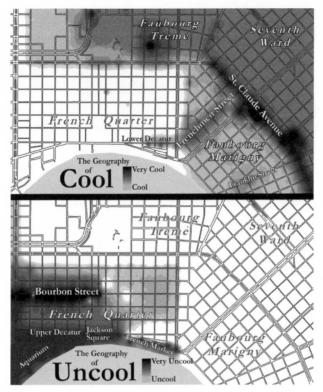

"Cool" and "uncool" spaces in downtown New Orleans, circa 2010s. Estimates by the author based on a variety of observations and metrics.

vintage attire, ironic mustaches, combat footgear, six-foot-high bicycles, and baroque tattoos measured in square footage. The patrons are a mix of visitors and residents, but the former tend to be the type who take offense at being called tourists, and the latter are disproportionately, probably overwhelmingly, transplants rather than natives of New Orleans. In short, Frenchmen Street today is the ultimate anti-Bourbon—what one reporter called the "the cool kids' alternative to Bourbon Street."[16] It calibrates its cultural superiority against the absolute zero that it perceives Bourbon to be.

But coolness is fickle, and, like authenticity, it can only be credibly claimed when propped against its opposite. As postdiluvian turmoil gave way to the "new normal" of the late 2000s and early 2010s, the neighborhoods below Esplanade Avenue began attracting hyperhip creative types and cultural envelope pushers, many of them Great Recession refugees from East and West Coast metropolises.

These youths expatriated to what they perceived to be an undiscovered Bohemia in the lower faubourgs of New Orleans. Instead they found its premier nightspot, Frenchmen Street, to be chic, trendy, entirely discovered, and all too reminiscent of similar spaces in the cities from which they had escaped. "The act of discovering what's cool," observed Malcolm Gladwell, "is what causes cool to move on."[17] And "move on" is exactly what the newcomers did. Agreeing that this was not what they moved down to New Orleans for, the cool kids moved away from Frenchmen Street and created an Anti-Frenchmen—or shall we call it the Anti-Anti-Bourbon—along disheveled St. Claude Avenue, particularly from St. Bernard to Franklin Avenues. Here hipsters could brood among their own, nurture their fixation on being ahead of the cultural curve, and distance themselves (their favorite dive is called Siberia) from the scorned mainstream. St. Claude is to Frenchmen what Frenchmen is to Bourbon: part snub, part alternative, part refuge; a utopia to the other's dystopia. The music played in each space accords with this cultural pecking order: St. Claude boasts experimental "indie" sounds— the operative word is "jam"—whereas Bourbon Street features mostly covered pop acts, and Frenchmen offers eclecticism with a preference for brass bands and funk covering retro sounds. Ditto the food, the décor, the prices, and the tourist/local ratio—very low on St. Claude, astronomical on Bourbon, and mixed on Frenchmen. The imaginary underworld that youths have created on St. Claude in the years after Hurricane Katrina, which includes public art, earthy galleries, grungy bars, and guerrilla performance spaces, recalls the Frenchmen Street of the 1980s, lower Decatur in the 1970s, and Bourbon Street and the Quarter in the 1920s and 1930s. To extend the lineage, Bourbon Street had inherited its nighttime scene from the Tango Belt of the 1910s–1920s, which had received it from Storyville (1897–1917), which derived from the Lorette Law and the soft-vice concentrations going back to antebellum times.

Hating Bourbon Street
On Iniquity and Inauthenticity

Contemplating Bourbon Street as a social artifact creates an opportunity to peer back at the society that created this space. Mostly what we see is people who enjoy it, as a momentary indulgence if not a lifestyle, else they would not visit it by the millions, spend billions, and make it famous. Thousands more make a living there, and hundreds call it home. What we also see is people who hate Bourbon Street and everything it stands for. Dispassion and ambivalence are rare in regard to Bourbon Street; usually the reaction is polarized: a mischievous smile and an arched eyebrow expressing delectable naughtiness, or a mouth twisted in disgust and a head shaking with agitation. People either run hot or cold on Bourbon Street, and that's usually the mark of something interesting.

What can we learn from Bourbon hating? Above all, the loathing transcends political and cultural spectrums. Haters may be conservative or liberal, and in general, the farther they range from the middle, the more intense their feeling.

Christian conservatives have shaken their fists at Bourbon Street at least since 1869, when religions reformers would slip into concert saloons and sing church hymns to save the souls of cancan fans. Temperance advocates saw Bourbon as justification for Prohibition. Evangelicals found it a convenient sound stage for their message, if not a productive source of converts. Bourbon has also provided rhetorical fodder and metaphorical reference for countless sermons and homilies, as it imparted to scriptural abstractions a clear mental image with a street address. Reverend Billy Graham, for example, gave Bourbon a shout-down during his 1954 New Orleans crusade, telling 61,500 faithful in Tulane Stadium that The Street emitted "a stench in the nostrils of God."[1] Local minister Grant E. Storms and his Christian Conservatives for Reform group railed annually against the gay Southern Decadence festival throughout the 2000s, at one point using video cameras to document public sex acts at Bourbon and St. Ann.[2] And in 2005, a handful of preachers and politicians publicly professed that Hurricane Katrina represented divine retribution for the wickedness of New Orleans in general, and Bourbon Street in particular.

Tonight, Pentecostals stake out a spot in the middle of Bourbon Street, usually around the extrawide Toulouse intersection, and use the surrounding sin-scape as an amphitheater for their evangelism. They are usually white males ranging from their twenties to sixties, organized under the aegis of the Vieux Carre Assembly of God Church or Raven Street Church Ministries. Upholding a large wooden cross with an electronic ticker mounted on the patibulum, the leader admonishes smirking pleasure-seekers of their folly and advises on their fate and salvation. Assistants distribute redemption literature and attempt to engage passersby in dialogue, as the ticker's light-emitting diodes spell out biblical verses in a glowing red Vegas-like crawl. Most revelers ignore the activists, some politely acknowledge them, and occasionally, according to one veteran pastor, "people spit on you, throw drinks at you, try to knock my cross over."[3] Recognizing, like everyone else trying to sell something on Bourbon Street, that an entirely new gaggle of potential customers arrives every ten seconds, the evangelist revisits his talking points and cinches his uncontested arguments cyclically. Like an itinerant preacher in reverse, he stands still and the congregation moves. Usually the nightly Bourbon Christians take a gentle, honey-over-vinegar approach in their proselytizing; being outnumbered, they have to. But they are hardly on enemy turf. Demographically and culturally, they are cut from the same cloth as most Bourbon revelers, and they readily clarify that they hate the sin—Bourbon Street—and not the sinners.

The soft suasions of the nightly crusaders stand in contrast to a new force on The Street: a particularly vitriolic brand of nondenominational zealots who arrive each Mardi Gras and Southern Decadence with a message that can only be described as hateful. They come from far and wide and organize via the website of a fire-and-brimstone street preacher named Ruben Israel, who targets large public and media events coast to coast. Equipped with bullhorns, safety glasses, and towering placards, they march single-file through the throngs, hands grasping the shoulder ahead of them like a SWAT team invading hell. Their principal target is the St. Ann queer space, but the condemnations go far beyond homosexuality:

WARNING: Fornicators, Drunkards, Liars, Thieves, God Haters, Sports Nuts, Ear Ticklers, World Lovers, Idolaters, Jesus Mockers, Mormons, Baby

Killers, Porn Watchers, Witches, Hindus, Muslims, Luke Warmers, Party
People, Homosexuals—*HELL AWAITS*

Other signs add Catholics to the list, ponder whether AIDS represented "Judgment or Cure?" and ask Bourbon revelers, "Are You God's Barf?"[4] Droves of
drunks engaging in shouting matches with incensed religious fanatics, at times
to the point of fisticuffs, has become one of the more disquieting spectacles of
Bourbon Street at the close of its third century. These Bourbon haters hate the
sin, the sinners, *and* The Street.

Those who hated the haters took legal action. When the City Council prepared an ordinance against "aggressive solicitation" in the French Quarter
in 2011, certain parties crafted a special clause and, with the endorsement of
VCPORA, French Quarter Citizens, the French Quarter Business Association,
and the French Quarter Management District, persuaded council members to
add it to the penultimate paragraph of the seven-page law: "It shall be prohibited
for any person or group of persons to loiter or congregate on Bourbon Street for
the purpose of disseminating any social, political or religious message between
the hours of sunset and sunrise."[5] In a remarkable demonstration of Bourbon
Street's power to reshuffle bedfellows, civil libertarians who normally pounce on
any fiddling with First Amendment rights—and this ordinance certainly qualified—instead dithered. Likewise, culture lovers who ordinarily rhapsodize about
New Orleans's exuberant use of public space when it takes the form of second-line
parades in Tremé instead fell silent when it took the form of proselytizing on
Bourbon Street. The police, on the other hand, who for decades raided Bourbon Street with alacrity, now discreetly refrained from implementing a law that
even its foremost supporter acknowledged was "unenforceable for free speech
reason[s]."[6] Christians nationwide, meanwhile, upon learning of the law via the
Internet, suddenly became civil libertarians and stakeholders in the very place
they despised. Only when police actually arrested nine highly confrontational
evangelicals during Southern Decadence 2012 did the American Civil Liberties
Union fully vocalize its dissent—thus putting the normally liberal group in bed
with Christian conservatives and at odds with gay-friendly French Quarter leaders.[7] In a letter published in the *Times-Picayune*, one of the authors of the Bourbon Street clause reminded readers that "a municipality may issue reasonable
regulations governing the time, place, and manner of speech." He also attempted
to defuse the underlying tension between secular Left and Christian Right by
shifting the problematic away from religion and back toward aggressive solicita-

Mardi Gras on Bourbon Street, 2012. *Photograph by author.*

tion, which constituted the bulk of the legislation.[8] When, that same weekend, police arrested a nonconfrontational preacher, the ACLU, obligated to challenge the law but leery of defending the most rancorously homophobic proselytizers, lunged at the opportunity to defend a more congenial one instead. The organization filed a lawsuit and promptly convinced a federal judge to block enforcement of the clause, although to date the ordinance remains on the books. The struggle was the latest in the long history of cultural, civic, religious, and legal battles over how people should behave in the curious space that is Bourbon Street.[9]

Americans on either side of the culture wars hate Bourbon Street. But they hate it for entirely different reasons. Traditionalists on the Right hate Bourbon Street for its iniquity. Progressives on the Left hate it for its inauthenticity. The Right hates it for its commercialization of sin; the Left, for its commercialization of culture. The Right hates it because it is dangerous pretending to be safe; the Left, because it is safe pretending to be dangerous. The Right, because it's funky and honky-tonk; the Left, because it's neither. The Right, because it makes the bourgeoisie indecent; the Left, because it appeals to indecent bourgeoisie. While the nature of the antipathy differs—the Right wags its finger, while the Left looks down its nose—the result is the same. Hating Bourbon Street is one of the few things traditionalists and progressives agree on, so long as they don't compare notes.

Intrinsic to the progressive brand of Bourbon hating is the notion of authenticity, or rather, the lack thereof. Authenticity may be viewed as the narrowness of the gap between one's innermost nature and that which gets expressed outwardly for external consumption. The wider the gap, and the more planning and scheming goes on to disguise that gap, the less the authenticity. Jean-Paul Sartre viewed jazz and the American musicians he heard in Greenwich Village as "speaking to the best part of you, the toughest, the freest, to the part which wants . . . the deafening climax of the moment"—utterly authentic, unlike what he heard from "sad imitators" in France.[10] Similarly, the existentialist viewed African American culture as free and genuine, and Western culture as affected and crafted.

Few people lost sleep over authenticity before the 1900s. Prior, most humans lived lives that were all too gritty and real to leave time to contemplate gritty reality. Those wealthy enough to distance themselves from daily drudgery mostly wanted to lengthen and flaunt that distance. This began to change with industrialization, which led to urbanization, the expanding ranks of the middle class, the spatial subjugation of the poor, and increased consumption of, among other things, modern leisure travel experiences. "Public relations" became a field; tourism became an industry; and image became everything. A gap seemed to widen between what people said they were—and what people said about places and products—and what they really were. The privileged, with time on their hands to ponder abstractions, became sensitive to their own artifice and grew intrigued by the apparent genuineness of common folk and their simple ways. Affluent youth started visiting the spaces of the poor, listening to their music, appropriating their language—"slumming," it was called. The most committed moved into their neighborhoods, like the French Quarter.

Postindustrialization furthered this process. The late-twentieth-century shift to an information society of white-collar professionals working in office parks and living in exurbs produced a generation insulated from risk and bound by structure. Education made youths aware of their privilege, and a certain segment grew bored and anguished with it. In the words of Adam Nathaniel Mayer, they "suffered a kind of postmodern malaise which in turn spurred a quest for meaning."[11] Previous generations had common causes like escaping poverty or fighting wars to satisfy this top tier of Maslow's Hierarchy of Needs; this generation did not. So they sought meaning through individualized quests for authentic experiences.

Because authenticity seemed to call for a certain demeanor, its seekers brooded, acted aloof, and squinted when they dragged on their cigarettes. Because it needed a certain look, they grew or chopped their hair defiantly, got tattoos, and donned ragged or vintage clothing. Music, food, cinema, literature, cars, religion: just about every aspect of culture had a "groovy" (1960s), "alternative" (1980s), or "critical" (2000s) counterpart which pitted itself against the mainstream and viewed itself as authentic. And because authenticity also had a geography, its seekers packed their knapsacks and hit the road—out of suburbia and into the wilderness, to distant countries, to communes, to college towns or mountain villages, and most commonly, to the decaying inner cities abandoned by their elders. In the past few decades, educated mostly white youths from prosperous backgrounds have transformed urban spaces in cities like Brooklyn and Oakland and Baltimore and Boston and London from shabbiness and indigence to restoration and gentrification.

New Orleans fit the bill perfectly. It had history, culture, and the poignancy of tragedy and past grandeur. It had a European look, a Caribbean feel, an expatriated vibe, an abundance of historic housing at low rent, a pervasive booziness, and music, food, and festivity to boot. It was authentic!

There was just one problem: authentic New Orleans depended wholly on the hideously inauthentic corporate conventioneers, SUV-driving suburbanites, and crass rubes who infested the inner city as tourists. Numbering close to 10 million per year, they ruined the progressives' quest for authenticity as absolutely as they absolutely loved Bourbon Street, which was *their* favored geography. Authenticity seekers responded by loving to hate Bourbon Street—ardently, almost histrionically, because outing the inauthentic enhanced their claim to its antithesis. They viewed Bourbon Street as a place where the spurious is sold to the phony to profit the sleazy at the expense of the real, and wanted everyone to know that they were on to it.

Not everyone plays the authenticity game. Many working-class natives of the metro area, particularly African Americans, have all the authenticity they need, and tend to view Bourbon Street as harmless, naughty fun. Middle-class folks throughout the region enjoy it for what it is and shrug off its faults. It's the cultural elite and their aspirants—image-conscious doyens, urbanophiles and preservationists, literati and academics, music connoisseurs and foodies, insecure transplants proving their *bona fides*, college students making a statement—who obsess about authenticity, going so far as to segregate nearly all aspects of city life into an authentic/inauthentic dualism. They would universally agree, for example, that the Seventh Ward, St. Claude Avenue, the bounce scene, second-line parades, Mardi Gras Indians, and anything to do with Creoles all sparkle with realness. And with equal unanimity they would give a thumbs-down to the upper Quarter, the French Market, Indian-owned T-shirt shops, and anything related to Bourbon Street. To be sure, most are willing to concede a few spots of Good Bourbon amid ten blocks of Bad Bourbon. Even the most rabid Bourbon haters, for example, revere Galatoire's, say nice things about Irvin Mayfield's Jazz Playhouse, maintain a polite neutrality regarding the St. Ann queer space, and enjoy Lafitte's Blacksmith Shop, whose candlelit interior wins over just about everyone. But these exceptions only prove the rule—and progressives rule that Bourbon Street is phony, period.

Although purely illusionary, authenticity is a powerful and omnipresent theme in both the intellectual and popular discourse about modern New Orleans. It and its evil handmaiden, inauthenticity, are used, in the words of sociologist Kevin Gotham, "to influence public debate, contest policies, neutralize counter-arguments and opposition, and mobilize constituents."[12] Buzz about authenticity can make or break a restaurant. It defines social circles and where they circulate. It underlies the credibility of artists, musicians, researchers, and writers. The authenticity argument helped win nationwide support for the rebuilding of New Orleans after Hurricane Katrina, and motivated thousands of authenticity-starved young professionals to move here unbidden to participate in the recovery. The city itself revels in its own realness, and sees no irony in statements such as that made by Chief Executive Officer Mark Romig, who extolled his New Orleans Tourism Marketing Corporation's "global efforts to bring the story of our authentic and unique culture to leisure travelers everywhere"—even as he canned a consulting firm with deep local roots in favor of a New York ad agency.[13]

Authenticity is seductive; we embrace it because it makes us feel exclusive. Declaring something to be authentic puts us in the know; it positions us in a place of power and authority, flatters our tastes, and flaunts our cultural savvy. So does condemning the inauthentic, under the syllogism that if I hate that which is fake, then I myself must be real. People's feelings about Bourbon Street inform on their actual or desired position in the socialcultural pyramid, and publicizing their disdain for Bourbon Street is an easy way to nudge that position upward. It is one of the first lessons learned by erudite newcomers: loving Bourbon Street is the shibboleth of a rube; disdaining it is the mark of a sophisticate. Hating Bourbon Street has valuable social currency, and it's an easy first step toward assuming co-ownership of "real" New Orleans culture.

So who's right? Who's the better Bourbon hater?

Clearly the traditionalists' abhorrence rests upon faith and creed. If one ac-cepts the Judeo-Christian notion of sin and writhes at the prospect of pleasure, then Bourbon Street qualifies as the proverbial den of iniquity. There's not much more content there beyond a simple faith-based virtue-versus-vice argument.

The progressives' argument for hating Bourbon Street is loaded with content, and, predicated as it is on the notion of authenticity, has its share of weaknesses. Declaring something to be inauthentic positions the critic in the dubious position of being the arbiter of reality. What qualifies any one individual—a "progressive," no less—to cast such bold judgment on another? The fact that no one person or community ever thinks of himself, herself, or itself as anything but fully real and genuine suggests that inauthenticity is at best a subjective and arbitrary construct, and at worse, an arrogant disparagement. It smacks of smugness; it is necessarily exclusionary; and it is usually elitist—yet it tumbles from the mouths of people who purport to be enlightened, inclusionary, and egalitarian. Worse, inauthen-ticity rests on the troubling supposition that not all human beings or human endeavors contribute equally to this thing we call culture; that some are more worthy than others.

Another weakness with authenticity is that it is ahistorical. A hundred years ago, scholars of the Old Guard like Charles Gayarré, Alcée Fortier, Grace King, and John Kendall took it upon themselves to scribe the "real" history and cul-ture of New Orleans. They esteemed the French founders, the aristocracy, the grand edifices, and the Confederate generals, and shunted aside the poor, blacks, women, laborers, shotgun shacks, and anything else they judged to be sidebars to the fault-free, triumphant, "authentic" New Orleans narrative. Now, it's precisely reversed: scholars today find plenty of fault in the historic inequities of wealth and power, roll their eyes at the cobwebbed icons of old, and adulate those mar-ginalized by the musty patricians of the past. What happened? Did the inauthen-tic become authentic? The fake real? Or did *we* change, as we came to view, with the passage of time, that what struck our predecessors as mere backdrop was in fact a legitimate and important part of New Orleans history and culture? Scholars a hundred years hence will likely intellectualize how New Orleanians back in the 2000s shopped at a place called Walmart, listed to the music of a lady who called herself Gaga, and generated income at the famous Bourbon Street—and perhaps they might ponder why scholars in the 2000s never wrote about these topics. The passage of time renders the inauthentic authentic. Put more bluntly, time puts the lie to authenticity. Dismissing the Bourbon Street of today as inauthentic commits precisely the same mistakes of ahistoricity and recentism as Old Guard elites made a century ago. It obtusely presumes that no one in historical times manipulated their image, hyped their business, contrived verisimilitude, or sold the sizzle; that everyone in the past was on the up-and-up, and what they displayed outwardly precisely represented their true innermost nature. It's utter nonsense. "Inauthenticity" is entirely human. It's real. Everything is real. Bourbon Street today is just as authentically part of real New Orleans culture as Storyville was a hundred years ago, and as Social Aid and Pleasure clubs, the housing projects, Creoles, and Tremé are today—no more, no less.

When viewed in this light, Bourbon Street emerges as a fascinating and refreshing phenomenon. The dizzying, deafening artifact we see today originated organically, without an inventor or a vision or a legislative act. There is no Bourbon Street logo, no headquarters, no board of directors, no visitors' center, no brochure, not even a website. The nightlife that made the street famous—after two hundred years of utter normalcy—was created spontaneously by a cast of local characters, who, in an uncoordinated attempt to make a living individually, succeeded collectively. Localism has always predominated on Bourbon Street; even today, in an era defined by corporate globalization, New Orleans–based proprietors own fully 74 percent of the units on Bourbon Street, while Louisianians, nearly all from the southeastern portion of the state, own 90 percent.[14] Bourbon Street is a self-organizing local network sans a central nervous system, a self-correcting system that recognizes its own imbalances, and a brutally efficient marketplace operating with a minimum of sentimentality. As such, Bourbon Street has proven to be pugnacious, adaptable, and resilient. It represents a triumph of localism, an argument for emergent over ordained order, and a case study of civic (if often uncivil) compromise. It has been famous for nearly one-third of the city's entire existence—longer than the French and Spanish colonial eras combined, and the entire antebellum era. Bourbon Street is New Orleans's most lucrative sustained homegrown commercial success.

Contrast this with the New Orleans Jazz and Heritage Festival, the annual springtime fete that attracts hundreds of thousands of people to the Fairgrounds in Gentilly. Jazz Fest takes great pride in its musical acts and regional foods, arts, and exhibits; cultural cognoscenti love it devoutly, and criticize it constructively only when it fails to live up to its own authenticity-reverent ideals. Among the unwritten rules of self-respecting festgoers are no beads, no Bourbon T-shirts, and no Bourbon antics; Jazz Fest sees itself as a cultural refuge from all that phoniness. Yet Jazz Fest was invented by a man from Massachusetts as part of a

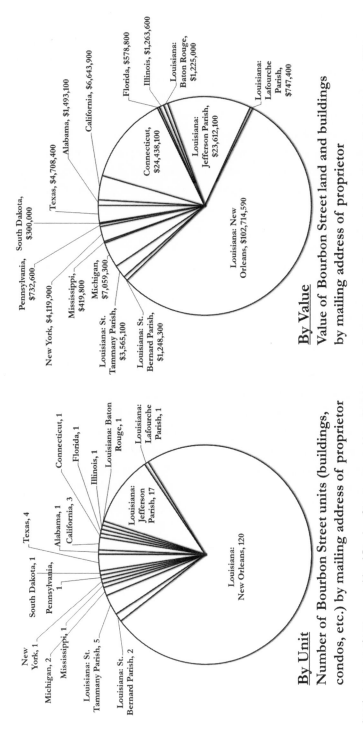

By Unit
<u>Number of Bourbon Street units (buildings, condos, etc.) by mailing address of proprietor</u>

By Value
<u>Value of Bourbon Street land and buildings by mailing address of proprietor</u>

Local versus out-of-state ownership of Bourbon Street, measured by unit and by value. *Analysis by author, based on data from Orleans Parish Assessor's Office, October 2012.*

worldwide megafestival circuit—essentially a local franchise of a global chain. Meticulously choreographed and carefully policed, it is managed out of New York, coordinated by crack professionals, "presented by Shell" (a phrase now officially appended to the event's name), increasingly dependent on global superstar acts, subsidized by an on-site Acura showroom, and funded by Big Oil—not to mention an entrance fee that has risen 400 percent in ten years, to fifty dollars per person, more than the median daily take-home pay for most New Orleanians. Trained staffers screen the acts, taste-test the foods of every concessionaire, and inspect the merchandise of all vendors before passing authentic/inauthentic judgment. The motifs of the event are all professionally designed to affect a funky juke-joint atmosphere—bottle caps nailed to rough-hewn clapboards, folk-style naïve art, helter-skelter multicolored lettering, that sort of thing. Jazz Fest is the epitome of invented, planned, centralized cultural control that leaves nothing to chance and covers its tracks with the trappings and aesthetics of authenticity. An existential philosopher would have to be particularly generous to describe Jazz Fest as authentic, and equally parsimonious to dismiss Bourbon Street as phony. Yet that is precisely what most Bourbon-hating culture lovers do.

A final rationale for Bourbon-hating transcends conservative and progressive worldviews. It's taste. Many people spurn Bourbon Street not necessarily because they see it as sinful or phony, but because it's crass and tasteless. In her essay "Notes on Camp," Susan Sontag viewed poor taste in art—kitsch—as aesthetically misguided to a comical extreme. But when set forth earnestly, devoid of all pretense and affectation, Sontag found kitsch to bear a certain honest and genuine appeal. Kitsch that is meant earnestly is campy; kitsch delivered lazily or cheaply is tasteless.

Bourbon Street from late 1930s to the mid-1960s was campy. The Oyster Girl and the Tassel Spinner were proudly proffered by impresarios as exemplars of stylish eroticism. People dressed to the nines and patronized Bourbon clubs craving the velvety cultural cachet that such clubs convincingly delivered. We laugh at them in retrospect, but they were not produced to be ridiculed; they were produced to dazzle. Midcentury Bourbon Street nightclubs presented themselves with enough decorum and pizzazz to make the kitsch campy.

What happened on Bourbon Street in the 1960s and 1970s was that the earnestness went out of the camp and left in its place only bad taste. It sold well nonetheless, because the eternal parade of tourists forever replenished itself and therefore had no collective memory. So the service got lazy, the merchandise cheapened, the bands lost their edge, the strippers let their bodies go, and Bourbon Street became, in the view of many, many people, a tasteless and vapid commercial conjunction with a bad case of cultural sclerosis.

And Bourbon Street doesn't necessarily disagree. Or agree. One of the benefits of being a self-organizing aggregation with no spokesperson is that Bourbon Street cannot take offense. Like disparagement of "the media" or "the establishment," criticism of Bourbon Street is diffused and abstracted to all its constituent parts, and that which belongs to everybody belongs to nobody. No Bourbon musician or chef retorts when detractors excoriate The Street's music or food, just as no Bourbonite protested when the writers of an "underground" (read: authentic) guidebook pointedly expunged Bourbon Street from the index, not to mention the content.[15] Bourbonites really don't give a damn; if they cry crocodile tears at all, they do so all the way to the bank. They'll address that tastelessness thing if and only if those trips to the bank start bearing shrinking sacks of cash. And sclerotic? Hardly. Bourbon Street operates on the principles of free-market capitalism. Those who don't flexibly adapt to demand go bankrupt; those who survive must be effectively and efficiently giving the people exactly what they want—and, yes, that may well be tasteless.

Las Vegas has been called America's most honest city for its undisguised pursuit of profit. Perhaps Bourbon rates as our most candid street, for the clarity of its deal: *accessible pleasures offered for a price to the passing parade.* For all its flamboyance and swagger, Bourbon Street is one of the least pretentious places in town. It's as utterly uncool as it is wildly successful, and in an era when "cool capital" is increasingly craved and fiscal capital is increasingly scarce, there's something refreshing about a place that flips off coolness and measures success the old-fashioned way: by the millions. And authenticity? Not only does Bourbon Street not try to be authentic, it doesn't even think about it. If, as Sartre once said, "you seek authenticity for authenticity's sake, you are no longer authentic," then perhaps the opposite is true as well. For all its ruses and illusions, Bourbon Street puts on no airs for anyone, requires no subsidies or handouts from anybody, has no need for the kindness of strangers, and lets the loquacious literati and the fuming fundamentalists fulminate alone. What you see when you peer past the neon is exactly what you get.

Replicating Bourbon Street
Spatial and Linguistic Diffusion

Perhaps the best evidence of Bourbon Street's success is the fact that, like jazz, it has diffused worldwide. It's a claim few other streets can make. As early as the 1950s, a nightclub named "Bourbon Street" operated in New York City, and apparently successfully, because in 1957 the Du Pont family formed a corporation to purchase it with plans to bring "Mambo City" entertainment to clubs named Bourbon Street in Miami and Chicago.[1] Today, at least 160 businesses throughout the United States and Canada have "Bourbon Street" in their names and themes; 77 percent are restaurants, bars, and clubs; 11 percent are retailers (mostly of party and novelty items); and the remainder are caterers, banquet halls, hotels, and casinos—more eating, drinking, and entertaining. They span coast to coast, from Key West to Edmonton and from San Diego to Montreal. Greater New York has eleven, while Calgary has six, as does San Antonio (mostly near the River Walk, "the Bourbon Street of San Antonio"). Greater Toronto has sixteen, most of them franchises of the Innovated Restaurant Group's "Bourbon St. Grill" chain—including one on Yonge Street, which has been described as "the Bourbon Street of Toronto." There are also Bourbon-named restaurants, bars, and clubs in London, Amsterdam, Hamburg, Naples, Moscow, Tokyo, Shanghai, Dubai, and many other world cities. These replicas enthusiastically embrace Bourbon Street imagery and material culture (lampposts, balconies, Mardi Gras jesters, beads) in their signage, décor, and websites. Menus attempt to deliver the spice and zest deemed intrinsic to this perceptual package, as does the atmospheric music. How convincingly do these meta-Bourbons replicate the original? A review of one such venue in Amsterdam ("the New Orleans of Europe") could easily apply to the actual street: "The jovial Bourbon Street Jazz and Blues Club . . . attracts a casual, jean-clad crowd of all ages [dancing to] cover bands with a pop flavor [or] blues

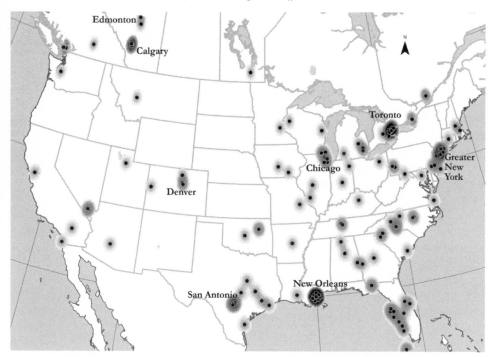

The name "Bourbon Street" is in the public domain, a valuable vernacular brand free for anyone to appropriate. Rich in imagery and connotations, it has thus diffused widely: shown here are locations of 160 active businesses named "Bourbon Street" throughout the United States and Canada in 2012. Scores more operate overseas.

rhythms. Three glass chandeliers hanging over the bar provide an incongruous dash of glamour to an otherwise low-key and comfortable scruffy décor."[2]

In this spatial dissemination we see a trend: while local replication of the Bourbon Street phenomenon usually takes the form of competition tinged with contempt (witness the "anti-Bourbons"), external replicas of Bourbon Street view themselves as payers of homage to the "authentic" original, and modestly present themselves as the next best thing without the airfare. No licenses are needed in replicating Bourbon Street; there are no copyrights, trademarks, or royalties due. The name, phenomenon, and imagery are all in the public domain, a valuable vernacular brand free for anyone to appropriate. Try doing that to the New Orleans Jazz and Heritage Festival Presented by Shell and you'd have a lawsuit on your hands.

Bourbon is also among the few streets to be replicated structurally—by the

State of Louisiana, which sponsored a three-acre exhibit at the 1964 World's Fair in Queens, New York. It featured all the standard architectural tropes of the French Quarter topped off with a huge arch emblazoned with LOUISIANA'S BOURBON STREET accompanied by towering Carnival royalty. In typical Louisiana fair tradition, however, the exhibit experienced construction delays and filed for bankruptcy, which caused the state to wash its hands of the fiasco and officially change the name of the exhibit to "Bourbon Street." "The so-called Louisiana area in its present condition," state officials solemnly proclaimed, "reflects discredit upon the State of Louisiana, its culture, heritage and people." Wags pointed out that this was pretty much what locals thought of the original Bourbon Street. But unlike the original, a corporate entity named Pavilion Properties, Inc. took over the exhibit, and after removing all references to Louisiana and spiffing up the props, it managed the Creole food booths, Dixieland trios, sketch artists, organ grinders, street performers, and nightclubs (including the popular "Gay New Orleans") for the remainder of the fair. Also unlike the original, Pavilion Properties' exhibit, just like the state's attempt, failed commercially and also filed for bankruptcy. Nevertheless, it introduced a generation of New Yorkers to the Bourbon Street brand.[3]

At the opposite end of the country two years later, another private-sector entity built a "New Orleans Square" at Disneyland. Based on field research conducted in the French Quarter by Walt Disney himself plus a staff of artists in 1965, the $13.5 million West Coast replica (nearly the cost of the Louisiana Purchase, Disney joked) eschewed the Bourbon moniker, presumably not to scare off parents, but nevertheless incorporated everything that worked on the real Bourbon Street minus the breasts and booze. Disney later replicated New Orleans Square at its Adventureland in Tokyo (1983), which may partly explain the popularity of the real New Orleans with Japanese visitors today. It did not, however, build a New Orleans Square at Disneyland Paris (Euro Disney) when it opened in 1992.[4]

Bourbon Street has also been thematically and structurally referenced in countless shopping malls, amusement parks, casinos, cruise-ship parties, festivals, convention banquets, and wedding receptions, not to mention on film and theatrical sets and in computer animation for movies like *The Princess and the Frog*. "Bourbon Street" as an adjective has found its way onto menus, usually for spicy dishes, and into household décor, generally to describe Old World filigree inspired by the iron-lace balconies. It's a case study of cultural diffusion which serves as free worldwide advertising for the original, across various media forms and demographic cohorts, all with zero encouragement and oversight from Bourbonites. Now that's success.

Imitation may be the sincerest form of flattery, but it also produces competition. Once there was a time when the forbidden pleasures available on Bourbon Street were in high demand and low supply nationwide, particularly in the South. That made Bourbon Street valuable. Today the nation is a whole lot less judgmental about pleasure and much better supplied with comparable pleasure districts. A visit to Galveston's The Strand, St. Louis's Soulard, and Mobile's Dauphine Street, all of which have adopted Bourbon-style Mardi Gras, may satisfy many people's desire for the escapism that Bourbon Street once monopolized. Even just a few blocks away in downtown New Orleans, Harrah's has quietly overseen the creation of a Bourbon alternative on the Fulton Street Mall, complete with outdoor dining, festival space, and a growing inventory of venues, all adjacent to the corporation's hotel and casino. Might such meta-Bourbons erode the market share of the original, in the same way that regional casinos have chipped away at Las Vegas's domination? Bourbonites would be ill-advised to rely on their fame; better to experiment with innovations, rediscover what worked in the past, and tame that which damages. That said, The Street does have certain inherent advantages: it's bigger and longer than the competition; it's embedded into the world-famous French Quarter and enjoys a symbiotic relationship with its tourism industry; and perhaps most important, it boasts that intimate historical streetscape and centuries-old civic reputation that conveys to visitors a certain credibility—shall we call it authenticity?—in a way unmatched by places like Las Vegas. On a dark note, Bourbon is also disturbingly vulnerable to accidental or intentional trauma, such as a balcony collapse, crowd stampede, or terrorist bombing, which, in addition to the human toll, could poison The Street's allure for years. Bourbon, in short, has bright prospects and a record of widespread economic and cultural influence, but it should not take its fame and success for granted.

Speaking of cultural influence, Bourbon Street has entered the language of American English, which, curiously, does not have a perfect word for the Bourbon Street phenomenon. Shall we call it an adult-entertainment area? A cluster? A strip? A pedestrian mall? A tenderloin, red-light, or vice district? All are awkward, some are imprecise, and none are perfect. The linguistic lacuna is particularly perplexing because nearly every city since Sybaris has developed such spaces.

To fill the gap, some speakers convert common nouns into proper toponyms; examples include Las Vegas's The Strip, Baltimore's The Block, and historic New Orleans's The Swamp or The Line. Others craft "antonamasias," which, in rhetoric, are attempts to describe the characteristics of a new phenomenon by invoking the name of a comparable known entity, e.g., "the Paris of . . . ," "the

Barbary Coast of . . . ," "the Greenwich Village of. . . ."[5] The antonamasia "the Bourbon Street of. . . ." is among the most popular ways for Americans to refer efficiently and effectively to pedestrian-scale drinking, eating, and entertainment districts. It's exceedingly common to hear Sixth Street, for example, described as the Bourbon Street of Austin. Ybor City is routinely characterized as the Bourbon Street of Tampa, as is Carson Street of Pittsburgh, and Duval Street of Key West (or of the entire Caribbean). Beale Street was completely redeveloped by a real estate corporation in the 1980s from a boarded-up eyesore to become, inevitably, the Bourbon Street of Memphis. A review of sixty-seven published articles since 1986, plus more than three hundred Internet sources, showed that at least eighty social spaces worldwide have been described as "the Bourbon Street of" their respective communities. They span from Hamburg's Reeperbahn to Bangkok's Patpong; from Spain's Pamplona during the Running of the Bulls to Las Ramblas in Barcelona, from Quay Street in Galway to Lan Kwai Fong in Hong Kong. They are not always urban; sometimes the phrase is used for frisky beaches at vacation destinations, for boating coves (most notoriously in Lake of the Ozarks, a popular rendezvous for nudity and inebriation), or the Mall of America in Minneapolis, the entire town of Hyannis ("the Bourbon Street of the Cape") or the city of Ogden ("the Bourbon Street of Utah," historically). Some use it as a warning ("Let's not turn the Underground into the Bourbon Street of Atlanta") or as an ambition ("the big goal is for the Mill Avenue District to become the Bourbon Street of the Southwest"). The phrase even found a home in its own backyard; a travel writer called "Jackson Square . . . the Bourbon Street of daytime New Orleans," and the *Times-Picayune* dubbed the Fulton Street Mall as "the Bourbon Street of the [1984] world's fair." Some uses emphasize the spatial clustering over the piquant aspect ("Canyon Road [is] the Bourbon Street of Santa Fe's art scene"); others do the exact opposite: "USA Network [is] the Bourbon Street of basic cable"; "Louisiana Fried Chicken [is] the Bourbon Street of chicken."[6]

One would be hard-pressed to think of another street so richly representational. The very matriculation of a street to the status of a metaphor (or, more accurately, a metonymy) is fairly rare. To be sure, we speak of Wall Street to mean corporate power, Madison Avenue to mean marketing, and Broadway for theater, but as we go further down the list, we find fewer linguistic uses and users. Bourbon Street is one of the American English language's handiest and most evocative place metaphors, a testament to The Street's widespread renown and iconic resonance.

Redeeming Bourbon Street
The Cheerful Defiance of Adversity

Saturday evening, August 27, 2005, could have passed for a typical summer night on Bourbon Street. It had less than the normal weekend traffic but was still noisy, rambunctious, and open for business. Next morning, however, was different. The beer trucks didn't arrive. No one hosed down the sidewalks. Plywood went up over doors and windows. Some rank-and-file Bourbonites, the type who live in the Bourbon Street Bubble, refused to take the talk of the town seriously. "Where's everybody going?" one straggler shouted to the emptying street. "It's just a little storm."

A hurricane ominously named Katrina had been strengthening in the Gulf of Mexico. After two days of westward nudges in its predicated path, now it unquestionably settled on a New Orleans–area landfall. For many locals, hurricanes brought with them more excitement than fright. It had been forty years since the city suffered a disastrous strike—by Hurricane Betsy in 1965—yet even that blow did not prevent Bourbon Street from reopening within hours. (Some people criticized Al Hirt for "dishonoring the dead" by performing during Betsy's aftermath; in a typically laconic Bourbon Street manner, he responded that he was "just trying to help people get on with their lives.")[1] Bourbon Street had weathered every storm before and since with equal aplomb. Just three years before Katrina, tropical storms Isidore and Lili had done little more than justify some hurricane parties, and only eleven months earlier, the evacuation for Hurricane Ivan had caused more problems than the storm.

Katrina, however, bespoke a certain dire admonition. The sight of Café Lafitte in Exile battening down its green shutters stopped one Bourbonite in his tracks. "When they close, you KNOW it's bad," he said. "They NEVER board up." More than a few clueless tourists, not having caught the news since their arrival, meandered about in a blissful ignorance they would soon come to rue.[2]

At dawn on Monday, August 29, Hurricane Katrina's winds pushed Gulf waters across the eastern marshes and drove them into the metropolis via manmade navigation canals. In quick sequence beginning around 7:00 a.m., a minor breach opened on the west side of the Industrial Canal, followed by two catastrophic failures on the eastern side. Over the next hour, two similar floodwalls collapsed on the London Avenue Outfall Canal in Gentilly, and shortly thereafter, on a stretch of the Seventeenth Street Canal, which had first fractured at dawn. By late morning, turbid salt water was pouring into every hydrological sub-basin on the east bank of Orleans Parish, plus one in Jefferson and all in St. Bernard and Plaquemines. Citizens perished in their own homes by the score, then by the hundreds, even as Katrina passed and Monday turned into Tuesday. A hundred thousand New Orleanians struggled to flee the watery apocalypse. World news outlets directed their cameras at terrible human suffering. A city once predicted to become the most affluent and powerful in the Western Hemisphere now stewed in its own filth. In the somber opening days of September 2005, millions of observers worldwide pondered the possibility that New Orleans, and all its rich history and colorful culture, might be dead.

Except, except, except . . . for a faint heartbeat that never quite flat-lined. It came from somewhere in the heart of the French Quarter, which did not flood thanks to the wisdom of Bienville and Pauger three centuries earlier. It emanated from one particular street, Bourbon Street, and one particular bar, Johnny White's. There, sixty-year-old bartender Perry Bailey and coworker Marcy Kreiter defied curfew orders and kept the dive open straight through the catastrophe, running on generators and serving more as community center than business enterprise. The heartbeat also came from a smattering of street musicians, who, having no tourists to entertain, played instead to an empty street. Their effort drew sympathetic journalists with cameras, who broadcast their life-affirming tunes—arguably the most important music ever played on Bourbon Street—to a nation otherwise preparing for a municipal funeral. The heartbeat came too from a handful of zany Southern Decadence revelers who somehow got into the city for the Labor Day festival that wasn't, and partied anyway. It came from the Royal Sonesta, which lodged hundreds of first-responders and cleanup workers. Together these brave Bourbonites incentivized the first businesses to return, and seeded the re-formation of an economy—not just Bourbon's, but that of the entire city.[3]

By mid-September, about a score of Bourbon Street businesses had tenuously reopened, selling beer on ice and charcoal-grilled burgers to FEMA, Red Cross,

HAZ-MAT crews, and soldiers with M-16s, some fresh from combat in Iraq or Afghanistan. "It was a little creepy," recalled one Bourbonite of those nights; "There was no light at first, [and] nobody in town."[4] By month's end, "topless women [were] hanging upside down from brass poles at a place called Déjà Vu," reported columnist Chris Rose, whose writings on the catastrophe would become canonical. "Gaudiness, flesh, neon and bad recorded music have returned to one small outpost on the Boulevard of Broken Dreams, [and] we can all be thankful for that."[5] By October, Big Al Carson, all five hundred pounds of him, was back singing the blues on Bourbon, despite having lost his home to the floodwaters. As the first residents ventured back to their damaged and often looted homes, Bourbon Street became the liveliest and happiest street in a city of death and misery.

Bourbon Street redeemed itself by keeping the human heart beating in this fragile, ancient experiment called New Orleans. It illustrated to the world that not only was the city still alive, it was plucky and resourceful. The cheerful defiance of adversity has universal human appeal, and Bourbon Street was the first to demonstrate that local ethos, which would become the essential narrative of the recovery, to the rest of humanity. "Music was important then," reflected Big Al of the Katrina aftermath; "It was important for people to know that Bourbon Street was back in action, that New Orleans hadn't lost its culture. *It meant everything.*"[6] Even Bourbon haters, who along with everyone else were scattered nationwide and hungered for updates, warmed to the impish strip.

Tough times lay ahead. The recovery would get off to a rocky start, and the widely broadcast images of destruction wreaked havoc on the all-important tourism industry. Visitation bottomed out for many months, and more than a few Bourbon Street enterprises folded. But within a year, a Saturday night on the strip would come reasonably close to prediluvian times, something very few other places in the city could say. Bourbon Street resumed sending paychecks into the pockets of New Orleanians, and tax dollars to the coffers of City Hall, well before nearly all other employers, including corporations, universities, big-box retailers, and Frenchmen Street. And unlike so many other entities, Bourbon Street recovered with little if any federal aid and zero charitable assistance. Bourbon Street was not only New Orleans's most successful invention, it was also its most resilient and self-reliant.

Yet Bourbon Street did not wait around to be thanked or awarded. It didn't even recognize its own heroism because no Bourbon Street Board of Directors existed to organize the ceremony, and no Bourbon Street CEO existed to receive the plaque. Bourbonites simply got back to work as quickly as possible, one tacky club or junk shop at a time, selling the ancient allure of sensual delights to a smaller but more appreciative parade.

When Johnny White's finally shuttered for the first time in nineteen years (the doors didn't have locks), staffers had to organize their own midnight jazz funeral. Fellow Bourbonites wished them well but were too busy making money *now* to join in the procession. Bourbon Street, after all, does not indulge in teary-eyed nostalgia or effusive introspection; it makes zero claims to cultural exclusivity or authenticity, and offers absolutely no apologies. Despite three centuries of rich history and priceless historical architecture, Bourbon Street's phenomenal success rests not on contemplating the past but on seizing the eternal present, and telescoping no farther into the future than *tonight*.

NOTES

1. A Straight Line in a Sinuous Space: Creating Rue Bourbon, 1682–1722

1. Samuel L. Clemens, *Life on the Mississippi* (1833; repr., New York: Harper and Row, 1958), p. 4.

2. Thomas Hall, *Planning Europe's Capital Cities: Aspects of Nineteenth-Century Urban Development* (Oxford: Alexandrine Press, 1997), pp. 9–15.

3. Thomas Gordon Smith, *Vitruvius on Architecture* (New York: Montecelli Press, 2003), pp. 9–25.

4. Shannon Lee Dawdy, *Building the Devil's Empire: French Colonial New Orleans* (Chicago: University of Chicago Press, 2008), p. 68.

5. Father Zenobius Membré, "Narrative of La Salle's Voyage down the Mississippi, by Father Zenobius Membré," in *The Journeys of René-Robert Cavelier Sieur de La Salle*, vol. 1, ed. Isaac Joslin Cox (1905; repr., Austin, Tex.: Pemberton Press, 1968), p. 145.

6. M. Cavelier de La Salle, "Memoir of M. Cavelier de La Salle," in *On the Discovery of the Mississippi*, ed. Thomas Falconer (London: Samuel Clarke, 1844), appendix, pp. 3–4, 24–27.

7. Sébastien Le Prestre, Seigneur de Vauban, *The New Method of Fortification, as Practiced by Monsieur de Vauban, Engineer General of France, with an Explication of All Terms Appertaining to that Art* (London: Abell Swall, 1693), topics culled from table of contents of second edition.

8. Dawdy, *Building the Devil's Empire*, p. 66.

9. Quoted in Tennant S. McWilliams in *Iberville's Gulf Journals*, ed. Richebourg Gaillard McWilliams (University, Ala.: University of Alabama Press, 1991), p. 4.

10. Ibid., p. 53.

11. M. de Pénicaut, "Annals of Louisiana, from the Establishment of the First Colony under M. D'Iberville, to the Departure of the Author to France, in 1722," in *Historical Collections of Louisiana and Florida, Volume VI*, ed. B. F. French (New York: J. Sabin & Sons, 1869), p. 46; "Historical Journal . . . of M. D'Iberville . . . ," in *Historical Collections of Louisiana and Florida, Volume VII*, ed. B. F. French (New York: J. Sabin and Sons, 1875), pp. 57–61.

12. Jay Higginbotham, *Old Mobile: Fort Louis de la Louisiane, 1702–1711* (Mobile, Ala.: Higginbotham, 1977), pp. 72–74; Peter Joseph Hamilton, *Colonial Mobile: An Historical Study . . . of the Alabama-Tombigbee Basin* (Boston: Houghton, Mifflin and Co., 1897), pp. 75–76.

13. Minutes of the Council, June 3 and July 1, 1716, *Mississippi Provincial Archives, 1701–1729: French Dominion*, vol. 2, ed. Dunbar Rowland and Albert Godfrey Sanders (Jackson: Press of the Mississippi Department of Archives and History, 1929), pp. 219–21; Susan Gibbs Lemann, *The Problems of Founding a Viable Colony: The Military in Early French Louisiana* (1982), reproduced in *The Louisiana Purchase Bicentennial Series in Louisiana History*, vol. 1, *The French Experience in Louisiana*, ed. Glenn R. Conrad (Lafayette: Center for Louisiana Studies, 1995), p. 360.

14. Lawrence N. Powell, *The Accidental City: Improvising New Orleans* (Cambridge: Harvard University Press, 2011), p. 28.

15. Quoted in Marc de Villiers du Terrage, "A History of the Foundation of New Orleans (1717–1722)," *Louisiana Historical Quarterly* 3, no. 2 (April 1920): 174 (emphasis in original).

16. The register lists the resolution to establish New Orleans next to an incomplete date ("9th"). It is probable that the month was September, since the company received its charter on September 6 and made a clear reference to the proposed city on October 1, 1717 (Villiers, "A History of the Foundation of New Orleans [1717–1722]," p. 174).

17. Jonathan Darby, "New Orleans, The Capital of the Colony and the Seat of Government and the Courts of Justice," trans. Rev. Conrad M. Widman, and published in "Some Southern Cities (in the U.S.) about 1750," *Records of the American Catholic Historical Society of Philadelphia* 10 (1899): 202.

18. Bienville to the Navy Council, June 12, 1718, *Mississippi Provincial Archives, 1704–1743: French Dominion*, vol. 3, ed. Dunbar Rowland and Albert Godfrey Sanders (Jackson: Press of the Mississippi Department of Archives and History, 1932), p. 228.

19. This line appears on Le Blond de La Tour's January 12, 1723, map, *Partie du plan de la Nouvelle Orléans* (French National Archives), drawn in red and labeled "Alignement suivant le projet de Mr. de Bienville des premieres maisons." See also Samuel Wilson Jr., *The Vieux Carre, New Orleans: Its Plan, Its Growth, Its Architecture* (New Orleans: Bureau of Governmental Research, 1968), p. 4.

20. Alfred E. Lemmon, "La Louisiane/La Luisiana: A Bourbon Colony," in *Charting Louisiana: Five Hundred Years of Maps*, ed. Alfred E. Lemmon, John T. Magill, and Jason R. Wiese (New Orleans: Historic New Orleans Collection, 2003), p. 46.

21. Thomas Jefferys, *The Natural and Civil History of the French Dominions in North and South America* (London: T. Jefferys, 1760), pp. 148–49.

22. Le Blond de La Tour, *Plan des ouvrages projettés pour le nouveau establissement du Nouveau Biloxy*, January 8, 1721, French National Archives.

23. Dawdy, *Building the Devil's Empire*, p. 65.

24. Le Blond de La Tour, *Partie du plan de la Nouvelle Orléans*, January 12, 1723, French National Archives.

25. Powell, *The Accidental City*, pp. 56–59.

26. Quoted in Wilson, *The Vieux Carre, New Orleans*, p. 11.

27. Adrien de Pauger, *Plan de la ville de la Nouvelle Orléans projettée en Mars 1721*, as reproduced in Wilson, *The Vieux Carre, New Orleans*, p. 6.

28. Charles R. Maduell Jr., *The Census Tables for the French Colony of Louisiana from 1699 to 1732* (Baltimore: C. R. Maduell, 1972), pp. 16–22, 81.

29. Villiers, "A History of the Foundation of New Orleans (1717–1722)," pp. 222–23.

30. Ibid., p. 229.

31. Pierre François Xavier de Charlevoix, *Journal of a Voyage to North-America Undertaken by Order of the French King, Volume II* (London: R. and J. Dodsley, 1761), pp. 275–76.

32. Marcel Giraud, *A History of French Louisiana*, vol. 5, *The Company of the Indies, 1723–1731* (Baton Rouge: Louisiana State University Press, 1987), pp. 498–99; Le Blond de La Tour, *Partie du plan de la Nouvelle Orléans*, January 12, 1723, French National Archives.

33. Quoted in Wilson, *The Vieux Carre, New Orleans*, p. 12.

34. Le Blond de la Tour, *Plan de la ville de la Nouvelle Orléans*, April 23, 1722, as reproduced in Wilson, *The Vieux Carre, New Orleans*, p. 12.

35. Charles Edwards O'Neill, "The French Regency and the Colonial Engineers: Street Names of

Early New Orleans," *Louisiana History* 39, no. 2 (Spring 1998): 209–10; Villiers, "A History of the Foundation of New Orleans (1717–1722)," p. 241.

36. O'Neill, "The French Regency and the Colonial Engineers," p. 213.

37. *Plan de la Nouvelle Orléans* (ca. 1722), as reproduced in *Charting Louisiana: Five Hundred Years of Maps*, ed. Lemmon, Magill, and Wiese, p. 309.

38. Bienville to the Council, February 1, 1723, *Mississippi Provincial Archives, 1704–1743: French Dominion*, vol. 3, pp. 343–44.

39. Adrien de Pauger, quoted in Wilson, *The Vieux Carre, New Orleans*, p. 13. A footnote in Dumont's journal and a number of tertiary sources date this hurricane to September 11, 1721, but 1722 is the more likely year.

40. M. Dumont, "History of Louisiana, Translated from the Historical Memoirs of M. Dumont," in *Historical Memoirs of Louisiana, From the First Settlement of the Colony to the Departure of Governor O'Reilly in 1770*, ed. B. F. French (New York: Lamport, Blakeman & Law, 1853), p. 24; Villiers, "A History of the Foundation of New Orleans (1717–1722)," pp. 235–36.

41. De La Tour, quoted in Villiers, "A History of the Foundation of New Orleans (1717–1722)," p. 236. Similar words have been attributed to Pauger.

42. Dumont, "History of Louisiana, Translated from the Historical Memoirs of M. Dumont," pp. 23–24.

43. Citywide, by 1731, only around half of the original sixty-six blocks had been subdivided into parcels, and many of them had little more than picket fences (Gonichon, *Plan de la Nouvelle Orléans telle qu'elle estoit au mois de dexembre [sic] 1731*, New Orleans; trans. Julie Hernandez; see also *Plan de la ville de la Nouvelle Orléans*, Edward E. Ayer Collection, Ms Map 30, Sheet 81, Newberry Library, Chicago, as reproduced in Powell, *The Accidental City*).

44. Dumont, "History of Louisiana, Translated from the Historical Memoirs of M. Dumont," p. 41.

45. Father Raphael to the Abbe Raguet, December 28, 1726, *Mississippi Provincial Archives, 1701–1729: French Dominion*, vol. 2, p. 521.

46. Powell, *The Accidental City*, p. 4.

2. A Streetscape Emerges: Rue Bourbon and Calle Borbon, 1722–1803

1. Quoted from Gonichon, *Plan de la Nouvelle Orléans telle qu'elle estoit au mois de dexembre [sic] 1731*, New Orleans, trans. Julie Hernandez.

2. Sister Mary Madeleine Hachard of St. Stanislaus to Her Father, April 24, 1728, in *The Ursulines in New Orleans and Our Lady of Prompt Succor: A Record of Two Centuries, 1727–1925*, ed. Rev. Henry Churchill Semple (New York: P. J. Kennedy & Sons, 1925), pp. 224–25.

3. Périer and De La Chaise to the Directors of the Company of the Indies, January 30, 1729, *Mississippi Provincial Archives, 1704–1743: French Dominion*, vol. 2, pp. 616–17 and 259–60; Giraud, *A History of French Louisiana*, vol. 5, *The Company of the Indies, 1723–1731*, p. 212.

4. Périer and De La Chaise to the Directors of the Company of the Indies, November 3, 1728, *Mississippi Provincial Archives, 1704–1743: French Dominion*, vol. 2, p. 592.

5. Based on December 1731 Gonichon map and detached index (in Archives Nationales, Paris, reproduced in Vieux Carré Survey, Historic New Orleans Collection, Binders 64 and 69, 300 block of Bourbon), linked by the author to household listings in the January 1732 census, as translated

by Charles R. Maduell Jr., *The Census Tables for the French Colony of Louisiana from 1699 to 1732* (Baltimore: Genealogical Publishing Co., 1972).

6. Le Page du Pratz, *The History of Louisiana*, ed. Joseph G. Tregle Jr. (1758; repr., Baton Rouge: LSU Press, 1976), pp. 54–55. Le Page du Pratz wrote this description (of the city in general, not necessarily of Bourbon Street) later in life, recollecting the years 1728–34.

7. Gonichon, *Plan de la Nouvelle Orléans telle qu'elle estoit au mois de dexembre 1731*; Marcel Giraud, *A History of French Louisiana*, vol. 5, *The Company of the Indies, 1723–1731*, p. 223; Jack D. Holden, H. Parrot Bacot, and Cybèle T. Gontar, *Furnishing Louisiana: Creole and Acadian Furniture, 1735–1835* (New Orleans: Historic New Orleans Collection, 2010), p. 81.

8. Based on 1731 Gonichon map linked with Archives Nationales index and cross-referenced with 1732 census.

9. Analyses of 1726 and 1732 censuses by the author based on data in Maduell, *The Census Tables for the French Colony of Louisiana from 1699 to 1732*.

10. *Records and Deliberations of the Cabildo, 1769–1803*, trans. Works Progress Administration, September 10, 1784, 7-A, pp. 19–20 of second microfilm roll, and Book 4, No. 3 (January 1, 1799, to September 12, 1800), February 7, 1800, 165-A, p. 130 of third microfilm roll of Cabildo records, Historic New Orleans Collection.

11. Ibid., Book 4, No. 3 (January 1, 1799, to September 12, 1800), September 1799, 150, pp. 74–75 and February 7, 1800, pp. 130 and 166–166A, p. 135 of third microfilm roll of Cabildo records; see also Book 1, p. 315, April 30, 1779, for delineations of wards.

12. Ibid., Book 3, No. 2 (January 1, 1788, to May 18, 1792), February 24, 1792, 174–174A, p. 195 of second microfilm roll; and Book 4, No. 3 (January 1, 1799, to December 12, 1800), February 15, 1799, 132A–133, p. 13 of third microfilm roll of Cabildo records.

13. Ibid., Book 4, No. 4 (September 19, 1800, to July 9, 1802), October 31, 1800, 199A–200, p. 31 of third microfilm roll of Cabildo records; Book 4, No. 3 (January 1, 1799, to September 12, 1800), September 6, 1799, 148-A, p. 68 of third microfilm roll; Book 3, No. 1 (July 2, 1784, to December 14, 1787), September 17, 1784, 9-A-10, p. 24 and April 15, 1785, 19-A-20, p. 48 of second microfilm roll; Book 2 (September 8, 1779, to June 25, 1784), May 19, 1780, 16A–17, p. 28 of first microfilm roll; Book 4, No. 4 (September 19, 1800, to July 17, 1802), May 7, 1802, 253A, p. 213 of fourth microfilm roll; September 10, 1784, 7-A, pp. 18–20 of second microfilm roll; and Book 1 (August 18, 1769, to August 27, 1779), April 12, 1771, 28B, p. 60, of first microfilm roll.

14. Ibid., Book 4, No. 2 (July 14, 1797, to December 20, 1798), May 11, 1798, 110–110A, pp. 137–38 and Book 4, No. 3 (January 1, 1799, to December 12, 1800), March 29, 1799, 135–135-A, p. 20, on third microfilm roll; Book 3, No. 3 (May 25, 1792, to April 17, 1795), October 5, 1792, 195-A, p. 24 of second microfilm roll; Book 3, No. 3 (May 25, 1792, to April 17, 1795), May 2, 1794, 247, pp. 130–31; May 23, 1794, 248-A–249, p. 136–37; August 1, 1794, 253–253-A, p. 147 of second microfilm roll; Book 4, No. 1 (April 24, 1795, to July 7, 1797), March 11, 1796, 30–30-A, p. 97; Book 4, No. 3 (January 1, 1799, to December 12, 1800), February 1799, 133A, p. 14, both on the third microfilm roll; Book 4, No. 1 (April 24, 1795 to July 7, 1797), March–April 1796, 31, p. 99 of third microfilm roll of Cabildo records.

15. Chevalier Guy de Soniat du Fossat, *Synopsis of the History of Louisiana from the Founding of the Colony to End of the Year 1791*, ed. and trans. Charles T. Soniat (New Orleans, 1903), p. 27; *Records . . . of the Cabildo*, March 26, 1788, 97-A/97-B, p. 13, second microfilm roll of Cabildo records.

16. *Records . . . of the Cabildo,* April 3, 1788, 99-A/100, p. 19 of second microfilm roll of Cabildo records.

17. Soniat du Fossat, *Synopsis of the History of Louisiana from the Founding of the Colony to End of the Year 1791,* pp. 27–28.

18. Property transaction, Pierre Lambert from Pedro Gautier, May 29, 1789 (notary: P. Pedesclaux), stored in Vieux Carré Survey, Historic New Orleans Collection, Binder 61, section on 636–640 Bourbon.

19. *Records . . . of the Cabildo,* Book 1 (August 18, 1769, to August 27, 1779), October 20, 1775, 113A–113B, p. 224, first microfilm roll of Cabildo records.

20. "Dreadful Fire," *New York Weekly Museum,* February 7, 1795; *Plano de la Ciudad de la N[ueav] a Orleans[;] Las lineas Rojas demuestran la parte destruida por el inc[endi]o acaecido de dia Ocho de Diziembre de 1794,* Archivo Historico Nacional, Madrid, Spain, as reproduced in *Charting Louisiana: Five Hundred Years of Maps,* p. 316.

21. *Records . . . of the Cabildo,* entries for mid-December 1794, 264-A/265, p. 177; 265/265-A, p. 178, 266/266-A, p. 180, and 266-A/267, p. 181, dated December 19, 1794, from second microfilm roll of Cabildo records; *Digest of the Acts and Deliberations of the Cabildo,* February 20, 1795, Book 3, Vol. 3, p. 198; *Records . . . of the Cabildo,* Book 4, Vol. 1, 18/18-A, p. 55 and 18-A/19, p. 56, October 9, 1795.

22. "Buildings, Numbering, Fire Limits, Etc.: An Ordinance Relative to Buildings, No. 95–96," in Henry J. Leovy, *The Laws and General Ordinances of the City of New Orleans* (New Orleans: E. C. Wharton, 1857), p. 30.

23. *The Navigator* (Pittsburgh: Zadok Cramer, 1806), p. 128.

24. Hugh Murray, *Historical Account of Discoveries and Travels in North America* (London: Longman, Rees, Orme, Brown, & Green, 1829), p. 426.

25. Daniel Blowe, *A Geographical, Historical, Commercial, and Agricultural View of the United States of America* (London: Edwards & Knibb, 1820), pp. 64–65.

26. Ibid., p. 128.

3. A Transect of Antebellum Society:
Ethnicity, Race, Class, and Caste on Bourbon Street, 1803–1860

1. "A Resolution of the City Council," May 11, 1805, as transcribed in *New Orleans in 1805: A Directory and a Census* (New Orleans: Pelican Gallery, 1936).

2. Forty-two percent were categorized as white; 18 percent were free people of color; 37 percent were enslaved; and the remainder unidentified.

3. The two streets closest to the backswamp, Dauphine and Burgundy, had the highest populations of free people of color.

4. Analysis of 1805 Matthew Flannery census by the author, as transcribed in *New Orleans in 1805: A Directory and a Census* (New Orleans: Pelican Gallery, 1936).

5. Pierre Clément de Laussat, *Memoirs of My Life* (1831; repr., Baton Rouge: LSU Press and Historic New Orleans Collection, 1978), p. 103.

6. Benjamin Henry Boneval Latrobe, *Impressions Respecting New Orleans: Diary & Sketches, 1818–1820,* ed. Samuel Wilson Jr. (New York: Columbia University Press, 1951), p. 32.

7. Analysis by the author. Names on map were categorized as being definite or probable French,

Spanish, or Anglo, with the assumption that most French and Spanish residents derived from co-lonial times and were therefore likely Creoles (as opposed to recent immigrants), and that most Anglo residents had arrived since the Louisiana Purchase. The percentages cited above represent full blocks on either side of Bourbon Street, from Royal to Dauphine (J. Pilié, *Plan de la ville de la Nouvelle Orléans avec les noms des proprietaires* [1808], Historic New Orleans Collection).

8. Friends of the Cabildo, Samuel Wilson, Mary Louise Christovich, Betsy Swanson, Roulhac Toledano, *New Orleans Architecture: The American Sector* (Gretna, La.: Pelican, 1972), p. 21.

9. Mildred Masson Costa, interview by Dorothy Schlesinger, January 30, 1985, Friends of the Cabildo Oral History Archive, Louisiana Division, New Orleans Public Library.

10. John Adems Paxton, *The New-Orleans Directory and Register* (New Orleans: Benj. Levy & Co., 1823), p. 137.

11. "For Sale. A fine house . . . ," *Moniteur,* August 14, 1802, p. 1, c. 2.; "For Sale. A new two story brick house . . . ," *Louisiana Courier,* November 11, 1812. This latter building still stands, at 701 Bourbon, and is now the Cat's Meow karaoke bar.

12. "An ordinance in relation to slaves in the city and suburbs of New-Orleans," October 15, 1817, *A General Digest of the Ordinances and Resolutions of the Corporation of New-Orleans* (New Orleans: Jerome Bayon, 1831), p. 133; Henry J. Leovy, *The Laws and General Ordinances of the City of New Orleans* (New Orleans: E. C. Wharton, 1857), p. 257.

13. Leovy, *The Laws and General Ordinances,* p. xxi.

14. *Daily Orleanian,* February 19, 1849, p. 2, c. 3.

15. Analysis of *Cohen's New Orleans & Lafayette Directory for 1851* by the author.

16. Among the prominent names who studied at the Jefferson Academy, which operated on upper Bourbon for most of the years between 1833 and 1886, was chess champion Paul Morphy, a Creole ("Jefferson Academy, 33 Bourbon Street, New Orleans, Conducted by J. G. Lord," *New Orleans Daily Creole,* July 3, 1856, p. 1; "Judah Touro's Will," *Daily Picayune,* January 24, 1854, p. 3.; Michael L. Kurtz, "Paul Morphy: Louisiana's Chess Champion," *Louisiana History* 34, no. 2 [Spring 1993]: 178).

17. That space remained city property even after the library moved elsewhere, the building was replaced, and the street was renamed Iberville. An ordinance in 1945 finally cancelled the public ownership of a narrow Bourbon Street alley that was the last remnant of the Fisk donation (Ordi-nance 16,135 Commission Council Series [C.C.S.], Mayoralty of New Orleans, City Hall, January 22, 1945; "Free Library," *Daily Picayune,* November 6, 1853, p. 8; Friends of the Cabildo, Samuel Wilson, Mary Louise Christovich, Sally Kittredge Evans, Roulhac Toledano, *New Orleans Architecture: The Esplánade Ridge* [Gretna, La.: Pelican, 1977], pp. 35–36).

18. Analysis and interpretation of *Cohen's New Orleans & Lafayette Directory for 1851* by the author.

19. Hodding Carter and Betty Werlein Carter, *So Great a Good: A History of the Episcopal Church in Louisiana and of Christ Church Cathedral, 1805–1855* (Sewanee, Tenn.: University Press, 1955), p. 75.

20. "Judah Touro's Will," p. 3; Friends of the Cabildo, Wilson, Christovich, Swanson, Toledano, *New Orleans Architecture: The American Sector,* pp. 21, 30.

21. Louis Fitzgerald Tasistro, *Random Shots and Southern Breezes,* vol. 1 (New York: Harper & Bros., 1842), pp. 73–94.

22. Contract No. 105, April 19, 1859, Building Contract, Gallier & Esterbrook with the New Orleans Opera House Company.

23. "The New Opera House," *New Orleans Delta,* May 23, 1859.

24. *Daily Picayune,* December 3, 1859.

25. "The Opera," *Daily Picayune,* October 24, 1869, p. 11, c. 4.

4. A Smell So Unsavory: Managing Bourbon Street in the Mid-1800s

1. A. C. Bell, "History and Selection of Street Paving in the City of New Orleans," as reproduced by William Joseph Hardee in "Street Paving in New Orleans: Its History for Nearly a Century," *Daily States Annual Trade Edition,* August 31, 1901, p. 20. Vincent Nolte recalled his experiences arranging the shaky finances of the 1822 paving project in his *Fifty Years in Both Hemispheres* (New York: Redfield, 1854), pp. 298–99.

2. "An Ordinance concerning the paving, and completing the footpaths (causeways) of the City of New-Orleans, and its incorporated suburbs," September 27, 1827, *A General Digest of the Ordinances and Resolutions of the Corporation of New-Orleans* (New Orleans: Jerome Bayon, 1831), pp. 279–85.

3. *New Orleans Argus,* July 21, 1829, p. 2, c. 2.

4. *Louisiana State Gazette,* July 29, 1826, p. 2, c. 1.

5. Resolutions of September 3 and November 24, 1835, *Digeste des ordonnances, resolutions et reglemens de la corporation de la Nouvelle-Orleans* (New Orleans: Gaston Brusle, 1836), pp. 185–86.

6. *Daily Picayune,* October 6, 1838, p. 2, c. 1.

7. Ibid., May 21, 1839, p. 2, c. 1.

8. Building transaction, Auguste O'Duhigg from Joachim Courcelle, August 7, 1839 (A. Ducatel, Notary), stored in Vieux Carré Survey, Historic New Orleans Collection, Binder 61, section on 626 Bourbon.

9. *Daily Picayune,* April 16, 1841, p. 2, c. 1.

10. Ibid., January 18, 1840, p. 2, c. 1 (emphasis in original).

11. Ibid., January 26 and April 16, 1841, p. 2, c. 1.

12. Bell, "History and Selection of Street Paving in the City of New Orleans," as reproduced by Hardee, "Street Paving in New Orleans," p. 20.

13. "An Ordinance to prevent nuisances, and to provide for the security of the public health of the city of New-Orleans," March 18, 1817, *A General Digest of the Ordinances,* pp. 343–45.

14. John H. B. Latrobe, *Southern Travels: Journal of John H. B. Latrobe 1834,* ed. Samuel Wilson Jr. (New Orleans: Historic New Orleans Collection, 1986), p. 47.

15. *Daily Picayune,* March 24, 1853, p. 2, c. 1, and April 23, 1853, p. 2, c. 1.

16. "Cleaning of the City," May 6, 1816, and September 1, 1819, *A General Digest of the Ordinances,* pp. 265–67.

17. "An Ordinance to prevent nuisances . . . ," March 18, 1817, *A General Digest of the Ordinances,* p. 345.

18. "Cleaning of the City," May 6, 1816, and September 1, 1819, *A General Digest of the Ordinances,* pp. 265–67.

19. John Adems Paxton, *The New-Orleans Directory and Register* (New Orleans: Benj. Levy & Co, 1823), p. 120; "An Ordinance concerning the lighting of the City," October 6, 1821, *A General Digest of the Ordinances,* p. 121.

20. "Lamps, Gas Lights, Etc.," No. 401, in Henry J. Leovy, *The Laws and General Ordinances of the*

City of New Orleans (New Orleans: E. C. Wharton, 1857), 141–42; "New Orleans 4th City in World to Have Gas Lights," *Times-Picayune*, January 25, 1937, sec. G, p. 15, c. 1–4.

21. W. M. Darling, "Street Numbers Have Been Headache to New Orleans since First 'System' Began," *Times-Picayune*, August 8, 1937, sec. 2, pp. 2 and 10, c. 2.

22. "A Resolution of the City Council," April 4 and 20, 1805, as transcribed in *New Orleans in 1805: A Directory and a Census* (New Orleans: Pelican Gallery, 1936).

23. "An Ordinance concerning the numbering of houses in the city of New-Orleans and its suburbs," February 22, 1831, *A General Digest of the Ordinances . . .* , pp. 271–75; "Names of the Streets and Numbering of the Houses," Resolution of August 12, 1835, *Digeste des ordonnances, resolutions et reglemens de la corporation de la Nouvelle-Orleans* (New Orleans: Gaston Brusle, 1836), p. 149.

24. Acts of the Legislature, Act 1852, Section 2, in Leovy, *The Laws and General Ordinances of the City of New Orleans*, pp. 51–52; Gray B. Amos. *Corrected Index, Alphabetical and Numerical, of Changes in Street Names and Numbers Old and New, 1852 to Current Date*, April 8, 1938 (New Orleans: City Archives, 1938).

5. A Place to "See the Elephant": Antecedents of Modern-Day Bourbon Street

1. Lafcadio Hearn, "Old-Fashioned Houses," January 12, 1881, in *Inventing New Orleans: Writings of Lafcadio Hearn*, ed. S. Frederick Starr (Jackson: University Press of Mississippi, 2001), p. 177.

2. Phillip Lopate, *Waterfront: A Walk around Manhattan* (New York: Anchor, 2004), pp. 203–4.

3. Walt Whitman, "Once I Pass'd Through a Populous City," *Leaves of Grass* (London: G. P. Putnam's Sons, 1897), p. 94.

4. David Metzer, "Reclaiming Walt: Marc Blitzstein's Whitman's Settings," *Journal of the American Musicological Society* 48, no. 2 (Summer 1995): 242.

5. Erving Goffman, *Stigma* (Englewood Cliffs, N.J.: Prentice Hall, 1963); David Redmon, "Playful Deviance as an Urban Leisure Activity: Secret Selves, Self-Validation, and Entertaining Performances," *Deviant Behavior* 24, no. 1 (2003): pp. 27–51.

6. "New-Orleans," *New-Bedford (Mass.) Courier*, August 16, 1831, p. 1; *New Orleans as It Is: Its Manners and Customs* ("By a Resident, Printed for the Publisher," 1850), p. 23.

7. Bennet Dowler, *Tableaux of New Orleans* (New Orleans: Daily Delta, 1851), pp. 22–23.

8. Asbury C. Jacquess, "The Journals of the Davy Crockett commencing December 20th, 1834," *Indiana Magazine of History* 102 (March 2006): 24 (underlined emphasis in original).

9. "City Intelligence—Highway Robbery," *Daily Picayune*, November 11, 1848, p. 2. *Having seen the elephant* also took on negative implications, implying that one had had enough of an overbearing experience which did not live up to expectations. Taken to its logical extreme, the expression also served as a euphemism for death, near-death experiences, and combat in warfare.

10. Lawrence N. Powell, *The Accidental City: Improvising New Orleans* (Cambridge: Harvard University Press, 2011), pp. 92–105.

11. "The Present State of the Country . . . of Louisiana . . . by an Officer at New Orleans to his Friend at Paris," in *Narratives of Colonial America, 1704–1765*, ed. Howard H. Peckham (Chicago: Lakeside Press, R. R. Donnelley & Sons, 1971), pp. 61–62.

12. "Extract of a Letter from an Emigrant in New-Orleans," *Newburyport (Mass.) Herald*, October 17, 1817, p. 3, c. 2.

13. John H. B. Latrobe, *Southern Travels: Journal of John H. B. Latrobe, 1834*, ed. Samuel Wilson Jr. (New Orleans: Historic New Orleans Collection, 1986), 42.

14. "Life in New Orleans," *Ohio Statesman* (Columbus), May 7, 1847, p. 3, c. 2.

15. Elisée Réclus, *A Voyage to New Orleans*, ed. and trans. John Clark and Camille Martin (1855; Thetford, Vt.: Glad Day Books, 2004), pp. 56–57.

16. *New Orleans as It Is*, 52–55.

17. *Journal of the American Temperance Union* (Philadelphia), 3, no. 1 (January 1839): 15.

18. *New-York Gazette & General Advertiser*, October 12, 1812, p. 2, c. 3.

19. Timothy Flint, *Recollections of the Last Ten Years . . . in the Valley of the Mississippi* (Boston: Cummings, Hilliard, and Co., 1826), pp. 305, 309.

20. *New Orleans as It Is*, p. 6.

21. Judith Kelleher Schafer, *Brothels, Depravity, and Abandoned Women: Illegal Sex in Antebellum New Orleans* (Baton Rouge: LSU Press, 2009), pp. 12–13, 126–44.

22. George W. Engelhardt, *New Orleans, Louisiana, the Crescent City: The Book of the Picayune* (New Orleans: n.p., 1903–4), pp. 11–22.

23. Spatial analysis by the author based on police reports, court records, and news articles of illegal sex arrests and related activities collected and interpreted by Judith Kelleher Schafer in *Brothels, Depravity, and Abandoned Women*. All reports with spatial references (by street, street address, or landmark) were mapped to determine these concentrations.

24. Journal of Welcome A. Greene, reproduced in "Being the Journal of a Quaker Merchant Who Visited N.O. in 1823," *Times-Picayune*, October 16, 1921, sec. 4, pp. 1, 6.

25. James Stuart, *Three Years in North America, Vol. II* (Edinburgh: Robert Cadell and Whittaker, 1833), p. 232.

26. "Curious Charge of Robbery," *Daily Picayune*, February 15, 1855, p. 1.

27. Charles E. Whitney, "Flatboating Days," *New Orleans Times-Democrat*, June 10, 1883, p. 5, c. 5.

28. "Girod Street, New Orleans," *Baltimore Sun*, September 22, 1838, p. 2.

29. "Girod Street," *Daily Picayune*, July 25, 1852, p. 1.

30. As cited by Schafer, *Brothels, Depravity, and Abandoned Women*, p. 6.

31. *Daily Picayune*, December 1 and 29, 1855, as referenced ibid.

32. A. Oakey Hall, *The Manhattaner in New Orleans; or, Phases of "Crescent City" Life* (New York: J. S. Redfield, Clinton Hall, 1851), p. 102.

33. "City Intelligence," *Daily Picayune*, September 23, 1849, p. 2.

34. These particular restrictions come from the *Digest of the Ordinances and Resolutions of the Second Municipality of New-Orleans* (John Calhoun, Comptroller, printed by F. Cook & A. Levy, New Orleans, 1840), which were typical of many other city laws.

35. Prostitutes in Paris in this era loitered near the Church of Notre Dame de Lorette, and became known as "Lorettes" throughout the Francophone world, including in New Orleans (Schafer, *Brothels, Depravity, and Abandoned Women*, p. 145).

36. "Lewd Women—An Ordinance concerning Lewd and Abandoned Women," in Henry J. Leovy, *The Laws and General Ordinances of the City of New Orleans* (New Orleans: E. C. Wharton, 1857), p. 376.

37. The restricted zone stretched from the Mississippi River to the upper limits of the city

(Toledano Street at that time), along the Carrolton railroad (present-day streetcar route) on St. Charles Avenue, lakeward on Felicity, then downriver along Hercules, Circus, Rampart, and Basin Streets (roughly today's Loyola Avenue–Elk Place–Basin Street corridor) until Toulouse Street, which aligned with the Old Basin Canal. All areas from that canal straight back to Bayou St. John and over to Esplanade Street were also included in the restricted zone, as were all areas from Esplanade down Broad and along Elysian Fields Street back to the Mississippi River.

38. Act Nos. 1084 and 1102, "Lewd Women—An Ordinance Concerning Lewd and Abandoned Women," in Leovy, *The Laws and General Ordinances of the City of New Orleans*, pp. 376–80.

39. Schafer, *Brothels, Depravity, and Abandoned Women*, p. 153.

40. Jefferson Davis to Varina Davis, March 15, 1876, in *Jefferson Davis: Private Letters, 1823–1889*, ed. Hudson Strode (repr., New York: Da Capo Press, 1995), p. 425.

41. *Gardner's New Orleans Directory for 1869* (New Orleans: Charles Gardner, Southern Publishing Co., 1868), p. 166. It is also possible that the "Gaskett" or "Gasquette" in question was the "Gasquet" family of present-day 324–328 Bourbon Street, who resided directly across the street from the Benjamin house.

6. How Bourbon Street Germinated: 1860s–1910s

1. *New-Orleans Tägliche Deutsche Zeitung*, November 21 1869, p. 8, c. 1; trans. Verena Rienke of Wilhelmshaven, Germany.

2. Ibid.

3. Ibid.

4. Register of Licenses, Comptroller Office, City of New Orleans, January 1–June 26, 1868, Volumes I and II (C670j), Louisiana Division, New Orleans Public Library. Tabulation and mapping of coffeehouses (saloons) by the author.

5. "Sight of New Orleans the Harpers Did Not See—A Scene at the Head of Canal Street," *Mascot*, January 29, 1887, p. 8.

6. William Ivy Hair, *Carnival of Fury: Robert Charles and the New Orleans Race Riot of 1900* (Baton Rouge: LSU Press, 1974), p. 76.

7. "Some Sights in New Orleans the Harpers Didn't See," *Mascot*, January 22, 1887, p. 2. I credit Alecia P. Long's research for bringing this article to my attention.

8. "Clio New Theater of Muses," *Daily Picayune*, October 20, 1867, p. 5. c. 5; "The Crescent City Circus," *New Orleans Times*, November 17, 1867.

9. Gleaned from 1876, 1885, 1896, and 1908 fire insurance maps produced by the Sanborn Map and Publishing Company and other sources.

10. "The Concert Saloons—The Pretty Waiter Girls—What They Do and What They Drink in Certain Places," *New Orleans Republican*, December 26, 1869, p. 1, c. 5.

11. "Reformation in Concert Saloons: Religious Songs in Vile Places," *New Orleans Republican*, November 18, 1869, p. 1, c. 5.

12. Register of Licenses, Comptroller Office, City of New Orleans, February 12–June 26, 1868, Volume II, C670j, Louisiana Division, New Orleans Public Library.

13. "The Concert Saloons—The Pretty Waiter Girls," p. 1, c. 5.

14. "Coffee House" listing in *Gardner's New Orleans Directory for 1869* (New Orleans: Charles Gardner, 1868), p. 179, based on data collected in 1868.

15. This ordinance "establish[ed] the rate of licenses for professions, callings and other business for the year 1879"; it did not deal with concert saloons or Wenger's per se (Ordinance No. 4789, Mayorality of New Orleans, December 13, 1878).

16. Analysis by the author of Register of Licenses, Comptroller Office, City of New Orleans, Jan. 1–Feb. 2, 1868, Volume I, C670j, and Licenses—Restaurants—1879–1880, No. 1, Department of Finance, City of New Orleans (C670j 1879, New Orleans Public Library—Louisiana Division); "Joseph Zeigler Beer Saloon," *Soards' New Orleans City Directory for 1880* (New Orleans: L. Soards, 1880), section "M" of opening section.

17. "War at Wenger's," *New Orleans Times*, May 18, 1875, p. 6.

18. "Wenger's Garden," *Daily Picayune*, January 8, 1876, p. 4.

19. "Mr. Wenger at Home Again," *New Orleans Times*, January 8, 1876, p. 8; "Wenger's Garden," p. 1.

20. James S. Zacharie, *New Orleans Guide: With Descriptions of the Routes to New Orleans, Sights of the City Arranged Alphabetically, and Other Information Useful to Travellers* (New Orleans: L. Graham & Son, 1885), p. 51.

21. "Pitfalls for the Unwary," *Mascot*, January 12, 1884, p. 580. I credit Alecia P. Long's research for bringing this article to my attention.

22. Liva Baker, *The Second Battle of New Orleans: The Hundred-Year Struggle to Integrate the Schools* (New York: Harper Collins, 1996), pp. 14, 31.

23. Based on the author's analysis of city license records of 1868 and 1879, city directory listings of 1869, 1880, 1885, and 1908–9; the Sanborn insurance maps of 1885, 1896, and 1908; and the Underwriters Inspection Bureau of New Orleans street rate slips of 1897 transcribed by the staff of the Louisiana Division of the New Orleans Public Library.

24. "Interests in the South . . . Gambling Houses in New Orleans," *Baltimore Sun*, January 10, 1885, p. 1.

25. "The Main Cause of the Depression of Trade in New Orleans: The Gambling Curse" and "Sights in New Orleans the Harpers Did Not See," *Mascot*, February 5, 1887, cover and p. 2; "The Keno Hells of Royal Street," *Mascot*, February 12, 1887, p. 5.

26. Lafcadio Hearn, "The Streets," in *Inventing New Orleans: Writings of Lafcadio Hearn*, ed. S. Frederick Starr (Jackson: University Press of Mississippi, 2001), pp. 18–22.

27. These examples come from George Washington Cable's *Strange True Stories of Louisiana* (New York: Charles Scribner's Sons, 1889), pp. 192–232; Grace King's influential *New Orleans: The Place and the People* (New York: Macmillan, 1895); and Cable's "Plotters and Pirates of Louisiana," *Century*, April 1883, vol. 25, issue 6, p. 860.

28. Hearn likely lived in the rear quarters of 719–725 St. Louis Street, which abut the dependencies behind 516 Bourbon ("Lafcadio Hearn's Domicile" and updating note by E. Long, filed in Vieux Carré Survey, Historic New Orleans Collection, Binder 62, section on 516 Bourbon, and other sources). See also Starr, ed., *Inventing New Orleans*.

29. Zacharie, *New Orleans Guide*, p. 5.

30. *New Orleans Times*, October 9, 1866, p. 1, c. 3.

31. Louis C. Hennick and E. Harper Charlton, *The Streetcars of New Orleans* (Gretna, La.: Pelican, 1965), p. 17.

32. "Bourbon Street Substation Property Donated to City for Park," January 1971 article from

Homemaking, stored in Vieux Carré Survey, Historic New Orleans Collection, Binder 69, section for 300 Bourbon.

33. *Visitors' Guide to the World's Industrial and Cotton Centennial Exposition, and New Orleans* (Louisville, Ky.: Courier-Journal Company, 1884).

34. Herbert S. Fairall, *The World's Industrial and Cotton Centennial Exposition, New Orleans, 1884–1885* (Iowa City: Republican Publishing Co., 1885), p. 12.

35. *New Orleans Republican,* November 18, 1869, p. 1, c. 5.

36. "Two Million Dollars' Worth of Property Destroyed by Fire Last Night at Canal and Bourn Street," *Daily Picayune,* February 18, 1892, p. 1.

37. Ibid.

38. "D. H. Holmes & Company Enlarge Their Store by the Purchase of the Wenger Property," *Daily Picayune,* March 16, 1892, p. 2; "Two Million Dollars' Worth of Property Destroyed by Fire," p. 1.

39. "A New Enterprise: Opening the Cosmopolitan Hotel and Café Restaurant," *Daily Picayune,* January 16, 1892, p. 3.

40. *Daily Picayune,* April 2, 1893, p. 5, c. 3.

41. A menu for one spring day in 1894 included broiled Spanish mackerel, veal chops à la Italienne, oyster patties, and strawberry short cake (*Daily Item,* April 27, 1894, p. 1, c. 2).

42. "The Husband Game, Played Successfully on a Country Visitor on Bourbon Street," *Daily Picayune,* April 28, 1885, p. 8.

43. Norma Badon (Wallace), quoted in Christine Wiltz, *The Last Madam: A Life in the New Orleans Underworld* (New York: Faber and Faber, 2000), pp. 15–16.

44. Alecia P. Long, *The Great Southern Babylon: Sex, Race, and Respectability in New Orleans, 1865–1920* (Baton Rouge: LSU Press, 2004), 104–5; Joy Jackson, "Prohibition in New Orleans: The Unlikeliest Crusade," *Louisiana History* 19, no. 3 (Summer 1978): 262.

45. Underwriters Inspection Bureau of New Orleans street rate slips of 1897, transcribed and classified by the staff of the Louisiana Division of the New Orleans Public Library.

46. Wiltz, *The Last Madam,* p. 26.

47. Long, *The Great Southern Babylon,* p. 106.

48. Ordinance 4118 C.C.S, City of New Orleans, February 7, 1917.

49. The first quote comes from Mayoralty of New Orleans, City Hall, Ordinance 13,604, September 1, 1897; the second quote comes from Long, *The Great Southern Babylon,* pp. 109–21 (quoted material on p. 121).

50. "A Costly Blaze on Bourbon Street, Starting in Osborne's Turkish Bath Building, and Destroying It," *Daily Picayune,* August 11, 1898, p. 2.

51. Ordinance No. 2155, New Council Series (N.C.S.), Mayoralty of New Orleans, City Hall, December 3, 1903; Long, *The Great Southern Babylon,* p. 158.

7. How Bourbon Street Blossomed: 1910s–1920s

1. Alecia P. Long, *The Great Southern Babylon: Sex, Race, and Respectability in New Orleans, 1865–1920* (Baton Rouge: LSU Press, 2004), p. 225.

2. Anthony Stanonis, *Creating the Big Easy: New Orleans and the Emergence of Modern Tourism, 1918–1945* (Athens: University of Georgia Press, 2006), p. 28, citing the *New Orleans Association of Commerce News Bulletin* of July 25, 1922.

3. Donald Gray, "An American Athens," *Overland Monthly and Out West Magazine,* July 1927, vol. 85, no. 7, p. 197; Stanonis, *Creating the Big Easy,* p. 28, citing the *New Orleans Association of Commerce News Bulletin* of July 25, 1922.

4. Mildred Masson Costa, interview by Dorothy Schlesinger, January 30, 1985, Friends of the Cabildo Oral History Archive, Louisiana Division, New Orleans Public Library.

5. Ibid.

6. Madeline Archinard Babin, interview by Christine Derbes, May 10, 1982, Friends of the Cabildo Oral History Archive, Louisiana Division, New Orleans Public Library.

7. Ibid.

8. Costa, interview by Schlesinger, January 30, 1985.

9. Ibid.

10. "Flame-Weakened, French Opera House Wall Crashed," *New Orleans Item,* December 4, 1919 (evening edition), p. 1; "Fire Probe Begun; Move for New Opera House," *New Orleans Item,* December 5, 1919, p. 8.

11. "Our Opera Misfortune," *Times-Picayune,* December 5, 1919, p. 8, c. 1.

12. Costa, interview by Schlesinger, January 30, 1985.

13. "To the Public," special notice posted in *New Orleans Item,* December 5, 1919, p. 21.

14. "Our Opera Misfortune," *Times-Picayune,* December 5, 1919, p. 8, c. 1.

15. This is today's Municipal Auditorium in the Faubourg Tremé. Frank Dallam, "Fire and Prohibition Rob New Orleans of Its Fame," *New York Tribune,* February 8, 1920, p. F7, c. 3.

16. Marie Pilkington Campbell, interview by Bernard Lemann, November 3, 1988, Friends of the Cabildo Oral History Archive, Louisiana Division, New Orleans Public Library.

17. "Fire and Prohibition Rob New Orleans of Its Fame," p. F7, c. 8.

18. "Dance Hall Feud Ends in Death of Two Rivals," *Daily Picayune,* March 25, 1913, p. 1; Christine Wiltz, *The Last Madam: A Life in the New Orleans Underworld* (New York: Faber and Faber, 2000), p. 7.

19. "The Tango Belt," *Times-Picayune,* June 21, 1916, p. 8; "Tango Belt Joys Turned to Gloom," *Times-Picayune,* February 18, 1920, p. 9; "No Action Taken: Women's Club Federation Has Not Considered Tango Belt Clean-Up," *Times-Picayune,* September 8, 1915, p. 5.

20. "Hail Behrman as Champion of Red Light," *Times-Picayune,* January 18, 1920, p. 1; Long, *The Great Southern Babylon,* pp. 225–28, and other sources.

21. Jack V. Buerkle and Danny Barker, *Bourbon Street Black: The New Orleans Black Jazzman* (London: Oxford University Press, 1973), pp. 24–25.

22. Norma Wallace, quoted in Wiltz, *The Last Madam,* pp. 17–18.

23. Elbert Samuel P'Pool, "Commercialized Amusements in New Orleans" (master's thesis, Tulane University, 1930, Tulane University Special Collections TT 1930 P4), p. 79; see also pp. 86–87.

24. "City Gaming Dens Close for Parade by Ring's Orders," *Times-Picayune,* January 18, 1920, p. 12.

25. Elsa A. Boole, quoted in Andrew Sinclair, *Era of Excess: A Social History of the Prohibition Movement* (Boston: Little, Brown, 1962), p. 408.

26. Joy Jackson, "Prohibition in New Orleans: The Unlikeliest Crusade," *Louisiana History* 19, no. 3 (Summer 1978): 261–65; Robert Hartsell Russell, "New Orleans and Nation-Wide Prohibition as Reflected in *Times-Picayune,* 1918–1920" (master's thesis, School of Journalism, Louisiana State University, 1956).

27. "Fire and Prohibition Rob New Orleans of Its Fame," p. F7, c. 8.

28. "Closing of Famous Passage Is Event in City's History," *Times-Picayune*, September 1, 1919, p. 14. This closure occurred on account of wartime prohibition laws, which predated the Eighteenth Amendment by one to two years. The effect was the same.

29. General Licenses, Treasury Division, 1920, Ledger B, Department of Public Finance, City of New Orleans (C670jg 1920 B, Louisiana Division, New Orleans Public Library), entries 1–29 for July 1, 1920, and entries 31–32 for February 5, 1920; Ledger A (C670jg 1920 A), entries for January 22, 1920, and April 16–22, 1920.

30. Louis Vyhnanek, *Unorganized Crime: New Orleans in the 1920s* (Lafayette: Center for Louisiana Studies, 1998), p. 73.

31. *Soards' New Orleans City Directory for 1918* (New Orleans: L. Soards, 1918), pp. 1535, 1921, and 1744.

32. Vyhnanek, *Unorganized Crime*, pp. 54–57; "Numerous Hiding Places for 'John,'" *Times-Picayune*, January 8, 1919, p. 16.

33. Tanya Marie Sanchez, "The Feminine Side of Bootlegging: Women, Drink, and Prohibition in New Orleans" (master's thesis, Department of History, University of New Orleans, 1998), p. 35.

34. Anti-Saloon League Yearbook data reported by Jackson in "Prohibition in New Orleans," 281.

35. "Numerous Hiding Places for 'John,'" p. 16.

36. As reported by Jackson, "Prohibition in New Orleans," p. 269; and Vyhnanek, *Unorganized Crime*, pp. 53, 75.

37. Jackson, "Prohibition in New Orleans," p. 270.

38. "Prieto Stands Pat He Had No Liquor," *Times-Picayune*, March 21, 1921, p. 4; "No 'Gold' Coins Found, But Still Is Discovered," *Times-Picayune*, March 22, 1921, p. 5.

39. The estimation of raids was conducted by searching *America's Historic Newspapers* online database, a repository of tens of millions of news pieces, for Louisiana news articles between 1920 and 1933 containing the words "raid" (which usually referred to Prohibition busts) and the names of the seven main French Quarter arteries. The results are intended only to give an idea of relative occurrence as reported in the news, and are not presented as enumerations.

40. Robert Tallant, *The Romantic New Orleanians* (New York: Dutton, 1950), p. 14.

41. Frenchy Brouillette and Matthew Randazzo V, *Mr. New Orleans: The Life of a Big Easy Underworld Legend* (Beverly Hills, Calif.: Phoenix, 2009), p. 151.

42. Frances Pedone Schiro (1917–2003), interview by Joseph N. Macaluso, August 23, 2000, in *Italian Immigrant Families: Grocer, Proprietors, and Entrepreneurs—The Story of the Italian/Sicilian Corner Grocers and Markets of Algiers, LA* (Pittsburgh: RoseDog, 2004), pp. 408–11.

8. How Bourbon Street Flourished: Late 1920s–Mid-1940s

1. Ronnie Virgets, "The Oyster Girl," *Gambit*, October 18, 1994, p. 13.

2. J. Mark Souther, *New Orleans on Parade: Tourism and the Transformation of the Crescent City* (Baton Rouge: LSU Press, 2006), p. 50.

3. "Foreigners Are Not Forbidden Privilege of Selling Liquors; Judge O'Neill . . . Takes Issue with Attorney General in Interpreting Gay-Shattuck Law," *Daily Picayune*, January 26, 1909, p. 3; Mara Laura Keire, *For Business and Pleasure: Red-Light Districts and the Regulation of Vice in the United States, 1890–1933* (Baltimore: Johns Hopkins University Press, 2010), pp. 64–66; Alecia P. Long, *The*

Great Southern Babylon: Sex, Race, and Respectability in New Orleans, 1865–1920 (Baton Rouge: LSU Press, 2004), pp. 180–82.

4. J. A. Walker, "Gaspar Gulotta—The Little Mayor of Bourbon Street," *New Orleans Magazine,* May 1971, p. 29.

5. Babe Carroll McTague, interviewed by Thomas Sancton in "Babe Sang Bourbon Street to Fame," *New Orleans Item,* December 29, 1949, p. 17.

6. "The Maxime," *Times-Picayune,* January 13, 1926, p. 14.

7. McTague quoted in Sancton, "Babe Sang Bourbon Street to Fame," p. 17.

8. Ibid.; "Four Padlocking Actions Started," *Times-Picayune,* September 12, 1926, p. 12; "Labels, Stamps for Bogus Rum Taken in Raid," *Times-Picayune,* April 10, 1927, p. 8.

9. David Winstein, interview by Peggy Scott Laborde, 1997, in *The French Quarter That Was,* televised documentary, WYES New Orleans, 1999.

10. General Licenses, Treasury Division, 1920, Ledger A, Department of Public Finance, City of New Orleans (C670jg 1920 A, Louisiana Division, New Orleans Public Library), p. 26, entry 7 made on January 24, 1920, and entry 26 on June 9, 1920.

11. Ordinance No. 395, C.C., New Orleans, November 20, 1852; Ordinance No. 7742, C.C.S., Mayoralty of New Orleans, City Hall, February 20, 1924.

12. City Planning and Zoning Commission—Advisory Commission, *The Handbook to Comprehensive Zone Law for New Orleans, Louisiana* (New Orleans, 1929–33), chap. 3, p. 1, Tulane University Special Collections, 976.31 (711) N469h 1933.

13. Ibid., chap. 4, pp. 5–6.

14. Some of these remarkable maps are stored in the archives of the New Orleans Public Library under materials filed with the early records of the City Planning and Zoning Commission. See also "The Plan for Zoning," chap. 7 of *City Planning Report* (New Orleans, 1930), pp. 4–6, Tulane University Special Collections, 976.31 (711) N469c.

15. See "Diagram of Present Uses of Property, 1926," from 1927 Major Street Report, filed in City Planning and Zoning Commission-Advisory Commission, chap. 5, prior to p. 7.

16. City Planning Commission of New Orleans, Executive Session on Zoning, February 19, 1963, pp. 2–5 and 2–6, filed in "Vieux Carré Zoning Case of Convent of Holy Family, 717 Orleans Avenue" Folder, Box 7 of Councilman Joseph V. DiRosa Papers, 1962–1966, 1970–1978, Louisiana Division, New Orleans Public Library. See also GIS zoning files produced and disseminated by the City Planning Commission; and Allen Johnson Jr., "Can't Stop the Music," "Dateline" column in *Gambit,* February 11, 1992, pp. 12–13.

17. New Orleans City Planning and Zoning Commission, "The Plan for Civic Art," chap. 6 of *City Planning Report* (New Orleans, 1930), pp. 31–38, Tulane University Special Collections, 976.31 (711) N469c; City Planning and Zoning Commission–Advisory Commission, chap. 5, p. 31.

18. *Map Showing Proposed Extension of Restricted Building District, as Sponsored by the Louisiana Chapter of the American Institute of Architecture,* March 30, 1928, original filed with the early records of the City Planning and Zoning Commission, Louisiana Division, New Orleans Public Library.

19. "The Proposed Civic Center: New Orleans, Louisiana," New Orleans City Planning and Zoning Commission/Bartholomew and Associates, St. Louis, undated, filed with early records of the City Planning and Zoning Commission, Louisiana Division, New Orleans Public Library.

20. Mary Elizabeth Morrison (Mrs. Jacob Morrison), interview by John Geiser, August 2, 1977, Friends of the Cabildo Oral History Archive, Louisiana Division, New Orleans Public Library.

21. "New Orleans Vieux Carré Proposed Housing Project," Frederick D. Parham Architects, May 1938, Historic New Orleans Collection, acc. no. 1994.101.4; Christine Wiltz, *The Last Madam: A Life in the New Orleans Underworld* (New York: Faber and Faber, 2000), p. 50.

22. Jeanette Raffray, "Origins of the Vieux Carré Commission, 1920–1941," *Louisiana History* 40, no. 3 (Summer 1999): 283–304.

23. New Orleans City Planning and Zoning Commission, "The Plan for Civic Art," chap. 6 of *City Planning Report* (New Orleans, 1930), pp. 4–5, Tulane University Special Collections, 976.31 (711) N469c.

24. "City Breweries Sell Out; Joyous Throngs Toast Old and New," *Times-Picayune*, April 14, 1933, p. 1.

25. Advertisement, "315–321 Bourbon Street, Offering You a Higher Type of Laundry Service," *New Orleans Item-Tribune*, June 14, 1926, p. 10; "Oriental Laundry Expands Business on Bourbon Street," *New Orleans Item-Tribune*, June 13, 1926, p. 8.

26. William H. Fitzpatrick, "City Chinatown Shifted as Aged Buildings Razed," *Times-Picayune*, September 21, 1937.

27. Elsie Brupbacher, "Kipling Was Wrong: N.O. Chinese Blend East with West," *New Orleans States*, December 12, 1953, p. 14.

28. Tennessee Williams, *A Streetcar Named Desire* (New York: Signet, 1947), p. 55.

29. "Costume Makers Kept Busy Not Withstanding War Times," *Times-Picayune*, August 3, 1919, p. 15.

30. Bettye Tucker, "Mme. Rapho's Casualty: Modern Times Force Institution's Closing," *New Orleans States and Item*, August 15, 1959; *Cohen's New Orleans & Lafayette Directory for 1851*.

31. *Soards' New Orleans City Directory for 1921* (New Orleans: L. Soards, 1921), pp. 1588, 1607, and 1624.

32. *New Orleans City Directory, 1938*; Federal Writers' Project of the Works Progress Administration, *New Orleans City Guide* (New York: Pantheon, 1938), "French Quarter Clubs and Bars" section.

33. "Map of New Orleans, 1938—Points of Interest on Tours" (Houghton Mifflin, 1938), stored in map drawer of Louisiana Collection, Earl K. Long Library, University of New Orleans.

34. Associated Press, "New Orleans Has Revival of Old Jazz," *Dallas Morning News*, August 20, 1940, sec. 2, p. 3.

35. "Opera, Jazz Music Just Four Blocks Apart in City," *Times-Picayune*, January 7, 1940, sec. 2, p. 6.

36. Based on the author's enumeration of 1938 *New Orleans City Directory* commercial listings by street.

37. Gleaned from the December 8, 1941, issue of the *Times-Picayune*; see also Brian Altobello, *New Orleans Goes to War, 1941–1945: An Oral History of New Orleanians during World War II* (New Orleans: Brian Altobello, 1990), pp. i–xxii.

38. A penthouse apartment, still visible today, was added to 835 St. Louis Street, a few doors from Bourbon. "Convert Vieux Carré Home for War Workers," *Old French Quarter News*, September 10, 1943, p. 3.

39. "545,041 New Population of New Orleans," *Old French Quarter News*, July 16, 1943, p. 1; "City Growing; Population [of Metro Area] is now 630,000," *Old French Quarter News*, November 30, 1945, p. 1.

40. Jerry E. Strahan, *Andrew Jackson Higgins and the Boats That Won World War II* (Baton Rouge: LSU Press, 1994); Jerry Purvis Sanson, *Louisiana during World War II: Politics and Society, 1939–1945* (Baton Rouge: LSU Press, 1999).

41. "60,000 Orleanians Discharges Given," *Old French Quarter News*, December 28, 1945, p. 7.

42. Morton Sosna, introduction to *Remaking Dixie: The Impact of World War II on the American South*, ed. Neil R. McMillin (Jackson: University Press of Mississippi, 1997), pp. xiii–xix.

43. Defense Department, Army, Center of Military History, *United States Army in World War 2, Technical Services, Transportation Corps, Movements, Training, and Supply* (Washington, D.C.: Government Printing Office, 1956), pp. 100 and 332; Meigs O. Frost, "Army Backs City as Official Port of Embarkation, General Reveals," *Times-Picayune*, June 28, 1941, pp. 1–3; "Orleans Chosen as Embarkation Port for Troops," *Times-Picayune*, July 4, 1941, pp. 1–2; "General Hunter Honored by Army," *Times-Picayune*, February 1, 1944, p. 7.

44. Ogden C. Bacon Jr., interview by Sean Harvey and Sandra Stewart Holyoak, May 3, 2000, New Brunswick, N.J., transcribed by D. Duarte, K. Tracy, Bacon, and Holyoak, Rutgers Oral History Archives, New Brunswick History Department.

45. Robert F. Moss, interview by G. Kurt Piehler and Bryan Holzmacher, October 13, 1994, Metuchen, N.J., transcribed by Holzmacher and Piehler, ibid.

46. Carl O. E. Bosenberg, interview by Shaun Illingworth and Sandra Stewart Holyoak, April 23, 2002, New Brunswick, N.J., transcribed by D. Duarte, D. D'Onofrio, M. Decker, Bosenberg, and Holyoak, ibid.

47. Edith Norris, "Service Men Go on Guided Tours," *Times-Picayune*, May 25, 1943, p. 10.

48. Kathleen F. Thomson Stoye, interview by Chris Simon (undated), Veterans History Project, American Folklife Center, Library of Congress, http://lcweb2.loc.gov/diglib/vhp/story/loc.natlib .afc2001001.33488/transcript?ID=sr0001.

49. "Society: Varied War Relief Activity Occupying Orleans Groups," *Times-Picayune*, March 24, 1943, p. 19.

50. Norris, "Service Men Go on Guided Tours," 10.

51. Ken Hulsizer, "New Orleans in Wartime," in *Jazz Review*, ed. Max Jones and Albert McCarthy (London: Jazz Music Books, 1945), p. 3; "Rent Controls to Continue in Effect in City," *Old French Quarter News*, August 31, 1945, p. 1.

52. Souther, *New Orleans on Parade*, pp. 43–45.

53. *Old French Quarter News*, January 14, June 4, and June 11, 1943; and subsequent editions (microfilm), Historic New Orleans Collection.

54. William Kenneth Smith, interview by Sandra Stewart Holyoak and Michael Ojeda, May 11, 2000, Brick Township, N.J., transcribed by G. D. Sabatini, S. Illingworth, W. K. Smith, and Stewart Holyoak, Rutgers Oral History Archives, New Brunswick History Department.

55. Arnold Spielberg, interview by Sandra Stewart Holyoak and Shaun Illingworth, May 12, 2006, New Brunswick, N.J., transcribed by D. Duarte, A. Spielberg, and Illingworth, ibid.

56. P. Richard Wexler, "My Version," Rutgers Oral History Archives, New Brunswick History Department, oralhistory.rutgers.edu/Docs/ . . . /wexler_p_richard_my_version.html.

57. M. Leon Canick, interview by G. Kurt Piehler and Patrick Goodwin, October 11, 1994, New York City, transcribed by P. Gordon, L. Lasko, and Piehler, Rutgers Oral History Archives, New Brunswick History Department.

58. "Serviceman Praises French Quarter to Popular New York Newspaper 'PM,'" *Old French Quarter News,* March 24, 1944, as cited by Souther, *New Orleans on Parade,* p. 44.

59. "Vieux Carré Nite Life: This Column Is Going to the Dogs," *Old French Quarter News,* February 8, 1946, p. 8.

60. John Pope, "Philanthropist, Civic Activist Kabacoff, 88," *Times-Picayune,* February 25, 2012, p. B6.

61. Souther, *New Orleans on Parade,* p. 107.

62. Crandon F. Clark, interview by G. Kurt Piehler, June 12, 1995, New Brunswick, N.J., transcribed by R. G. O'Connor, L. Lasko, and Piehler, Rutgers Oral History Archives, New Brunswick History Department.

63. Tambasco's service during World War II, which placed him on a flagship throughout the island-hopping campaign, gave the young Brooklynite his first exposure to the South, New Orleans, and Bourbon Street, just like a million others of his generation. His best friend from Brooklyn, Mario Campanella, trained at Fort Benning in Georgia in 1945, his first southern experience as well. John Tambasco is my uncle, and Mario Campanella (1926–2012) is my father (John Tambasco, interview by Richard Campanella, March 27, 2012).

64. New Orleans Hostess Committee, Beauregard House Center for Service Men, scrapbook archived at Historic New Orleans Collection, 2002-94-L.1.

65. Nadia Moise, interview by Mark Cave, July 19, 2002, Historic New Orleans Collection, 2002-94-L.

66. Murray K. Finley to "The Girls of the Beauregard House," October 12, 1942, stored in New Orleans Hostess Committee, Beauregard House Center for Service Men scrapbook, archived at Historic New Orleans Collection, 2002-94-L.1.

67. "Beauregard Home Welcomes Soldiers from Another Army," *Times-Picayune,* August 30, 1942, sec. 3, pp. 3–6; Elizabeth Kell, "Beauregard House Servicemen's Center Closes Its Doors as Usefulness Ends," *New Orleans States,* September 13, 1945, p. 16. See also various clippings and materials stored in the New Orleans Hostess Committee, Beauregard House Center for Service Men scrapbook, archived at Historic New Orleans Collection, 2002-94-L.1.

68. "Seeks Hospitality for Service Men," unattributed and undated clipping stored in the New Orleans Hostess Committee, Beauregard House Center for Service Men scrapbook.

69. "Museum Visitors Break Record; 546,606 Flow inside Gates of Cabildo," *Old French Quarter News,* October 29, 1943, p. 1; "Vieux Carré Charm of Old World Cited: Orleans Is Placed First in List of 10 Best by Magazine," *Old French Quarter News,* December 31, 1943, p. 3.

70. Curly Lima, "Vieux Carré Nite Life," *Old French Quarter News,* December 3, 1948, p. 4.

71. Kathleen F. Thomson Stoye, interview by Chris Simon (undated), Veterans History Project, American Folklife Center, Library of Congress, http://lcweb2.loc.gov/diglib/vhp/story/loc.natlib .afc2001001.33488/transcript?ID=sr0001.

72. This nuisance continued after the war. One such incident in November 1946, which caused an estimated $100,000 in mechanical damages, led to a tightening of the antisoot ordinance that had been on the books. Another case in 1949, involving a British vessel docked at the foot of Dumaine Street, blackened everything within a six-block radius ("Push Rigid Anti-Soot Ordinance," *Old French Quarter News,* November 8, 1946, pp. 1–8; "Ship Soot Rains on Vieux Carré; Charges Shaped," *Old French Quarter News,* July 15, 1949, p. 1).

73. "Late Lights on Again in Orleans Night Spots," *Times-Picayune,* May 10, 1945, p. 1; "Bar

Maid Is Booked under Curfew Law," *Times-Picayune*, January 6, 1944, p. 10; "Distressed Citizen," "Enforcing of Liquor, Noise Laws Urged," letter to the editor, *Times-Picayune*, April 9, 1943, p. 10.

74. Hulsizer, "New Orleans in Wartime," p. 4.

75. Marjorie H. Roehl, "Southern Hospitality, Fried Chicken Making Army Feel at Home Here," *New Orleans States-Item,* and "Home Dinners for Soldiers Plan of Hostesses," undated wartime clippings stored in New Orleans Hostess Committee, Beauregard House Center for Service Men scrapbook.

76. M. Leon Canick, interview by G. Kurt Piehler and Patrick Goodwin, October 11, 1994, New York City, transcribed by P. Gordon, L. Lasko, and Piehler, Rutgers Oral History Archives, New Brunswick History Department.

77. Hulsizer, "New Orleans in Wartime," p. 3.

78. "Oyster Time's Here Again; Already Talk of Raising Prices," *Old French Quarter News,* September 3, 1943, p. 6.

79. Curly Lima, "Vieux Carré Nite Life," *Old French Quarter News,* August 3, 1945, p. 8.

80. Edith Norris, "Service Men Go on Guided Tours," *Times-Picayune*, May 25, 1943, p. 10; "At the Ringside Table" column in the *Old French Quarter News* throughout war years; personal recollections of Mary Lou Widmer, *New Orleans in the Forties* (Gretna, La.: Pelican, 1990), p. 65.

81. "Heard at Tugy's Famous Bar," *Old French Quarter News,* August 20, 1943, p. 7; "Hitler Shot Nightly at Tugy's Famous Bar," *Old French Quarter News,* September 3, 1943, p. 6.

82. "Heard at the Famous Door," *Old French Quarter News,* June 11, 1943, p. 7.

83. "Heard at Club Bourbon," *Old French Quarter News,* December 17, 1943, p. 6.

84. "Heard at Jimmy's Gay 90's," *Old French Quarter News,* October 8, 1943, p. 6; "Heard at Gaspar's Bar," *Old French Quarter News,* October 29, 1943, p. 6.

85. "At the Ringside Table," *Old French Quarter News,* January 14, 1943, p. 6; December 10, 1943, p. 7; December 17, 1943, p. 6.

86. Ken Hulsizer, "New Orleans in Wartime," p. 4.

87. "It's a Lie, Suh! Orleans Girls Not Hussies," *Old French Quarter News,* January 28, 1944, p. 2.

88. "Gypsies, Marooned by War, Settle in Quarter," *Old French Quarter News,* August 20, 1943, p. 3.

89. *Polk's New Orleans City Directory of 1945–46,* p. 35 of pink-colored section.

90. "House Full, Help Short, Hotels' Plaint," *Old French Quarter News,* August 13, 1943, p. 1.

91. Hulsizer, "New Orleans in Wartime," p. 6.

92. "Up and down the Street—Spasm Band," *Times-Picayune*, May 8, 1943, p. 23; "Help Wanted—Female," *Times-Picayune*, February 20, 1944, sec. 4, p. 3; "Help Wanted—Male," *Times-Picayune*, October 18, 1942, sec. 5, p. 2; "Visitors' Guide to New Orleans, The Paris of America," *Times-Picayune*, October 30, 1941, p. 23; "Vieux Carré Restaurant Doing $75,000 Last Year," *Times-Picayune*, October 6, 1946, sec. 4, Classified Real Estate.

93. "Puneky Quits Night Club Tax Collection Job," *Old French Quarter News,* January 25, 1946, p. 1; advertisement, *Old French Quarter News,* February 1, 1946, p. 8.

94. "At a Ringside Table," *Old French Quarter News,* February 11, 1944, p. 6.

95. The proposed law failed on grounds of unconstitutionality. "Vieux Carré Nite Life," *Old French Quarter News,* August 23, 1946, p. 8.

96. Quoted and depicted in Pete Daniel, "Going among Strangers: Southern Reactions to World War II," *Journal of American History* 77, no. 3 (December 1990): 886–911.

97. *Old French Quarter News,* August 13, 1943, p. 7; October 22, 1943, p. 5; "Blaboteurs Warned by FBI," *Old French Quarter News,* January 7, 1944, p. 1.

98. "Soldier Patients Are Taken on Motor Tour of Quarter," *Old French Quarter News,* August 27, 1943, p. 1.

99. "Airman Survives 32,000-Foot Fall," *Times-Picayune,* January 24, 1945, p. 1.

100. Hulsizer, "New Orleans in Wartime," pp. 3–6.

101. Ibid.

102. Eula Lole MacPherson McMillan, interview by Patricia Redmond, January 24, 2008, Veterans History Project, American Folklife Center, Library of Congress, http://lcweb2.loc.gov/diglib/vhp/story/loc.natlib.afc2001001.62475/transcript?ID=sr0001.

103. "Chinese Shoot Fireworks in Celebration of V-J Day," *Times-Picayune,* September 3, 1945, pp. 1, 3.

104. "Late Lights on Again in Orleans Night Spots," *Times-Picayune,* May 10, 1945, p. 1.

105. Paul Rork, interview by G. Kurt Piehler, July 18, 1994, Mahwah, N.J., transcribed by C. Fleischer, L. Lasko, Piehler, Rork, and S. Holyoak, Rutgers Oral History Archives, New Brunswick History Department.

106. Fred Pickett, "At a Ringside Table," *Old French Quarter News,* June 21, 1946, p. 6.

107. Defense Department, Army, Center of Military History, *United States Army in World War 2,* p. 207.

108. Morrison (Mrs. Jacob Morrison), interview by Geiser, August 2, 1977.

109. "Mardi Gras Is Revived," *Windsor Daily Star,* Ontario, Canada, February 25, 1946, p. 8; "Bourbon Bounders to Elect Queen at Mardi Gras Frolic," *Old French Quarter News,* February 22, 1946, p. 1.

110. "Routes of Mardi Gras Parades," *Old French Quarter News,* March 1, 1946, p. 1; "Young M. Gee, Owner of Chinese Restaurants." *Times-Picayune,* Thursday, June 10, 2004, sec. B, p. 4.

111. Associated Press, "Boom in Night Life Hits New Orleans Where All Is Gay," *Bend (Ore.) Bulletin,* January 26, 1948, p. 3.

112. "For a Greater New Orleans—and Vieux Carré," *Old French Quarter News,* January 18, 1946, p. 4.

113. U.S. Census Bureau, analysis by the author; see also "545,041 New Population of New Orleans," *Old French Quarter News,* July 16, 1943, p. 1; "City Growing; Population [of Metro Area] is now 630,000," *Old French Quarter News,* November 30, 1945, p. 1; "Population of New Orleans over 565,000," *Old French Quarter News,* May 3, 1946, p. 1.

114. United Press, "Mardi Gras Carnival Week Appears Jinxed," *Sunday Wilmington (N.C.) Star-News,* February 27, 1949, sec. B, p. 8; United Press, "700,000 Persons Open New Orleans Blowout," *Wilmington (N.C.) News,* February 23, 1949, p. 9.

115. Virgets, "The Oyster Girl," p. 13; Liz Scott, "Evangeline, the Oyster Girl: When Stripping Was an Art," *New Orleans Magazine,* August 1995, pp. 45–46.

116. Fred Pickett, "At the Ringside Table," *Old French Quarter News,* May 10, 1946, p. 6.

117. Mary Bruns, "Bouquets for Vieux Carré's Bourbon Street," *New Orleans Item,* August 18, 1948, p. 22.

118. "Vieux Carré Nite Life," *Old French Quarter News,* October 25, 1946, p. 8.

119. "All Around the Quarter," *Old French Quarter News,* March 19, 1948, p. 7.

120. Analysis by the author using Bourbon Street listings in *Polk's New Orleans Directory* for 1938, 1940, 1945–46, and 1952–53; "At the Ringside Table," *Old French Quarter News*, March 15, 1946, p. 8.

121. Curly Lima, "Vieux Carré Night Life," *Old French Quarter News*, September 3, 1948, p. 6; November 5, 1948, p. 4; December 17, 1948, p. 4.

122. Curly Lima, "Vieux Carré Night Life," *Old French Quarter News*, August 13, 1948, p. 6.

123. Ordinance No. 16,906 Commission Council Series (C.C.S.), Mayoralty of New Orleans, June 6, 1947.

124. "Vieux Carré Nite Life," *Old French Quarter News*, April 16, 1948, p. 6.

125. Photograph by Charles Frank, June 17, 1952, Historic New Orleans Collection, acc. no. 1979.325.4865.

126. Curly Lima, "Vieux Carré Night Life," *Old French Quarter News*, June 21, 1946, p. 7.

9. How Bourbon Street Exploded: Late 1940s–Early 1960s

1. "All Around the Quarter," *Old French Quarter News*, July 9, 1948, p. 7.

2. Mary Elizabeth Morrison (Mrs. Jacob Morrison), interview by John Geiser, August 2, 1977, Friends of the Cabildo Oral History Archive, Louisiana Division, New Orleans Public Library.

3. "Student," "Local Vendors of Vice," letter to the editor, *Times-Picayune*, March 8, 1949, p. 12.

4. "Group Seeks to Curb Noises in Vieux Carré," *Old French Quarter News*, October 4, 1946, p. 2; "Agent Who Made Blackout of Quarter Threat Jailed," *Old French Quarter News*, June 14, 1946, p. 2; "Wake Up French Quarterites," *Old French Quarter News*, October 12, 1945, p. 4.

5. "At a Ringside Table," *Old French Quarter News*, March 22, 1946, p. 6.

6. Joe Herman, quoted in Curly Lima in "Vieux Carré Nite Life," *Old French Quarter News*, May 7, 1948, p. 6; "Blackeye to City," *Old French Quarter News*, February 22, 1946, p. 1; Curly Lima, "Nite Club Future Scanned," *Old French Quarter News*, November 16, 1945, p. 1.

7. Norma Wallace, quoted in Christine Wiltz, *The Last Madam: A Life in the New Orleans Underworld* (New York: Faber and Faber, 2000), p. 73.

8. Curly Lima, "Vieux Carré Nite Life," *Old French Quarter News*, February 15, 1946, p. 8. Morrison had been elected but not yet sworn in when this article was written.

9. Mark J. Souther, *New Orleans on Parade: Tourism and the Transformation of the Crescent City* (Baton Rouge: LSU Press, 2006), p. 46.

10. "Parade Route for Morrison Inauguration," *Old French Quarter News*, May 3, 1946, p. 2.

11. Edward F. Haas, *Delesseps S. Morrison and the Image of Reform: New Orleans Politics, 1946–1961* (Baton Rouge: LSU Press, 1974), pp. 98–109.

12. "Club Operators Agree to Clean Up Night Shows," *Old French Quarter News*, April 30, 1948, p. 2; Hyp Guinle, quoted in Curly Lima in "Vieux Carré Nite Life," *Old French Quarter News*, May 7, 1948, p. 6.

13. Earl Dworecki, letter to the editor, *Times-Picayune*, October 5, 1948, p. 10; Ray Samuel, "What's Happened to Bourbon Street?" *Times-Picayune*, November 28, 1948, magazine section, pp. 8–11.

14. "Gal without Stitch on Goes for Quarter Stroll," *Old French Quarter News*, October 14, 1949, p. 7.

15. Ellen Middlebrook, "Clean Up Bourbon Street, Jazz Old-Timers Advise; Faces 52nd Street Fate, Warn Musicians," *Times-Picayune*, November 11, 1949, p. 18, c. 3.

16. Samuel, "What's Happened to Bourbon Street?" pp. 8–11.

17. Thomas Sancton, "Babe Sang Bourbon Street to Fame," *New Orleans Item*, December 29, 1949, p. 17.

18. "Quarter Rail Removal Sought," *Old French Quarter News*, May 10, 1946, p. 1; Curly Lima, "Vieux Carré Nite Life," *Old French Quarter News*, January 7, 1949, p. 4; "French Quarter Residents Demand More Protection," *Old French Quarter News*, April 9, 1948, p. 8.

19. "Property Owners Map Plan to Halt New Bars," *Old French Quarter News*, October 14, 1949, p. 1.

20. Morrison (Mrs. Jacob Morrison), interview by Geiser, August 2, 1977.

21. Bob Harrington with Walter Wagner, *The Chaplain of Bourbon Street* (Garden City, N.Y.: Doubleday, 1969), p. 101.

22. Curly Lima, "Vieux Carré Nite Life," *Old French Quarter News*, May 28, 1948, p. 6.

23. Ibid., September 3, 1948, p. 6 (emphasis added).

24. Ibid., August 13, 1948, p. 6.

25. Ibid., December 3, 1948, p. 4.

26. Ibid., July 12, 1946, p. 8; "Brennan Seeks an 'Uncle Tom,'" *Old French Quarter News*, May 10, 1946, p. 1.

27. Robert Sylvester, "Let's Move New Orleans Up Here," *Old French Quarter News*, June 7, 1946, p. 7.

28. Curly Lima, "Vieux Carré Nite Life," *Old French Quarter News*, October 7, 1949, p. 7.

29. Advertisement, *Old French Quarter News*, February 27, 1948, p. 8; Curly Lima, "Vieux Carré Night Life," *Old French Quarter News*, January 7, 1949, p. 4, and other sources.

30. Howard Jacobs, "A City of Character—in Fact, a Whole Slue of 'Em," condensed and published in "Owner of Club Provides Souvenirs for Stealing," *Times-Picayune*, January 11, 1970, p. 19.

31. Anthony Stanonis, *Creating the Big Easy: New Orleans and the Emergence of Modern Tourism, 1918–1945* (Athens: University of Georgia Press, 2006), p. 224.

32. Charles Suhor, "New Jazz in the Cradle, Part I," *Down Beat Magazine*, August 17, 1961, reprinted in *Jazz in New Orleans: The Postwar Years through 1970*, ed. Charles Suhor (Lanham, Md.: Scarecrow Press and the Institute of Jazz Studies at Rutgers University, 2001), p. 252.

33. "Zachary Scott Booked in Raid; Nine Held for Drinking in Negro Establishment," *Times-Picayune*, November 17, 1952, p. 19. See also testimonies of William Claxton and Joachim E. Berendt in *New Orleans Jazzlife, 1960* (Hong Kong: Taschen Press, 2008), pp. 22–23.

34. American Automobile Association, *Guide to America: A Treasury of Information about Its States, Cities, Parks, and Historical Points of Interest* (Washington, D.C.: Public Affairs Press, 1953), p. 261; Frenchy Brouillette and Matthew Randazzo V, *Mr. New Orleans: The Life of a Big Easy Underworld Legend* (Beverly Hills, Calif.: Phoenix, 2009), p. 92.

35. Frank Ray Perilli, interview by David Cuthbert, "Frankie Speaking: From Bourbon Street to Lenny Bruce and 'Dracula's Dog,' Frankie Ray Has Seen It All," *Times-Picayune*, January 15, 2000; Jacobs, "A City of Character," p. 13; "Royale Flush," *Life* magazine, November 28, 1949, pp. 127–28; Ronnie Virgets, "The Oyster Girl," *Gambit*, October 18, 1994, p. 13.

36. Michael L. Kurtz and Morgan D. Peoples, *Earl K. Long: The Saga of Uncle Earl and Louisiana Politics* (Baton Rouge: LSU Press, 1992), pp. 214–16.

37. "Warns Cat Girl Her Act Is Naughty," *New Orleans Item*, June 9, 1952, p. 1; "Bourbon Dances Confused," *New Orleans Item*, June 10, 1952, pp. 1–10.

38. Confidential Investigator #9, Investigative Report dated September 28, 1953, Box 4, Folder 5, Vice Activities Gambling—Other, City Council Special Citizens Investigating Committee Records, 1953–1963, Louisiana Division, New Orleans Public Library.

39. Weegee (Arthur Fellig), *Weegee by Weegee: An Autobiography* (New York: Ziff-Davis, 1961), pp. 111–13; Brouillette and Randazzo, *Mr. New Orleans,* p. 50.

40. Weegee (Arthur Fellig), *Weegee by Weegee,* pp. 111–13.

41. Harrington and Wagner, *The Chaplain of Bourbon Street,* p. 140.

42. The term "vidalia," unique to New Orleans vernacular and now extinct, has two origin hypotheses. One holds that the Mississippi lumber town of Vidalia once supplied a stream of wealthy tycoons to the brothels of the Crescent City, and because many amorous tourists hailed from similar small southern communities, "Vidalia" came to mean any out-of-towner with sex on his mind and money in his pocket. Madam Norma Wallace, source of the other theory, contended that she had named one of her bordello lapdogs Vidalia and attached the name to the other hapless dogs who came to her door craving sex. "Pansies," which appears occasionally in the *Old French Quarter News* in reference to gay sex-seekers, presumably originated as a floral counterpart to vidalias (Brouillette and Randazzo, *Mr. New Orleans,* pp. 47–48; Wiltz, *The Last Madam,* pp. 10, 29).

43. Confidential Investigator #9, Investigative Report dated November 10, 1953, Box 4, Folder 5, Vice Activities Gambling—Other, City Council Special Citizens Investigating Committee Records, 1953–1963, Louisiana Division, New Orleans Public Library.

44. Ibid.; Brouillette and Randazzo, *Mr. New Orleans,* pp. 123–25.

45. Ione Doris Bourde, interview by Aaron M. Kohn, July 22, 1953, Box 4, Folder 16, p. 42, City Council Special Citizens Investigating Committee Records, 1953–1963, Louisiana Division, New Orleans Public Library.

46. Ibid.

47. Ibid.

48. "Billy Graham Now 'Loves' New Orleans," *Dallas Morning News,* November 1, 1954, p. 10.

49. Virgets, "The Oyster Girl," p. 13.

50. Culled from papers in Folders 7 and 8, Larry Fontaine Papers, 95-73-L, Collection Number N950911.6, Historic New Orleans Collection.

51. Perilli, interview by Cuthbert, "Frankie Speaking."

52. "Gunman Battles Cops, Wounds One, after Stabbing Dancer," *Times-Picayune,* June 17, 1951, p. 18; "Dancers Booked after Gun Fight; Two Young Women Face B-Drink Charges," *Times-Picayune,* June 18, 1951, p. 1; "Bond of $33,500 Set in Stabbing," *Times-Picayune,* June 19, 1951, p. 13; "Knifing Attack Told by Dancer," *Times-Picayune,* June 23, 1951, p. 3.

53. John Collier, "New Orleans Numbers Racket," *New Orleans Item,* 1949, undated newspaper clipping filed in Box 4, Folder 4, Vice Activities Gambling–Lottery, City Council Special Citizens Investigating Committee Records, 1953–1963, Louisiana Division, New Orleans Public Library.

54. Clippings filed in Box 4, Folder 4, Vice Activities Gambling–Lottery, City Council Special Citizens Investigating Committee Records, 1953–1963, Louisiana Division, New Orleans Public Library.

55. Kurtz and Peoples, *Earl K. Long,* pp. 86–90.

56. Rosemary James, quoted in Wiltz, *The Last Madam,* p. 85.

57. Confidential Investigator #8, Investigative Report dated November 7, 1953, Box 4, Folder 1,

Vice Activities Gambling—Lottery, City Council Special Citizens Investigating Committee Records, 1953–1963, Louisiana Division, New Orleans Public Library.

58. Edward F. Haas, *Delesseps S. Morrison and the Image of Reform: New Orleans Politics, 1946–1961* (Baton Rouge: LSU Press, 1974), pp. 103, 138.

59. A former bodyguard for Huey P. Long, Bracato could not have achieved this position without the assistance of Huey's brother, Louisiana lieutenant governor Earl K. Long, and New Orleans mayor Robert Maestri (Kurtz and Peoples, *Earl K. Long*, pp. 88–89).

60. Brouillette and Randazzo, *Mr. New Orleans*, pp. 40–42, 62–66, 88–90; Rosemary James, quoted in Wiltz, *The Last Madam*, p. 85; Kurtz and Peoples, *Earl K. Long*, pp. 86–90.

61. William Tell, *The Beat of Bourbon Street* (New Orleans: Bormon House, 1949), p. 1.

62. Ibid., pp. 16, 24.

63. Curly Lima, "Vieux Carré Nite Life," *Old French Quarter News*, May 27, 1949, p. 4.

64. Mary Bromfield, quoted in Dominic P. Papatola, "A Strip down Memory Lane," *Times-Picayune*, June 26, 1998.

65. Curly Lima, "Vieux Carré Night Life," *Old French Quarter News*, December 17, 1948, p. 4; Brouillette and Randazzo, *Mr. New Orleans*, p. 67.

66. Photograph, 325 Bourbon, late 1940s, by Walter Cook Keenan, 1–400 Bourbon Folder 78, Southeastern Architectural Archives, Tulane University.

67. "Roof Garden Grows in Quarter," *Old French Quarter News*, July 22, 1949, p. 7.

68. Patsy Bonnette-Mire, "Catch of the Day—Pigeon," "Your Opinion," *Times-Picayune*, July 25, 2012, p. B4.

69. Interview of an "unnamed old time Bourbon Streeter," by J. A. Walker, "Gaspar Gulotta—The Little Mayor of Bourbon Street," *New Orleans Magazine*, May 1971, p. 57.

70. Gaspar Gulotta, interview by Aaron M. Kohn, Public Hearing before the Commission Council of the City of New Orleans, January 5, 1954, Box 10, Folder 5; Ione Doris Bourde, interview by Aaron M. Kohn, July 22, 1953, Box 4, Folder 16, p. 153; City Council Special Citizens Investigating Committee Records, 1953–1963, Louisiana Division, New Orleans Public Library; Brouillette and Randazzo, *Mr. New Orleans*, pp. 72–74.

71. Liz Scott, "Evangeline, the Oyster Girl: When Stripping Was an Art," *New Orleans Magazine*, August 1995, pp. 45–46.

72. Thomas Sancton, "Revelry at Gaspar's Club Just as He Would Have It," *New Orleans Item*, January 1, 1958, p. 2.

73. Sociologist Jack V. Buerkle, who studied the local music scene in the 1960s and 1970s and worked closely with the likes of Danny Barker, wrote: "To the best of our knowledge, there are no black club owners or employers along Bourbon Street or within the Vieux Carré." Such was the case in the 1940s and 1950s (Jack V. Buerkle and Danny Barker, *Bourbon Street Black: The New Orleans Black Jazzman* [London: Oxford University Press, 1973], p. 121).

74. Curly Lima, "Vieux Carré Night Life," *Old French Quarter News*, June 21, 1946, p. 7; Brouillette and Randazzo, *Mr. New Orleans*, pp. 99–103.

75. Scott, "Evangeline, the Oyster Girl," pp. 45–46

76. "Business Loss Blamed on Law," *Times-Picayune*, August 15, 1962, p. 25; barker banter culled from the memories of Frenchy Brouillette in Brouillette and Randazzo's *Mr. New Orleans*, p. 49, and other sources.

77. "All Around the Quarter," *Old French Quarter News,* November 19, 1948, p. 3.

78. Scott, "Evangeline, the Oyster Girl," pp. 45–46; Virgets, "The Oyster Girl," p. 13.

79. Gleaned from a variety of sources, including newspaper ads; Carol Flake, "Stripper Gossip," *New Orleans Magazine,* September 1975, pp. 74–76; Jacobs, "A City of Character"; and interviews and vignettes by Peggy Scott Laborde, *Bourbon Street: The Neon Strip,* televised documentary, WYES New Orleans, 1993.

80. Interview of Kitty West by Peggy Scott Laborde, in *The French Quarter That Was,* televised documentary, WYES New Orleans, 1999, and other sources.

81. Virgets, "The Oyster Girl," p. 13.

82. Harrington and Wagner, *The Chaplain of Bourbon Street,* pp. 124–27.

83. Folder 2, "Night Clubs Dad Worked At," and scrapbook and photo album in the Larry Fontaine Papers, 95-73-L, Collection Number N950911.6, Historic New Orleans Collection.

84. Suhor, "New Jazz in the Cradle, Part I," 252.

85. Buerkle and Barker, *Bourbon Street Black,* pp. 41–45.

86. Ibid., p. 83.

87. Ibid., p. 116.

88. Ibid.; Tom Bethell, "Books . . . Reviewing Two Louisiana Traditions: Judge Perez and Bourbon Street's Black Musicians," *New Orleans Magazine,* December 1973, pp. 94–96.

89. Brouillette and Randazzo, *Mr. New Orleans,* p. 48

90. Claxton and Berendt, *New Orleans Jazzlife, 1960,* pp. 6–7, 17, 56–57, 60–61.

91. Ibid., pp. 6–7, 17, 56–57, 60–61.

92. Ibid., p. 22.

93. Suhor, "New Jazz in the Cradle, Part I," p. 252.

94. Anonymous, quoted in Buerkle and Barker, *Bourbon Street Black,* p. 98.

95. Jazz segment on *David Brinkley's Journal* (1962), viewed at Hogan Jazz Archive, Special Collections, Tulane University.

96. The editorialist chided: "This is what the Vieux Carré commission has been justifiably complaining about. . . . Maybe now [City Hall] will give cognizance to this ever-growing problem" (Sim Meyers, "On the Square: Elvis Premiere," *Times-Picayune,* May 14, 1958, p. 42; emphasis added).

97. Ibid., p. 31.

98. Hedda Hopper, "Looking at Hollywood," *Times-Picayune,* September 18, 1958, p. 87.

99. "Absinthe House Deal Is Closed," *Times-Picayune,* June 13, 1959, p. 30.

100. Maud O'Bryan, "Up and down the Street," *Times-Picayune,* May 12, 1959, p. 15; "Attention" (classified ad), *Times-Picayune,* May 21, 1959, p. 44; see also photographs stored in Vieux Carré Survey, Historic New Orleans Collection, Binder 73, section on 701 Bourbon.

101. "Dupont Dough Backs Murphy," *Billboard,* December 2, 1957, p. 19.

102. Pete Fountain, interview by Nick Compagno, reproduced in *Experience New Orleans;* "Pete Fountain," *Down Beat Magazine,* November 23, 1961, reprinted in *Jazz in New Orleans: The Postwar Years through 1970,* ed. Suhor, pp. 165–68.

103. Hirt's talent had so inspired a fifteen-year-old saxophonist from Arkansas that, when he was in New Orleans in 1961, the youth sought him out at his Bourbon Street club and got permission to catch two sets—accompanied by his mother because of his age. Hirt lived long enough to see that teenager become president of the United States. "I've never forgotten that," President Clinton

recalled with a smile (President Bill Clinton, interview by Peggy Scott Laborde, in *The Nightlife That Was,* televised documentary, WYES New Orleans, 2004).

104. "Narrowing of Sidewalks in Vieux Carré Studied," *Old French Quarter News,* October 29, 1948, p. 1.

105. Jacobs, "A City of Character" and "Owner of Club," *Times-Picayune,* January 10, 1970, p. 13, and January 11, 1970, p. 19.

106. New Orleans City Planning and Zoning Commission, "The Plan for Civic Art," chap. 6 of *City Planning Report* (New Orleans, 1930), p. 10, Tulane University Special Collections, 976.31 (711) N469c.

107. See, for example, informant interviewed in the 1962 *David Brinkley's Journal* broadcast on the state of jazz in New Orleans. See also Adam Fairclough, *Race and Democracy: The Civil Rights Struggle in Louisiana, 1915–1971* (Athens: University of Georgia Press, 2008), pp. 336, 428.

108. Chris Owens, e-mail interview by Richard Campanella, January 14, 2013.

109. "AFL Pulls Out for Houston," "Cancellation of Game Community Loss—Dixon," and "Mayor's Statement," *New Orleans States-Item,* January 11, 1965, pp. 22–25; "Houston Rushing Preps for AFL" and "Negro Walkout Termed Regrettable," *New Orleans States-Item,* January 12, 1965, p. 25; "City Must Look Forward, Not Back," "Deplores Action of Negro Ball Players," *New Orleans States-Item,* January 13, 1965, p. 10; Fairclough, *Race and Democracy,* pp. 336, 428.

110. Haas, *Delesseps S. Morrison and the Image of Reform,* p. 268.

111. Pat and Deane Mernagh, *Mammy Liza's Appeal to Her People (On the Question of Integration in Southern Schools),* 1954 pamphlet, Historic New Orleans Collection, acc. no. PS 3525.E7 M3 1954.

112. "'Segregation' Booklet Commended," *Times-Picayune,* December 7, 1954, p. 26; Ralph E. Ellsworth and Sarah M. Harris, "The American Right Wing: A Report to the Fund for the Republic, Inc." *Occasional Papers,* University of Illinois Library School, No. 59, November 1960, p. 6; "Fiesta Returns to Patio Trail," *Times-Picayune,* April 29, 1954, p. 6; "Literary Party Honors Robert Tallant," *Times-Picayune,* November 26, 1953, p. 33.

113. "Literary Party Honors Robert Tallant," p. 33; "'Segregation' Booklet Commended," p. 26.

114. "Public Access Contested in Court Action; Judge Temporarily Bans Enforcement Here," *Times-Picayune,* December 31, 1969, pp. 1–2.

115. "Business Loss Involves Laws; Segregation Found Slashing Conventions," *Times-Picayune,* September 8, 1962, p. 11; Howard Jacobs, "News of the Week in Review," *Times-Picayune,* May 26, 1963, sec. 2, p. 4; "Puerto Rican Delegation Walks Out of Conference," *Times-Picayune,* April 28, 1964, pp. 1–3; "Hotel Segregation Law Held Invalid; Action May End Long-Standing Practice," *Times-Picayune,* May 19, 1963, p. 1; "Report on Race Incidents Filed," *Times-Picayune,* August 14, 1969, p. 10; "N.O. Public Access Law Upheld Again by Ruling; Federal Court Refuses Injunction Plea," *Times-Picayune,* January 16, 1970, p. 1; Fairclough, *Race and Democracy,* p. 428; Carroll Joseph Dugas, "The Dismantling of De Jure Segregation in Louisiana, 1954–1974," vol. 1 (Ph.D. diss., Louisiana State University Department of History, 1989), pp. 336–49.

116. "Dancers Wanted," *Times-Picayune,* July 23, 1971, p. 47; "Colored, Light Complexion," *Times-Picayune,* April 8, 1971, p. 86; "Dancers Wanted," *Times-Picayune,* March 21, 1972, p. 40.

117. Jack Davis, "No Blacks/Whites Need Apply," *Figaro,* May 27, 1972, pp. 1–5.

118. Madeline Archinard Babin, interview by Christine Derbes, May 10, 1982, Friends of the Cabildo Oral History Archive, Louisiana Division, New Orleans Public Library.

119. We cannot quantify Bourbon Street's residential population changes throughout the late twentieth century because the data needed for such a study—the door-to-door population schedules of the decennial census—are not released by the Census Bureau until seventy-two years after collection, for reasons of privacy. What are released are aggregated statistics by census tract (for midcentury censuses), of which there are three in the French Quarter. Bourbon Street transects all three, again depriving us of concise statistics. The tracts cover from Canal to Conti (upper Quarter), Conti to St. Philip (central Quarter), and St. Philip to Esplanade (lower Quarter).

120. Analysis by the author using U.S. Census Bureau data from 1940 to 2010 censuses, as well as College of Urban and Public Affairs, *Changing Land Use in the Vieux Carré: Managing Growth to Preserve a National Landmark District* (New Orleans: University of New Orleans, 1992), pp. 2-3 to 2-5, a-7 to a-15; H. W. Gilmore, *Some Basic Census Tract Maps of New Orleans* (New Orleans, 1937), map book stored at Tulane University Special Collections, C5-D10-F6.

121. For a discussion on these topics, including the alliance between conservative women and gay progressive men in the preservation movement, see "In Search of Gay Preservationists" and "Cherishing Old New Orleans and Louisiana" in Will Fellows, *A Passion to Preserve: Gay Men as Keepers of Culture* (Madison: University of Wisconsin Press, 2005), pp. 217–42.

122. Tell, *The Beat of Bourbon Street*, p. 12.

123. So named because unemployed sailors ("monkeys") would hang out there and press their working mates to help make ends meet ("wrenching") (Federal Writers' Project of the Works Progress Administration, *New Orleans City Guide* [1938; repr., New Orleans: Garrett County Press, 2009], pp. 240–41).

124. Frank Perez and Jeffrey Palmquist, *In Exile: The History and Lore Surrounding New Orleans Gay Culture and Its Oldest Gay Bar* (Hurlford, Scotland: LL-Publications, 2012), pp. 37–44.

125. Lucy J. Fair, "New Orleans" entry to *Encyclopedia of Homosexuality*, ed. Wayne R. Dynes (New York: Garland, 1990), p. 895, posted online at http://williamapercy.com.

126. Jacobs, "A City of Character" and "Owner of Club," *Times-Picayune*, January 10, 1970, p. 13, and January 11, 1970, p. 19.

127. Violations Card Index (1955–1956) filed in Box 35, and Confidential Investigator #9, Investigative Report, November 7, 1953, Box 4, Folder 1, Vice Activities Gambling—Lottery, City Council Special Citizens Investigating Committee Records, 1953–1963, Louisiana Division, New Orleans Public Library.

128. "Boast in Fatal Beating Is Told," *Times-Picayune*, January 22, 1959, pp. 1–3; Perez and Palmquist, *In Exile*, p. 49.

129. Cabrini Park certainly had this reputation in the late 1960s, and probably in previous decades (*New Orleans Sunflower* newsletter, vol. 1, no. 1, January 1971, Louisiana Division, New Orleans Public Library).

130. Ron Swoboda, "Strip Search: Bourbon's Past, Live on Stage," *New Orleans Magazine*, July 1998, pp. 46–47.

131. "Dowling Knew of Aid, Charge; Sent Nightclub Operators Thanks, Says Garrison," *Times-Picayune*, March 3, 1962, p. 47.

132. "D.A. Candidates State Their Views," *Times-Picayune*, April 1, 1962, p. 15.

133. "Schiro Winner over Buckley by Big Margin," *Times-Picayune*, April 4, 1962, p. 1.

134. Kent "Frenchy" Brouillette, who recollected the organized criminality of midcentury Bour-

bon Street unburdened by understatement, described Garrison as "the biggest fucking hypocrite ever to live" (Brouillette and Randazzo, *Mr. New Orleans*, pp. 126–31; see also Wiltz, *The Last Madam*, pp. 145–47).

135. Culled from various police and news reports, plus descriptions in Brouillette and Randazzo, *Mr. New Orleans*, p. 51.

136. Lawrence LaMarca, Bourbon Street Association of Night Clubs, to Honorable Joseph I. Giarrusso, Superintendent of Police, November 10, 1962, filed in "Bourbon Street Association of Night Clubs, 1962–1963" Folder, Box 1 of Councilman Joseph V. DiRosa Papers, 1962–1966; 1970–1978, Louisiana Division, New Orleans Public Library.

137. Jack Kneece, "Many Clubs in Quarter Still Dimly Lit as Ever," *Times-Picayune*, August 11, 1962, p. 1; "Nightly Checks Are Still Made, No Arrests in Quarter in Several Days," *Times-Picayune*, August 22, 1962, p. 11.

138. "Obscenity Told at Quarter Bar; Solicited for Prostitution, Investigator Testifies," *Times-Picayune*, January 8, 1963, p. 18; "22 Women Face Morals Cases," *Times-Picayune*, December 4, 1962, p. 6.

139. "Bourbon St. Clubs Raided; 12 Arrested as War on B-Drinking Continues," *Times-Picayune*, August 23, 1962, p. 3; "Will Not Quarrel, Giarruso States," *Times-Picayune*, August 30, 1962, pp. 1–3; "Garrison Sees Strip Clubs' End; Pledges Enforcing Laws Against B-Drinking," *Times-Picayune*, September 20, 1962, p. 1.

140. Bourbon Street Association of Night Clubs to Councilman-at-Large Joseph V. DiRosa, September 21, 1962 (emphasis added), filed in "Bourbon Street Association, 1962," Folder, Box 1 of Councilman Joseph V. DiRosa Papers, 1962–1966; 1970–1978, Louisiana Division, New Orleans Public Library.

141. Larry LaMarca, Gunga Den Night Club, to Honorable Joseph DiRosa, November 10, 1962, filed in "Bourbon Street Association of Night Clubs, 1962–1963" Folder, Box 1 of Councilman Joseph V. DiRosa Papers, 1962–1966; 1970–1978, Louisiana Division, New Orleans Public Library.

142. Lawrence LaMarca, Bourbon Street Association of Night Clubs, to Honorable Victor H. Schiro, November 13, 1962, filed in "Bourbon Street Association of Night Clubs, 1962–1963" Folder, Box 1 of Councilman Joseph V. DiRosa Papers, 1962–1966; 1970–1978, Louisiana Division, New Orleans Public Library.

143. "Bourbon Spots to Reopen—DA; Says Raids to Continue at Any Violating Law," *Times-Picayune*, September 25, 1962, p. 32; "Padlock Confronts Skin Mills," *Times-Picayune*, December 23, 1962, p. 32; "22 Women Face Morals Cases," *Times-Picayune*, December 4, 1962, p. 6; James Savage, *Jim Garrison's Bourbon Street Brawl* (Lafayette: University of Louisiana Press, 2010), 12–13.

144. "Police Continue War on Vice in Night Spots," *Times-Picayune*, May 4, 1963, 1–3.

145. "Defense Given by Evangelist; Bourbon St. Needs Soul Saving, He Says," *Times-Picayune*, August 15, 1963, p. 34, "Anti-Mingling Measure Upset; Unconstitutional, Judge Decides on Appeal," *Times-Picayune*, September 13, 1963, p. 36.

146. "Judge Views DA Accusations as 'Wild Charges,'" *Times-Picayune*, November 2, 1962, pp. 1–17; Edgar Poe, "High Court Upsets Conviction of D.A., Voids La. Statute in Case of Jim Garrison," *Times-Picayune*, November 24, 1964, pp. 1–17; Savage, *Jim Garrison's Bourbon Street Brawl*.

147. "Bourbon Blaze Injures Two," *Times-Picayune*, June 9, 1964, p. 6.

148. Charles Yoder, "Disappointed," *Times-Picayune*, December 17, 1964, p. 14.

149. Brouillette and Randazzo, *Mr. New Orleans*, pp. 120–21, 130.

150. Clarence Doucet, "Bourbon House Declared Dead," *Times-Picayune*, October 1, 1964.

151. Wiltz, *The Last Madam*, p. 149; James H. Gillis, "In Minds of Politicians, It Was Garrison on Trial," *Times-Picayune*, March 9, 1969, p. 37.

10. How Bourbon Street Degenerated: Late 1960s–1970s

1. "Vieux Carré Hotel Proposed," *Old French Quarter News,* August 16, 1946, pp. 1–3.

2. Mary Elizabeth Morrison (Mrs. Jacob Morrison), interview by John Geiser, August 2, 1977, Friends of the Cabildo Oral History Archive, Louisiana Division, New Orleans Public Library.

3. Vieux Carré Commission member James Lamantia, quoted in article, "Quarter Hotel Ideas Outlined," *Times-Picayune*, July 17, 1963; Frank Schneider, "N.O. Investors to Begin Hotel; Aim to Complete Vieux Carré Facility in '69," *Times-Picayune*, December 14, 1967, pp. 1–22.

4. Oliver W. Hammonds to Councilman-at-Large Joseph V. DiRosa, September 16, 1963, filed in "Vieux Carré 300 Bourbon Street" Folder, Box 7 of Councilman Joseph V. DiRosa Papers, 1962–1966; 1970–1978, Louisiana Division, New Orleans Public Library. See also "Vieux Carré Hotel–Regal Brewery Site" Folder.

5. James Morrison to Guy Seghers, re: "Bourbon Street Hole," October 10, 1966, in Bourbon Street Hole Folder, Southeastern Architectural Archives, Tulane University. Special thanks to Keli Rylance for bringing these sources to my attention.

6. Guy Seghers to James Morrison, re: "Bourbon Street Hole," December 1, 1966, in Bourbon Street Hole Folder, Southeastern Architectural Archives, Tulane University.

7. Rosemary James, "Quarter Buildings Crack; Excavation Perils Sites; Emergency Work Approved," *New Orleans States-Item*, August 30, 1966.

8. Louisiana Council for the Vieux Carré (Martha G. Robinson, President), "The Requiem of the Vieux Carré," undated ca. 1966 flier, in Bourbon Street Hole Folder, Southeastern Architectural Archives, Tulane University.

9. James J. Morrison to Honorable Victor H. Shiro, re: "Necessity and Legality of Immediate and Decisive Action to Prevent Ruination of Large Area of the Vieux Carré by the Greater and Greater Diversa Bourbon Street Hole," September 26, 1966, in Bourbon Street Hole Folder, Southeastern Architectural Archives, Tulane University.

10. Samuel Wilson Jr., interview transcribed by Abbye Alexander Gorin in *Conversations with Samuel Wilson, Jr., Dean of Architectural Preservation in New Orleans* (New Orleans: Samuel Wilson, Jr. Publications Fund of the Louisiana Landmarks Society, 1991), p. 45.

11. This was the case in 1980, according to Larry and Mary Kell's *Vieux Carré Atlas*. Don Lee Keith, "Who Owns the French Quarter?" *Figaro*, December 22, 1980, pp. 8–9.

12. Gleaned from 1876, 1885, 1896, and 1908 fire insurance maps produced by the Sanborn Map and Publishing Company and other sources.

13. "Sisters of the Holy Family Asking for Public's Support," *Times-Picayune*, March 14, 1963.

14. Ivor Trapolin, quoted in "Council Denies Bid for Zoning Change; Blocks Motor Hotel at Bourbon, Orleans," *Times-Picayune*, March 15, 1963.

15. Hartnett T. Kane and Martha G. Robinson, testimony at City Planning Commission of New Orleans Special Public Hearing, January 15, 1963, pp. 3-15 and 3-18, filed in "Vieux Carré Zoning Case of Convent of Holy Family 717 Orleans Avenue" Folder, Box 7 of Councilman Joseph V. DiRosa Papers, 1962–1966; 1970–1978, Louisiana Division, New Orleans Public Library.

16. John W. Lawrence, Dean of the Tulane School of Architecture, testimony at City Planning Commission of New Orleans Special Public Hearing, January 15, 1963, p. 3-10, filed in "Vieux Carré Zoning Case of Convent of Holy Family 717 Orleans Avenue" Folder, Box 7 of Councilman Joseph V. DiRosa Papers, 1962–1966; 1970–1978, Louisiana Division, New Orleans Public Library.

17. "Bourbon Orleans Hotel Initial Work Will Begin," *Times-Picayune*, April 15, 1964; "Ceremonies Mark Opening of Bourbon Orleans Hotel," *New Orleans States-Item*, July 18, 1966.

18. Morrison (Mrs. Jacob Morrison), interview by Geiser, August 2, 1977.

19. Frank Schneider, "Winthrop Rockefeller Here for Building Event; $3 Million Structure to Be Erected," *Times-Picayune*, August 1, 1964, p. 55.

20. "Le Downtowner Dedicated Here; Parade Shows Dignitaries, Pretty Girls, Old Cars," *Times-Picayune*, December 5, 1965, p. 46.

21. Morrison (Mrs. Jacob Morrison), interview by Geiser, August 2, 1977.

22. E. Lysle Aschaffenburg to Councilman Joseph V. DiRosa, March 12, 1963, filed in "Vieux Carré Zoning Case of Convent of Holy Family 717 Orleans Avenue" Folder, Box 7 of Councilman Joseph V. DiRosa Papers, 1962–1966, 1970–1978, Louisiana Division, New Orleans Public Library; Ed Nebel and Fritz Wagner, *Facing Change in the French Quarter of New Orleans: Trends and Developments*, Report of the UNO School of Urban and Regional Studies (June 1984), pp. iii, 29–31, Louisiana Collection, Earl K. Long Library, University of New Orleans; Tom Bethell, "Business . . . Tourism . . . More Hotels Mean Tourists Mean More Hotels. . . . ," *New Orleans Magazine*, June 1974, pp. 94–100.

23. David Winstein, interview by Peggy Scott Laborde, 1997, in *The French Quarter That Was*, televised documentary, WYES New Orleans, 1999.

24. Howard Jacobs, "A City of Character—in Fact, a Whole Slue of 'Em," and "Owner of Club Provides Souvenirs for Stealing," *Times-Picayune*, January 10, 1970, p. 13, and January 11, 1970, p. 19.

25. Art Seidenbaum, "Fleshy French Quarter—Treat or Trap?," *Atlantic Constitution*, May 18, 1973, p. 1; Maurice Kowalewski, "Flies in the Bourbon: A Walking Tour of Bourbon Street without the Benefit of Rose Colored Hurricane Glasses," *New Orleans Magazine*, March 1973, pp. 75–93; Charles Suhor, "The Problems of Modern Jazz in New Orleans," *New Orleans Magazine*, August 1967, reprinted in *Jazz in New Orleans: The Postwar Years through 1970*, ed. Charles Suhor (Lanham, Md.: Scarecrow Press and the Institute of Jazz Studies at Rutgers University, 2001), p. 259.

26. Edward J. Lepoma, "Law to Cork Window 'Bars,' Sidewalk Tippling Schiro Aim," *New Orleans States-Item*, September 15, 1969, p. 1.

27. "Instant Coney Island" and accompanying cartoon, *New Orleans States-Item*, September 19, 1969, p. 8.

28. Bill Rushton, "H.E.A.D.—The French Quarter's Only Health Dispensary," *New Orleans Magazine*, March 1971, pp. 32–71.

29. Ordinance No. 4162, Mayor Council Series (M.C.S.), amending Chapter 42 of Ordinance No. 828 M.C.S., City of New Orleans, September 18, 1969, adopted by the Council October 9, 1969, effective November 1, 1969; "French Quarter Bar Wins Ruling on Sales," *Times-Picayune/States-Item*, May 30, 1981, sec. 1, p. 20; Marks, Lewis, Torre Associates, *Bourbon Street Study* (New Orleans: Vieux Carré Commission, 1977), pp. 15–16.

30. Analysis by the author based on Joe Wilkins 1965–1966 Mardi Gras Photograph Collection, acc. no. 2011.0378.1–66, Historic New Orleans Collection.

31. William K. Stevens, "New Orleans Loses All Parades for Mardi Gras in Police Strike," *New York Times*, February 21, 1979, p. A1.

32. Wesley Shrum and John Kilburn, "Ritual Disrobement at Mardi Gras: Ceremonial Exchange and Moral Order," *Social Forces* 75, no. 2 (December 1996): 430.

33. Unnamed individuals quoted in Kowalewski, "Flies in the Bourbon," pp. 77, 90.

34. Chris Owens, interview by Peggy Scott Laborde in *Bourbon Street: The Neon Strip*, televised documentary, WYES New Orleans, 1993.

35. Carol Flake, "Stripper Gossip," *New Orleans Magazine*, September 1975, pp. 74–76.

36. Kathy Kitten, interview by Kowalewski, "Flies in the Bourbon," pp. 77, 90.

37. Lee Fox, quoted in Flake, "Stripper Gossip," pp. 74–76.

38. Art Seidenbaum, "Fleshy French Quarter—Treat or Trap?," *Atlanta Constitution*, May 18, 1973, p. 1.

39. "NOPSI Gives Building in Quarter to the City," *Times-Picayune*, October 29, 1970.

40. Sid Moody, "Mardi Gras in New Orleans: Is It Worth It? Fat Tuesday in the Big Easy," *Lima (Ohio) News*, April 2, 1972, pp. D1–D5.

41. Kowalewski, "Flies in the Bourbon," pp. 75–93.

42. "Drug Raid Nets 19 in French Quarter," *Times-Picayune*, February 1, 1970, pp. 1–4; Jack Lloyd, "The Grateful Dead: Still Alive at 15," *Times-Picayune/States-Item*, October 17, 1980, magazine section, p. 3.

43. Lynda C. Friedmann, Director of Vieux Carré Commission, to Julian Craggs, WYES-TV, August 18, 1978, in Bourbon Street Task Force Folder, Box VCC-1, Vieux Carré Commission Papers, Louisiana Division, New Orleans Public Library.

44. Mister Food, "Bourbon Street's Elite Eat Beat," *New Orleans Magazine*, September 1975, pp. 99–100.

11. How Bourbon Street Stabilized: 1980s–Present

1. Joe Massa, "Quarter Task Force Is Formed," *Times-Picayune*, January 26, 1977, p. 1.

2. Lynda C. Friedmann, Director of the Vieux Carré Commission, to Mike Early, Richard Kernion, Ed McNeill, Tom Purdy, and Harold Katner, interoffice memorandum, November 24, 1976; Lynda C. Friedmann to Raquel Ramati, Director, Department of City Planning of the City of New York, July 26, 1978, in Bourbon Street Task Force Folder, Box VCC-1, Vieux Carré Commission papers, Louisiana Division, New Orleans Public Library.

3. Minutes, "Bourbon Street Meeting—Al Hirt's Club, February 24, 1977," Bourbon Street Task Force Folder, Box VCC-1, Vieux Carré Commission papers, Louisiana Division, New Orleans Public Library.

4. Tables 1–12 of Bourbon Street Task Force Survey, Bourbon Street Task Force Folder, Box VCC-1, Vieux Carré Commission papers, Louisiana Division, New Orleans Public Library; Marks Lewis Torre Associates, *A Plan for Revitalization: Bourbon Street* (New Orleans, Marks Lewis Torre Associates, 1977), pp. 20–12; "French Quarter Survey: How Do You Rate Bourbon Street,?" *Times-Picayune*, June 11, 1977, sec. 1, p. 18; Joe Massa, "Study Shows People Want Big Name Bourbon St. Acts," *Times-Picayune*, August 2, 1977, sec. 3, p. 4.

5. Marks Lewis Torre Associates, *A Plan for Revitalization*, p. 128.

6. Ed Nebel and Fritz Wagner, *Facing Change in the French Quarter of New Orleans: Trends and*

Developments, Report of the UNO School of Urban and Regional Studies (June 1984), pp. 40–41, Louisiana Collection, Earl K. Long Library, University of New Orleans.

7. The system described here, which remains in place today, reflects a 1982 improvement over the closure system recommended by the task force (Joe Massa and Dan Bennett, "City Putting Stronger Barriers on Bourbon," *Times-Picayune,* September 28, 1982, sec. 1, p. 13).

8. Motion M-78-59 by Councilman Early, March 2, 1978; Resolution R-78-112, July 13, 1978; Lynda C. Friedmann to Mike Early, interoffice memorandum, March 30, 1978; Marks, Lewis, Torre and Associates memorandum entitled "Re: Bourbon Street Study, September 7, 1977"; and related materials in Bourbon Street Task Force Folder, Box VCC-1, Vieux Carré Commission papers, Louisiana Division, New Orleans Public Library.

9. After a handful of editions and a shortage of new content, the periodical was renamed *French Quarter Sights & Sounds* and disappeared shortly thereafter. Surviving originals are rare (Bourbon Merchants Association, *Bourbon Street Sights & Sounds,* June 1978, vol. 2, no. 6, stored at Louisiana Division, New Orleans Public Library; Mary Johnson, "The Bourbon Street Elite vs. Inflation," *Bourbon Street Sights & Sounds,* November 1978, vol. 2, no. 9, p. 1, stored at Historic New Orleans Collection).

10. Handwritten notes on yellow legal pad entitled "Bourbon Street Task Force Meeting, November 19, 1976," filed in Bourbon Street Task Force Folder, Box VCC-1, Vieux Carré Commission papers, Louisiana Division, New Orleans Public Library.

11. Marks Lewis Torre Associates, *A Plan for Revitalization,* p. 33.

12. Lynda C. Friedmann, Director of the Vieux Carré Commission, to Ruth Ann Menutis, Bourbon Merchants Association, November 28, 1977; Lynda C. Friedmann to Bourbon Street Task Force, interoffice memorandum, October 12, 1977, in Bourbon Street Task Force Folder, Box VCC-1, Vieux Carré Commission papers, Louisiana Division, New Orleans Public Library.

13. Karen Nabonne, "They Boogied on Bourbon," *Times-Picayune,* November 23, 1977, sec. 1, p. 5.

14. Nebel and Wagner, *Facing Change in the French Quarter of New Orleans,* pp. iii–iv.

15. Earl Bernhardt, interview by Richard Campanella, October 11, 2012.

16. Bob Murret, interview by Peggy Scott Laborde, in *The Nightlife That Was,* televised documentary, WYES New Orleans, 2004.

17. Al Hirt, quoted in James Hodge, "Al Hirt Returning to Bourbon Street," *Times-Picayune,* September 18, 1991.

18. Henry Lambert, quoted in Angela M. Carll, "Café Opens in Park," *Times-Picayune,* July 30, 1983.

19. Based on various materials in Vieux Carré Survey, Historic New Orleans Collection, Binder 69, section for 300 Bourbon.

20. Gary Esolen, quoted in Don Lee Keith, "Sassafras: Last of the Stripteasers," *New Orleans Magazine,* July 1989, p. 77.

21. Earl Bernhardt, quoted in Jan Ramsey, "The Bourbon Street Blues: Club Owner Earl Bernhardt's Worried That Bourbon Street Could Go the Way of Fat City," *OffBeat Magazine,* January 2011, p. 22.

22. Tom Bethell, "Business . . . Tourism . . . More Hotels Mean Tourists Mean More Hotels . . . ," *New Orleans Magazine,* June 1974, pp. 94–100.

23. Nebel and Wagner, *Facing Change in the French Quarter of New Orleans,* pp. 27–29; U.S.

Census Bureau data from 1940 to 2010 censuses, as well as College of Urban and Public Affairs, *Changing Land Use in the Vieux Carré: Managing Growth to Preserve a National Landmark District* (New Orleans: University of New Orleans, 1992), pp. 2-3 to 2-5, a-7 to a-15; Robert Ratcliffe, "The Rise of Lower Decatur Street," *Gambit*, April 3, 1990, vol. 11, no. 14, pp. 9–10.

24. Nebel and Wagner, *Facing Change in the French Quarter of New Orleans*, pp. iii–iv.

25. Frank Donze and Clancy DuBos, "Opinions Differ on Street Show Ban in Quarter," *Times-Picayune/States-Item*, September 23, 1980, p. 13.

26. Associated Press, "Main Quarter Street Will Lose Pedestrian Mall," *AP News Archive*, November 4, 1988.

27. Rebecca Mowbray, "The New Bourbon Royalty: Even Though Bidding Wars and Big Money Are Becoming Staples on Bourbon Street, Could the Street's Old Styles Be Poised for a Renaissance?" *Times-Picayune*, February 10, 2002; Earl Bernhardt, quoted in Ramsey, "The Bourbon Street Blues," p. 22.

28. Leslie Tamar Snadowsky, "French Quarter Losing Landmark; Some Say Trend Toward New Spots Is Ruining New Orleans' Flavor," *Dallas Morning News*, October 5, 1997, Texas & Southwest section, p. 43A; Keith Spera, "A-Bar Reunion: Old Absinthe Bar Veterans Relive Their Bourbon Street Blues with a Free Show at Tipitina's," *Times-Picayune*, June 22, 2007.

29. "Our Opera Misfortune," *Times-Picayune*, December 5, 1919, p. 8, c. 1.

30. George Gurtner, "Chris Owens: Surviving and Thriving on Bourbon Street," *New Orleans Magazine*, January 1996, pp. 122–23.

31. Vincent Fumar, "The Bourbon Street Beat," *Times-Picayune*, July 29, 1988, "Lagniappe" section, pp. 18–20.

32. Ibid.

33. "An Ordinance concerning Inns, Boarding-houses, Coffee-houses, Billiards-houses, Taverns, Grog-shops, and other houses with the city of New-Orleans," March 8, 1831, *A General Digest of the Ordinances and Resolutions of the Corporation of New-Orleans* (New Orleans: Jerome Bayon, 1831), pp. 63–70.

34. "Distressed Citizen," "Enforcing of Liquor, Noise Laws Urged," letter to the editor, *Times-Picayune*, April 9, 1943, p. 10; "Group Seeks to Curb Noises in Vieux Carré," *Old French Quarter News*, October 4, 1946, p. 2.

35. Vincent Lee, "Minyard Denounces Crackdown on Music," *Times-Picayune*, May 31, 1977, p. 5.

36. Bruce Eggler, "Dire Diagnosis: The Prognosis Is Not Good for These Historic Structures on the Louisiana Landmarks Society's Endangered List," *Times-Picayune*, June 7, 2012, p. 1. In the interest of disclosure, I was on the committee selecting the nine sites; while I participated in the discussion, I refrained from opining and voting on the selection of Bourbon Street.

37. John Simerman, "Quarter Bar Wins Ruling in Noise Case," *Times-Picayune*, March 9, 2012, p. B1; Sydni Dunn and Michelle Krupa, "French Quarter Proposal Takes Aim at Nightclubs' Loudspeakers," *Times-Picayune*, March 17, 2012, p. 1; "Speakers' Corners: City Council Regulates Amplified Music in Quarter, CBD," *Gambit*, April 10, 2012, p. 11; David S. Woolworth, "Revision of New Orleans' Noise Ordinance: Efforts toward Simplification and Enforceability," unpublished report by Oxford Acoustics for the City of New Orleans, 2012, provided by Woolworth to author; and other sources.

38. Clancy DuBos, "T-Shirts, Massages Targeted," *Times-Picayune/States-Item*, July 31, 1981, p.

21; "Zoning Versus Quarter Blight," *Times-Picayune/States-Item,* August 3, 1981, p. 14; John Pope, "Wanted: Businesses on Bourbon Sing the Recession Blues," *Times-Picayune/States-Item,* September 27, 1982, pp. 1–4; Frank Donze, "Bourbon Street T-Shirt Ban Defeated Again," *Times-Picayune,* December 9, 1988, p. B3.

39. Richard A. Webster, "Last Dance? Support Mounting for Proposal That Could Shutter Bourbon Street Strip in N.O.," *New Orleans City Business,* November 3, 2008.

40. Ron Swoboda, "Strip Search: Bourbon's Past, Live on Stage," *New Orleans Magazine,* July 1998, pp. 46–47.

41. Analysis by the author based on Joe Wilkins 1965–1966 Mardi Gras Photograph Collection, acc. no. 2011.0378.1-66, Historic New Orleans Collection.

42. Wesley Shrum and John Kilburn, "Ritual Disrobement at Mardi Gras: Ceremonial Exchange and Moral Order," *Social Forces* 75, no. 2 (December 1996): 423–58.

43. David Redmon, "Playful Deviance as an Urban Leisure Activity: Secret Selves, Self-Validation, and Entertaining Performances," *Deviant Behavior* 24, no. 1 (2003): 31–32.

44. Christopher Cooper, "Carnival Panel Targets Nudity," *Times-Picayune,* February 28, 1995.

45. Paul Purpura and Natalie Pompilio, "Officials: Nudity 'Crackdown' Isn't; 50 Arrested for Baring Flesh over Weekend," *Times-Picayune,* February 29, 2000; Pam Louwagie, "Revelers Expose Lenience on Nudity; At Sight of Skin, Cops Look the Other Way," *Times-Picayune,* March 8, 2000.

46. Earl Bernhardt, interview by Richard Campanella, October 11, 2012.

47. Michael Perlstein, "The Old Razzle Dazzle: With Key NOPD Cops Suspected of Protecting a Gambling Scam That Was Fleecing French Quarter Tourists, It Took State Troopers to Bust the Con," *Times-Picayune,* May 2, 2004; "Ex-Con: Officers Shielded Scam; He Seeks Plea Deal in Probe of NOPD," *Times-Picayune,* June 13, 2004, and "Bourbon Street Hustler Plays Last Con Game; 93-Year-Old Career Criminal Dies on Day of His Sentencing," *Times-Picayune,* April 15, 2005.

48. Variations of this wording appeared on at least a dozen club doorways in the 2010s.

49. Andrew Buncombe, "Old South Racism Lives On in Big Easy's Bourbon Street," *Independent,* May 20, 2005; Shawn Chollette, "Investigation Finds Bias at Bourbon Street Bars," *New York Times Institute,* June 2005, http://nola10.nytimes-institute.com/archive/2005/xbias.html; Matthew Cardinale, "White Protesters Shunned at Rally over Racist Murder," *OpEd News,* July 2005, www.opednews.com/cardinale_022205_white_protesters.htm; "N.O. Police Are Taped Beating Man, 64; AP Producer Also Punched on Film," *Times-Picayune,* October 10, 2005.

50. Bernhardt, interview by Campanella, October 11, 2012.

51. Earl Bernhardt, quoted in Ramsey, "The Bourbon Street Blues," 22, and by Scarlett Rayner, "No Journey," *OffBeat Magazine,* September 2011, p. 10.

52. Pawan Dhingra, *Life behind the Lobby: Indian American Motel Owners and the American Dream* (Palo Alto, Calif.: Stanford University Press, 2012); Emma Sapong, "The 'Patel-Motel' Phenomenon: Immigrant Entrepreneurs from India, Many with the Same Last Name, Now Dominate the Hospitality Industry," *Buffalo News,* May 13, 2012; Bruce Eggler, "T-Shirt Kingpin under Fire on ATM's," *Times-Picayune,* January 10, 2008; Bruce Eggler, "Panel Cheers Tear-Down Proposal," *Times-Picayune,* July 16, 2012, p. B1.

53. Frank Perez and Jeffrey Palmquist, *In Exile: The History and Lore Surrounding New Orleans Gay Culture and Its Oldest Gay Bar* (Hurlford, Scotland: LL-Publications, 2012), pp. 117–18.

54. Analysis by the author using U.S. Census Bureau data from 1940 to 2010 censuses, as well

as College of Urban and Public Affairs, *Changing Land Use in the Vieux Carré: Managing Growth to Preserve a National Landmark District* (New Orleans: University of New Orleans, 1992), pp. 2-3 to 2-5, a-7 to a-15. The 1980 estimate is cited in "Gay Bar Raid Raises Specter of Crackdown," *Figaro*, September 22, 1980, p. 6.

55. Bernhardt, interview by Campanella, October 11, 2012.

56. Curly Lima, "Vieux Carré Nite Life," *Old French Quarter News*, December 3, 1948, p. 4.

57. Bernhardt, interview by Campanella, October 11, 2012.

58. Ibid.; *OffBeat* 2012 Best of the Beat Bourbon Street Award, *OffBeat Magazine*, February 2013, p. 19.

12. Locating Bourbon Street: Why Here?

1. James S. Zacharie, *New Orleans Guide: With Descriptions of the Routes to New Orleans, Sights of the City Arranged Alphabetically, and Other Information Useful to Travellers* (New Orleans: L. Graham & Son, 1885), p. 93; "'Quarter' Glows with Old Romance, History, Beauty; Vieux Carré Is Only Intact Section of Its Kind," *Times-Picayune*, February 7, 1929, p. 39.

2. Walt Disney, quoted in Howard Jacobs, "A City of Character—in Fact, a Whole Slue of 'Em," and "Owner of Club Provides Souvenirs for Stealing," *Times-Picayune*, January 10, 1970, p. 13, and January 11, 1970, p. 19.

3. Arlene Stanton, "Let's Meet on Royal Street," *New Orleans Magazine*, March 1989, p. 34.

4. Eve Zibart, Tom Fitzmorris, and Will Coviello, *The Unofficial Guide to New Orleans* (Hoboken, N.J.: Wiley, 2009), p. 109.

5. Patricia Fretwell, interview by Allen Johnson Jr., in "Can't Stop the Music," "Dateline" column in *Gambit*, February 11, 1992, pp. 12–13.

6. Mary Elizabeth Morrison (Mrs. Jacob Morrison), interview by John Geiser, August 2, 1977, Friends of the Cabildo Oral History Archive, Louisiana Division, New Orleans Public Library.

13. Working Bourbon Street: How the Machine Runs

1. Richard Thompson, "Millions of Tourists Spend Billions in N.O.," *Times-Picayune*, October 7, 2012, p. A26; Mark Waller, "N.O. Hits 9.01 Million Visitors in 2012," *Times-Picayune*, March 13, 2013.

2. Because these data are aggregated by block, some jobs on Royal, Dauphine, and around Bourbon's corners are included in this figure. They are, however, more than offset by the many unreported or nonqualifying jobs on Bourbon proper, not to mention suppliers and deliverers with Bourbon clients.

3. The building housing Galatoire's, for example, drew an offer for $5 million in 2008, about $3 million more than its appraised value (Claire Galofaro, "'Classic N.O. Food Fight' Simmers," *Times-Picayune*, December 23, 2012, pp. A1–A6).

4. Based on queries made on each property through the Orleans Parish Assessor's Office online property records database, September–October 2012, http://nolaassessor.com/. Special thanks to Elyse Monat for assistance in compiling these data.

5. Mary Johnson, "The Bourbon Street Elite vs. Inflation," *Bourbon Street Sights & Sounds*, November 1978, vol. 2, no. 9, p. 1, Historic New Orleans Collection.

6. Active Alcohol Beverage Outlet (ABO) Licenses for 2012 analyzed by the author; data provided by the Department of Finance, City of New Orleans.

7. Data computed by the author based on 2008 State of Louisiana employment data produced in collaboration with the U.S. Census Bureau and provided to the author by the Greater New Orleans Community Data Center; Todd A. Price, "Spike TV's 'Bar Rescue' Makes Over Bourbon Location in New Orleans," *Times-Picayune*, November 5, 2012; Evan G. Nicholl, interview by Richard Campanella, July 24, 2012.

8. Nicholl, interview by Campanella, July 24, 2012.

9. Price, "Spike TV's 'Bar Rescue' Makes Over Bourbon Location in New Orleans."

10. Earl Bernhardt, interview by Richard Campanella, October 11, 2012.

11. Ibid.

12. Howard Jacobs, "A City of Character—in Fact, a Whole Slue of 'Em," and "Owner of Club Provides Souvenirs for Stealing," *Times-Picayune*, January 10, 1970, p. 13, and January 11, 1970, p. 19.

13. Ibid.

14. Thomas Ashe, *Travels in America Performed in the Year 1806* (London: Richard Phillips, 1809), pp. 310–11.

15. Mel Leavitt, quoted in Brian Clarey, "Bourbon Street Smarts: An Insider's Guide to Grandma's Interesting Neighborhood," *Gambit*, December 26, 1995, pp. 25–29.

16. Hannah Miet, "To the Party Patrol: Too Pushy," *Times-Picayune*, August 19, 2011, p. 1.

17. Jon Taffer, as reported in Price, "Spike TV's 'Bar Rescue' Makes Over Bourbon Location in New Orleans."

18. Ad for Rick's Cabaret "New Bourbon Bar," *Where Y'At Magazine*, December 2012, p. 32.

19. David S. Woolworth, "Revision of New Orleans' Noise Ordinance: Efforts toward Simplification and Enforceability," unpublished report by Oxford Acoustics for the City of New Orleans, 2012, provided by Woolworth to the author.

20. Wesley Shrum and John Kilburn, "Ritual Disrobement at Mardi Gras: Ceremonial Exchange and Moral Order," *Social Forces* 75, no. 2 (December 1996): 423–58.

21. These figures are averages of six Wednesday and Friday nights with no special events.

22. Based on the author's analysis of hundreds of thousands of service calls made to the New Orleans Police Department during 2012, provided by the City of New Orleans.

23. Within the four 2010–11 surveys, variations ranged from 62 to 80 percent for people from the United States outside Louisiana; 2 to 8 percent for Louisianians outside New Orleans; 6 to 26 percent for residents of Greater New Orleans; and 7 to 14 percent for foreigners. Special thanks to Julie Hernandez for her critical role in this survey. See also tables 1–12 of Bourbon Street Task Force Survey, Bourbon Street Task Force Folder, Box VCC-1, Vieux Carré Commission papers, Louisiana Division, New Orleans Public Library; and Marks Lewis Torre Associates, *A Plan for Revitalization*, pp. 20–22.

24. Nicholl, interview by Campanella, July 24, 2012; Bernhardt, interview by Campanella, October 11, 2012.

25. Mario Cruz, "Impact Hits Home: NFL Players on Strike," and John Pope, "Wanted: Businesses on Bourbon Sing the Recession Blues," *Times-Picayune/States-Item*, September 27, 1982, pp. 1–4.

26. Informants (anonymous), interview by Richard Campanella.

27. Nicholl, interview by Campanella, July 24, 2012. Evan worked at two typical large music clubs in 2009.

28. Allison Fenterstock, "Bourbon Street Clubs Pulling Out the Stops for Super Gras," *Times-Picayune,* January 30, 2013, pp. 1, 9.

29. Nicholl, interview by Campanella, July 24, 2012.

30. Earl Bernhardt, quoted in Jan Ramsey, "The Bourbon Street Blues: Club Owner Earl Bernhardt's Worried That Bourbon Street Could Go the Way of Fat City," *OffBeat Magazine,* January 2011, p. 22; photograph, 331 Bourbon, June 8, 1949, by Walter Cook Keenan, 1-400 Bourbon Folder 78, Southeastern Architectural Archives, Tulane University.

31. Amy Trail, quoted in Courtney Young, "Location, Location, Location: Amy Trail Discovered That Where You Play Matters More Than You Think," *OffBeat Magazine,* July 2010, p. 22; David Hyde and Shawn O'Neal, "Letters—Frenchmen vs. Bourbon," *OffBeat Magazine,* September 2011, p. 6.

32. Keith Spera, "Outspoken Drummer and WWOZ Deejay Had Roots in Traditional Jazz," *Times-Picayune,* November 14, 2012, pp. 1 and 16; Keith Spera, "Bob French Forges an Unlikely Bourbon Street Alliance with Irvin Mayfield," *Times-Picayune,* June 19, 2009.

33. Big Al Carson and Irvin Mayfield, quoted in John Swenson, *New Atlantis: Musicians Battle for the Survival of New Orleans* (New York: Oxford University Press, 2011), pp. 191–92.

34. NOPD service-call data for 2012 provided by City of New Orleans and analyzed by the author. Figures include all calls regardless of disposition.

14. Challenging Bourbon Street: The Rise of the Anti-Bourbons

1. Charles Suhor, "New Jazz in the Cradle, Part I," *Down Beat Magazine,* August 17, 1961, reprinted in *Jazz in New Orleans: The Postwar Years through 1970,* ed. Charles Suhor (Lanham, Md.: Scarecrow Press and the Institute of Jazz Studies at Rutgers University, 2001), p. 253.

2. Howard Mitchum, "Jazz Festival," "Views of Readers," *Times-Picayune,* April 15, 1968, p. 8; Joe Leydon, "Preservation Is Goal and Name of Jazz Ensemble," *Dallas Morning News,* June 1, 1980, p. 68.

3. Stephanie Riegel, "Locals and Tourists Feed Rebirth of Decatur: It Has Less Glitz Than Bourbon, but Merchants See Quarter's Future Unfolding on This Street," *CityBusiness,* July 15–28, 1991, pp. 1–22; Robert Ratcliffe, "The Rise of Lower Decatur Street," *Gambit,* April 3, 1990, vol. 11, no. 14, pp. 9–10.

4. Bill Rushton, "H.E.A.D.—The French Quarter's Only Health Dispensary," *New Orleans Magazine,* March 1971, pp. 32–71.

5. Riegel, "Locals and Tourists Feed Rebirth of Decatur," pp. 1–22; Ratcliffe, "The Rise of Lower Decatur Street," pp. 9–10.

6. Roy Anselmo and John Newlin, interviews by Peggy Scott Laborde, in *The Nightlife That Was,* televised documentary, WYES New Orleans, 2004; "Fat City Protects Its Party Vibe," *Times-Picayune,* "Lagniappe's Bar Guide," July 27, 2012, p. 4.

7. Drew Broach, "Helping Fat City Get with the 'Times,'" *Times-Picayune,* November 11, 2012, Metro section, p. 1.

8. Wendy Hollger, quoted in Brett Anderson, "The Street to Eat: Restaurants Are Springing Up Everywhere on Frenchmen Street," *Times-Picayune,* April 19, 2002.

9. "Faubourg Marigny," a term coined in 1805, had fallen out of use by the early 1900s with the decline of the French language. It was revived in the 1970s, when preservationists, local historians, and real estate agents reintroduced old Francophone neighborhood names.

10. "Gambling Raids Made by Police," *Times-Picayune*, May 13, 1969, p. 1; Kelly Tucker, "Big-Name Jazz Dies Again in N.O.," *Times-Picayune*, July 4, 1980, p. 8.

11. Mary Howell, quoted in Allen Johnson Jr., "Can't Stop the Music," "Dateline" column in *Gambit*, February 11, 1992, pp. 12–13.

12. Typewriter poets have recently set up outside Lafitte's Blacksmith Shop, which is generally viewed as the only place on Bourbon cool enough for the Frenchmen crowd.

13. Richard A. Webster, "Frenchmen Street Proposal Ignites Worries; Neighbors Fear Street Will Reach Tipping Point," *Times-Picayune*, December 16, 2012, p. A22; Bruce Eggler, "Plan for New Club on Frenchmen Runs into Opposition; Residents Fear Area Too Congested," *Times-Picayune*, January 11, 2013, Business section, p. 1.

14. Jan V. Ramsey, "Paying Musicians on Frenchmen—How Do We Do It?," *OffBeat Magazine*, July 7, 2011, and other sources.

15. Michelle Nicolosi, "Easy Street: Frenchmen's Magic Is Simple: This Strip Is Crowded with an Eclectic Cluster of Clubs and Bistros," *Orange County Register*, September 7, 1997.

16. Riegel, "Locals and Tourists Feed Rebirth of Decatur," pp. 1–22; Ratcliffe, "The Rise of Lower Decatur Street," pp. 9–10; "Frenchmen Street Is on the Map," *Times-Picayune*, "Lagniappe's Bar Guide," July 27, 2012, p. 5.

17. Malcolm Gladwell, "The Coolhunt," *New Yorker*, March 17, 1997, pp. 78–88.

15. Hating Bourbon Street: On Iniquity and Inauthenticity

1. "Billy Graham Now 'Loves' New Orleans," *Dallas Morning News*, November 1, 1954, p. 10.

2. Said Storms after publicizing a sex tape: "We simply walked around the corner onto Bourbon Street and within minutes started videotaping dozens of men huddled around each other engaging in oral sex and masturbation . . . in the middle of the street." Nine years later, Storms himself was arrested for public masturbation near a playground in the suburbs (Rev. Grant E. Storms, "Not Just Inappropriate: Illegal," "Your Opinions," *Times-Picayune*, October 12, 2002).

3. Pastor Paul Gros, quoted in Frank Etheridge, "Cross to Bear," *Gambit*, November 6, 2012, p. 18.

4. Signs hoisted on Bourbon Street, Mardi Gras 2012.

5. Ordinance No. 24636, Mayor Council Series, adopted by the Council of the City of New Orleans October 20, 2011, and approved by the mayor on October 26, 2011.

6. James Gill, "Speech Is Free, No Matter the Hour," *Times-Picayune*, February 1, 2012.

7. Katherine Fretland, "Preachers Challenge Speech Ban in Quarter; 9 Arrested during Southern Decadence," *Times-Picayune*, September 10, 2012, p. B1.

8. Robert Watters, "Anti-Solicitation Ordinance Crafted with Care," letter to the editor, *Times-Picayune*, September 15, 2012, p. B4.

9. Bruce Nolan, "ACLU Wins Round in Fight for Preachers," *Times-Picayune*, September 22, 2012, p. 1.

10. Jean-Paul Sartre, "Jazz in America," in *Frontiers of Jazz*, ed. Ralph De Toledano (Gretna, La.: Pelican, 1994), pp. 64–66.

11. Adam Nathaniel Mayer, "Pondering Urban Authenticity: A Look at the New Book 'Naked City,'" *New Geography*, April 2010, online journal, www.newgeography.com/.

12. Kevin Fox Gotham, *Authentic New Orleans: Tourism, Culture, and Race in the Big Easy* (New York: New York University Press, 2007), p. 12.

13. Mark C. Romig, "Thorough Review Led to New Ad Agency," "Your Opinions," *Times-Picayune,* July 25, 2012, p. B4.

14. These percentages are based on units. When we look at value, New Orleans–based proprietors in 2012 owned 56 percent of the appraised land and building value of Bourbon Street; those based in Jefferson Parish owned an additional 13 percent; and Louisianians in general held 72 percent of the value (analysis by the author based on property values and ownership information from the Orleans Parish Assessor's Office, queried October 2012).

15. The reference is to *New Orleans: The Underground Guide,* by Michael Patrick Welch with Alison Fensterstock (New Orleans: UNO Press, 2010).

16. Replicating Bourbon Street: Spatial and Linguistic Diffusion

1. "Dupont Dough Backs Murphy," *Billboard,* December 2, 1957, p. 19.

2. Corinne LaBalme, "Night Moves of All Kinds: The Club Scene in Seven Cities—Amsterdam," *New York Times,* September 17, 2000.

3. Francis Stilley, "Visitors to World's Fair Will 'Ride Magic Carpet,'" *Times-Picayune,* April 15, 1964; "Hot Flashes," *Times-Picayune,* May 31, 1964, p. 37; Charles M. Hargroder, "Governor, Firm Announce Plant," *Times-Picayune,* June 17, 1964, pp. 1–16; Richard Phalon, "Bourbon Street Operator at Fair Is 11th Bankrupt Exhibitor," *New York Times,* February 5, 1965, p. 32.

4. "Disneyland N.O. Replica, Aim," *Times-Picayune,* April 11, 1965, p. 17.

5. I thank sociolinguist Christina Schoux Casey for informing me of this obscure but useful term.

6. Research by the author using hundreds of news and online sources, 1986–present, searched throughout 2012.

17. Redeeming Bourbon Street: The Cheerful Defiance of Adversity

1. Peter Finney, "Aftermath of Katrina unlike Betsy," *Times-Picayune,* September 4, 2005.

2. Based on the author's personal experiences and research, and "Hurricane Katrina—The Approaching Storm," staff reports for *Times-Picayune* Weblog, August 28, 2005.

3. James Varney, "Looters Update," *Times-Picayune,* August 31, 2005; Michael Perlstein, "Urban Survivalists Create a Community amid Chaos; Life Revolves around Generators, Ingenuity," *Times-Picayune,* September 6, 2005; John Swenson, *New Atlantis: Musicians Battle for the Survival of New Orleans* (New York: Oxford University Press, 2011), p. 30.

4. Big Al Carson, quoted in Swenson, *New Atlantis,* p. 191.

5. Chris Rose, "Where Nudity Meets Normalcy: The Strippers Are Back on Bourbon, and We Can All Be Thankful for That," *Times-Picayune,* September 27, 2005.

6. Big Al Carlson, quoted in Swenson, *New Atlantis,* p. 191 (emphasis added).

INDEX